1453

1453

THE CONQUEST AND TRAGEDY OF CONSTANTINOPLE

ANTHONY KALDELLIS

OXFORD UNIVERSITY PRESS

OXFORD
UNIVERSITY PRESS

Oxford University Press is a department of the University of Oxford.
It furthers the University's objective of excellence in research, scholarship,
and education by publishing worldwide. Oxford is a registered trade mark of
Oxford University Press in the UK and certain other countries.

Published in the United States of America by Oxford University Press
198 Madison Avenue, New York, NY 10016, United States of America.

CIP data is on file at the Library of Congress

ISBN 978–0–19–782750–5

DOI: 10.1093/oso/9780197827505.001.0001

Printed by Sheridan Books, Inc., United States of America

The manufacturer's authorized representative in the EU for product safety is
Oxford University Press España S.A. of Parque Empresarial San Fernando de Henares,
Avenida de Castilla, 2 – 28830 Madrid (www.oup.es/en or product.safety@oup.com).
OUP España S.A. also acts as importer into Spain of products made by the manufacturer.

To the memory of the most extraordinary man I have known,
Manolis Kaldellis (1935–2025)

Contents

Acknowledgments

Although I did not know it at the time, many long conversations with Marios Philippides and Walter Hanak at successive meetings of the Byzantine Studies Conference of North America primed me for thinking about 1453 and its cast of characters. They spoke about the events so intimately it was as if they had been present there themselves and were determined also to find the humor in them, a breath of fresh air regarding a topic that typically elicits solemn rhetoric and gloomy reflections. My work is greatly indebted to theirs, and if at times I disagree with their conclusions, I remain grateful for their immense labor and share their ambition to separate history from legend.

Siren Çelik has been a wonderful interlocutor for discussions of this period, and she read and commented on the first chapter. I have also benefited from many discussions with Hakan Karateke, especially in the class that we co-taught on Roman and Ottoman Constantinople. Marion Kruse read the entire book and, as always, offered astute advice on both substance and presentation. Ian Mladjov prepared the excellent maps and, in double-checking the positions of the defenders, saved me from a critical error at the last minute. Lorenzo Miletti advised me on all matters pertaining to Alfonso V and his court and graciously helped to obtain the image of Rumeli Hisarı from the Trivulziana manuscript. Thanks are due also to David Hendrix for providing many of the images used throughout this book. His service in making images available through his project on "The Byzantine Legacy" should be recognized beyond the acknowledgments of the many books they have enriched. Anastasia Koumousi generously provided the recently identified image of the last basileus, Konstantinos XI Palaiologos, and made the identification itself, of course. I also thank the anonymous readers of the press, who read the book carefully and made a number of useful suggestions for revision. Audiences at the Marco Institute of the University of Tennessee, the Departments of History and Classics of the University of Iowa, and the Lin Center of McGill University asked questions that led me to refine some of the arguments made in the book. I thank the organizers for the invitations to speak and the conversations that ensued over dinner.

Special thanks go to my editor at Oxford University Press, Stefan Vranka. More important than his advice on how to improve the book was the fact that he suggested the project in the first place. I was initially skeptical, believing that the topic was amply and sufficiently discussed in the scholarship. It was exciting to discover how wrong I was about that.

THE OTTOMAN EMPIRE IN 1453
1 Albanian lords
2 Tocchi/Kephalonia
3 Palaiologoi/Morea
4 Acciaiuoli/Athens
5 Dukes of Naxos
6 Gattilusi
7 Gabrades/Theodoro
8 Komnēnoi/Trebizond
G Genoese possessions; H Hospitaller possessions
R Roman possessions; V Venetian possessions
HUNGARY
WALLACHIA
SERBIA
BOSNIA
BULGARIA
MOREA
CANDAR
KARA KOYUNLU
KARAMAN
DULKADIR
RAMAZAN
AK KOYUNLU
MAMLUKS
CYPRUS
Black Sea
Mediterranean Sea
Danube
Euphrates
Sirmium
Belgrade
Golubac
Smederevo
Severin
Târgoviște
Hârșova
Dorostolon
Vidin
Nikopolis
Kruševac
Pločnik
Niš
Priština
Kosovo
Kotor
Skadar
Sofia
Tărnovo
Šumen
Varna
Kaliakra
Mesembria
Anchialos
Zlatica
Beroe
Skopje
Philippoupolis
Černomen
Edirne
Krujë
Durazzo
Ohrid
Prilep
Strumica
Didymoteichon
Vize
Çorlu
Rodosçuk
Selymbria
Constantinople
Berat
Avlona
Pelagonia
Serres
Xantheia
Kastoria
Thessalonike
Ainos
Gallipoli
Argyrokastron
Butrint
Ioannina
Kerkyra
Larissa
Trikala
Arta
Lemnos
Zetounion
Leukas
Kephalonia
Salona
Bodonitsa
Negroponte
Thebes
Patras
Corinth
Athens
Zakynthos
Argos
Mystras
Modon
Koron
Monembasia
Kythera
Crete
Candia
Naxos
Chios
Mytilene
Phokaia
Halikarnassos
Rhodes
Theodoro
Amastris
Sinop
Samsun
Trebizond
Kastamonu
Ereğli
Nikomedeia
Bolu
Çankırı
Amasya
Tokat
Sivas
Erzincan
Nikaia
Bursa
Biga
Söğüt
Eskişehir
Ankara
Kütahya
Bergama
Manisa
İzmir
Alaşehir
Tire
Ayasuluk
Ladik
Milas
Muğla
Antalya
Alanya
Karahisar
Akşehir
Konya
Aksaray
Kırşehir
Kayseri
Larende
Tarsus
Adana
Korykos
Ayas
Maraş
Malatya
Harput
Amid
Edessa
Aleppo
Antioch
Laodikeia
Hamah
Raqqa
150 km
100 mi
Map by Ian Mladjov

Map 1

CONSTANTINOPLE
Kosmidion
Ottoman pontoon bridge
Diplokionion
Blachernai
Phanarion
Golden Horn
Galatas/Pera
Lykos River
Walls of Theodosius II
Mesoteichion
Maltepe
boom
Bosporos
Arkla
Scutari
"N. Mese"
Mese
"S. Mese"
Pege
Golden Gate
Hebdomon
Sea of Marmara
0 1000 m
0 3000 ft
Map by Ian Mladjov
1 Holy Apostles
2 Forum of Constantine
3 Hippodrome
4 Great Palace
5 Hagia Sophia
6 Hagia Eirene
7 St Demetrios
Chalkedon

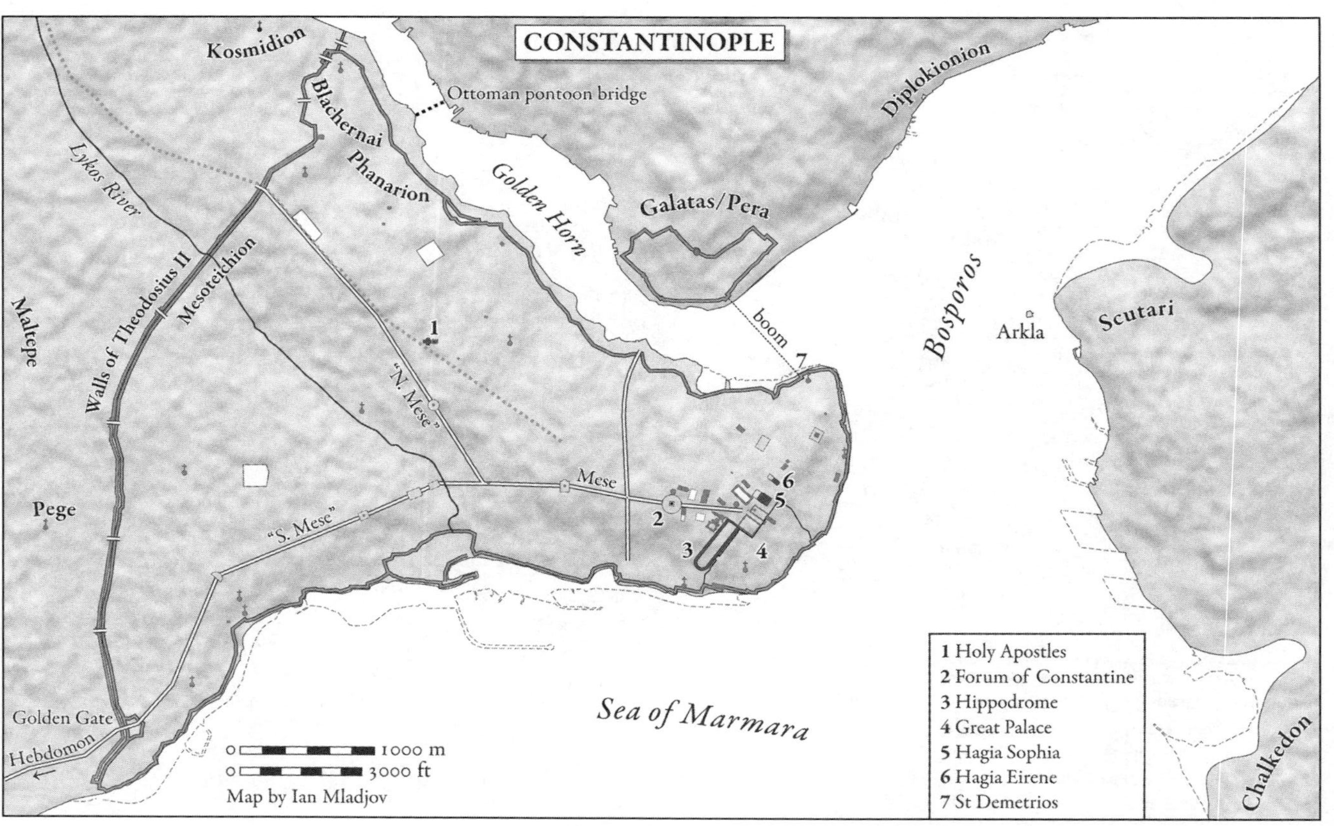

Map 2

THEODOSIAN WALLS
NORTH SECTION
The number of every 5th tower is indicated.
N
Golden Horn
Xyloporta Gate
Girolamo Italiano
Leonardo di Langasco
Manuel Palaiologos?
Blachernai Gate
Anemas Tower
St Mary Church
Dolfino Dolfin
Blachernai Palace
Karaca Paşa
Theodoros Karystenos
Theophilos Palaiologos
Johannes Grant
Manuel Goudeles?
Kaligaria Gate
Gate of the Porphyrogennetos
Palace of the Porphyrogennetos
Kerkoporta Gate?
95
Cemetery
Chora Church
90
Charisios Gate
Andronikos Leontares Bryennios
Fabrizio Corner
85
St Georgios Church
Moat
80a
80
Halil Paşa Çandarlı
Mesoteichion
St Kyriake Church
5th Military Gate (Pempton)
Giovanni Longo Giustiniani
Lykos River
Mehmed II
75
0
300 m
0
1000 ft
Map by Ian Mladjov, adapted from Van Millingen

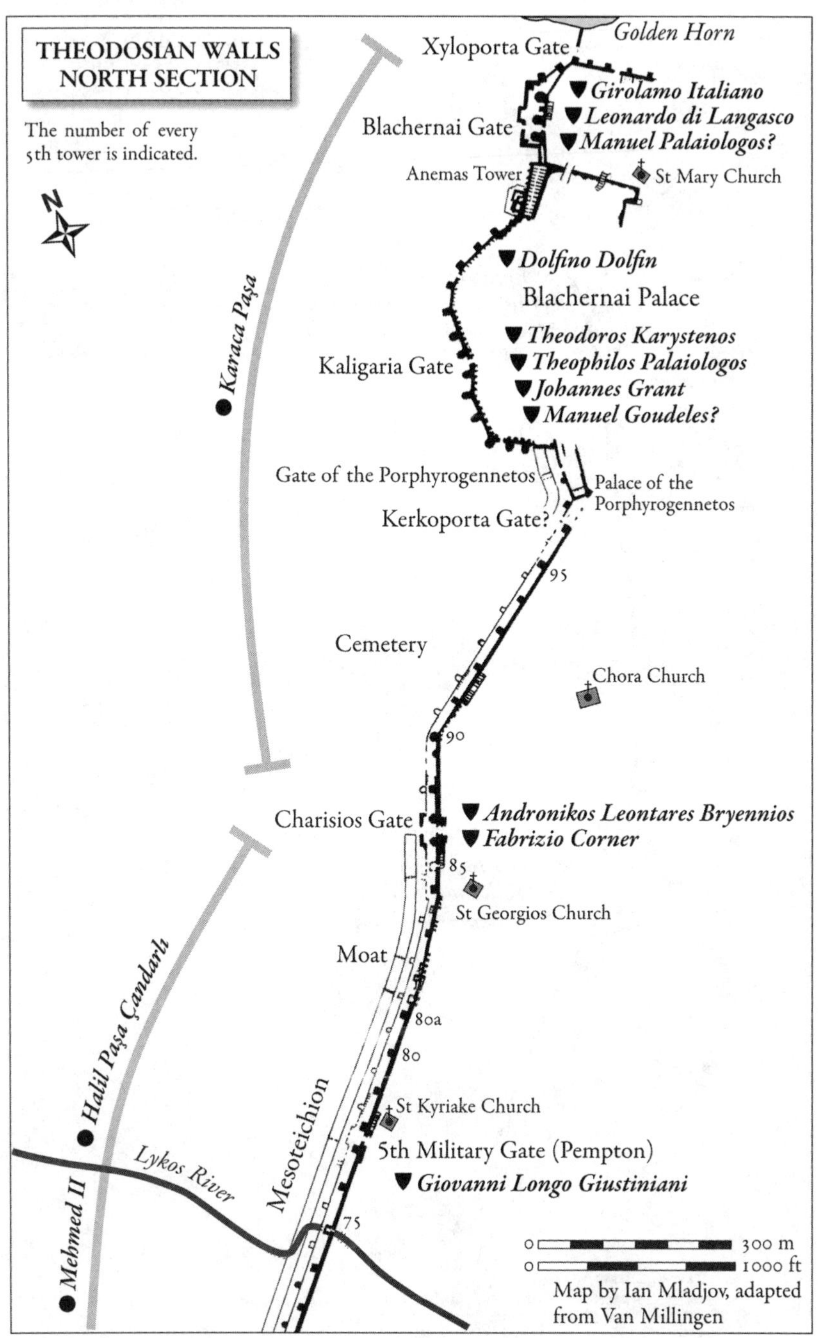

Map 3

THEODOSIAN WALLS
MIDDLE SECTION
The number of every 5th tower is indicated.
Mesoteichion
70
Konstantinos XI Palaiologos
St Romanos Church
St Romanos Gate
65
Ioannes Kantakouzenos
Andronikos Kantakouzenos
Saraca Paşa
Halil Paşa Çandarlı
Mehmed II
60
4th Military Gate
55
Region Gate = ? Myriandron Gate
50
Paolo Bocchiardi
Troilo Bocchiardi
Antonio Bocchiardi
45
Moat
Ishak Paşa
40
3rd Military Gate = Kalagros Gate
0 300 m
0 1000 ft
Map by Ian Mladjov, adapted from Van Millingen

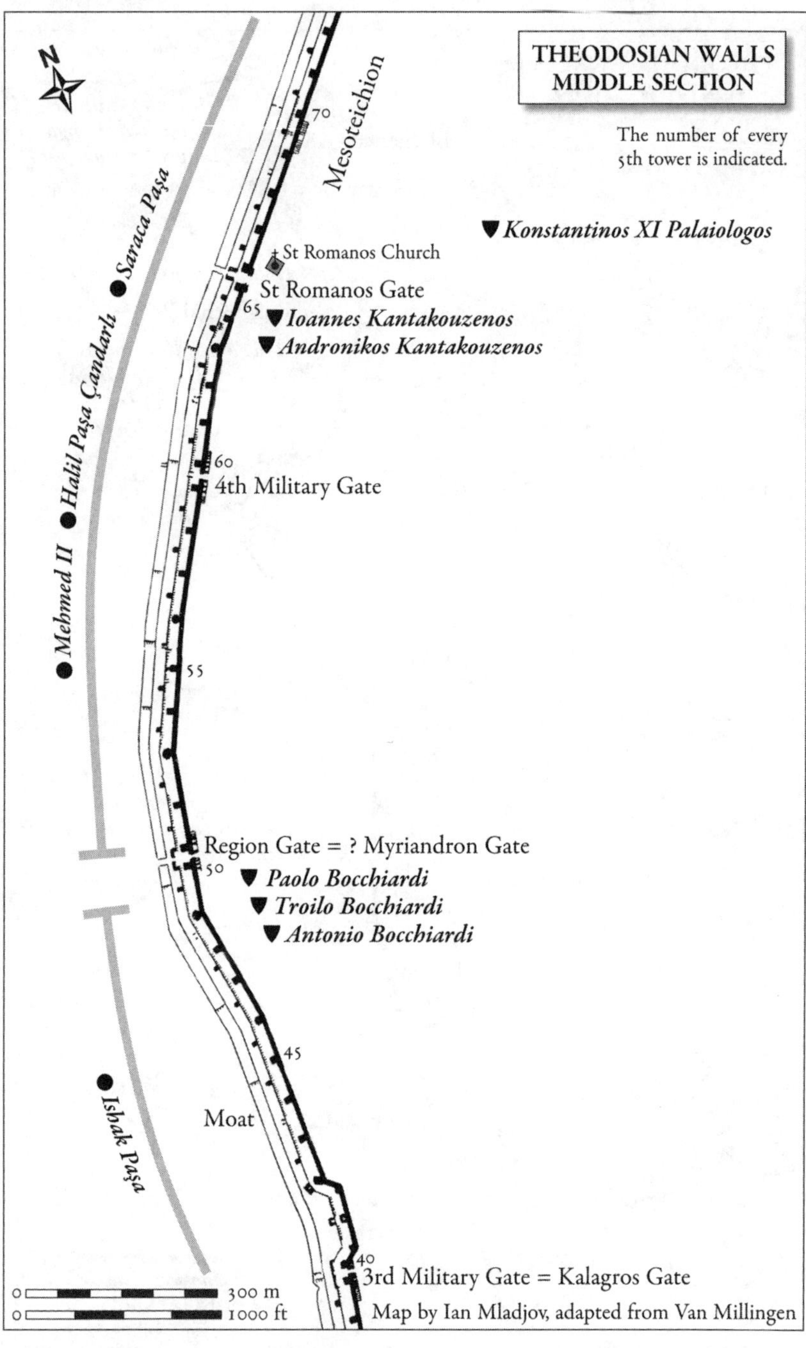

Map 4

THEODOSIAN WALLS
SOUTH END
The number of every 5th tower is indicated.
N
Pege Church
Pege Gate
35
Nikolaos Goudeles
Battista Gritti
Nicolò Mocenigo?
2nd Military Gate
30
Maurizio Cattaneo
25
Xylokerkos Gate
(walled up)
20
Ishak Paşa
15
Heptapyrgion Fortress
Heptapyrgion Gate
10
Golden Gate
Andronikos
Kantakouzenos
Catarino
Contarini
5
Moat
1st Military Gate
1
Marble Tower
Mole
Sea of Marmara
0
300 m
0
1000 ft
Map by Ian Mladjov, adapted from Van Millingen

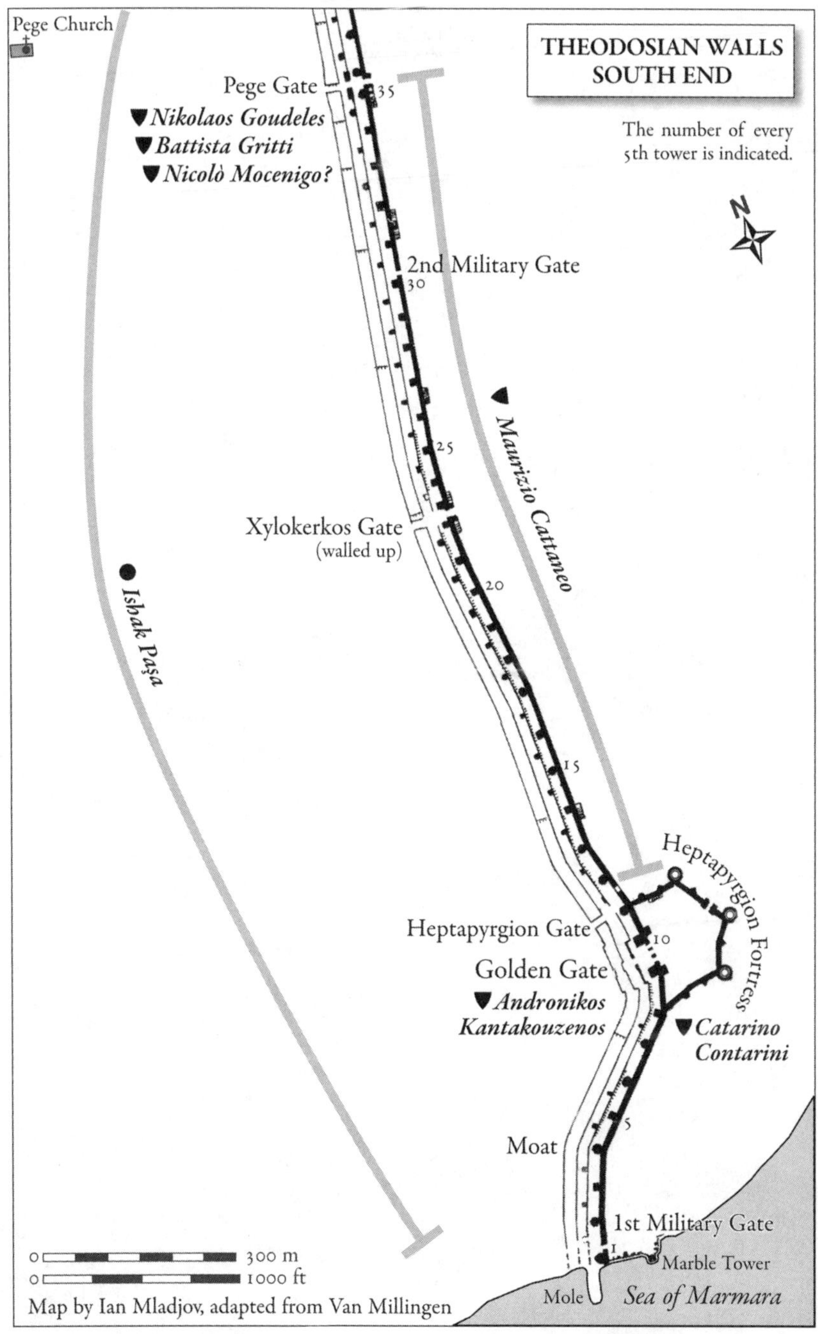

Map 5

Introduction

On May 29, 1453, the city of Constantinople disappeared. For over a millennium, it had been the capital of the east Roman polity and a center of Greek learning and the Orthodox faith. New Rome, or just "The City" as it was commonly called, was adorned with imperial monuments and classical art, unrivaled collections of Greek manuscripts, precious Christian relics, and the most majestic church in the world, Hagia Sophia. It was still a bustling center of international trade, with one of the largest and safest natural harbors in the world, the Golden Horn (see Color Plates 3 and 4). Thousands of visitors still traveled to it every year to study, venerate, trade, and gaze upon its wonders. By 1453, it was visibly in decline and ruled almost no territory, but its people proudly clung to their heritage and traditions. Those came to an end on that May day. A few thousand of its inhabitants were killed during the morning fighting, while the rest—Constantinople's entire populace—were rounded up and marched outside the walls. Their homes and churches were plundered. Tradition granted victorious Muslim armies three days to plunder a city that fell to their arms, but Constantinople was a ghost town by nightfall. The victors' celebrations echoed in its empty streets with the distant sound of feasting, dancing, and singing mixed with the wails and groaning that rose from the slave pens. It was a day of tragedy and triumph. A few days later, most of the captives were led away to their captors' homes in distant lands. The City's fate remained uncertain. Only a few garrisons left by the conqueror remained behind.

Many heart-rending laments were written and sung over Constantinople in the aftermath of its fall. It was not just any city, after all, but a symbol for an entire people, the Romans of the east (or *Romaioi*), most of whom were already living under Turkish rule and some still under Latin rule. For almost two months, the City had defended itself fiercely against an army ten times larger and vastly better equipped and supplied than its own. Its foe brought massive cannons to demolish the ancient walls. After May 29, the ceaseless and deafening bombardment that the City had endured gave way to an eerie silence. For the first and only time in its history, Constantinople was emptied of people. The victors did not immediately move in to occupy it; instead, they dispersed back to their homes. It took the sultan Mehmed II years to decide what to do with the empty husk that he had conquered, and years more after that to repopulate it. May 29 is thus a fulcrum between the City's life as New Rome and its subsequent career as Konstantiniyye, the capital of the Ottoman empire.

In the immediate aftermath, some survivors of the siege wrote accounts suggesting that Constantinople was fated to fall, that divine punishment could not long tolerate the many sins of its inhabitants. They cited the omens and prophesies that foretold the City's doom in advance. Theologians quickly interpreted it as a punishment sent by God because the Orthodox had abandoned their faith to join in Union with the Catholic Church of Rome (so said the opponents of Union) or because they had failed to unite with Rome (so said the proponents of Union). It was easy to look back and conclude that the conquest was inevitable. Gennadios Scholarios, the first patriarch of Constantinople appointed by the sultan after the fall, did just that. Our country could not have lasted longer, he opined. Everyone was certain that it would fall as we beheld the growth of the enemy's power and the City's decline and senescence. It was nothing but vain hope to believe that the end could be postponed or that God would forgive us. Certain insightful people—no points for guessing who—had spoken about this before its last ruler, the basileus Konstantinos XI Palaiologos. The latter was only doing what he could to safeguard the freedom and salvation of his people, but his efforts were doomed.[1]

While eschewing theological interpretations, most modern accounts of 1453 follow our sources and regard the City's fall as inevitable. They view the defense as "ineffectual," "futile," and "doomed to fail" before the forces of the sultan. The present history of the siege pushes back against that narrative. Konstantinos XI did not choose to resist the sultan because he wanted to die fighting, nor did his people and their Latin allies support him, with almost no dissenters, thinking that they would likely be enslaved. They had good reason to believe that victory was possible. Contrary to what all modern accounts suggest, they almost won. They managed to counter all the sultan's assaults and stratagems until the very last day. By the same token, their success makes the sultan's last-minute victory all the more consequential. He was not pushing against an open door. His victory was far less assured than is often thought and a testament to his tenacity, determination, and strategy.

The nature of the resistance speaks volumes about the civilization that fell on that day. The narratives of decline that we associate with "Byzantium," which is what we call the east Roman polity, predispose us to see it as an already defunct civilization. But its people believed it was worth fighting for. Their determination refutes our teleological perspective on the last phase of its history. We see it as a sad slide into powerlessness, poverty, misery, and defeat. From that standpoint, it is easy to view the Romans' decision to fight to the bitter end, when they had been given the chance to surrender, as either delusional or heroically tragic. This book, however, will counter both impressions. The defenders knew what they were doing and were not looking to be martyred. They were proud, but realistic. Their defeat was heroic, but by no means inevitable. They made Mehmed work for the prize, and he rose to the occasion.

To be sure, Constantinople had lost its provinces. It had been enveloped by the growing Ottoman empire. Its ruler (basileus) had little money and few soldiers. The population of Constantinople had shrunk to less than a tenth of its past high mark. It was commonplace among its authors to lament the sorry condition of their state, society, and finances.

And yet, as we will see, Roman Constantinople was by no means ready to exit the stage of history. It remained a vibrant, interconnected hub offering unparalleled cultural assets that drew visitors, pilgrims, and students from far afield. These late Romans prized their freedom and sovereignty and were proud of their culture. They knew that times were tough, that something had gone wrong. But their writings from this period, which are numerous and thoughtful, powerfully proclaimed that their cherished City was worth saving. They did not believe what modern historians told them in retrospect, that it was time to give up, accept terms of surrender, and go quietly into the night.

The fall of Constantinople was not inevitable in 1453. Yet that narrative was convenient to both Ottomans and western Europeans for whom the survival of east Rome was an ideological nuisance, a relic of the ancient world that stood in the way of the stories that new powers wanted to tell about themselves. Its fierce resistance at the end stands as a final protest against narratives that would render it irrelevant. The Romans asserted a right to survive and, by not surrendering, they refused to consent to their obsolescence. They chose to risk destruction over the ignominy of surrender and voluntary extinction. To be sure, they believed that the odds were in their favor—and in this they were probably correct—but they also knew the cost of defeat. Such assertions of will cannot be morally extinguished, even if they are physically overcome. Thus, 1453 continues to reverberate as a kind of open question, a contest of wills that history alone failed to settle. It unsettles the narrative that we like to tell of Roman decline and decrepitude. That narrative would have preferred an ignominious surrender. Instead, while Mehmed won the glory, Konstantinos gained the honor. His self-sacrifice redeemed the dismal tale of his dynasty. And his people, long scorned or overlooked, suddenly turned heads, earned last-minute respect, and inspired tragic reflections.

The year 1453 resonates emotionally today in conflicting ways, as modern nations and religions still regard themselves as the heirs of the conquerors and conquered. In Turkey it has been celebrated officially as "the Conquest" (*Fetih*) since 1953, the 500th anniversary of the siege. These celebrations are a function of modern nationalism and, currently, of political Islam. Thus, Fetih Day is more prominent in the early twenty-first century than it ever was during the twentieth.[2] It is accompanied by stirring rhetoric about the world-critical mission of the Turkish people, films and novels, janissary cosplay, and a special panoramic museum of the Conquest that is pitched more toward locals than international tourists (see Introduction Image 1). It is unusual for a modern nation-state to celebrate the actions of its imperial forebear, actions carried out almost 600 years ago, and its defensive tones betray a curious anxiety about whether the conquest really "took" the first time around. On May 29, 2025, the President of Turkey reiterated that "Constantinople and Hagia Sophia will forever be ours." One cannot imagine, say, the Prime Minister of Spain feeling the need to say the same about Andalusia. The Conquest's reenactment in Istanbul provides reassurance and confirmation, paradoxically exposing doubts. Istanbul—which has been a Muslim city for six centuries—must be symbolically reconquered through grandiose proclamations and the ongoing conversion of former

Image 1 May 29, 2012, Istanbul: An Ottoman army band performs during the celebrations of Conquest Day. The obelisks of the hippodrome are visible in the background. Source: fulya atalay/Shutterstock.

churches into mosques in imitation of the Conqueror. It is as if the tenacity of the defenders in 1453 and the tragedy that befell them never lost their moral force and must be periodically re-defeated.

By contrast, in Orthodox circles, especially in Greece, the *Alosis* or "taking of the City by force," is perceived as a dark day. But to the limited extent that it is commemorated, it is somberly relegated to ancient history as part of a long and dusty tale of triumphs and tragedies. Laments about the fall of the City come only from hyper-Orthodox or nationalist circles—usually as email—and induce eye-rolling in everyone else. It is not a national holiday. In 2021, in a ceremony that was quite small—partly due to COVID-19 and partly due to limited interest—the President of the Greek Democracy laid a wreath before a statue of Konstantinos XI Palaiologos at the small town of Mystras, near Sparta, where he ruled before moving to Constantinople in 1449 (see Introduction Image 2). The *Alosis* is associated with the genre of lament, but it is set in a distant world with limited relevance to the present.

Image 2 The President of the Hellenic Republic lays a wreath before a statue of Konstantinos XI Palaiologos at Mystras in the Peloponnese, in 2021. Source: Presidency of the Hellenic Republic.

The present narrative of 1453 will validate both perspectives—conquest *and* tragedy—but will skirt modern politics to restore the vitality of the actual experience. The fall of Constantinople was not inevitable, and the defense was not doomed. For most of the siege, the burden of failure was in fact on Mehmed. This makes his victory consequential: it was a feat of arms, ingenuity, innovation, and determination. At the same time, the sad fate of the City on the day of its fall and afterward was far worse than people imagine. Both experts and laypeople with whom I have spoken believe that the Ottoman armies moved in and, after the initial slaughter subsided, occupied the City, whose population then carried on under Turkish rule. In reality, Constantinople was not immediately occupied by the conqueror. It was emptied out and its population dispersed as captives across the Ottoman empire. It is a picture that one rarely encounters in existing publications. It was a story of both desperate triumph and unspeakable tragedy.

It is widely assumed that the siege of Constantinople has been exhaustively studied by modern scholarship, and that there is no reason to do it again. That is perhaps why so much recent work has focused on its reception; that is, on how the events were perceived at the time and later, in other societies. However, this impression is wrong. The most recent narrative reconstruction of the siege by a historian, Steven Runciman, was published in 1965, over 60 years ago. Much of it focuses on the context and consequences of the event, leaving little space for an analysis of the siege itself, which is not told in full detail. It is also, by now, outdated in many respects, more than I can list here. Yet it is still cited as an adequate reconstruction of events.[3] In fact, Runciman misjudged the dynamics of the siege. His chapter on its end is entitled "Fading Hope," referring to the defenders, when it should have referred *to the sultan*.

The siege has also been recounted by generalist historians, but they tend to reproduce the same picture, hitting the same dramatic beats, without re-assessing the testimony of the sources or questioning the building blocks of the story.[4] The siege has also been a popular topic for journalists, novelists, and ideologues of various stripes. It is featured briefly in general histories that focus on the end of Byzantium or the rise of the Ottoman empire as well as in studies of Mehmed II and the origins of Muslim Constantinople. These works do not offer original perspectives or a deep scrutiny of the testimony of the individual sources. Many of them contain serious factual errors. As mentioned, there is also now a significant body of scholarship on the reception, impact, and reactions to 1453. In particular, there is apparently no limit to how many times we can retell the story of how the West reacted to news of the City's fall. Little of this bears directly on the siege.

In the meantime, two massive publications have laid the groundwork for new approaches. One is a tome by Marios Philippides and Walter Hanak, *The Siege and the Fall of Constantinople in 1453: Historiography, Topography, and Military Studies* (2011). This brought together the life's work of two scholars who studied the sources, topography, and prosopography of the siege. It clears up many misunderstandings and puts our research on a new footing. However, it does not offer a new synthesis and is a chaotic book. Over the decades of its gestation, the authors lost control of the material, so the book contains many repetitions and contradictions. The authors make numerous mistakes and draw conclusions with which the following reconstruction will sometimes disagree. Yet everyone who works on 1453 remains in their debt, especially for their effort to clear up many confusions and willingness to reconsider supposedly settled matters. Marios and Walter's eagerness to talk shop for hours at the Byzantine Studies Conference of North America will be remembered fondly by the present author, as will their irrepressible good cheer. They are both missed.

The second tome is a collection of sources in French translation, edited by Vincent Déroche and Nicolas Vatin. It is called *Constantinople 1453* and was published in 2016. It almost reaches the 1,453 page-mark! This volume makes accessible many sources that are otherwise never featured in narratives of 1453, especially documentary and notarial sources on the Italian side, as well as a full translation of the relevant portions of the history of the Ottoman writer Tursun Bey (his English version from 1978 is not a translation but a condensed, loose paraphrase). A great virtue of this anthology is its annotation, which provides critical information on individuals, institutions, and events, many of them unrepresented, so far, in 1453 scholarship. Special mention must be made of the extraordinary work of Thierry Ganchou, one of the contributors to the volume, who has unraveled many important stories from this period by working carefully through documentary sources. His contributions to prosopography have been decisive and illuminating, both in that volume and in separate publications.

The main sources for the siege are listed and briefly explained in a section at the end of this book, before the bibliography. The names of their authors will recur throughout the narrative, so, until the reader becomes acquainted with them, this list can serve as a handy reference. It is a treat for a premodern historian to have so many eyewitness accounts of an event. As one of them, Leonardo of Chios, stated: "there is advantage in having a multitude of accounts, and the evidence of an eyewitness is always more reliable than hearsay."[5] Most of the eyewitness sources were written by Latins and are biased against the Greeks. The Greek historians wrote in the 1460s, a decade later, although they had spoken with survivors. Apart from Tursun Bey, the Ottoman historians wrote later and either do not provide much concrete information about the siege, being more interested in ideologizing it, or include too many fictional elaborations to be treated as reliable.[6] They are interesting in their own right, but less so for the historian of the siege itself.

One text that has been strictly excluded from my reconstruction is the longer (so-called *Maius*) version of the (Greek) chronicle of Georgios Sphrantzes (i.e., pseudo-Sphrantzes). This is now known to be a sixteenth-century forgery by Makarios Melissourgos, pretending to be the work of a confidant of Konstantinos XI. To flesh out the narrative, he adapted other known sources and supplemented them with his imagination. His inventions are plausible and answer questions that the other, non-fictional sources leave open. It is tempting to use his information, which is why so many historians have done so, but the work is a fraud and should be avoided on principle. Uncorroborated information in pseudo-Sphrantzes cannot be used safely, and if it is corroborated, then we don't need it. Unfortunately, his inventions contaminate many modern narratives, including that by Runciman and later historians.

Our knowledge of the siege and its aftermath relies mostly on literary and documentary sources. There is no archaeology of the siege, except for research on the Theodosian walls. This is also not a story in which women appear prominently in the sources. Occasionally we glimpse them among the people of Constantinople and among the captives after the fall, but there are no prominent individual women to showcase, as is sometimes done as a second-best option when genuine women's history lies beyond reach. Konstantinos XI was unmarried during his reign (although not for a lack of trying to find a bride) and the Ottoman harem was secretive about the identities of the mothers and concubines of the sultans.

A final note on terminology. The majority population of Constantinople was Roman. They called themselves that and so do I. They were Greek-speaking, Orthodox Christians. In contexts or statements where they might be confused with the ancient Romans or the Romans of Rome in Italy, I call them east Romans.[7] By contrast, western Europeans called them Greeks, and I follow this usage when I am presenting events through the eyes of western observers or referring to authors via the language in which they wrote (e.g., the "Greek historians" of the fall). The term "Latins" refers to any western European whose churches used the Latin rite; in this story, most of them were Italians, and the two terms will sometimes be used interchangeably. I have spelled Venetian names in their standardized Italian forms, and I call the ruler of Constantinople a basileus (plural: basileis), from the Greek. "Emperor" is a misleading western translation of basileus, which I use only when presenting events through the eyes of western observers to represent their perspective.

I do not provide references for events before 1402. The reader may consult my general history, *The New Roman Empire: A History of Byzantium* (Oxford 2023).

I

The Queen of Cities, Still

In the late 1430s, a Spanish gentleman named Pero Tafur set out from his native Andalusia to see the world, hitching passage on a sequence of trading and passenger vessels, moving from port to port. His four-year journey took him around the Mediterranean, and he arrived at Constantinople in 1438. As his ship approached the City at dawn, "we saw a high mountain, more than a hundred miles off, and they told us that it was Santa Sophia" (see Color Plate 5). Tafur was eager to meet the basileus, who in his mind held the rank of "emperor." This was easy to arrange because the rulers of Constantinople were willing to speak with anyone who brought news of the outside world. Tafur's ship docked at Pera (also known as Galatas), the Genoese colony situated across the City's harbor. There he ran into an old friend from Seville, a captain plying the eastern trade routes. In both Pera and Constantinople, Tafur encountered many of his countrymen, as did other Latin visitors, especially Italians. A few days later, his friends, dressed in their finery, accompanied him to the Blachernai palace to meet the basileus. Ioannes VIII Palaiologos (1425–1448) was seated on a throne with a lion skin spread under his feet and spoke through a Castilian interpreter, a man who could also sing Spanish songs for the pleasure of the court. Hunting was another pastime of the basileus, who regularly invited visiting gentlemen to join the chase for deer and boar in the surrounding fields and forests.[1]

Tafur had come to Constantinople for personal reasons. An ancestor had supposedly emigrated from Constantinople to Spain in the late eleventh century and Tafur wanted to learn more about him. During his stay there, he felt most welcome as he "found many Castilians and persons of other Latin nations in the emperor's service" who "showed me much honor." One day he was invited to dinner by a "knight of the [emperor's] household" who revealed to him, when the two spoke privately after the meal, that he could speak Castilian Spanish. "If I have not spoken to you until now in your tongue in public it is because we hold it a disgrace to give up our own language and speak a strange one." The Romans of Constantinople, whom Tafur and all Latins called "Greeks," were proud of their cultural heritage, but they also lived in a highly interconnected world. Many of them knew foreign languages. A dense network of exchange, contact, and trade extended all around their City from the Atlantic to Central Asia and from Russia to Egypt. Even after the loss of its empire, Constantinople was still situated at the center of its own world.

Constantinople had once ruled much of this world. Tafur's travels—including his native Andalusia—rarely took him outside of the former Roman *oikoumene*. That word literally meant "the inhabited world," but for the Romans it referred to the territories of their empire, which they had once called *Romanía* (i.e., "Romanland"). Soon after Constantinople was dedicated in 330 AD, the Romans began to refer to it as the "heart" and "center" of that world.[2] Many did so still a thousand years later, even after the empire itself was lost. In the early fourteenth century, when the territory of the east Roman state was a patch of land in the Balkans approximately the size of England, the philosopher and statesman Theodoros Metochites wrote a spectacular oration in praise of Constantinople in which he reemphasized the City's centrality. For him, Constantinople had been built by the first Christian emperor, Constantine the Great, to rule the world. The City was modeled on, and attuned to, the cosmos itself. It was beautiful beyond comparison, even beyond Metochites' (considerable) rhetorical ability to describe. Its ruins ennobled it. "Other nations would pay real money to have our ruins."[3]

Roman authors continued to praise the City's superlative beauty and importance in the fifteenth century. Yet foreign visitors described a more drab reality. For Tafur, Constantinople was underpopulated. The old Great Palace by the former hippodrome was in ruin, although it once "must have been magnificent." The emperor maintained a splendid court, but "he is like a bishop without a diocese." The people of the City were "not well clad, but sad and poor, showing the hardship of their lot," although "they deserved even worse because they are steeped in sin." Here Tafur reveals a typical Latin bias against "the Greeks," much of which originated in their refusal to submit to the pope and accept him as the head of their Church.[4]

Metochites and other Romans were not in denial when they praised the City as central to the *oikoumene*. They knew that the empire was gone and that their polity had little power. Yet in his massive oration Metochites subtly redefined the idea of the *oikoumene* to showcase Constantinople as a global center of trade, travel, information, and culture. In this sense, his image of it accurately captured Tafur's experience. After describing Hagia Sophia as the soul of the City, Metochites turns next, in an unusual move, to the harbor in the Golden Horn, which, he says, welcomed ships from all over the world conveying every kind of merchandise. Ordinarily, his oration should have stopped at the pinnacle that was Hagia Sophia. But instead, he descends into the harbor, casting Constantinople as a nurturing mother that receives her "children" into its bosom, becoming "the common harbor of mankind." It served this function in part because of its strategic location between the Black Sea and the Mediterranean (on the north–south axis) and between Asia and Europe (on the east–west axis). The City itself straddled both sea and land like a kind of "mainland island." All people find safety and repose here from their voyages at sea. All come to obtain whatever they need, from material goods to information. As a "marketplace for the whole of mankind," Constantinople continues to "unify the world." All languages are spoken here by members of every nation, where they mingle and learn about each other without having to travel to so many separate destinations. The City is their "common fatherland." Metochites triumphantly concludes that this is "a new kind of commonwealth for the whole of mankind."[5]

This was a panegyrical image, to be sure, but not entirely wrong. In the first half of the fifteenth century, Constantinople was still one of the most visited places on earth. Tafur and others confirmed that the Golden Horn provided unparalleled anchorage: it is "the most safe and the finest harbor in the world," wrote another Spanish visitor (see Color Plates 3 and 4).[6] It was a major transit node for Venetian and Genoese trade from the Black Sea, including a traffic in slaves from the north.[7] Both republics maintained a large presence there, the Venetians in Constantinople proper and the Genoese in their colony at Pera. Pera was a regional branch-office of Genoa. It was established by imperial permission and technically subject to the authority of Constantinople, but in practice it was independent. Tafur noted that the "common people [in Pera] are Greeks, but they are governed by the Genoese, who hold all the offices."[8] The highest office was the podestà, or "power-holder," an official sent from Genoa. The Venetians lived in the City proper, in quarters by the harbor, and were governed by an official named the bailo who was sent from Venice (the term is cognate with the English bailiff).

Catalans and Castilians were also present, as Tafur discovered, although not on the same scale as the Venetians and Genoese. A Catalan duchy subject to the crown of Aragon had been established at Athens in the fourteenth century. While that was now extinct (the Florentines had taken over), the Catalan presence revived in the mid-fifteenth century because of the ambitions of Alfonso V of Aragon in the central and eastern Mediterranean. A steady stream of western diplomats passed through the City, bringing news and proposals. They ranged from papal nuncios, who were trying to organize or enforce Union between the Churches of Rome and Constantinople, to what were effectively explorers seeking to establish relations with distant Muslim powers. In 1403, the Castilian envoy Ruy Gonzáles de Clavijo stopped at Constantinople on his way to the court of the Mongol conqueror Timur (also known as Tamerlane) at Samarkand in Asia. He too wrote an account of his stay and subsequent travels. Others were scouting out the prospect of a crusade against the Turks on behalf of their lords, such as the Burgundian pilgrim-spy Bertrandon de la Broquière, who passed through in 1432. Bertrandon also wrote about his experiences in Constantinople, exhibiting the usual anti-Greek bias of so many Latin authors of this period. A version of his travel book, *The Voyage to Outremer*, was produced in 1455, two years after the fall of the City, and one of its accompanying images (by Jean Le Tavernier) shows the siege, getting much of the topography right. It is one of the first images to ever be produced of the siege of Constantinople, and it is printed on the cover of this book.[9]

Constantinople was also visited by adventurer-travelers such as Tafur and scholars such as Kyriacus of Ancona, who spied on the east on behalf of his Italian lords while also collecting ancient inscriptions, visiting classical sites, and sketching their antiquities. As Constantinople was by this time enveloped by the Ottoman empire, Christian captives of the Turks who wished to escape also found a refuge there as they sought a way home. The Bavarian Johann Schiltberger was one such fugitive in the 1420s. He was kept in protective custody in the patriarch's residence lest he be recognized and re-enslaved. "I would gladly have seen [the City] but the emperor had forbidden it; even then we sometimes went out with the patriarch's servants."[10] We note again the interest shown by the basileus in people passing through, even the most humble, who might have useful information. This story confirms that Turks also walked the streets of the City, although we have no accounts written by them. There were so many Turks that providing a *kadi* for them—a religious judge—was an item of frequent negotiation between the basileus and the sultan.[11]

Most Turks in the City were there to trade,[12] but some had more interesting motives, especially lesser members of the Ottoman dynasty who wanted to escape its lethal politics. Yusuf was a son of the sultan Bayezid who opted to live quietly in Constantinople as his brothers fought and murdered each other in a succession struggle that raged for a decade after Bayezid's defeat by the Mongol conqueror Timur in 1402. He studied the Greek classics and was even baptized as Demetrios, signaling to his kin that he was not a threat to them.[13] Likewise, Orhan was an Ottoman prince who was being kept in Constantinople in 1453 as a hostage, or bargaining chip, with a retinue of a few hundred other Turks. They were there when the City was besieged by Mehmed and were part of the reason behind the war.

The chief foreign students of classical culture in Constantinople were not Turkish princes but Italian scholars. Training in Greek was not widely available in Italy. They also came to acquire ancient books. Some, such as the antiquarian Kyriacus of Ancona, could not wait to explore the local holdings and get their hands on them. "He saw many libraries famous for their many gold-illuminated and pictured manuscripts, both sacred and profane, in diverse monasteries."[14] He was primed by his reading to have classical experiences during his visit. When he approached the City by sea in 1447, his ship was "accompanied by a joyous school of dolphins that adorned the swelling sea."[15]

Enea Silvio Piccolomini was an Italian humanist who later, as pope Pius II (1458–1464), tried to organize a crusade for the liberation of Constantinople. In his view, "no Latin may deem himself to be educated unless he has studied in Constantinople."[16] (He himself had not done so.) The east Romans would have wholeheartedly agreed. They considered their native Hellenic learning to be the best education available in the world. One of Metochites' arguments for Constantinople being the common hearth of mankind was that true wisdom, both secular and divine, could be found only there: it was the last remaining "museum of reason" and "treasury of wisdom" that survived from the ancient world.[17] By the early fifteenth century, however, some Romans had realized with regret that both Fortune and Wisdom were migrating to Italy, as the Latins were pulling ahead.[18]

The famous humanist Francesco Filelfo spent seven years in Constantinople during the 1420s, learning Greek while working for the bailo of the Venetians and the basileus Ioannes VIII as a secretary and diplomat. He married the daughter of his Greek teacher, Ioannes Chrysoloras, nephew of the great Manuel Chrysoloras, who had been among the first to teach Greek in Italy a generation earlier.[19] While in Constantinople, he too explored its monuments, antiquities, and inscriptions, and reported that ancient Attic Greek was spoken at the court.[20] This linguistic conservatism resonates with what Tafur was told by his contact, that in public the emperor's men were expected to speak only their own language.

Religious attractions also brought a host of pilgrims to Constantinople. All the dignitaries, travelers, spies, and students mentioned above were also fascinated by the City's Christian antiquities, its relics and churches. They were eager to visit Hagia Sophia and gaze in awe at its majesty, marble paneling, architecture, and impressive collection of sacred relics. The church had famously been built in the sixth century by the emperor Justinian. To Tafur it had seemed like a "mountain" when he saw it from a distance. A century earlier, Metochites had used the same term, comparing it to "a fragment of a mountain that somehow found itself in the midst of the City." For him, it was the pinnacle of the City, the splendor of the sky reflected upon the earth, and the dwelling of God. It was the soul of the City just as the City was the soul of the world.[21] In a later poem, Metochites imagined his own soul being replaced with a personification of Hagia Sophia.[22]

To be sure, Metochites' rhetoric was more rapturous than the accounts of foreign visitors, but only because they lacked his rhetorical prowess, not because their experience of the place was less moving. The Castilian traveler Clavijo (1403) wrote an especially detailed description of Hagia Sophia. He was struck by the quality of the mosaic art, both here and elsewhere in the City, and noted that "the church is so immense in size, and so wonderful are the sights to be seen there, that it was impossible to make a complete examination." The escaped prisoner Johann Schiltberger, who had traveled across Asia with the Mongols, declared that "it is the most beautiful church, so that nothing like it can be found in India." For his part, Tafur found Hagia Sophia to be in such good shape that it seemed to have been recently built.[23] The urban authorities were prioritizing their restorations to keep this showpiece in good repair, just as they were upholding the purity of court Greek.

A major attraction of Hagia Sophia were the relics of the Passion and the various saints, and other relics were dispersed among the churches and monasteries of the City. At this time, there might have been eighteen functioning monasteries (in the past there might have been over a hundred).[24] A Russian guidebook from the 1390s claims that "there are thousands upon thousands of relics of saints and many wonders which it is impossible to describe."[25] Western visitors knew well that the City's collections had been plundered by the Venetians and others after the Fourth Crusade in 1204, but they did not question the authenticity of the relics on display and sought to venerate them. Relics from Constantinople were still prized in the West and were given by the court as precious diplomatic gifts, accompanied by authenticating paperwork signed by the patriarch.[26]

Westerners do not appear to have come specifically to venerate the City's relics. It was the Russians who did that, and they were far more interested in the holy icons than the Latins, especially those that were reputed to be miraculous, to the same degree that they were uninterested in classical culture. These northern Orthodox visitors were exclusively focused on pious attractions, paying almost no attention to the rest, as if Constantinople were but an Orthodox theme park. Their accounts are guidebooks to the churches and relics for the benefit of their countrymen back home, with Hagia Sophia always coming first. There is a similar brief text of this kind in Armenian, written before 1434.[27] The Russians' interest in these churches went back to the early conversion of the Rus' to Christianity, when the envoys of their ruler Volodymyr of Kiev (978–1015) supposedly reported back to him that when they attended services in the shrines of Constantinople "we knew not whether we were in heaven or on earth . . . We only know that God dwells there among men, and their service is fairer than the ceremonies of other nations."[28] The Russian community in Constantinople seems to have consisted mostly of clergy and monks, and it was quite small compared to the Italians.

Constantinople had always received thousands of visitors per year, but it is from the first half of the fifteenth century that most foreign travel accounts survive, in many languages. It is not clear whether this reflects an uptick in traffic or the rise of travel literature in western Europe,[29] but certainly the City had never been more interconnected with the rest of the world. It boasted a robust tourist industry, in the form of local guides for hire. They not only knew the places that each foreign nationality wanted to see, but they could also secure access and tell stories about the sites, monuments, works of art, relics, and icons. These guides are surely the main source for the mostly unhistorical tales—some including dragons—that our travelers brought back to regale their readers. These tales did not necessarily reflect what Constantinopolitans believed or knew about their history. It was only what local guides believed their clients wanted to hear. A pilgrim from distant Novgorod advised future travelers from the north that "it is impossible to get around without a good guide; and if you attempt to get around stingily you will not be able to see or kiss a single saint."[30]

These, then, were the reasons that brought people to Constantinople in the early fifteenth century: trade, pilgrimage, diplomacy, espionage, exploration, and classical study. In many cases, they overlapped, explaining why many Latins were there when Mehmed appeared before the walls. It also explains why the authors of our main accounts were there. The Catholic cardinal Isidoros, an ethnic east Roman, and his friend, the Genoese bishop of Mytilene, Leonardo of Chios, were representing the pope and hoping to advance the cause of Church Union. Nicolò Barbaro was serving on a Venetian trade galley. Benvenuto of Ancona was representing his city as its consul. Ubertino Posculo was there to study Greek. And the Russian Nestor-Iskander . . . well, we don't know who he was, but the tale that was produced later under his name exhibits an Orthodox bias, which counters the Latin, Catholic bias of the others. Thus, the siege is told to us primarily by non-natives. Yet people impacted primarily by the siege were its native Roman inhabitants, so we turn to them now.

After 1430, the east Roman polity ruled by the Palaiologos dynasty encompassed few territories: Constantinople and a corner of Thrace around it, including parts of the coastal strip that extended along the Sea of Marmara to Selymbria, and parts of the coast that extended north along the Black Sea to Anchialos and Mesembria; the small Aegean islands of Thasos, Imbros, Lemnos, and the Sporades (Skiathos, Skopelos, and Skyros); and the Peloponnese, which was the largest territory still in Roman hands, though not the coastal towns of Methone (Modon), Korone (Coron), and Nauplion, which were held by Venice. Two more territories were held in a kind of vassalage to the basileus by the Genoese family of Gattilusio, namely the island of Lesbos and the coastal city of Ainos in Thrace, but these were de facto independent and made no move to help in 1453.[31]

Thus, the majority of free Romans in the world—that is, those who lived under their own rulers and were not treated, because of their ethnicity and religion, as second- or third-class subjects in other empires and colonies—were in the Peloponnese, followed by Constantinople and its hinterland. The basileus himself was always based in Constantinople and appointed his brothers or sons to govern the outlying areas as "despots." The largest despotate was the Peloponnese, also called the Morea, but despots could also be sent to Selymbria and Mesembria.

On both the Balkan and Anatolian side, Constantinople was surrounded by the Ottoman empire. The City was like an island not only because of its strategic location on the Bosporos but because it was surrounded by Ottoman territories. The main Ottoman naval base was at Gallipoli, in the Hellespont just south of Panion, and the nearest trading settlement on the Asian side was Scutari, visible from Constantinople and occupying the site of one of its former suburbs, Chrysopolis. There was regular ship traffic between the two.[32] The City itself was well-defined by its famous walls (which we will discuss in detail in Chapter 4). The walls enclosed an area of thirteen square kilometers, or five square miles, which was immense by medieval and early modern standards, rivaled only by the likes of Rome and Baghdad. Its population, however, was not proportionate to its size. Past estimates of the population in this period varied widely between 15,000 and 140,000 before stabilizing at around 40,000 or 50,000. A recent estimate revises that number down to 30,000 or 35,000.[33] Either way, the figure is significantly smaller than the City's peak population in the 530s under Justinian, when it reached half a million. In the seventh century, it hit another low, down to 40,000 to 100,000, and then grew again until it reached 300,000 in the later twelfth century. This means that, in 1453, the population of Constantinople was a tenth or less of its historical maximum.

This decline was due to many factors, which had left scars on the City's history, memory, and urban fabric. When the Fourth Crusade took Constantinople in 1203 and 1204, its armies deliberately set fires that rendered possibly a fourth or more of its populace homeless.[34] This, followed by two generations of colonial Latin rule, prompted a mass exodus. The Romans retook Constantinople in 1261, and many returned. But in the fourteenth century, the collapsing fortunes of the Roman state, including frequent bouts of civil war, led many to emigrate and to seek their fortune elsewhere.[35] Among them was Michael Doukas, the grandfather of the historian of the fall, who was disgusted by the "wicked actions of the Romans," and chose to serve the Muslim emir of Aydın in western Anatolia, who treated him well.[36] Then, the Black Death of 1347 carried away at least a third of those who remained and possibly more. The plague recurred at intervals, with about ten visitations before 1453.[37] Moreover, people who ventured outside the safety of the walls for trade, travel, or agriculture were liable to be captured and sold into slavery in the interlocking slave markets that were run by the Ottomans, Venetians, and Genoese.[38] A final exodus was caused by the blockade of the City by the Ottoman sultan Bayezid, which lasted for eight years (1394–1402), causing famine and hardship. It stripped many Romans of their livelihoods, inducing them to leave.[39] Bayezid was defeated by the Mongol conqueror Timur at Ankara in 1402, which extended the life of Roman Constantinople for half a century. But the cumulative impact of these crises left the City with a decidedly run-down and abandoned feel.

As a result, the inhabitants of Constantinople, in early 1453, lived amidst the monuments and abandoned dwellings of a city that had once accommodated a population ten times larger. This does not mean that nine out of every ten homes and apartments lay empty. Many would have fallen into ruin in the centuries since the heyday of the twelfth century, overgrown or buried under. Extensive recycling had also turned the ruins of the past into quarries for materials and new homes. In 1411, the classical scholar Manuel Chrysoloras wrote an essay comparing Old and New Rome in which he observed that, "like our city, Rome uses itself as a mine and a quarry . . . it both nourishes and consumes itself" in a process of urban self-cannibalism.[40] Even so, Constantinople had the feel of a ghost town, haunted by a missing population and by bygone eras of imperial glory.

An impression of ruin and abandonment was shared by Romans and Latins, although they placed it within contrasting moral frameworks. The Orthodox writer Gennadios Scholarios, a leader of the anti-Union resistance, admitted that the City was poor, mostly uninhabited, lived in fear, and had been stripped of its famous patrimony, but at least it was free and nourished its residents "in Christ."[41] The Florentine traveler and cartographer Cristoforo Buondelmonti, who published his description and maps of the Aegean islands and Constantinople in the 1420s, introduces it as "the ruined city of Constantinople." Like Tafur and other Latins, he notes that it had "few inhabitants" and he channels typical western biases when he says that "they are the enemies of the Latins" and "if they promise something they do not keep their promises." He meant primarily promises to submit to the pope (see Image 1.1).[42] Buondelmonti makes Galatas seem much larger than it really was, reflecting both his Latin bias and the commercial importance of the place, and he makes it seem more densely inhabited, which may have well been true.

Therefore, those thirteen square kilometers, enclosed by the most impressive walls of the medieval period, were mostly empty land and open spaces, much of it cultivated to feed the existing population.[43] Clavijo reflected the experience of other visitors, both Christian and Muslim, when he wrote that:

> though the circuit of the walls is great and the area spacious, the city is not densely populated. There are within many hills and valleys with corn fields and orchards, and among the orchards there are hamlets and suburbs . . . Everywhere there are great palaces, churches, and monasteries, but most are now in ruin. It is plain that in former times when Constantinople was in its pristine state it was one of the noblest capitals of the world.[44]

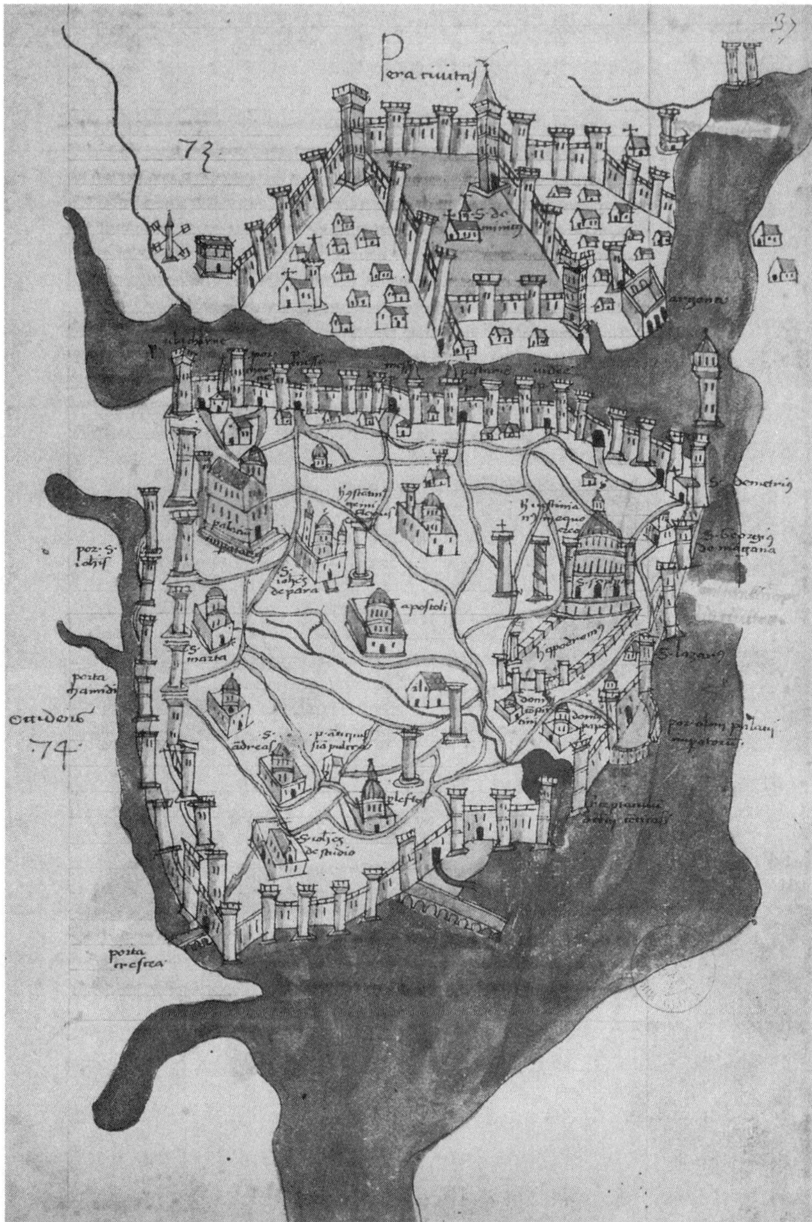

Image 1.1 Cristoforo Buondelmonti, map of Constantinople from his *Liber insularum Archipelagi* (ca. 1422): Bibliothèque nationale de France, Département des Cartes et Plans, Ge FF 9351 Rés., fol. 37r. Source: Paris, Bibliothèque nationale de France, Département des Cartes et Plans, Ge FF 9351 Rés., fol. 37r/ Wikipedia.

In an invented speech, the historian Kritoboulos makes the sultan Mehmed II tell his men before the siege that:

> it is no longer a real city, but only bears the name of one. In other respects, it is full of fields, gardens, and vineyards, as you can see, as well as uninhabited buildings and empty walls, most of which are in ruins.[45]

It was a paradox for a city's walls to enclose both its urban core *and* part of its agricultural hinterland.

Those "hamlets" inside the walls were separate neighborhoods, or clusters of dwellings, that had their own mayors, or *demarchs*. The basileus liaised with the population at large through these local officials, who attended ceremonies at the court. According to a protocol for their appointment, the basileus charged them with maintaining law and order in their districts and with adjudicating disputes impartially, admonishing them not to take bribes. They also kept lists of residents, which would be consulted in 1453 to call up defenders to the walls.[46]

Constantinople's centers of gravity had shifted during this later phase of its existence. Until the eleventh century, its imperial, religious, and commercial focal points were clustered in the east, around the palace and patriarchate adjacent to the hippodrome and Hagia Sophia. Even now, in the late period, these two places hosted assemblies of the population, while workshop and retail venues extended outward from there along the paved and colonnaded Mese boulevard and into the surrounding streets. This was the monumental and ceremonial core of imperial New Rome. But by the fifteenth century much activity had dispersed to other regions, with the palace, court, and mansions of the elite clustered around the Blachernai district in the northwest. The patriarch remained in the east, managing Hagia Sophia and other important churches, like that of the Virgin Hodegetria, where important processions were organized. Meanwhile, most commercial transactions took place in the harbor of the Golden Horn and the warehouses and Italian districts that lined it, including the commercial streets above it. These sectors had acquired lives of their own.

The old Great Palace was a sprawling "campus" of buildings, courtyards, and churches that sloped, on terraces, down from the hippodrome to the sea. By this time, most of it was an abandoned ruin, although some halls were apparently still maintained for ceremonial purposes. The German fugitive Johann Schiltberger (present in the 1420s) says that they were very beautiful and adorned with precious stones; he saw this because he was holed up in the adjacent patriarchal residence. Tafur says that at the entrance there was a loggia with stone benches that housed an extensive collection of books and board games, the latter for the basileus' use (although perhaps this is a reference to the Blachernai palace).[47] The hippodrome had not hosted chariot races in the ancient style since the twelfth century. Most of the structure seems to have still been intact, including the massive columns around the *sphendone* (the curved section in the southwest); the marble stands (or at least some of them); the two obelisks and the bronze Serpent Column; and the imperial box, a separate building in its own right. At this time, the hippodrome hosted not chariot races but jousts and other tournaments. In 1432, the Burgundian spy Bertrandon de la Broquière saw a young Konstantinos Palaiologos engaged in equestrian games there with his companions:

> Each was carrying his bow and galloping the length of the square. They threw their hats ahead of them, and then the one who could strike closest, shooting backward, was considered the best. This is one of the talents they have learned from the Turks.[48]

These hippodrome pastimes reveal the convergence of Latin and Turkish influences on the Roman aristocracy.

In former times, this part of the City was dense with monuments, palaces, amenities, and residences. But an entire neighborhood next to the hippodrome was abandoned during Bayezid's blockade, after which a notable turned it into an agricultural estate as an endowment for a local church to John the Baptist that he wished to restore. This estate abutted on the colonnade of the Mese itself.[49] Just up the street on the Mese was the forum of Constantine with its famous porphyry column topped by a massive cross (see Image 1.2). This was still a major marketplace for the City's inhabitants, including even bookstalls. But right next to it now were vineyards.[50]

Image 1.2 The remains of the porphyry Column of Constantine, banded in steel hoops for support. Its base was encased in Ottoman times, and the forum around it has disappeared along with the large cross that it stood at its top between the twelfth and fifteenth centuries. Source: The Byzantine Legacy/David Hendrix.

The beating heart of this part of the City was Hagia Sophia—its "soul," as Metochites called it—and the emblematic column of Justinian with his famous equestrian statue in the adjacent Augoustaion square. All around there were many stalls and shops selling wine, bread, and fish, especially shellfish, along with stone tables "where they eat, both rulers and common people, together."[51] Tafur is likely referring here to the day-to-day bustle and social mixing of the place and not to set feast days. Another occasion for gathering, mixing, and socializing was provided by religious celebrations and processions, especially those organized by the church of the Virgin Hodegetria ("Leader" or "Guide"), "our Lady" as locals called her. Her famous icon was paraded every Tuesday before large crowds and foreigners were told to expect miracles.[52]

The court of the basileus was located four kilometers away in the Blachernai district. This palace was more compact, with taller buildings overlooking enclosed courtyards. It offered splendid views of the Kosmidion grounds outside the walls and the Golden Horn. We can reconstruct life in this palace only as late as the mid-fourteenth century, when we have the protocol-book known as pseudo-Kodinos and the detailed narratives of two historians who spent much time in the palace.[53] It is likely that much had changed in the intervening century, in part because of the shortage of funds. Major repairs were impossible. For example, the important church in the vicinity, the Virgin of Blachernai, had burned down in 1434 and was abandoned. (When it had burned in 1069, it was promptly rebuilt). Isidoros, one of the defenders of Constantinople during the siege of 1453, was the abbot of a monastery in the City when it burned and he wrote a rhetorical lament for it. According to Tafur, who visited only a few years later, God had burned the Virgin of Blachernai with a lightning bolt because of all the sodomy that used to happen in its entrance.[54]

Rhetorical speeches praising the basileus were still performed in the palace. Learned men caught his attention by delivering such orations before assemblies of notables, churchmen, and other members of the polity. The nobility would also send their children to intern as pages at the court, where they learned the skills of elite society, formed useful networks, and gained experience by accompanying embassies abroad. If we judge by the reports of foreign travelers, the basileus and his retinue spent most of their time interviewing foreign visitors and hunting. In 1403, Manuel II brought back a boar that he had personally killed and gave it to Clavijo's company.[55] A detailed description of such a hunt in the forests and hills of Thrace is given by Kyriacus of Ancona, who accompanied one in 1444 at the invitation of Manuel's son, the basileus Ioannes VIII. Present were not only many Roman nobles but leaders of the Genoese and Venetian communities.[56] By hunting together, the leaders of these communities formed tighter and more cooperative bonds. The basileis may not have fielded large armies but were expected to lead their men and fight in person if necessary. Hunting was a good way to hone these important skills, as were the equestrian games in the hippodrome that Bertrandon witnessed.

However, Romanía no longer possessed a military aristocracy or, for that matter, a regular army. For over a millennium before the mid-fourteenth century, the empire had been defended by regular armies consisting of units that were paid by the state and commanded by generals who rotated in and out of office. But that ancient system had been swept away by the crippling loss of territory and revenue. The soldiery now increasingly consisted of the ad hoc retinues of the basileus and his brothers and sons—the despots—who were sent out to govern the outlying cities and provinces. With whatever revenues they could scrape together, they hired soldiers, both native Romans and foreign. Therefore, little information survives about the military institutions of that era, nor did these military forces consist of units with discrete identities that remained stable over time.[57]

Nor was there much of a landed aristocracy either, as there was hardly any land left. This was unprecedented. In all of Roman history so far, elites were either military or landed or both. Yet now the only group with any wealth was one that had always existed but had never gained the political and social prominence that it enjoyed after 1400: these were the traders, merchants, and investors. They become more important around the turn of the century and began to hold key positions at the court by the side of the basileis. The Goudeles and Notaras families exemplify this trend. They and others made their fortunes largely by participating in the trade networks of Genoa and Venice. These Romans were typically minor partners of the Italians, but, starting sometimes from provincial backgrounds, they grew wealthy in comparison to their countrymen and became pillars of the court hierarchy in Constantinople, funding many of its activities. It is unlikely that they were paid salaries by the basileus, another break from Roman tradition caused by the lack of state resources.

In the late fourteenth century, Georgios Notaras was a court interpreter who traded in dried fish, probably his main source of revenue. His grandson, Loukas Notaras, was the *megas doux* and *mesazon* of Konstantinos XI (a kind of chief minister). Loukas does not seem to have engaged in trade himself but lived off the interest generated by the substantial accounts that his father had deposited with various Genoese and Venetian banks, including investments in their public bonds. This class of new men mixed private with state business, so when they went on diplomatic missions to Italy they also engaged in trade and personal banking. The Goudeles family were also merchants who had carried out diplomatic missions on behalf of the basileis. Nikolaos Goudeles, who fought in the siege of 1453, had risen to the position of eparch of the City (a kind of mayor and so court official).[58]

Understandably, these men were tight with Italian merchants and bankers and so were, at least politically, in favor of Church Union when that was official court policy (for the question of Union in detail, see the following chapter). Some of them even acquired Venetian and Genoese citizenship in the process; Notaras had both. This posed a problem because it enabled them to take advantage of the tax exemptions that the basileis had granted to the Italian republics, or else they used Italian intermediaries to circumvent the trade taxes that Romans still owed. Thus, the basileis lost revenues that they would otherwise have received from taxing the business activities of their own subjects. The basileis complained about this to the Venetian Senate. Conversely, in 1451 some Venetian citizens managed to have themselves registered as Constantinopolitans to skirt Venetian jurisdiction.[59]

Monied elites, whatever the source of their wealth, made their presence known in Constantinople by building mansions. Decades before the siege, a popular anti-Union preacher had spoken passionately before the court and patriarch in the Blachernai palace, reprimanding the City's elites for wasting their money on fancy three-story homes while neglecting the upkeep of the Theodosian walls that were keeping them all safe.[60] A relative of the ruling family, Theodoros Kantakouzenos, who had also acquired Venetian citizenship, built a magnificent domicile in the most desirable location in the City, on a hill with an unobstructed view all around. Its expensive wood, polished marble, and rows of columns made it a wonder to behold, and he commissioned poets to praise it.[61] It is likely that these mansions were either in the Blachernai district or nearby, so that these men could participate in the life of the court. By contrast, the house of the richest man in the City, Notaras, was likely situated about half a mile south of the Golden Horn harbor, closer to the source of his wealth. It was built around a tall, centuries-old tower, known as the Tower of Eirene. It appears that this house was a thousand years old and had been inhabited by famous generals, foreign princes, and court luminaries during all periods of east Roman history, although certainly it had undergone repairs and renovations over time. Notaras' version would have been unrecognizable to its former inhabitants.[62] Still, Constantinople was one of few places in the world where a residence could have accumulated such a history.

It was not only "new men," such as Goudeles and Notaras, whose wealth was generated from Italian trade and connections. Men with the most aristocratic names were joining in too. We have the accounts books for 1436 to 1440 of one Giacomo Badoer, a Venetian who did business in Constantinople. Local Romans make up about a third of his local buyers and sellers. We find a Goudeles and a Notaras, as we might expect, but also men named Palaiologos, Kantakouzenos, Argyros, Doukas, and Laskaris.[63] So while the manors of the aristocracy might have been at Blachernai, their business was in the harbor. Badoer's ledgers reflect the diverse origins of his clients, who came from across the Mediterranean, from Spain to the Levant. Of interest also are Romans who hailed from the territories under Turkish or Latin rule. For them Constantinople was a place of opportunity, a hub where they could profit from their native ability to interface among Greek-, Latin-, and Turkish-speakers and make deals happen. The City, under Roman rule, also held out the prospect of social and political mobility, something that could not happen for them at home because of the colonial or imperial regimes that relegated them to permanent subordination. This resulted in a partial "reverse migration" of Romans to the capital, which is also visible in Venetian archival records.[64]

In fact, many of the Venetians in Constantinople were not originally from the Rialto but from Crete, and some were ethnic Romans using their Venetian citizenship.[65] Trade was only one reason bringing them to Constantinople. The Cretan icon-painter Angelos Akotantos drew up his will in 1436 because he intended to travel to Constantinople and it was prudent to put his affairs in order before such a journey, which was likely connected to his craft. Akotantos may be the same man as the famous painter Angelos of that period, over a dozen of whose paintings survive. He signed them with the moniker "by the hand of Angelos," which means "angel" in Greek.[66]

The balance of trade, however, was uneven. Romans tended to buy finished western products and sell primary resources, and they bought more than they sold, although Badoer's accounts may not be representative. Certainly, most trade passing through what Metochites called "the harbor of the world" benefited Italians more than Romans, due to the concessions that Venice and Genoa had extracted from the basileis, namely complete exemption from taxes and fees. Most trade probably passed through Pera, not Constantinople proper. By 1350, the former was pulling in seven times more revenue than the latter. Moreover, even the Venetians, who used the Constantinopolitan side of the harbor, were tax-exempt, which means that the Roman–Italian revenue gap was even greater than those figures suggest. To attract trade to his side, the basileus had to lower taxes on his own subjects from 10% to 2%.[67] This low-tax environment partly explains why so much traffic was passing through the Golden Horn.

This economy benefited the minority of Romans who were junior partners in Italian trade much more than it did the majority of the City's inhabitants. To be sure, there was a trickle-down effect as someone had to load and unload cargos, weigh and measure them, maintain ships, docks, and warehouses, and provide equipment and services needed for transit, storage, and logistics.[68] Much of this was done by locals. But it did not result in a significant transfer of wealth. Tafur may not have been biased when he noted that the inhabitants of Constantinople were poor and sad whereas Pera saw constant "traffic in goods brought from the Black Sea, the West, Syria, and Egypt, and there everyone is wealthy."[69]

This imbalance caused resentment and may explain a series of episodes of minor violence and theft that were perpetrated against Venetians by local Romans. In their typical fussy legalism, the authorities in Venice documented these in detail and lodged formal protests to the basileus, seeking redress and compensation.[70] But we must be careful with this data. Only this Venetian documentation survives about street crime in Constantinople, as its compilers were eager to record offenses against Venetians, and no others. We cannot know whether these episodes reflect an anti-Venetian bias on the part of their lower- and middle-class Roman perpetrators, or only the bias of our documentation. Moreover, Venice had a long history of bringing such litigious demands for compensation before the basileis and using them as leverage in negotiations.[71] Their data may not be representative, or accurate.

These stories do, however, reflect the complex jurisdictions that the basileis had to navigate. When Tafur was in Constantinople, the Castilians protested to the despot Konstantinos Palaiologos, the future basileus who was governing the City in the absence of his brother Ioannes VIII. A Greek sailor had killed a Castilian and tried to take his ship. They demanded that justice be done, although the Greeks were reluctant. In the end, the despot had the murderer's hands cut off and his eyes put out. Tafur thought that they should just have killed him, but the Greeks with whom he spoke said that they did not believe in capital punishment.[72]

In the end, it is likely that most Romans did not benefit much from the Italian trade networks, apart from the pittances that trickled down to them from their social betters who did. The people of Constantinople had their own economy and local markets, as befitted any city of that size. We catch incidental references to retail shops, workshops, and specialists of almost every type, including even a gunpowder workshop.[73] As they had in centuries past, women also owned and ran businesses in the City, investing their funds and even forming cooperatives to manage their outlets.[74] But these were mostly small shops for local consumption, not export. A colorful description of the market down by the harbor is provided by a satirical text that lambastes a corrupt judge who grew rich through corruption, extortion, and theft, acquiring horses, slaves, and silken garments for himself in the process. He would step outside the harbor walls through a small gate and fleece the fish-, vegetable-, and cheese-vendors along the coastline, then go back inside and do the same to the butchers and craftsmen on his way home.[75] So, some of the money that trickled down trickled back up again.

On the eve of its fall, Constantinople was a paradoxical place. It was empty yet bustling, both a capital and a frontier, a city and its hinterland in one, where orchards grew next to majestic imperial monuments that had stood for over a thousand years. It was a place scarred by loss where massive profits could still be made. It was materially poor yet culturally rich, while its incomparable patrimony drew scholars and pilgrims from all across Christendom to access its scholarship, venerate its relics and icons, and gaze upon Hagia Sophia. Having lost its empire, Constantinople was still situated at the center of a vast new *oikoumene*, receiving news and information from distant lands on all sides.

Constantinople was also more multi-cultural than ever before. A variety of Italian, Turkish, and Roman silver coins circulated in its economy. Everyone spoke some Italian, Greek, and Turkish. In defending himself against the accusation of going Catholic because he studied Latin texts, the theologian Gennadios Scholarios argued that "by this logic all of us are Muslims, for almost all of us use their language."[76] But anxiety was justified. The Romans had once been solidly Orthodoxy, but now many of their best scholars were embracing Catholicism and even moving to Italy, including Isidoros, Bessarion, and Ioannes Argyropoulos. Even the basileis Ioannes VIII and Konstantinos XI were pro-Union, at least nominally. Other Romans were converting to Islam, perhaps in the belief that Ottoman successes reflected God's favor. Orthodox theologians tried to persuade them not to stray from the one true faith of their ancestors, but Islam was making sense to many.[77]

The City was living in all tenses simultaneously. It was still rooted in its own past, both physically and in self-awareness. Constantinople was a museum to past centuries of imperial glory. Yet it was also coping as best as it could with the challenges of the present, playing a weak hand in a rapidly evolving world. It was not, as it is often depicted, trapped in a dreamscape of the past, unable to adjust pragmatically. Past, present, and future collided. In the most recent calculations by expert theologians, the date of the Second Coming of Christ was anticipated for the year 7,000 since Creation, which is our 1492 AD.[78] That was not a far distant future, but in truth the end was even nearer.

2

Turks, Romans, and Italians

In the 1460s, two Greek historians of the rise of the Ottoman empire, Kritoboulos of Imbros and Laonikos Chalkokondyles of Athens, modeled their narratives on that of the ancient historian Thucydides.[1] They imitated his prose and the narrative forms of his *History of the Peloponnesian War*, but there was another reason that drew them to him. Thucydides had recounted a war between two asymmetrical powers, the Spartans and the Athenians, the former of whom were almost unbeatable on land while the latter had the advantage at sea. To counter the Spartan land army, the Athenians built a wall around their city, treating Athens like an island, and used their fleet to harass Spartan territories and allies. A similar strategic asymmetry played out in 1453: a seemingly invincible Ottoman army faced the unconquered land walls of the City and the superior ships of its Italian defenders.

The Ottomans were supreme on land. The Romans had not dared to fight them in battle since 1329. The Serbs and Bulgarians had been conquered entirely through land operations. Catholic Christians had also launched several crusades against the Ottomans that marched across the Balkans but were roundly defeated at Nicopolis in 1396 and Varna in 1444. The Hungarians and Wallachians were defeated again at Kosovo in 1448. No one was eager to fight an Ottoman army in battle after that. But Constantinople did not necessarily have to in order to survive. It could use its impregnable walls to turn itself effectively into an island, as writers at the time called it.[2] The Romans had tried the same strategy in their other major territory too, the Peloponnese (Morea), by refortifying the Hexamilion wall across the Isthmos. They pursued this project rather obsessively in an effort to turn the Peloponnese into an island, even though the Hexamilion wall repeatedly failed to halt Ottoman advances. Constantinople, in particular, could not be fully secured without control of the sea around it. So far, the Ottomans had failed to build an effective fleet. The sea still belonged to the Italians, with whom the Turks could not compete even when they did build navies of their own. So long as the City was allied to the Italian republics, it could hope to fend off the Turks from behind its walls. This interplay of armies, walls, and ships was exactly what Thucydides' history was all about, making him an ideal model.

Konstantinos XI Palaiologos was counting on walls and ships to protect his city against land armies. But when the sultan Mehmed II arrived, in April 1453, he brought a new generation of cannons, planning to test this new technology against the most formidable city walls in the world. Thucydides' analysis suddenly needed an update. While imitating his ancient Attic prose, Laonikos and Kritoboulos rose to the challenge of describing this terrifying new weaponry, which altered the old balance of power among armies, walls, and ships.

The Ottoman empire would eventually become one of the largest in the world. But its origins are obscure, and its first steps were modest and incremental rather than explosive. The Ottomans did not burst onto the stage of history as conquerors led by a great empire-builder, as had the Persians, Macedonians, Arabs, and Mongols. They emerged in the instability of late thirteenth-century Anatolia, and they were only one among many nomadic Turkish groups that were seeking to find pasturelands and extract revenues from the settled agricultural populations whom they targeted with raids and threats. These nomadic groups were exploiting the chaos that was caused by the decline and fall of the Seljuk sultanate of Rum. The latter had emerged in central Anatolia after the battle of Mantzikert (1071), when the Great Seljuk sultan Alp Arslan defeated and captured the Roman basileus Romanos IV Diogenes. Alp Arslan's dynasty was based in the Near East, but a lateral branch of it moved into Anatolia, conquering its upland core from the Romans. The

Seljuk sultans of Rum then ruled over a mostly Christian and Roman population, hence the name Rum. The Seljuks also fought a constant series of civil wars among themselves, faced several crusading armies that arrived from the West, and also tried to manage the influx of additional Turkmen and Persian immigrants.

This delicate balancing act failed when Seljuk Anatolia was targeted by the Mongols in the mid-thirteenth century. The Seljuks became Mongol vassals and lost control over Anatolia, which disintegrated during the tail end of that century. At the same time, more Turkmen streamed into Anatolia and away from areas under Mongol control. Many of them pushed into the west and northwest, where the Romans still maintained their hold in the coastal lands. The last pockets of Roman control there collapsed by ca. 1300 and Anatolia was carved up among a number of Turkish emirates.[3] The Ottomans were only one among them and they were not a particularly powerful group, at least not at first. However, the land they seized, Bithynia, was agriculturally productive and contained major cities, such as Nikaia (İznik in Turkish), Nikomedeia (İzmit), and Prousa (Bursa), which became the first Ottoman capital.

This is not the place to rehearse the wars, battles, and circumstances that led to the growth of the Ottoman empire. It is more important to identify the sources and institutions of Ottoman power, for they were eventually inherited by Mehmed II and brought to bear against Constantinople.

The origins of Ottoman power lay in the local protection racket that was run by the first chiefs, Osman (d. 1323/4), after whom the dynasty is named, and his son and heir Orhan (d. 1362). With a growing band of followers, they would raid for plunder or accept tribute to refrain from raiding. Eventually, they formed close working relationships with local notables, some of whom joined the chief's followings, contributing their local know-how and broader networks of clients to the enterprise, even if they did not always convert to Islam.[4] Eventually, the cities of Bithynia, some of which resisted the Ottomans for decades, surrendered as well. Osman and Orhan did not have an easy task. They had to reward their men with plunder, land, and riches, while also protecting the settled populations that had agreed to pay tribute in exchange for peace and security. The Ottomans were often at war with the other emirates of Anatolia and did not always control the raiders, tribesmen, and holy warriors who moved into Bithynia. But they had an advantage over other emirates, which was that they could funnel surplus raiders and their own ambitions across the straits into the collapsing remnants of the Roman state in the Balkans.

Many Turkish warriors raided the Balkans on their own initiative, while at other times they took up service as mercenaries under the various Roman factions that were fighting their own civil wars. They could wear a number of different hats depending on which one suited them at the moment. Thus, in one campaign they were holy warriors for Islam (*gazi*), which, in their own eyes at least, justified their predations. Holy warfare did not aim to convert people to Islam, only to raid and plunder their lands and enrich the raiders. Another year, these same raiders could be hired by Christian rulers in the Balkans on a seasonal or per-campaign basis. Alternately, they could affiliate themselves with the Ottomans in their wars against other emirates or against their erstwhile Christian employers, especially once Ottoman ambitions extended into the Balkans in the second half of the fourteenth century. The dynasty thus built up its powerbase in northwest Anatolia and was gradually expanding, conquering the lands of its Muslim rivals in the east and of the Christian states in the Balkans, mostly the Romans but eventually also the Serbs and the Bulgarians. By the later fourteenth century, the Ottoman project was looking more like a state, although its ruler remained itinerant, always at war against his neighbors, regardless of their religion. A Balkan capital of sorts was established at Edirne (Adrianople), which was a forward operating base for further conquests at the expense of weak Christian states. Murad I (1362–1389) was called a sultan and, through his non-stop wars, he subordinated several Christian principalities to vassal status. Among other dues, they had to provide soldiers to his campaigns.

The early Ottoman state was centered on the dynasty, whose sultans had to manage their diverse assets and relationships carefully. Christian subjects were given assurances of safety and protection in exchange for paying tribute, and this gradually turned into a regular system of taxation. The sultans continued to coopt Christian notables into their court to tap their skills, connections, and local networks of dependents. Meanwhile, they began to assign lands (*timars*) to their soldiers, both infantry and cavalry, who could be called up in time of war and who enforced sultanic authority locally during peacetime. Eventually, two broad commands emerged, Rumeli (referring to Ottoman lands in the Balkans) and Anatolia. The soldiers of each were placed under the command of a *beylerbey*, or "lord of lords." Thus, on large campaigns, such as the siege of Constantinople, the sultan was accompanied by the *beylerbey* of Rumeli and the *beylerbey* of Anatolia, who commanded the empire's regular forces.

From its inception, the Ottoman project represented a loose alliance between the dynasty and its retainers and armies on the one hand and the quasi-independent raiders on the other (the *akıncı*), who wanted to raid Christian lands for plunder and slaves. Even in the developed empire of the fifteenth century, the raiders acted to "soften up" targets for the sultan and his armies, while raking in huge profits for themselves through the slave trade. "They receive neither wages nor office from the sultan, but are always striving for plunder and loot."[5] Their human captives were sold on the slave markets, some of which were operated by the Venetians and Genoese. The raiders would also fight at the sultan's side in battle when summoned. The sultan's own armies were also deeply invested in the slave trade. The conquest period was thus "fueled not by the zeal of a religious brotherhood, but by the greed and ambition of a predatory confederacy."[6]

To assert central control over this messy process, Murad I and his son, Bayezid (1389–1402), created the janissary corps. This was the sultans' personal elite force, which, by 1453, numbered around 5,000 men. Its name meant "new army," and it was a centralizing counterweight to the raiders, tribal contingents, local recruits, and allied vassal forces that made up the rest of the Ottoman army. The janissaries were the products of a peculiar form of recruitment, the *devşirme* system, which means "collection." Children of conquered Christian populations would be removed from their parents, enrolled as slaves of the Ottoman court, converted to Islam, and raised to become the sultan's soldiers and officials. One of the earliest references to this system comes from a sermon, *On the Abduction of Children*, by the bishop of Thessalonike in 1395, soon after the city had come under Ottoman rule:

> What suffering might one not experience, seeing his own child, whom he raised, over whom he shed tears praying for his happiness, being torn away from him violently by the hands of foreigners and forced to adopt a barbaric language, dress, and religion? . . . A child who once attended churches is taught to murder his own kind![7]

The janissaries exemplified the assimilative nature of the Ottoman elite, in which the old Turkish nobility rubbed shoulders with newly minted Muslims, who might have been conscripted as children or converted as adults. Many janissaries had risen from Christian and slave origins to become the sultan's elite soldiers and high officials. Yet they were prone to causing trouble, like an Ottoman Praetorian Guard, protesting policies they did not like, mutinying to demand better pay, and generally causing disturbances to press their demands. They would continue to cause trouble down to 1826, when the sultan Mahmud II massacred them all on one day (subsequently dubbed the "Auspicious Incident"). A reliance on elite soldiers who rose up from captive origins was not unique to the Ottomans. Other Muslim states relied on similar armies. In Egypt at that time, one such army, the Mamluks, had seized control of the state and ruled it in its own name.[8]

The Ottomans used (former) slaves of Christian origin for another purpose, too, namely as wives and concubines for the sultan's harem. As a result, we know little about the early sultans' women, including the mother of Mehmed II. Among other benefits, this eliminated the pressure on the court that could be brought by powerful and influential in-laws. Thus, the Ottomans rarely engaged in diplomatic marriages, at least not such as could constrain the sultans' freedom of action. The empire's elites were not a hereditary aristocracy that prided itself on pedigree. Men who came from established Muslim families rubbed shoulders at the court with high officials who had risen from slave status, many of them ex-Christians from the conquered Christian populations of the provinces. The sultans themselves were scions of the dynasty, to be sure, but they too often had slave mothers. The leading members of Mehmed's court in 1453 came from this assimilative system.

Mehmed II acceded to the throne of the Ottoman empire in February 1451 (see Color Plate 2 for a later painting of him). He was only nineteen years old, and his grasp on power was insecure. The death of his father, Murad II, had been kept a secret in Edirne (Adrianople) to give Mehmed time to race there from Anatolia and claim the throne before anyone could disrupt the succession, including conquered subjects of the empire who might seize the moment to rebel. The janissaries often bullied the sultans to extract concessions, and it appears that they did mutiny when Murad II died. There were also possible threats to Mehmed's position within the dynasty. One of his first actions was to order the murder of his infant half-brother, thus eliminating a potential dynastic rival who might be used against him. In the years from 1402 to 1413, the sons of the sultan Bayezid had fought a series of bitter and destructive civil wars among themselves, after their father had been defeated and captured by the Mongol conqueror Timur. Those wars were a test of the resilience of the Ottoman empire. It was Mehmed's grandfather Mehmed I (1413–1421) who had managed to reunify the empire after that bout of fratricidal conflict, but a decade of war had exposed the potential for intra-dynastic strife. This made the sultans wary of having too many brothers. Mehmed II did not want to have any.[9]

There were other powers behind the throne that Mehmed could not afford to offend, at least not yet. Chief among them was the grand vizier, Halil Pasha. At this time the sultans were served usually by three viziers, who functioned as their chiefs-of-staff and lead ministers, managing all areas of government and deciding which business should be brought to the sultans' attention. The head vizier, Halil, came from the Çandarlı family, a fabulously wealthy, patrician clan of Turkish aristocrats who had produced grand viziers four generations in a row. Halil was the mover and shaker at the court of Murad II; in fact, he was the arbiter of the succession. It was he who handled the transition of power and countered the janissaries when they tried to take advantage of the brief interregnum in 1451. It was the second time that he played that role. Back in 1444, after defeating the Varna crusade, Murad II had abdicated, retiring to an estate in Anatolia and appointing Mehmed, who was then twelve years old, to be sultan under Halil's supervision. The child naturally proved to be a weak ruler. As enemies assembled against the empire and the janissaries mutinied, Halil orchestrated Murad's return to power in 1446. Mehmed meekly went back to being the designated heir, possibly nursing resentment and grievances against Halil. This bizarre episode in the history of the dynasty is hard to explain. Some accept the testimony of the sources, which present it as a personal decision by Murad to retire, whereas others suspect that it resulted from factional strife at the court that pushed Murad out. As the Ottoman court is opaque, we cannot identify the factions involved.[10] At any rate, when Mehmed II returned to power in 1451, for the second time, it was under the cloud of a past failure and embarrassment.

Halil was a sophisticated courtier, administrator, and diplomat. He is cast in the sources as averse to war with the Romans, repeatedly counseling the sultans against conflict. He is even supposed to have secretly thwarted and sabotaged their designs against Constantinople, including during the siege of 1453. It was rumored that he was being bribed by the Romans. This cannot be proven, but we do know that Halil was actively involved in the trade that passed through the City, so he had a stake in the status quo.[11] Mehmed had to carefully maneuver Halil into supporting the war against Constantinople, or at least not resisting it. But our accounts of their relationship are dramatized and cannot be taken at face value.[12] In reality, we cannot peer into the inner workings of the court. Halil's contacts with the Romans could, alternately, be an asset for the sultan. Mehmed was a skillful diplomat and it suited him to project friendship toward a given foreign power, depending on his strategic objectives, until the moment came for him to attack. It was useful to have a vizier who credibly wore a pro-Roman face. The sultan needed to keep his options open, which meant having men by his side who credibly represented different approaches.

The janissary corps was another source of instability, as was the tension between them, who were recent converts, and the established Turkish elites. Many Romans and other Christians served the sultans as tax collectors, secretaries, and administrators,[13] and some had taken the extra step of converting to Islam to get ahead at the court, although they retained close contacts with their former coreligionists. This made them assets for the sultans as well. The Ottoman leadership had always been of mixed ethnic background. But the Muslims of the *devşirme*—the "collection" system for Christian slave children—were sometimes more eager to wage war on behalf of Islam than the old nobility. If Halil was the dove at Mehmed's court, the hawk was Zaganos Pasha, a convert who had risen through the janissary ranks.[14] He was apparently close to Mehmed and had been dismissed when the latter fell from power in 1446. He was appointed second vizier when Mehmed ascended the throne again in 1451. The court was divided between Halil, the advocate of peace, and Zaganos, who pushed for war. This likely reflected a broader structural cleavage in the Ottoman elite.[15]

The raiders were another potential problem. The Ottoman administration had by this point established a regular military presence in the conquered lands. Thousands of Muslim Turks had been settled throughout the Balkans, and soldiers formed the core of these clusters. Some, albeit a minority, were still Christians.[16] But the sultans still lived a semi-nomadic lifestyle, even when they resided at the palace at Edirne. The Andalusian traveler Pero Tafur was left with the impression that "the Grand Turk and his people are always in the field in their tents, both in winter and summer."[17] This was an exaggeration, but the court remained highly mobile and retained strong traces of its nomadic origins. That is why the frontier warlords felt threatened by the prospect of the conquest of Constantinople. The City could easily pull the court in and transform it into a more settled, bureaucratic power-structure that was further detached from their interests. In the long run, this is precisely what happened. The warlords wanted the periphery to remain central, whereas Mehmed was eyeing the geographical heart of his empire, which remained untamed, its inner frontier as it were.[18]

To be sure, Muslims had dreamed of conquering Constantinople from the beginning of their expansion into the Mediterranean in the seventh century, even though they had been forced to defer that dream for many centuries. In one of his sayings, a *hadith*, the Prophet himself had allegedly declared that Muslims would conquer Constantinople: "Hail to the prince and the army to whom this is given." This "conquest hadith," which is now famous, was apocryphal and is sometimes seen as an Ottoman invention. However, it is probably older, going back to the ninth century, although it was certainly marginal before the Ottomans, who made it famous after the conquest of Constantinople.[19] It is unclear whether traditions such as these inspired Mehmed to attack Constantinople. He did reference them immediately after the conquest, in the victory letters that he sent to other Muslim rulers, such as the sultan of Egypt.[20] Moreover, present at Mehmed's court was the dervish holy man Ak Şemseddin. His biography was written later and contains embellishments. It is said that he prophesied the fall of the City and supported the sultan's decision to besiege it against the objections of many in the court who said that the project was futile ("so many other Muslim leaders have tried it and failed," they said). The holy man's role in these discussions, as well as a surviving letter that he wrote to Mehmed at a critical moment in the siege, expose more fissures within the Ottoman leadership.[21]

To gain mastery over these competing elements, the sultans had elevated themselves by claiming a charismatic mystique and authority. A sultan was the *gazi*-in-chief, expanding the domain of Islam; he was the heir to the Seljuk sultans of Rum; he was a ruler favored by God and prophesied by ancient dreams; and, perhaps most importantly, he was the representative of the dynasty that held the whole project together.[22] After all, there was no sense yet that the Ottoman empire was a polity with a common purpose independent of the coercion that was exerted by the dynasty's armies. Without the dynasty, even its Muslim elites would fragment into rival factions, and its Christian populations would immediately try to regain their lost independence. So, everyone who benefited from the project knew that a degree of central control was necessary to keep it going. The sultans had based and expanded their power upon that understanding. But still, Mehmed had to maintain the loyalty or at least the obedience of all these elements—unruly janissaries, powerful viziers, new and old Muslims, holy men, frontier warlords, and resentful Christians—while also preventing a grand new coalition of Christian powers coming from the West and smashing it to pieces. It was a delicate balancing act.

A successful attack on Constantinople could enhance Mehmed's authority. Alternately, it could destabilize the empire and distract it from pressing problems. That risk was probably why the grand vizier Halil opposed the project, not because he was on the take. Pero Tafur had observed that, "if the Turks did not lay hands upon the City, it was for fear of the Christian peoples of the West, lest they should take up arms."[23] An attack on Constantinople might again unify the West against the empire. This fear is confirmed by the basileus' confidant Georgios Sphrantzes. In his memoirs, he says that Halil advised Murad II not to attack Constantinople because that would push the Romans to accept Union with the Catholic Church and "then, behold, what we fear most will come to pass."[24]

The basileis of the Romans were balanced precariously on the other side of that equation. Manuel II Palaiologos had clearly explained to his heir Ioannes VIII the cynical game that the Romans had to play:

> What the infidel fears most at the bottom of his heart is that we will come to an agreement and unite with the Franks, because they know that, should that happen, great harm will come to them from the Christians of the West on our account. So when it comes to a Council for Union, look into the matter and make a great noise about it, especially when you have to frighten off the infidel, but never carry it through to its conclusion, because our people are not inclined to find a way forward with union, peace, and harmony . . . I fear lest they create an even worse schism and we are left exposed to the infidel.[25]

This gives away what the Latins had long suspected, namely that the Greeks were not sincere about Union but were only leading them on because they wanted help, or at least a credible threat, against the Turks. A number of basileis and their high officials were ready to accept Union on the terms required by the papacy, but they knew that they could not enforce it on their people and that trying to do so would create only more social division at home that would probably worsen relations with the West. Best to just play the game of keeping the Latins and the Turks in a tense balance.

Yet, against his father's advice, Ioannes VIII went to Italy with a massive delegation of Orthodox clergy and some leading intellectuals. In 1439, at Florence, an agreement regarding the Union of the two Churches was hammered out, after long debates and great difficulty. This alarmed the sultan, Murad II. However, when Ioannes returned to Constantinople he neither enforced nor proclaimed the Union officially. It quickly became apparent that the issue was too explosive, that Union was unpopular with too many people, and that it would split society and the Church into factions. A number of signatories repudiated the consent that they had given. The theologian Georgios Scholarios, who had accepted Union at Florence, also changed his mind and eventually became the leader of the most intransigent opposition to Union with Rome (he took the name Gennadios when he became a monk in 1448). Thus, while the basileus himself remained personally committed to Union, the pope saw no sign that the Church and people of Constantinople had accepted it.[26] The Varna crusade that was launched in 1443–1444 was intended not to help the Greeks primarily but the Hungarians. However, Ottoman observers could connect the Council of Florence to the Varna crusade, and at least one contemporary, possibly a janissary, did just that.[27] Union was a security threat for the Ottomans. Even if the agreement at Florence did not bring material aid for Constantinople, Ioannes VIII had managed to aggravate both the Turks *and* the Latins, a lose-lose outcome.

The issue of Union was extremely divisive in Constantinople. To be clear, all Christians were theoretically in favor of it, but the Devil lay in the conditions required by Rome, including acceptance by the Orthodox of an addition to the Creed regarding the Procession of the Holy Spirit (from the Father *and* the Son—*filioque*—not only the Father). Constantinople also had to accept the pope as supreme leader of Christendom, although what this meant in practice was unclear. It certainly entailed mentioning the pope's name in the prayers after the liturgy, which became a litmus test in Constantinople for one's position. These and other terms were flatly unacceptable to many Orthodox. Thus, in a strange twist, the problem of military defense against the Turks was inextricably bound up with obscure doctrinal disputes between the Churches, disputes that, however, had by now become red lines of Orthodox identity.

There were non-theological issues at play, too. The Romans could not forgive the unjustified atrocities perpetrated on Constantinople by the armies of the Fourth Crusade in 1203–1204, or the subsequent dismemberment of Romanía into feudal territories ruled by racist colonial dukes and barons from the West. It would not have been forgotten that the Crusaders justified this aggression also in religious terms, by claiming that they were "reducing" the Greeks "back to obedience" to the pope. It was not easy to forgive and forget this history of violence, resentment, cynicism, and suspicion. The Romans regarded the Latins as insufferably arrogant for seeking to enforce their religion on them, while the Latins regarded the Greeks as insufferably arrogant for refusing to submit to the pope. Both sides viewed each other's Church as deviant, verging on heretical. Many Latins also regarded the Greeks as cowards, devious dissemblers, unreliable, and sexually effeminate.[28]

A small minority of ethnic Romans sincerely accepted Catholicism. They included prominent intellectuals, including Bessarion and Isidoros, who were appointed cardinals by the pope; teachers such as Ioannes Argyropoulos; and even clergy, such as the patriarch Gregorios III (1443–1450). All four of those men, and many others, eventually emigrated to Italy. Another group consisted of politicians who professed Union for pragmatic reasons. They included Ioannes VIII and many high officials, such as the *mesazon* (i.e., chief minister) Loukas Notaras.

These men valued western assistance more than Orthodox purity, and so were pro-Union, but at the same time they knew that aid was unlikely to come unless they repressed domestic opposition to Union. This they were disinclined to do, temperamentally and morally, but also pragmatically: persecuting Orthodox hardliners in the name of Union with the Catholic Church would cause greater problems than it would solve. It had been tried by the pro-Union basileus Michael VIII Palaiologos back in the 1270s and had failed miserably. They did not want to repeat that experience, although the popes and their spokesmen seemed to expect it.

Sociologically, Roman elites, such as Notaras, who had business relationships with the Italians—and held Genoese or Venetian citizenship—were more likely to accept Union.[29] Most Romans, however, rejected it, although their attitudes were diverse and liable to change depending on circumstances. We cannot access them because we have only the writings of people with a strong agenda. But a common attitude was likely reflected by Sphrantzes in his memoirs. He wished that Florence had not happened:

> Let the experts debate the doctrines. But the faith I received from my father is good enough for me . . . Suppose that for many years, in the company of some friends, I have been walking to Hagia Sophia through the City along the main boulevard, and one day they tell me that they have discovered another way to get there and want to take me that way. Well, I will tell them that this way that I have been on suffices for me. You go that way in peace and reach Hagia Sophia however you like, but I will continue to go this way, which is an old and good way.[30]

Đurađ Branković, the contemporary despot of Serbia, gave a similar response to a Catholic friar: "I have lived for ninety years and know no other religion than the one I received from my forefathers . . . I would rather end my life with a noose than abandon the traditions of my ancestors."[31]

If the political leadership was amenable to Union, the majority of Orthodox clergy was likely not.[32] An anti-Union pressure-group quickly formed. By writing letters and pamphlets and preaching fiery sermons, they tried to persuade, shame, or bully their peers into rejecting Union, and their influence soon spread far and wide across lay society, too. Their first leader was Markos Eugenikos of Ephesos, the only bishop who had steadfastly refused to sign off on Union at Florence. His brother Ioannes was a skilled agitator and advocate for the cause. After Markos' death, Gennadios Scholarios became the group's leader. By the mid-1440s, it was calling itself the Holy Synaxis ("Assembly") and was acting as a "shadow" rival of the official Holy Synod of the court and patriarch.[33] The Synaxis boycotted Unionist services and urged everyone else to do so too. Ioannes Eugenikos scolded Notaras merely for visiting the residence of the patriarch Gregorios III and told Konstantinos XI that high officials were not sincere when they claimed to support Union as they were also attending avowedly anti-Union services.[34]

This broke the Church and made it dysfunctional. Basic court ceremonies became politicized and sometimes could not be performed for fear of polarizing society even further. When Ioannes VIII died late in 1448, he was buried without the full rites befitting a basileus. Then, when Konstantinos XI arrived in 1449 to replace him, he chose not to be crowned by the patriarch as was customary, probably because Gregorios III was too isolated and polarizing a figure.[35] Any such high-profile event would become a flash-point of controversy, exacerbating the division. Whoever has witnessed a modern culture war will know what it felt like. Even so, Konstantinos was depicted with a crown during his reign (see Color Plate 1). But the patriarch Gregorios III was so disgusted at this state of affairs, and so blocked from doing his job, that he left the City for good in 1450. He didn't resign or give an official explanation. He just . . . left, eventually ending up in Rome on a papal stipend. There was no patriarch in Roman Constantinople after that. The Church was paralyzed.[36]

So how did opponents of Union believe that Constantinople could be saved from the Turks? The leadership of the Synaxis does not tell us because they did not think in pragmatic terms when it came to secular matters. They saw everything in terms of theodicy and the narrow goals of their culture war. They believed (or said) that Turks were prevailing *because* of Union, which angered God. The implication was that if the

Synaxis' views prevailed then somehow the problems would go away. The solution was prayer. But unless Union was repudiated, there was no hope. Besides, the West had not delivered on its promises of aid, nor would it. So, by sticking to the current policy, the Orthodox would lose *both* their faith *and* their freedom.[37] Besides, anti-Latin agitators cared less about being conquered by the Turks than about having Catholicism forced upon them. Ioannes Eugenikos told Notaras that "Latinism would be a far more bitter captivity than falling to the barbarians."[38] According to Doukas, when Mehmed's forces arrived some hoped that Constantinople would fall into the hands of the Latins, who were at least Christians, whereas others declared that Turkish rule was preferable to that of the Latins.[39]

The most notorious of these statements is the least likely to be historical. Doukas attributes to Notaras a saying that has become infamous and emblematic of fanatical adherence to Orthodoxy. "Better to see the Turkish turban in the middle of the City than the Latin headgear." It is not clear what that last word refers to: a papal miter? a Latin crown? Was Notaras referring to western political rule or Church Union?[40] At any rate, he probably did not make this statement at all. As a pragmatic politician, Notaras followed the basileus' pro-Union policy. His correspondence with the leading anti-Unionists reveals that they did not regard him as one of their own but as a temporizer. They condemned his "flexibility" in the matter. Yet he tried to keep open channels with both them and their opponents.[41] Besides, it is unlikely that Notaras looked favorably on the prospect of Turkish rule. Back in 1411, during a brief siege of Constantinople Turks had killed his brother and publicly beheaded the body. The family had to pay a huge ransom to retrieve it.[42]

The Romans were weighing the pros and cons of Latin vs. Turkish rule because they had been stuck between the two rising powers for four centuries. No one *wanted* to be conquered by either side; both options were horrible.[43] By this time, Romans around the Aegean had long experience of Latin and Turkish rule. Both were exploitative, reducing them to second-class status with fewer rights than they had before. The Latins were Christians, but they refused to recognize the Romans' ethnic identity, calling them "Greeks," often pejoratively, and regarded their Orthodoxy as deviant. The Turks, on the other hand, recognized both their Romanness and their religion, as they did not seek to change their subjects' identity, only to subjugate them. As early as the thirteenth century, opponents of Union insisted that "Muslims will dominate your body, but the heretics [i.e., Latins] will take over your soul."[44] After the fall of the City, Gennadios similarly argued that Latins force the Orthodox to accept their mode of worship, whereas their current masters, the Turks, may be oppressive but at least they allow us to worship in our ancestral way.[45]

Orthodox hardliners were suggesting that Turkish rule was the lesser of two evils. Gennadios was essentially saying that we can work with these people and find a way forward under them. But he would quickly be disillusioned on that point. Even before the fall, some Romans had recognized that life under Muslim rule also threatened the pillars of Roman Orthodox identity. Toward the start of the century, the emperor Manuel II Palaiologos had observed that getting ahead under Turkish rule meant adjusting to their laws and customs and eventually losing one's own. Many converted to Islam under such conditions. And in other works, written after the fall, Gennadios presents a different picture, according to which the Turks are insufferably oppressive and have caused many of the Orthodox to convert to Islam. Regular Christian life was difficult in Turkish-ruled lands, he realized.[46] Perhaps neither option was really workable in the end.

Orthodox monasteries had already learned to reach accommodations with the Ottomans.[47] This was made easier by the fact that the sultans did not feel threatened by monasteries and preferred to organize their subjects' lives around their religion rather than their secular-political institutions. The latter were always a potential threat because military opposition could rally around them. Therefore, monasteries managed to strike deals with the sultans or their representatives that allowed them to survive, albeit with diminished landholdings. The more radical membership of the Synaxis may have had this kind of accommodationist model in mind for the rest of their fellow Romans. Before the siege, Gennadios was in touch with Romans who worked for the Ottoman court, men who ransomed him after the fall and brought him before the sultan as an ideal leader for the Orthodox Church.[48] Relations between the anti-Unionists and the Turks might in fact have been tight. A mediator between the two was Demetrios Palaiologos, the basileus' brother. He was in touch with precisely the same men at the sultan's court who later ransomed Gennadios. When he attempted a coup in 1442 with Turkish aid, he also had anti-Unionists backing him in the City. By 1450, Demetrios, Gennadios, and the Synaxis were corresponding about overturning the Union. There may well have been a pro-Turkish, anti-Union faction waiting for its moment.[49]

That moment came after the fall. Yet when the siege was upon them, most Romans did not stop for a second to ponder whether they preferred the Latins to the Turks. It was not the Latins who were attacking the City. They had not done so in a century. Since then, Italians, Catalans, Castilians, and Frenchmen had lived among the Romans, trading with them and bringing them food and other goods, employing them, and had even allowed some of them to profit from their business, if only marginally. When the Turks came, Romans and Latins stood together, as both Constantinopolitans and Christians. As we will see when we look at the events of the siege, it is erroneous to believe that religious divisions undermined the defense effort, whether we mean the divisions between Catholic and Orthodox or between pro- and anti-Union Orthodox. This position was taken by at least one contemporary historian and many modern ones.[50] However, there is no evidence that religious division hampered the defense once the siege began. The culture war paled into insignificance when the sultan's armies arrived.

Few rulers in history have come to power in conditions as unenviable as those of Konstantinos XI. In early 1449, he traveled to Constantinople from the Morea to rule over the Roman polity, leaving behind his two quarreling brothers, Thomas and Demetrios, to govern the Peloponnese between them. An agreement between them was worked out, which is presumably commemorated in the main church of the Old Taxiarches monastery in Aigialeia, near Aigion on the northern coast. In connection with a major donation, images of Konstantinos as basileus and his brothers as despots were painted inside the church (see Color Plate 1).[51] This is the only known contemporary image of the basileus, and it was identified only recently. His regalia feature the double-headed eagle used by the basileis of this period as an emblem. The Palaiologoi also issued silver coins bearing their image, although it was rudimentary and typecast, and sometimes certified their official documents with gold seals that also bore their image and title (see Image 2.1).

Konstantinos inherited a capital with almost no territory and a Church that would soon have no patriarch. He had no empress, and his two wives had died before they could give him an heir. He was a basileus but had not been crowned, nor could he be crowned, because of the division in the Church. At least that was a blow only to his pride, not his position. Formal coronations had no constitutional significance in the Roman monarchy, as a basileus was created by the consensus of his subjects and their acclamations. Coronations were symbolic ceremonies, and we should not project western beliefs about them onto the east Romans. No one doubted that Konstantinos was the legitimate basileus of the Romans. All recognized him as that, although anti-Union

Image 2.1 Gold seal of Ioannes VIII Palaiologos (1425–1448), used to authenticate documents (the groove through which the string passed runs visibly down the middle). The obverse depicts Christ while the reverse depicts Ioannes with the title *autokrator*. His brother, Konstantinos XI Palaiologos, used the same design. Source: © Dumbarton Oaks, Washington, DC.

agitators rubbed in the humiliation of his failure to be crowned, pretending that it had been caused by the Union with Rome rather than by their own troublemaking.[52]

Pro-Union writers were more deferential. Ioannes Argyropoulos greeted Konstantinos' arrival with traditional speeches of praise. As a Catholic, he viewed his people as Hellenes (i.e., Greeks), rather than Romans. In one speech, he laments that the Hellenes, who used to rule the world, had lost their dominion over land, seas, cities, and revenue to the barbarians. They lack allies and fear losing their City, their common hearth. What is worse, he adds, instead of fighting the barbarians we are fighting among ourselves over the most important matters, by which he means religion. May help come from the West and may the basileus inspire hope that our people will yet behold the light of freedom "at this late hour."[53]

Was hope warranted? Could Konstantinos actually govern? It can easily appear that he had no room in which to maneuver and no resources with which to do so. He chose to do nothing about Union so as not to exacerbate the prevailing social division. It was probably a wise policy. He was sensitive to public opinion in the City. The people of Constantinople could be a savage and disruptive force. On the financial side, the Roman state was broke and in debt to the Venetians.[54] Konstantinos tried to impose some minor taxes on goods that the Venetians were importing, but they furiously protested this action.[55] The basileus of the Romans was struggling to assert himself over small change. (Such petty squabbles, however, quickly evaporated in 1453. When the enemy arrived, Konstantinos entrusted his palace and harbor to the Venetians to defend.) It is also likely that the basileus did not—and could not—pay salaries to his leading officials, and that they supported themselves privately. It is probably no accident that his richest subject, Notaras, who was living off his father's investments in the dried fish trade, was also his most powerful official.

In his memoirs, Sphrantzes recounts a moving if pathetic scene in which the basileus confesses to him in despair that he was unable to push back against the demands and opinions of his grandees, leaving him with no one to consult, apart from Sphrantzes himself, of course. Notaras ran the place and, as the saying went, "could move every rock." Supposedly, Konstantinos could not bestow a high court title on Sphrantzes openly because it would offend Notaras, and so he ridiculously asked Sphrantzes to accept the title in private only and keep it a secret between the two of them.[56] But we must be careful with this testimony. Sphrantzes disliked Notaras and wanted to present himself as the basileus' closest confidant. But there is no other sign of tension between the basileus and his *mesazon*; they worked together quite well. This, however, does not mean that Konstantinos was calling the shots. Leonardo of Chios said that he was a good man, but he lacked firmness and so everyone around him did whatever they wanted; no one was punished for disobeying him and he pretended not to see what was happening.[57]

Even so, Konstantinos had grounds for hope. He was personally well liked and broadly regarded as a decent and patient man. He had no bitter enemies. Even Italians, who disliked the Greeks, spoke of him with respect. Konstantinos projected the gravity of an "emperor" in the Latins' eyes, managing to persuade Italians who were in the City to stay and help him defend it. Moreover, it is only in hindsight that we see him as a tragic and doomed figure. His memory has been inextricably bound to the fall of Constantinople, making it difficult to see him in other terms. Moreover, we are so used to seeing this phase of "Byzantine" history in hopeless terms, as a pointless extension of a failed state, that we fail to assess its prospects. Konstantinos might have had a more optimistic outlook. He was, after all, born into a time of renewed hope for the Romans. We may not see it that way, but at the time it was a plausible perspective. Two years before his birth, Bayezid had been defeated by Timur, and the Ottoman empire was shattered. The Romans regained territory, including the city of Thessalonike, and Konstantinos' father, Manuel II, played a major role in the prolonged Ottoman civil war.

For reasons that will be explained in the following chapter, Roman–Turkish relations soured in 1421. The following year, the young sultan, Murad II, besieged Constantinople with canons and janissaries. The siege was a failure, forcing Murad to withdraw. Konstantinos, seventeen years old at the time, was probably present in the City and witnessed this failure. When Ioannes VIII traveled to Italy in 1423–1424 to seek aid, he left Konstantinos in charge as his vicegerent.[58] This was the first of three times that Konstantinos governed the City. Meanwhile, the Romans were strengthening their position in the Morea and gradually expanding their rule there to the entirety of the peninsula by absorbing the territories of its remaining Latin lords, excepting Venetian strongholds along the coastal routes. Konstantinos himself played a key role in this process in 1427–1432 through feats of arms, naval battles, diplomacy, and a strategic marriage. The reconquest of the Peloponnese was a messy process and not without setbacks, but it was he who won the greatest victory when he took Patras in 1429, and then its citadel in 1430.[59] Based on his own experiences, Konstantinos had reason to believe that Roman fortunes could be revived.

Konstantinos governed Constantinople again in from 1437 to 1439 while Ioannes VIII traveled to Italy for the Council of Florence. During this time, Konstantinos met and greeted Pero Tafur, among other travelers, envoys, and pilgrims.[60] In 1443, he returned to the Peloponnese. His actions as the despot at Mystras reveal an ambitious sense of what could be accomplished. In 1444, taking advantage of the Varna crusade and Murad II's abdication, he refortified the Hexamilion wall and overran Boiotia and parts of Attica, forcing the (Florentine) duke of Athens to pay tribute to him. Possibly he extended his reach into Lokris, Phokis, and even Thessaly, thereby infringing on the territories of the sultan and the Venetians, too, and not just the Florentine duke. This aggressive move proved to be misguided. When Murad returned to power, he wiped out these gains in a single campaign in 1446. The Hexamilion wall at the Isthmos turned out, once again, to be militarily useless. The janissaries overran it, in part by using guns and cannons, then raided widely across the Peloponnese, dragging thousands of captives away while Konstantinos ran for cover.[61] It was a sobering slap in the face of what Argyropoulos would call "hope." Konstantinos had made serious miscalculations and probably came to the City in a sober state of mind. But his tenure there shows that, as late as the mid-1440s, Konstantinos was not pessimistically resigned to decline and fall, to living within narrow means and contracting horizons.

The reason why Konstantinos had no money, despite the excellent harbor of the City and its strategic location on a number of major trade routes, was that the Venetians and Genoese had, over the centuries, extracted tax exemptions from his predecessors that enabled them to grow fabulously rich at the Romans' expense. Their trade routes consisted of strategic nodes strung out along the coastlines of the Black Sea and Aegean. Each Italian republic had created its own "in-house" network, while the fiscal exemptions that made it profitable had been created not by diplomacy and trade alone but primarily through violence. Venetians and Genoese had forcibly removed islands and coastal forts from Roman control and extorted ever greater concessions when it came to taxes and residency in the City itself. The deal that Michael VIII Palaiologos had cut with the Genoese in the 1260s, allowing them to settle at Pera as their own colony, was intended to deploy them as a counterweight to the Venetians. But this only allowed them to enter Roman waters in force and entrench themselves at the Romans' expense.

The eastern trade networks of Venice and Genoa in the fifteenth century were quite different. Venice was dominant in the west, along the Adriatic and Ionian Seas, in the south, on Crete, around the coast of the Peloponnese, and on Euboia in the western Aegean. Its holdings were governed directly by Venice itself, as colonial outposts. This reflected its own evolution as an integrated, sovereign state.[62] By contrast, Genoa was more like a coalition of wealthy noble families and an urban populace. In the east, it was represented by opportunistic families and adventurers who made their own arrangements. They were present in the eastern Aegean, with the Gattilusi ruling the island of Lesbos and Ainos on the coast of Thrace, ostensibly in the name of the basileus, and they ran the profitable alum mines and port at Phokaia on the coast of Asia Minor.[63] A corporation of Genoese shareholders, the Mahona, mostly of the Giustiniani family, ruled Chios, generating huge profits from the mastic trees that are unique to the island.[64] The Genoese were also more dominant in the Black Sea, with colonies in the north at Tana and Kaffa, although the Venetians had a strong presence too. Both groups were heavily invested in the slave trade, obtaining their human cargos from the north or from the captives that were generated by Ottoman expansion. Many thousands of Romans were captured by Turks and sold to Genoese or Venetian middlemen, who exported them to slave markets around the Mediterranean.[65]

The Venetians and Genoese in Constantinople were organized differently, too. The Venetians formed a self-governing, largely autonomous community that lived in the City proper, mostly around the harbor. They were governed by the bailo, an official sent from Venice (in 1453 this was Girolamo Minotto); he was advised by the local Council of Twelve (the Venetians generally loved committees and subcommittees).[66] Venetians abroad also liked to replicate their home city, so their main church in Constantinople was San Marco. Their number included not only Italians but also Greeks from Crete who held Venetian citizenship. Venetian citizenship was also held by many subjects of the basileus, including his *mesazon* (Notaras) and treasurer (Andronikos Koumouses). Thus, many bridges existed between Romans and Venetians, including business partnerships, employment (mostly of Romans by Venetians), intermarriage, common entertainments, and worship. But the Venetian community was mixed in another way, too. It included permanent residents of the City, merchants and sailors who passed through on a regular basis, and those who were truly transient, perhaps docking there only once or twice. Many Venetians who participated in the siege of 1453, especially on the ships in the harbor, were possibly there for the first time.

Venetian convoys were also organized by the state. The state owned the galleys, set the routes and schedule for each run, and auctioned off the rights to operate its ships to members of the nobility who bid for them. The convoys were simultaneously mercantile and military because the ships had to be able to fight off pirates and hostile states, including the Genoese. This proved to be advantageous in 1453, as some of the galleys harbored in Constantinople were also formidable war machines with crews trained to fight.[67]

By contrast, the Genoese had an actual city of their own on the northern side of the harbor, Pera/Galatas. It was small in size but prosperous. Pera had been granted as a concession to them by Michael VIII Palaiologos in 1267, on the condition that it remain nominally subject to him and his heirs, at least in symbolic ways; for example, its ships were required to raise the basileus' banner first upon entering the harbor. Yet over time it became functionally independent, expanded, and surrounded itself with walls, violating its agreements with the basileus. Pera was governed by a podestà sent from Genoa, who resided in an official palace; in 1453, this was Angelo Giovanni Lomellino. In its own way, Pera, too, evoked its metropolis, Genoa, perhaps through the lofty towers of its nobility.[68] Many of its residents were Greeks, some with Genoese citizenship. According to Tetaldi, the town's population was 7,000; according to Pero Tafur, it was 2,000.[69] It also housed Dominican monks, who had been trying to persuade the Greeks to accept the pope since the thirteenth century.[70]

Some of the Italians in Constantinople and Pera were permanent residents with full lives there. But many were there solely for trade and profit. That was their priority and they subordinated everything else to it. Moreover, the priority of their distant governments of Genoa and Venice was to maximize profits, regardless of what that might mean sometimes for local ties, religion, and basic ethics. In the past, Genoa and Venice had fought vicious wars against each other over control of the most important trade nodes, but in the fifteenth century they had settled into a peaceful state of rivalry, mutual hatred, and occasional piracy. They avoided open war, because it was too costly and had proven to be indecisive.

The Italians' relations with the Romans were utilitarian and exploitative. Between them, Venice and Genoa had contributed greatly toward turning Romanía into a powerless state that could not limit their profit margins, an empty husk from which they had sucked the marrow. They resented any effort by the basileis to tap into the proceeds of the trade that passed through Constantinople. As mentioned, one of Konstantinos' small battles was to impose minor taxes on Venetian imports to the

City, in 1450–1451. He explained that they were necessary for the City to function. This elicited a furious protest from Venice, whose envoy threatened to remove the Venetian community to a city not under the basileus' jurisdiction, reminding him for good measure of the debts that he already owed to Venice.[71]

Neither Venice nor Genoa was a reliable ally. Instead, they made deals with the Turks too, seeking short-term gains regardless of future consequences. In 1421, Venice instructed its bailo to hide from the Romans the fact that he was negotiating with the sultan over trade rights. The following year, Genoa was happy to sell its services to the sultan, ferrying his army across the straits as he was about to besiege Constantinople. In 1430, Venice tried to block Roman–Ottoman trade.[72] In 1444, the Genoese once again ferried Murad's army across the straits so that he could defeat the crusade at Varna. In 1452, they provided him with materials to build the fort of Rumeli Hisarı, the opening act of the siege of Constantinople.[73] At that very moment, the Venetian Senate was debating whether it was worth trying to help Constantinople at all.[74]

And yet, when Mehmed's armies and fleet appeared before the walls in early 1453, the Venetians and many of the Genoese who were present stepped up and helped to defend the City, giving their lives and risking their freedom to prevent it from falling into the hands of the sultan. In part, this was for calculated reasons. Mehmed had already used Rumeli Hisarı to attack Venetian shipping and was essentially at war with Venice. Genoese Pera maintained the fiction that it was at peace with the sultan and so neutral in the fight, but many of its citizens fought for the defense. Both the Venetians and the Genoese realized correctly that the fall of Constantinople would greatly harm their business interests. But there was more. The Italians who were present in the City were not just merchants and sailors but also nobles and fighters, and they valued their honor in matters of war. Their decision to stay was influenced by the basileus himself. Both Venetian and Genoese sources portray him as a man of honor and Christian dignity. He had the proper gravitas of an "emperor." When he asked them to help defend a Christian city from the "infidel," they did so, despite their misgivings.

In and around Constantinople, Romans, Turks, and Italians lived in a shared world with few cultural and material boundaries. They learned each other's languages, borrowing words freely in all directions. They ate each other's food and wore each other's clothes. The Ottoman leadership wore garments imported from Italy.[75] They traded goods, traveled, and knew each other's cities intimately. Ethnicity and citizenship did not overlap neatly and there was a lot of movement across categories, as individuals and families sought new opportunities. On the eve of 1453, the Romans were divided over Union, and their culture was already partly Turkified.[76] The Venetians and Genoese were bitter rivals and used to making flexible deals across religious boundaries for the sake of profit.

Yet when Mehmed's armies approached the City, all this fluidity mattered for little. The sultan's imperial objectives were neither fluid nor flexible. Nor, it turned out, were the deepest commitments of the people he targeted. Rather than surrender to him, the Romans, regardless of their stance on Union or the hybridity of their culture, chose to fight, risking all to preserve their freedom. Food and clothes did not define identities. The Italians, at the urging of the basileus, also put aside their mutual differences and their common dislike of the Romans. They too risked their lives, freedom, and cargos for, as Barbaro put it, "the honor of God and the Christian faith."[77]

3

The Outbreak of War

For a generation before the accession of Mehmed II, Roman–Ottoman relations had been governed by the treaty of 1424. This, in turn, represented a revision of the terms of the treaty of 1403 in a way that favored the Ottomans. The treaty of 1403 had been concluded after the catastrophic defeat of the sultan Bayezid by the Mongol conqueror Timur at the battle of Ankara. Bayezid's heirs immediately embarked on an eleven-year civil war among themselves. Each of them sought Roman support, as Constantinople was a crucial strategic node between the two halves of the now shattered Ottoman empire. The treaty of 1403 made territorial concessions to the Romans, including Thessalonike, which had surrendered to the Ottomans in 1387, and the Thracian coast along both the Sea of Marmara and Black Sea. The basileus was no longer treated as a vassal who had to pay tribute but rather as the sultan's honored "father." During the ensuing decade of war, the Romans intervened in Ottoman politics and developed a taste for playing king-maker, backing one claimant after another.[1] Eventually Mehmed I (1413–1421) emerged victorious and consolidated his rule over the entire empire. In 1416, Manuel II secured from him an annual payment of 300,000 Turkish silver coins (akçe) to maintain, but also keep under guard, a pretender to the Ottoman throne, Mustafa.[2]

However, the strategy of meddling in the Ottoman succession backfired badly when it was tried again in 1421, upon Mehmed I's death. Against the sound advice of an ailing Manuel II, Ioannes VIII unleashed the pretender Mustafa against Mehmed's designated successor Murad

II. The outcome was disastrous for the Romans. Murad swiftly defeated and killed Mustafa, besieged Constantinople and Thessalonike, and sent forces to invade the Peloponnese. Thessalonike was so hard-pressed that the Romans had to turn it over to the Venetians in 1423, who lost it after a seven-year blockade in 1430. The siege of Constantinople in 1422 lasted for only three months because Murad had to deal with yet another pretender in Asia Minor backed by Roman gold. Constantinople's ambassadors, including Loukas Notaras and Georgios Sphrantzes, worked out a treaty with Murad in 1424, in which the Romans made significant concessions. They surrendered the coastal strip along the Black Sea, excepting fortified cities such as Mesembria, as well as the lands around the Strymon river in Macedonia that they had gained by the treaty of 1403. They also agreed to *pay* an annual tribute of 300,000 akçe.[3]

For the Romans, the days of playing Ottoman king-maker and generally acting "large" on the international stage were over. This is what Manuel II meant when, criticizing his son's actions in the Mustafa debacle, he told Sphrantzes that the Roman state needed a prudent steward more than a basileus. The Romans had to adopt to a more modest foreign policy.[4]

The peace established in 1424 held for almost thirty years, excepting some minor provocations and clashes. When Ioannes VIII went to Italy to ratify Union between the Churches at the Council of Florence in 1439, Murad II assumed that a broader Christian alliance against him was in the making. But Ioannes assured him that his journey had to do only with the faith and not politics. Murad accepted this at face value, likely with a grain of salt.[5] When Ioannes died in 1448, his younger brother Demetrios, who was anti-Union and either pro-Turkish or just an out-and-out Turkish puppet, made a bid to seize the throne. But he was blocked by the rest of the Palaiologos family, his mother included, as well as by the entire court, all the high officials, and the populace of the City, who preferred Konstantinos.[6] The latter dispatched Sphrantzes to the sultan with gifts and assurances of friendship, which the sultan accepted gracefully.[7] Murad is praised by Roman authors as mild and true to his agreements with Christians. At any rate, those qualities of his were stressed later, once they experienced his son Mehmed II, who lacked them.[8]

Mehmed II succeeded his father in February 1451. Initially, he, too, was gracious. Konstantinos congratulated him on his accession and asked him to pay for the expenses associated with the upkeep of another Ottoman prince, Orhan, held in the "protective custody" of Constantinople. Mehmed granted this request by earmarking revenue worth 300,000 akçe from some lands along the Strymon river. As this was the sum that the Romans owed by the treaty of 1424, it was in effect a remission of the annual tribute.[9] As we saw in the previous chapter, Mehmed was in an insecure position, acceding to the throne at a young age for the second time and with a cloud hanging over his reputation. He was equally gracious and accommodating to the Serbs, Hungarians, Wallachians, Venetians, Bulgarians, the Gattilusi of Lesbos, the Hospitaller Knights of Rhodes, the Genoese of Pera and Chios, and all others who came to congratulate him, sound him out, and lobby him.[10] Meanwhile, he was inspecting the treasury and learning the ropes of his new position.

At the same time, Mehmed was making plans for a campaign against the unruly emirate of Karaman in Asia Minor. It is unclear how early in 1451 he made this decision, so it is possible that he was planning the campaign while negotiating with the foreign embassies. In this case, he would have wanted to reassure them so as to secure his other fronts while focusing on Karaman. Later, if necessary, he could revise his agreements, appeasing everyone else again while focusing his aggression on an isolated target. He used this tactic often, earning a reputation for untrustworthiness—"a wolf under a sheep's hide."[11] His biographer Kritoboulos insinuated that, in Mehmed's view, might made right.[12]

Mehmed was still regarded by many as a weak and simple boy who posed no threat. It was not only Latins who held this view. The ruler of Trebizond in the southeast corner of the Black Sea implied as much to Sphrantzes, who went there in search of a bride for his master Konstantinos XI.[13] Thus, there is no reason to think that Constantinople was unduly worried over Mehmed's accession. In 1451, Konstantinos

XI sent envoys to a number of foreign powers, including Venice, the papacy, and other Italian cities, as well as to king Alfonso V of Aragon in Naples, a major player who wanted to expand his presence in the eastern Mediterranean. Some historians attribute this burst of diplomatic activity to "alarm" in Constantinople over the Ottomans.[14] But there is no sign of that. The Roman envoys went to Venice mostly to wrangle over some minor taxes that Konstantinos wanted to levy on Venetians in the City. "There is no word of emergency in the documents . . . no warning of especial danger."[15] To the pope they brought a (futile) proposal from the Synaxis for a Council to be held in Constantinople that would settle the issue of Union.[16] It is not clear what they wanted from Alfonso of Aragon. His response, at any rate, politely declines to help, citing preoccupations in Italy, but does not specifically mention the Turks.[17]

We have pope Nicholas V's response to Konstantinos, which was sent in late September 1451. It, too, does not mention the Turks and merely reiterates the standard papal position: the basileus must enforce the decision of the Council of Florence and his Church must accept the papacy as "unquestionably supreme." If the Greeks want to receive anything from the West, they must restore the unionist patriarch Gregorios III. Gregorios was in Rome, having left Constantinople in protest at the obstructionist tactics of his opponents in the Synaxis. They must also include the pope's name in their liturgical prayers. Nicholas blamed the Schism on Photios, a patriarch of Constantinople in the ninth century, whom he identified with Satan.[18]

An episode reported only by Doukas suggests that, far from being afraid of Mehmed, Konstantinos and his advisors believed that they could push him around, a fatal miscalculation, if the story is accurate. During the Karaman campaign, the basileus sent envoys asking Mehmed to raise the annual stipend for Orhan, hinting that otherwise they might have to release him, and who knew what he might do? This was thinly disguised extortion. The Romans had likely concluded from their success in early 1451 that Mehmed was weak and would make concessions rather than face a civil war instigated by yet another Roman-backed pretender. The vizier Halil, who was otherwise sympathetic to the Romans, was appalled at this brazen demand, and the sultan flew into a rage. He canceled the gift of the Strymon revenues for Orhan's upkeep and decided to build the fortress of Rumeli Hisarı on the European side of the Bosporos, a first step toward the conquest of the City.[19]

We do not know when Mehmed decided to conquer Constantinople. It may have been his "dream" all along and the Orhan fiasco was only a pretext, or else that demand may have pushed him to it. Rumors were circulating about Rumeli Hisarı already by the fall of 1451.[20] Konstantinos immediately sent an urgent appeal to Venice for help, but the Senate claimed that it was too preoccupied with affairs in Italy; they would authorize some gunpowder and breastplates to be sent his way.[21] But why did aggression suddenly make sense to Mehmed now, when it had not to his father for over a generation?

We can only speculate about psychological motives, such as Mehmed's need to prove himself as a young ruler or his supposed ambition to fulfill long-standing Islamic prophesy and win glory. He still had a shaky grasp on his father's throne and possibly felt the sting of his first, failed reign. The janissaries had mutinied when his father died, and they caused more trouble during the Karaman campaign. The sultan had to make concessions to them, although he punished some of the officers later.[22] A major offensive and logistical operation, such as a siege of Constantinople, would enable the young sultan to assert his authority over them, impose discipline, and, ideally, show them that he was a great general. An attack, then, would be a means by which Mehmed could mobilize and consolidate control over his empire's resources. As we will see, the campaign required resources on a truly prodigious scale.[23]

Besides, war against non-Muslims was authorized in advance by the notion of *gaza*, or holy war to expand the frontiers of Islam. Mehmed cast himself as such a holy warrior when he announced his victory in 1453 to other Muslim rulers. But we should be cautious about projecting that stance onto his decision to attack the City. He would have presented himself that way in communications with fellow Muslim rulers no matter what his real motives were.[24] We cannot take his claims at face value. The conquest of the City made strategic sense on its own terms, too. The reasons for this, while always present to some degree, had become acute since the treaty of 1424. They are eloquently articulated by the sultan's biographer, Kritoboulos, in a fictitious speech that he puts into Mehmed's mouth, making him sound like an orator out of Thucydides. Situated at the juncture point of Europe and Asia, Constantinople was a highly fortified bunker lodged at the very heart of the Ottoman empire. It could be used to drive a wedge between its two halves and leave the sultan isolated on one side while his foes ravaged the other and instigated his subjects to rebel. This is precisely what happened during the Varna crusade in 1443–1444, when Murad II faced the prospect of being stranded on the Asian side while his enemies attacked him in Europe.[25] As a Christian city, Constantinople solicited intervention from western powers who had stronger fleets than the Turks and could cut off their passage across the straits, using Constantinople as a naval base to entrench themselves in the east.[26]

Mehmed himself, while returning from the Karaman war in 1451, had also been blocked by Christian ships from crossing and had to improvise to cross the straits. That experience may have done more to convince Mehmed to cut off the straits and conquer the City than the alleged fiasco over Orhan's stipend.[27] The Ottoman historian of the City's conquest, Tursun Bey, called Constantinople "a scar on the forehead of Islam," largely because it enabled the Franks to control the straits and the sea. In his view, Galatas was an extension of Frangistan (i.e., Latin western Europe).[28]

Based in Edirne, Mehmed spent the winter of 1451–1452 gathering workmen, materials, and equipment from across his empire for the rapid construction of Rumeli Hisarı. He moved to the straits in the spring of 1452, when construction began under the protective cover of an Ottoman fleet of between thirty and forty ships that came up from their base at Gallipoli. The work was finished in record time, some four months, by August 1452. It had to be done quickly, before the Latins could mobilize an effective naval response. Mehmed assigned different sectors of the project to his viziers—Halil, Zaganos, and Saraca—and made it a competition among them. Some local residents tried to resist

Image 3.1 Anadolu Hisarı, the fort built by the Ottoman sultan Bayezid on the Asian side of the Bosporos in connection with his long blockade of Constantinople in 1394–1402. Mehmed II later built Rumeli Hisarı across the straits from it. Source: Flickr/flowcomm.

when the columns of their church were taken away for the project, and they were killed. Rumeli Hisarı was built at the narrow point of the Bosporos, where it was 850 meters across. It faced Anadolu Hisarı (see Image 3.1), a matching fort built on the Asian side by Bayezid in the 1390s before his siege of Constantinople. Mehmed installed a garrison of 400 men and placed cannons in the forts, pointing in all directions and "belching fire like dragons." He was now master of the straits. All ships had to stop and pay a toll. If they tried to force their way through, the commander of the fort, Firuz Bey, was under orders to sink them. The fort quickly came to be called Throat Cutter. In theory, it shut the straits up so tightly that "not a bird could fly from the Mediterranean to the Black Sea."[29] In reality, ships could successfully run the gauntlet, but it was extremely dangerous.

Today Rumeli Hisarı is a major tourist attraction (see Image 3.2), but in fact it is a badly executed restoration of the original. A Venetian spy

Image 3.2 Rumeli Hisarı, the fortress built by Mehmed II in 1452 on the European side of the Bosporos straits in preparation for his attack on Constantinople. Source: Flickr/Dennis Jarvis.

managed to produce a detailed drawing of its original shape within a year of its construction, if not immediately, showing the cannon emplacements (see Color Plate 7). This image survives at the end of a manuscript (Codex membranaceo 641, Biblioteca Trivulziana, Milan) that was produced only a few decades afterwards and contains texts relating to the fall of Constantinople, including Leonardo of Chios, Isidoros, Nikolaos Sekoundinos, and others. It is, in effect, one of the first (if not the first) anthologies of texts about the fall, a genre that is still published today.[30]

While the construction of Rumeli Hisarı was underway, the basileus sent envoys to the sultan to protest this action as contrary to their treaty. The fort could be used to exclude the Latins from the Black Sea, a major source of grain, and thereby starve out the City. In Kritoboulos' telling, Mehmed denied that his actions violated the treaty and claimed that he was defending his right to cross freely from one part of his domain to the other. He remembered as a child when the Latin fleets prevented his father from crossing during the Varna crusade. However, Kritoboulos has also given his readers enough reason by now to realize that the sultan was lying about this being a defensive measure.[31] No one at the time was fooled. The Venetian Nicolò Barbaro, serving on a trade convoy at the time, was emphatic on this point: the fort "was made for the express purpose of taking the city of Constantinople." The Ottoman sources do not contradict him.[32]

Hostilities had already begun during the fort's construction, which required the presence of an Ottoman army close to Constantinople, whose soldiers scavenged, foraged, and looted in its environs. They began to seize farmers who were working in the fields outside the City and trampled their crops with their coming and going. The basileus sent envoys and gifts to Mehmed begging him to respect the rights of his subjects. The sultan, wishing to delay an open conflict until after the work was completed, promised to send men to supervise his crews and keep inventories of the damage that they caused. The situation was tense, and violence broke out at Epibates, a fort near the city of Selymbria. Some Turks loosed their animals on the crops of some Romans, who resisted, leading to deaths on both sides. When he heard this, Mehmed sent one of his officers to punish the village. Forty people were slaughtered.[33]

With Turkish soldiers roaming the countryside freely, Konstantinos took the reasonable precaution of shutting the City gates. There happened to be some Turks inside the City, including eunuchs from the sultan's household. Tursun Bey, the Ottoman historian, suggests that they were taking this last chance to sight-see in Constantinople before the war broke out. It is also possible that they were there to buy supplies for their men outside. The student Posculo, who was in the City at the time, was outraged that Greeks and Genoese from Galatas were selling supplies to the Turks, putting their own greed above everything. But, if true, this was not as outrageous as he believed. Constantinople was a mostly free market, and those merchants may have had long-standing relations with Turkish clients. There was yet no official state of war and developments that were moving fast at the level of the political leadership may not have percolated down to the markets. (Note, by way of comparison, that in 1990–1991 US arms continued to be shipped to Saddam Hussein, a US client until then, even while the US war against him was in motion.) At any rate, Konstantinos set those Turks free, perhaps as a gesture of good will, although Tursun Bey assures us that they meant nothing to the sultan, mere drops in the sea. But Konstantinos had prudently brought the grain from the harvest of that year into the City.[34] The gates thereafter remained shut.

Mehmed declared war on Constantinople soon after the completion of Rumeli Hisarı, at the start of September 1452. He did so by beheading two envoys sent by the basileus. He then brought his army up to the walls of the City, where it encamped for three days, ravaging the hinterland as he inspected the fortifications and terrain. Meanwhile, Karaca Bey, his general for Europe (*beylerbey* of Rumeli), ranged as far as Selymbria and captured a number of towns and villages.[35] "Thus did Mehmed initiate the war."[36]

On September 13, 1452—when Rumeli Hisarı was completed and war had begun—Theodoros Agallianos, an anti-Union theologian and ally of Gennadios Scholarios, wrote a note reflecting on his people's grim circumstances. He observed that:

> Constantinople used to be mighty and prosperous, the Queen of Cities and Mother of Churches, but now it has fallen into slavery, as God is punishing us for our sins . . . The most impious Mehmed will return in the spring hoping to besiege Constantinople with every imaginable kind of artillery and siege-engine. He just completed the construction of a fort that will enable him to destroy the City; then, he sat before the City for three days, cutting up our vineyards, ravaging the suburbs, and taking various forts with his engines. He killed not a few people. Woe, for God is letting him do this on account of my sins! The City is bereft of any kind of assistance, whether from inside or outside, as it lacks money and men and has been ravaged by poverty, depopulation, enemy attacks, and by fear of what the future holds. Its only hope is to trust in God's compassion and in the all-pure and holy Virgin.[37]

Agallianos goes on to blame the current misfortune on the Union of Churches that was signed at Florence. In the margins of the manuscript in which he wrote this note, someone else added a comment that the fort, namely Rumeli Hisarı, was also known as "The Murderer."[38]

Terror and despair gripped many of the inhabitants of Constantinople. They knew what was in store for them.[39] First, they would have to decide whether to surrender to Mehmed or resist. Eventually he would offer them this stark choice, as required by Islamic tradition, although he does not appear to have done so yet. The two choices held significantly different outcomes, which everyone living in this part of the world understood well. The Ottomans had been conquering Asia Minor and the Balkans for over a century and had established a consistent track record on this point. The option to surrender was outlined in a brief ultimatum sent to the city of Ioannina by the Ottoman general Sinan Pasha, a vizier of Murad II, in 1430, immediately after the conquest of Thessalonike. Cities that opened their gates, he pledged, would not be ravaged or harmed. Those that resisted, however, would be torn down to their foundations:

> Don't listen to the words of the Franks, it will do you no good; they will bring you to ruin as happened at Thessalonike. I swear by the Prophet Muhammad that you need have no fear; no one will be enslaved, your children will not be taken away, your churches will not be destroyed, nor will we convert them into mosques. Your bishop can continue to act as your judge according to Roman law . . . and your lords can keep their properties.[40]

This was not entirely true. Children would be "collected" for the janissary corps. The city would not be able to keep *all* its properties as some would be reassigned to Turkish settlers. Moreover, the sultan could revise these terms and agreements at a later time. Those who surrendered were at the conqueror's mercy.

Sinan was coming straight from the violent conquest of Thessalonike earlier that year. In fact, Thessalonike represented a kind of historical experiment on this point. It had both surrendered to the Ottomans in 1387 and then been conquered by them in 1430, so the two options could be compared.[41] Obviously, the city was not demolished in 1430, as Sinan threatened Ioannina, but the differences were still stark. To be sure, surrender was not as rosy as Sinan made it sound. Those who surrendered were, in theory, not enslaved or harmed. They kept most of their property, though the conqueror was free to confiscate land or impose taxes as he deemed fit (and the sultans did so, sometimes with a heavy hand). Freedom to practice one's religion was respected and local communities, defined usually by religion, were granted a measure of local self-governance under their own leaders, though the latter had to be approved by the conqueror and could be replaced at his discretion. Thus, surrender did entail subordination, both political and social. Christians became second-class subjects in a foreign empire. Legal restrictions on their rights and opportunities could (and did) mount over time. However you looked at it, it was a loss of freedom and dignity.

But the alternative was far worse. Cities that were taken by storm had no guarantees and no rights. Their inhabitants could be enslaved, families dispersed, and properties redistributed among the conquerors. It did not *have* to happen that way; the conqueror could be more merciful, but that was at his discretion. When Murad took Thessalonike in 1430, he told his soldiers that they could enslave the people for their own profit and take away anything they could physically carry; the city's infrastructure, however, belonged to him. It was also his right to take a cut of the slaves, whom he then resettled back in their city, which was now his (Mehmed did the same when he captured Constantinople).[42] Thessalonike did not cease to exist, but even decades later its population was only a fraction of what it had been before 1430.[43] "Enslavement" in this case was literal, not a metaphor for political subordination. Families were split up and possibly never saw each other again, their members dispersed across the Ottoman empire, wherever their captors took them. In 1422, when Murad besieged Constantinople, its inhabitants feared death less than mass enslavement, the rape of the women, the circumcision and conversion of their children, and the loss of their churches.[44] The same terrors returned now, in 1452, when many were still alive who remembered the earlier siege well as well as the grim fate of Thessalonike in 1430.[45]

This dread was exacerbated by prophesies that circulated about the City's inevitable demise. During its thousand-year history, many predictions had already been made about the fall of Constantinople. All had been proven wrong, so the genre was not altogether credible. Moreover, for decades theologians had been predicting that the Second Coming would happen in 1492 AD, which was still relatively far in the future.[46] But other dark prophesies added to the climate of gloomy foreboding in 1452. These included the idea that Constantinople would fall when a Constantine, the son of Helene, was basileus, just as the City had been founded by a Constantine, son of Helene. The so-called *Oracles of Leon the Wise* contained various apocalyptic scenarios about the Last Emperor that could be applied to the current situation. Certain scriptural passages that were read aloud in church, when interpreted loosely, also seemed to hint at the worst outcome. Constantinople's monuments were implicated in these narratives, too. The column in the forum of Constantine had long been a focal point for apocalyptic scenarios (see Image 1.2), while the extended hand of the equestrian statue of Justinian next to Hagia Sophia seemed to either block or invite the onrush of eastern foes. If cities survived a siege, such predictions were forgotten, but if they fell then they were brought forth as proof that it was inevitable and foretold. All our sources for the siege of 1453 succumb to this confirmation bias. They list these omens and prophecies right before the final attack to heighten the drama at the climactic moment.[47]

On the other hand, there was a good chance that resistance could succeed. It had succeeded in 1422 against Murad. This is what the defenders, in 1453, hoped for, and it is certain that the majority of the population of Constantinople backed the basileus' decision to resist. In this era, after all, it was impossible for a basileus to get anything significant done without the active or tacit consent of the majority of his fellow Constantinopolitans. The people of the City could always make their preferences known when they opposed a decision by their rulers. Konstantinos could not properly bury his brother, or be crowned, or have a patriarch, or enforce the Union of the Churches because too many of his people might object. In 1387, when his father, Manuel II, wanted to hold Thessalonike against the Ottomans, the people of the city overrode him, forced him to leave, and surrendered the city.[48] But in 1452–1453 there is no credible evidence that anyone, let alone an entire faction, advocated surrender.

Besides, the dark forebodings of occult prophecies were mitigated by the trust that the people of the City placed in the Virgin, who had come to their rescue so many times before. The unknown factor here was Roman sinfulness, which, if severe enough, might cause her to withhold her favor. Unionists believed that the sin in question was the non-enforcement of Union, whereas anti-Unionists believed it was the fact that Union had been signed in the first place. (In retrospect, after the City's fall, both sides claimed to be right.) But the Virgin could work in mysterious ways. She was even credited with sending Timur to defeat Bayezid in 1402, just as the City was about to surrender—hard though it is to hold the Virgin and Timur in the same thought.[49]

A fourth option was to turn a city over to a Latin power and hope that it would do a better job of defending it against the Turks. In 1397, during an intense phase of Bayezid's blockade of Constantinople, Manuel II offered to turn the City and some islands over to the Venetians, though this offer was firmly declined and its precise nature remains obscure.[50] In 1400, Manuel's brother, the despot of the Peloponnese, Theodoros Palaiologos, contemplated selling his entire domain to the Hospitaller Knights and retiring to Venice. His subjects vociferously opposed this plan and he backed off.[51] In 1423, Thessalonike was turned over to the Venetians to defend against Murad II, which they did for seven years before the city fell, having made themselves unpopular with its inhabitants in the meantime.[52] In a certain sense, Konstantinos XI was thinking along these lines when he entrusted the defense of his harbor to the Venetians and the most critical sector of the walls to the Genoese captain Giustiniani. On April 2, 1453, when he spoke to leading Venetians about the City's defense, he said "that Constantinople had come to belong more to the Venetians than to the Greeks . . . so he was willing to give the four gates of the City with all their keys into their charge."[53]

By the fall of 1452, the Romans knew that they were facing an existential threat. Konstantinos now sent out urgent appeals for help, especially to Venice, just as he was receiving pope Nicholas V's unhelpful response to his earlier, dead-on-arrival overture about Union. The Senate of Venice, he learned in October, had voted to not abandon the City to its fate—although the motion was apparently proposed!—and it authorized Gabriele Trevisan to help in its defense, though only if the City came under direct attack. Venice was already aware, since July 1452, that Constantinople was about to be attacked. But the Republic was distracted by a costly war with Milan, and its leader, the doge Francesco Foscari, was old and slow to react. He was building a new palace and coping politically with his son's scandals. Trevisan arrived in Constantinople in early October with two galleys, each with about 200 men, although his priority mission in the eyes of the Senate was to escort three cargo galleys from Tana. Presumably, they paid the toll at Rumeli Hisarı before arriving at Constantinople. The Senate's next communication to the basileus, in November, suggested that plans were being made to send relief but, in the meantime, he should appeal to the pope, who might organize a broader Christian effort.[54]

The pope, meanwhile, had dispatched a cardinal to Constantinople as his representative. This was Isidoros, an ethnic Roman in his sixties. He was possibly from the Peloponnese, had received a classical Greek education, and had entered the religious life in Constantinople. He was appointed bishop of Kiev and All Rus' by the patriarch, in which capacity he attended the Council of Florence as a member of the Greek delegation. Isidoros was staunchly pro-Union and had learned Latin, but when he tried to persuade Moscow to accept Florence he was imprisoned. He eventually returned to Rome and now, as a cardinal, he was being sent back to his homeland to advance the cause of Union. It is not clear whether the pope had charged him also to assist in the defense of Constantinople, but he did so anyway. It is fitting that a man with such an adventurous life, who crossed the boundaries between the Greeks and the Latins, would be a protagonist of the siege as well as an important eyewitness to it.

Isidoros arrived on October 26, after a journey of six months from Rome, with two ships. Along the way he recruited 200 mercenaries armed with guns and crossbows, to assist in the defense as a gesture of Catholic good will. He brought also the Latin archbishop of Mytilene, Leonardo of Chios, who was Genoese by origin (both Mytilene and Chios were under Genoese rule). Leonardo, too, was classically educated, albeit in Latin, with a background in the Dominican order, and something of a philosopher. He was distrustful of the Greeks. In 1450–1451, he had already written against Gennadios Scholarios on the matter of the Procession of the Holy Spirit, which may be why Isidoros chose him as a companion. After the City's fall, Leonardo wrote a letter to the pope with a first-hand account of the siege. Leonardo and Isidoros worked closely during the siege and shaped each other's perceptions of it.[55]

More ships continued to arrive that would play a role in the siege. A few days after Isidoros, eight ships came bearing wine from Venetian Crete. On November 10, two great galleys from Caffa under the command of the Venetian captain Girolamo Morosini managed to run the gauntlet of the Ottoman forts in the Bosporos, losing many men in the process but evading the tolls. Then, on November 26, the ship of the Venetian Antonio Rizzo, also coming from the Black Sea with food for Constantinople, was sunk by the fort cannons. Rizzo and thirty of his men were captured by the garrison and sent to the sultan. On December 4, a Venetian galley from Trebizond under Giacomo Cocco also managed to make it past Rumeli Hisarı without paying, after an altercation with the garrison. A few days later, probably in response to this incident, the sultan had Rizzo impaled—this entailed pounding a sharp stake through the anus until it came out the chest or neck—and decapitated the rest of his men, possibly using a saw. The Venetian bailo in Constantinople, Girolamo Minotto, sent one Fabrizio Corner to the sultan to negotiate for their release, but the men had already been executed. The historian Doukas saw their bodies a few days later, as he was passing through that region. This action was effectively a declaration of war against Venice.[56]

During the winter of 1452–1453, Venice, Genoa, and Rome exchanged envoys regarding Constantinople, but came to no decision.

Konstantinos appealed again for help to Rome and to the rulers of western kingdoms, including Hungary and Alfonso V at Naples, but received no assurances of aid, at least none that would come in time.[57] In his memoirs, Sphrantzes later railed against all these so-called Christians that did not come to the defense of the capital of eastern Christianity, including Serbia, Venice, the papacy, Trebizond, Wallachia, Georgia, Hungary, Alfonso V, and the Genoese of Chios. He could have added many more.[58] All of them, of course, had reasons for not rushing to the City's aid. Pope Nicholas was sending a crusade against the Hussites in Bohemia. Hungary had been trounced twice by Murad (in 1444 and 1448), was regrouping, and did not want to risk further retaliations. Alfonso V was preoccupied with Italian affairs, and he actually had plans to conquer Constantinople for himself. The despot of Serbia was a vassal of the sultan who sent soldiers to assist him *against* the City. The despots of the Peloponnese, Konstantinos' brothers Thomas and Demetrios, were coping with a Turkish invasion that the sultan had ordered precisely to distract them.[59] It is, moreover, unclear that their armies consisted of more than part-time peasant soldiers, and Demetrios was not inclined to help Konstantinos anyway. Further afield, France and England were at the tail end of the Hundred Years War. But why, Sphrantzes wondered, could they not have sent money to Constantinople, which they could have done secretly?

Konstantinos realized that he had better chances of securing western aid if he officially proclaimed the Union of Florence, something that his brother Ioannes VIII had been reluctant to do. Isidoros had come to Constantinople precisely for that purpose. But the basileis rarely acted unilaterally in such matters, especially in the face of determined opposition, and the lack of a patriarch complicated matters further. A consultative process was required to create the legitimacy of consensus. In November, Konstantinos summoned his clergy, including monastic abbots, to discuss Union in the Xylalas palace. Gennadios Scholarios was not invited, likely because, as a simple monk, he had no official standing, and because he certainly would be disruptive, although his absence from the meetings was the elephant in the room. He had, however, given talking points to some of his followers who did attend, including Agallianos, whom we met earlier as the author of the manuscript note about the building of Rumeli Hisarı. Gennadios was producing anti-Union treatises, pamphlets, and proclamations throughout this period, one of which he pinned to his cell door. These were read and disseminated among his followers throughout the City. Their tone was hysterical: not only were the people of the City being asked to give up their faith, he wrote, they were incurring God's wrath, which would soon be visited upon them. Gennadios held that devotion to the pure faith—or his version of it—was more important than securing western aid for the siege.[60]

To the chagrin of Leonardo and others, Konstantinos did not clamp down on this anti-Union agitation. The Xylalas palace meetings resulted, predictably, in a decision in favor of Union, and the basileus was content merely to proclaim it. He did not seek to enforce it by repressing the Synaxis dissidents and their followers, which is what Leonardo wanted, even though he realized that most Greeks opposed the Florence Union. As a result, Leonardo came away thinking that the basileus, while a sincere Catholic, was a coward. Konstantinos was no coward, as events would clearly show. However, his view, which he shared with his confidant Sphrantzes, was that "it would be terrible to instigate an internal war when we already have a foreign one hanging over us."[61] He was not about to attack his own subjects. Unlike Leonardo, Konstantinos was not a fanatic.

Union was proclaimed at a service in Hagia Sophia on December 12 (see Color Plate 6). In the presence of the court and clergy of the Great Church, Isidoros presided as both a Catholic cardinal and native Greek-speaker and commemorated the pope. Then he spoke to the assembly, pledging to defend his fatherland. Konstantinos spoke next. This was a major event in the history of the two Churches and possibly the last Christian service conducted in Hagia Sophia before the fall. Our sources oddly say little about it. The Synaxis regarded this event as a desecration of the precious church and urged the people of the City to avoid the service and shun the Great Church thereafter. Doukas and Leonardo, who implied that most inhabitants of the City were hostile to Union, believed that the service was compromised by this ugly climate. Leonardo called it a piece of theater. So, no one felt like celebrating it after the fall. Only the young Brescian student Posculo wrote a long account of the proceedings in his allusive and often opaque Vergilian verse.[62] Yet it is likely that many Constantinopolitans did attend. Even if public opinion was anti-Union, the die-hard followers of the Synaxis who would boycott a ceremony in Hagia Sophia were a minority. We hear of no large demonstrations of the sort that the populace made on other occasions to voice its discontent. Isidoros later told the pope that only Gennadios Scholarios and eight monks refused to participate, although here the cardinal was exaggerating the success of his mission.[63] For his part, Gennadios claimed that only a handful of papists attended Catholic services.[64]

The basileus had ably threaded the needle of proclaiming Union without sparking popular resistance. Contrary to the assertions of modern scholars, the rift over Union did not compromise the defense effort once the armies of the sultan arrived. No one refused to fight during the siege, or fought less strenuously, on the grounds that the basileus proclaimed Union (on the one hand) or that he had not enforced it vigorously enough (on the other). Konstantinos let the matter lie after that, leaving it to Isidoros to change people's mind through persuasion, with the help of local scholars who were pro-Union, most prominently Argyropoulos and Michael Apostoles.[65] Gennadios drops out of the story of the siege at this point, as he secluded himself in his cell, praying and writing diatribes.

With his authority among the Latins enhanced, the basileus and his officials decided at a public meeting in Hagia Sophia that the Venetian ships in the harbor should stay and join in the defense. "The public forum suggests that the emperor wished to demonstrate to his subjects that Church Union would immediately produce tangible results."[66] In this request to the Venetians he was backed by Isidoros (a papal representative), Leonardo, and the Venetian bailo. Some of the captains and crews balked at this request, requiring long debates. Eventually their objections were overridden by the bailo and his council of advisors "for the honor of God, Venice, and the Christian faith." Our information comes chiefly from the diary of Nicolò Barbaro, a young Venetian serving on a ship in Alvise Diedo's trade convoy, which had been escorted to Constantinople by the two galleys of Trevisan. Barbaro was a crossbowman and possibly also a medic. His diary, written in the Venetian dialect, is the single most important source for the day-to-day chronology of the siege, although it is biased against the Greeks and Genoese.[67]

The Venetian galleys in the harbor comprised the two of Trevisan, the three of Diedo from Tana, eight from Candia (Crete), two from Caffa, and one from Trebizond. There were also many Genoese ships of various sizes on the Pera side. The basileus owned ships too, although we do not know exactly how many. He now sent men to bring grain from the islands and dispatched four ships—his own?—to Chios specifically, where they would wait for one of his own that had gone to the Peloponnese.[68] Pera had decided on a policy of official neutrality in the war, a fiction that Mehmed accepted, probably so as not to increase the number of active enemies at this critical stage. He could always deal with them separately later. But unofficially the Genoese of Pera intended to help the City, for they realized that the fates of their two communities were intertwined. They asked for assistance from Genoa and were told that a ship was coming with 200 armed men, presumably to be used for the defense of Pera itself. After the fall, however, the podestà Angelo Giovanni Lomellino said that he had used the soldiers from Genoa for the defense of Constantinople, along with many of his own citizens, including his own nephew (who went missing afterward) and the Genoese from Chios.[69]

A diplomatic mission was also sent to the sultan after the celebration of Union on December 12. It is mentioned only by Posculo, who did not have inside knowledge of its purpose and who tends to distort events through the prism of his Catholic bias. Specifically, he reports a last-minute effort to make peace that was entrusted by the basileus to one Basilikos, a Greek merchant living "in the enemy camp" (Edirne?). He conveyed "secret letters," and his mission was allegedly unknown to Isidoros. Posculo wants to imply that the mission was some kind of betrayal of Union.[70] At any rate, it went disastrously wrong, as we learn from a later, still unpublished text written by Leonardo. He says that Ioannes Basilikos and a business partner, Thomas Pyropoulos, both of whom were staunch anti-Unionists and friendly with Gennadios (which we can confirm independently), were widely suspected of treason. The City populace became so angry at them that the basileus exiled them and demolished their homes in the City. In January 1453, they turned up in Pera, engaging in business but legally prevented from crossing the harbor to Constantinople proper.[71] This episode leaves us with many unanswered questions. It seems as though Konstantinos made a diplomatic push for peace by using anti-Union Romans at the sultan's court, which would make strategic sense, but somehow the whole thing went badly wrong. Basilikos and Pyropoulos would show up again after the fall to have the last laugh.

One more group arrived at Constantinople before the start of the siege, and this was to prove possibly the most consequential for the course of events. On January 26, 1453, the Genoese mercenary captain Giovanni Longo Giustiniani arrived in Constantinople. He was thirty-five years old and led a force of between 400 and 700 soldiers from Genoese Chios in two ships, which also became part of the defense fleet. Giustiniani was related to leading families in Genoa and had probably been encouraged by its doge to help Konstantinos in the defense of Constantinople. Before that, he had spent a few years practicing piracy in the Aegean, preying on the shipping routes and acquiring a fierce reputation. Piracy was not an entirely dishonorable occupation in the fifteenth century. He had passed through Constantinople and met the basileus in 1451. Konstantinos now placed him in command of the City's land defenses along the walls, giving him the position of *protostrator* and formally offering him the island of Lemnos in case the defense was successful. Giustiniani and his men, armored in the heavy plate mail of that time, proved to be a formidable defense force (see Image 3.3). Giustiniani became the hero of the siege, that is, until the last moment. Even a witness as hostile to the Genoese as Barbaro admitted that Giustiniani came "because he realized the need in which Constantinople stood, and for the advantage of the Christian faith."[72]

Image 3.3 Giustiniani and his soldiers were likely wearing heavy armor similar to that shown on the arch of Alfonso V of Aragon in Naples (1470, Castel Nuovo, Maschio Angioino). Source: Sailko/Wikipedia.

Konstantinos melted down some silver church plate to mint coins (see Image 3.4). Other emperors of Constantinople had resorted to this measure in past crises, treating the churches as emergency treasuries. Some of his coins have been found: they have a higher silver content than the coins of his father and brother, indicating that they originated in liturgical vessels and dedications. In addition to the other expenses of the siege, the basileus agreed to pay stipends to the Venetian crews he had retained. He also borrowed money from the Genoese of Pera. A document in the archives of Genoa records a loan of 9,000 hyperpyra negotiated in January 1453 in the manor of Notaras, with Notaras acting as guarantor.[73] This is the only loan that we know about, but there may well have been more, with additional sums borrowed from the Venetians. This refutes the accusation that was then (and is still now) made against

Image 3.4 Silver coins of Konstantinos XI Palaiologos, whose unusually high silver content indicated that they were possibly minted from Church plate in the run-up to the siege. © Dumbarton Oaks, Washington, DC.

Notaras that he withheld his personal assets from the war effort and thereby contributed to the fall of the City. Latins such as Leonardo accused the Greeks of squirreling their money away selfishly. A note added to Barbaro's journal claims that an unnamed Greek noble hid away 30,000 ducats (an impossibly large sum). When the Turks sacked the City, some of them did find valuables in the houses that they plundered. Thus, it has been argued that this withholding of personal assets contributed to the City's fall.[74] With more money, Konstantinos could have hired more mercenaries or retained the services of Orban, an engineer who allegedly went over to Mehmed instead.[75]

However, we need to be cautious in making this argument. To be sure, Notaras did not pledge his entire fortune to the war effort, nor did anyone else. But in no war in history have people of means voluntarily pledged the entirety of their fortune to the cause. It is unreasonable to hold the Romans up to such a standard, especially based on biased Latin reports. After all, one of the arguments that will be made in our account of the siege is that the Romans could realistically expect to survive it, so planning for the future was prudent. Moreover, just because cash and precious metals were found in people's houses does not mean that these resources were not accessible to the basileus. It is unlikely that he kept all his money with him all the time, especially during the siege, when he was encamped by the wall. We know that he gave sums to his people to carry out works related to the siege. After all, that is how money works: you use it to pay for material or services. The money then ends up in the hands of other people. Consider the hoard of 158 late Palaiologan silver coins that surfaced in Istanbul in 1990.[76] It does not prove that selfish Romans were hoarding cash. The majority of these coins were minted by Konstantinos himself right before the siege, probably from church plate. So, this was either cash that he had not yet spent or that he had spent—for the defense. Hoards of cash do not support the argument about Roman selfishness.

Roman elites likely contributed more to the war effort than we know. The details of loan guarantees were not public knowledge, and so we are lucky to know about the deal with the Genoese. In a letter to Gennadios, Notaras remarked that "my chief concern is the common good . . . I too am upset that our country is in a bad state on account of being badly governed."[77] Well, Notaras was now one of the most powerful men in the realm. Perhaps it was beyond his ability to fix the deep systemic problems that had brought the Roman polity so low, but he could at least help it survive the coming storm. The defense of the City that he, the basileus, the Venetians, and Giustiniani devised was probably the best that could be managed under the circumstances. To their strategy we can now turn.

4

The Strategy of the Defenders

The strategy of the defenders intelligently anticipated Mehmed's strengths and made efficient use of their limited resources to counter them. Whether they were informed by spies or guessed intelligently, the defenders correctly estimated the forces that the sultan would deploy against them, and they assessed the risk that each branch of his army posed to them. At the same time, they were clear-sighted about their own weaknesses and counted on Mehmed to attack them precisely there, which is exactly what he did. They had the benefit of experience from recent sieges of Constantinople, Thessalonike, and smaller cities. They also had access to a long tradition of military science, codified in a series of manuals that continued to be copied in Constantinople well into the fifteenth century. At least one such manuscript belonged to the family of a leading general of the first decades of the fifteenth century, Demetrios Leontares, and his descendants were in the City during the siege.[1] We do not know if these manuals were consulted in preparation for the siege, but many of the tactics employed during the defense echoed the stratagems recommended by a long tradition of ancient and medieval military science.

The defenders anticipated that Mehmed's large infantry army would target the Mesoteichion ("Mid-Wall") section, where the Theodosian walls dip into the shallow valley of the Lykos stream around the Fifth Gate (see Color Plate 8 and Image 4.1). The defense would then have to concentrate there. As this was a siege, the much-feared Ottoman cavalry would be neutralized. Reports had also reached the defenders that

Image 4.1 The Theodosian land walls at the point where they dip into the Lykos valley and come up again, where most of the fighting took place. This is the view on the inside; the outside is difficult to photograph because of an overpass. Source: The Byzantine Legacy/David Hendrix.

Mehmed was casting larger cannons than his father, Murad II, had deployed in 1422 against the Mid-Wall. But the effectiveness of this next generation of artillery was inevitably an unknowable factor, until they were tested in practice. Against it the defenders could do little more than store materials with which to repair the walls during the fighting. The defenders had their own cannons, but it would have been pointless to invest in more and bigger ones, as they would not have helped much against the dispersed Turkish encampment. Cannons still fired solid rocks, not explosive ordinance.[2] The defense barely used the cannons that it did have during the siege.

The defenders' other main weakness was their limited numbers. They knew that Mehmed would force them to spread themselves thin by testing other lines of attack, especially against the other sectors of the land walls, and also by using his fleet to gain entry into the Golden Horn. These flanking attacks would not aim to break through but were primarily distractions because, to counter them, the defense would have to pull men away from the crucial pressure point at the Mid-Wall. However, the defense could safely de-prioritize the sea walls along the Sea of Marmara. No invader had ever managed (or even tried) to scale the walls there, and doing so would require a capacity for sophisticated amphibian operations that Mehmed lacked. The currents, winds, and rocks there made approaching the walls too difficult, as the Venetians, "who had more experience of the sea," understood even in 1204.[3]

The sea walls in the harbor were more vulnerable. A naval assault against them, however, required specialized platforms deployed upright on ships that were lashed together and manned by crews that were trained to carry out complex naval maneuvers. The Venetians had pulled this off in 1203 and 1204. Mehmed did not have either the ships or the crews for something like this. Also, to block him from even reaching the walls in the Golden Horn, the defenders closed the harbor with a chain and posted their galleys to guard it (see Color Plate 3).[4] As we will see, these galleys were largely invulnerable to Ottoman naval attack, so the harbor was as safe as it could be. Therefore, the defenders would not have to thin themselves out too much along the sea walls and could concentrate on defending the Mid-Wall.

The defense's greatest asset was the land walls of Constantinople. Wave after wave of foreign invaders had broken on their ramparts over the centuries, allowing not only Constantinople but the Roman state to survive for over a millennium. The Romans made a point of piously praising the Virgin Mary for saving the City on those occasions. Credit was less often given—but was surely owed—to its human defenders, too, both soldiers and civilians who stood on the battlements and fought off attackers. But many knew that the City's safety was ultimately due to the walls themselves. It wasn't just that they caused attacks to fail: they caused attacks to not happen in the first place. In 1345, the raider Umur Bey, the ruler of Aydın, a Turkish beylik in western Asia Minor, involved himself in a Roman civil war and approached Constantinople "in order to look upon it and, if necessary, to attack it." However, a contemporary historian recounts that:

> as he stood before the City and inspected it from an appropriate distance, at times standing and at times walking about, he was amazed at its size and the height and beauty of the walls, as well as by the wonderous construction of the ditches around it and the position and arrangement of the defensive works.[5]

Even though there were no soldiers patrolling the battlements, Umur declined the opportunity to attack and sought out other targets instead.

Umur's reaction to the walls was as much aesthetic as it was strategic. The walls instilled a sense of awe. Up close they were titanic, whereas from a distance their incredible length only magnified the massive size of the City they enclosed. Few people alive at the time had ever seen anything like it. Even those who came with hostile intentions and prejudice against the Greeks confessed their awe. Witness Villehardouin, a French marshal who helped to orchestrate the deviation of the Fourth Crusade to Constantinople:

> All those who had never seen Constantinople before gazed intently at the city, having never imagined there could be so fine a place in all the world. They noted the high walls and lofty towers encircling it, and its rich palaces and tall churches, of which there were so many that no one would have believed it to be true if he had not seen it with his own eyes; and they viewed the length and breadth of that city which reigns supreme over all others. There was indeed no man so brave and daring that his flesh did not shudder at the sight.[6]

In their own literature, Romans liked to imagine the effect that the walls had on visitors and travelers. In the tenth century, a poet praising the wonders of the City described a weary traveler at the end of a long journey beholding the row of towers and the roofs of lofty buildings behind them. When he "reaches the City wall and approaches the gates, what wayfarer does not salute the City and, bending his neck downwards to the ground, embrace the celebrated earth and say: 'Hail, glory of the world!'"[7] In 1204, when the City fell to the Crusaders, the high official and historian Niketas Choniates threw himself to the ground before the walls in an utterly different spirit. He was being forced to leave Constantinople as a refugee and asked the walls how they could just stand there without feeling anything, neither weeping nor lying in ruins, having failed to protect the City and its inhabitants. "Why do you still stand, then? Whom are you protecting now?"[8]

The land walls of Constantinople stretched from the Sea of Marmara in the south to the Golden Horn in the north in a line approximately six kilometers long. Most of this line was built under the emperor Theodosius II (408–450), although the northernmost sector, which enclosed the palace and district of Blachernai, was by this time protected by a series of walls and towers that had been erected between the seventh and twelfth centuries. Apart from that corner of the City's fortifications, which was defined by its uniquely uneven terrain, the main land walls consisted of a triple line of defense (see Color Plate 9). Moving from the inside out, there was a taller inner wall, a lower outer wall, and finally a ditch or moat backed by a small wall of its own (see Image 4.2). These walls were made of stone, brick, and mortar, and were faced on the outside mostly with tightly fitted stone blocks. The inner wall, which

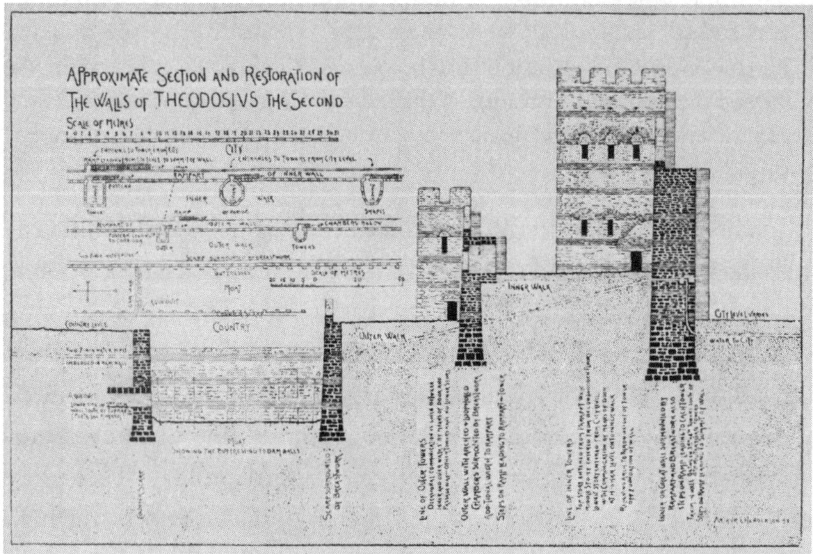

Image 4.2 Cross-section and top-view diagram of the Theodosian land walls, showing the double wall system, walkways, and moat. It was published by A. Van Millingen, *Byzantine Constantinople: The Walls of the City and Adjoining Historical Sites* (Cambridge University Press 1899), facing p. 106.

was about five meters thick (or 16 feet), rose 15 meters (40 feet) or more above the walkway (*peribolos*) that ran between the inner and outer walls. This inner wall was studded with 96 towers, spaced unevenly as the terrain required, although mostly they were between 40 and 60 meters apart. The towers were 11 meters wide, rose another five to 10 meters above the inner wall, and they projected into the *peribolos* walkway, allowing archers on top to shoot down on foes who made it past the moat and outer wall.[9]

The towers of the inner wall were spaced together more closely around its gates, to enable flanking fire from both directions on anyone trying to break in. Access to the ground-floor rooms of the towers, which were often used for storage, was mainly from inside the City, although some had a small postern gate that let out onto the *peribolos* to facilitate the movement of the defenders and allow them to attack from the side anyone who broke through the outer wall. The rooms on the second floor of the towers let out onto the battlements of the inner wall, while their roofs could be used as firing bases for ballistae and catapults.

The *peribolos* walkway was, on average, about 17 meters wide (55 feet). The outer wall, which was about two meters thick at its base, rose about nine meters (30 feet) above the clearing between the outer wall and the moat. It, too, was studded with towers, at least 62 of them, which were generally placed between the towers of the inner wall. Some towers of the outer wall around the Fifth Gate (Pempton), which sustained the most intense bombardment during the siege, have disappeared entirely, so their full number is unknown. These towers were, on average, 13 meters tall and four meters wide (or 42 feet by 13). Posterns in the base of these towers, as well as the regular gates in the walls, let out onto the outer terrace or walkway (the *parateichion*) that ran between the outer wall and the moat. This, too, was about as wide as the *peribolos*, or wider (around 20 meters or 65 feet), although it also narrowed where the towers of the outer wall projected out into it.

The moat was 18 meters wide and at least seven meters deep (or 59 feet by 23), and it was lined with thick stonework. On the inner side, its retaining wall rose up another meter and a half above the *parateichion*, so it could also be used as a defensive line, the first to meet a foe who made it past the ditch, or to shelter defenders returning from a sortie against the enemy.[10]

Therefore, from the start of the ditch to the inner walls, the attacker had to run a 60-meter gauntlet of overlapping fire across ascending terraces. As one lament put it, written shortly after the fall of the City by a scholar who had studied there, after crossing a long and deep moat the attacker faced a tall sturdy wall, behind which there was an even taller, more awe-inspiring wall.[11] No medieval city, which was otherwise situated so accessibly at sea level, was even remotely as well fortified as Constantinople. It was in a league of its own.

The moat was designed to hold water, at least in some of its stretches, as shown by the pipes that led to it and the transverse retaining walls that divided it into segments that could hold water on sloping ground. Several fifteenth-century texts refer to the moat as a "river," although of course it did not flow. In 1411, the classical scholar Manuel Chrysoloras wrote a rhetorical comparison of Old and New Rome—he had lived in both cities—in which he claimed that the moat of Constantinople held so much water that it made the City seem like an island, except for a small dry segment (he probably meant the Blachernai district in the northwest and possibly also the Mid-Wall section).[12] Chrysoloras frequently presents Constantinople in an idealized way that harked back to its former glories, even while acknowledging that it had fallen on hard times. Other contemporaries also compared the moat to a river, including Andronikos Kallistos, a scholar who had lived there before moving to the West, in a lament that he wrote soon after the City's fall.[13] The map of Constantinople drawn in ca. 1420 by the Florentine Cristoforo Buondelmonti clearly shows the moat filled with water, as an extension of the Sea of Marmara (see Image 1.1).[14] Yet despite these abundant textual and visual references, no account of the siege of 1453 mentions water in the moat. It is possible that the Mid-Wall segment, which dips into the Lykos valley where most of the fighting took place, was dry (see Color Plate 8), but the southern reaches of the moat toward the Sea of Marmara did hold water, at least enough to justify the river comparison.

The Blachernai district in the northwest corner of the City was fortified in a different way (see Image 4.3). Most of it was enveloped by the wall and towers built in the twelfth century by Manuel I Komnenos (1143–1180) to protect his principal palace.[15] It is a single circuit whose height varies between eight and 20 meters depending on the terrain, which slopes in this district away from the wall in a way that favors the defenders, although determined attacks on it were made both by the Fourth Crusade and the Turks in 1453. For much of the length of the wall here a ditch would have been impossible to excavate or pointless. While the slope generally favored the defenders, it also allowed attackers to more easily tunnel under the wall. This is indeed where Mehmed directed his miners and sappers.

The walls of Constantinople had been maintained in reasonably good shape over the centuries. They were routinely repaired and improved by

Image 4.3 Photograph (taken ca. 1875) of the walls around the Blachernai district of Constantinople, at the point where the ground slopes down toward the Golden Horn harbor. Source: Guillaume Berggren.

emperors who prominently placed inscriptions on the towers to record their labors and proclaim their solicitude for the Romans' safety. The walls' greatest enemy were earthquakes and neglect rather than enemy attacks. Extensive repairs had been carried out by Konstantinos XI's brother and predecessor Ioannes VIII Palaiologos (1425–1448), as documented by a number of his inscriptions (see Image 4.4).[16] His repairs concentrated on the outer wall and its towers, which made sense because that was the wall that the defenders had chosen to hold during the siege by Murad II in 1422 and were likely to man again in the event of another siege (as, indeed, they did in 1453). Ioannes was praised for this maintenance work by an orator who specifies that the basileus had work teams clear out the moat, which had been filled up in places by debris deposited by winter storms and seasonal flooding. The work was completed in two months.[17] These works were necessary because, in the siege of 1422,

Image 4.4 Inscription of Ioannes VIII Palaiologos placed on a tower of the outer walls, attesting to its restoration. It says, "Ioannes Palaiologos, *autokrator* in Christ, restored this tower in the year 6941" (i.e., 1432/3). The inscription is in the Istanbul Archaeological Museum. Source: The Byzantine Legacy/David Hendrix.

Murad had found part of the moat in the Mid-Wall filled in with debris and, directly in front of it, the tower had cracked.[18]

Konstantinos XI also repaired and upgraded the defenses in anticipation of the siege. Leonardo of Chios says that the basileus entrusted considerable sums of money to one Manuel Iagaris and a monk, Neophytos, but they instead stole the money, so eventually it fell into the hands of the Turks. But Leonardo is biased in such matters and was looking for ways to blame the Greeks for their City's fall.[19] An inscription near the Fifth Gate bearing Iagaris' name suggests that he did use at least some of the funds for their intended purpose (see Image 4.5).[20] Elsewhere Leonardo reveals that the cardinal Isidoros, his hero, paid for the restoration of the walls and towers in the Blachernai district, which he could have done only after his arrival in the City in late October 1452.[21]

Konstantinos also sought Venetian help in upgrading the defenses of the Blachernai district. He approached Alvise Diedo, the captain of the three galleys from Tana, and asked if his crews would dig a ditch around the Kynegos Gate, at the point where the Blachernai walls turn into the

Image 4.5 Inscription from the Theodosian land walls proving that Manuel Iagaris did carry out at least some restoration work before the siege of 1453, as instructed by Konstantinos IX Palaiologos, despite claims to the contrary. The inscription is in the Istanbul Archaeological Museum. Source: The Byzantine Legacy/David Hendrix.

sea walls that run along the Golden Horn. "The captain replied to the emperor, 'I shall do it willingly, for the honor of God and the Christian faith, and in obedience to your Majesty.'" On Monday, March 14, just three weeks before the main Ottoman army arrived, Diedo brought his three galleys to that point and disembarked his crews, possibly as many as 600 men. They were joined later that day by the crews of the two light galleys under Gabriele Trevisan:

> Then everyone willingly went on shore, some with spades, some with picks, and some with boxes to carry the earth; and the emperor with all his nobles stood watching this fine piece of work. Each of the masters of the galleys had his own flag planted in the ground to serve as a rallying point for his men, and that day a great length of ditch was dug.

The work was finished after a second day of energetic work by the Tana crews on Easter Saturday; that is, March 31. They dug a ditch 34 meters long and almost three meters deep. By that point, the basileus had posted patrols to watch for the arrival of Turkish forces. This information is provided by the Venetian Barbaro, who may well have been part of these work-crews.[22] He does not explain why the basileus had to post military cover for them, but we know from Doukas that Karaca Bey, the *beylerbey* of Rumeli, was active in the area, raiding the City's outskirts with reinforcements from Anatolia to ensure that the Romans could not come out.[23]

How many men could the defense muster? The eyewitness sources consistently say that there were around 7,000 to 9,000 men, including both Romans and Italians. Specifically, the Anconitan consul Benvenuto says that there were 7,000 defenders, including the soldiers brought by the cardinal Isidoros.[24] Leonardo of Chios says that the Greeks numbered at most 6,000 and the Italians at most 3,000.[25] Giacomo Tetaldi estimated that the population of the City was 25,000 or 30,000 men—presumably he means people—an estimate that is consistent with the latest scholarship on the question; he adds that only 6,000 or 7,000 were fit for combat.[26]

A key testimony occurs in the autobiographical notes of the basileus' political advisor and chief diplomat, Georgios Sphrantzes. He says that the basileus asked the City's demarchs—the heads or local mayors of its neighborhoods—to bring him a list of all the men in their respective districts who could bear arms, including the monks, and what weapons were available. He gave these lists to Sphrantzes to tally, and also to keep secret because the total was depressingly low: 4,773 able-bodied men, plus just under 200 foreigners.[27] Most scholars have emended that second figure to 2,000, as we know that there were more foreigners active in the defense than just 200. But Sphrantzes' figure is likely correct. These lists were drawn up by the demarchs of full-time residents of their neighborhoods, not of Venetian and Genoese galley crews and companies who had just arrived, such as those with Isidoros and Giustiniani. It is possible that Sphrantzes' figure for the Romans omits the basileus' guards and any professional soldiers that he employed, for the basileus knew those numbers and did not need the demarchs to count them. Thus, if he had about 1,000 soldiers and the Venetians and Genoese contributed 3,000 in total, including the galley crews, we reach a tally of almost 9,000, as reported by Leonardo.

This conclusion is reinforced by Leonardo of Chios' claim that most of the Greek defenders were not professional soldiers but civilians who had to use their weapons "according to the light of nature rather than with any skill." Their fathers had done the same in the siege of 1422, when many civilians and even monks and priests had fought on the walls with improvised weapons, some by using kitchen tables as shields, strapped to them by ropes. Now, in 1453, there were not enough trained archers to man the ramparts, but they were all doing "the best they could." Leonardo gives fairly generic information about the arms and armor of the Greek defenders of the City: they wielded an assortment of shields, spears, bows, and swords, and most of them had helmets and metal or leather armor. He says that it was difficult to keep some of these Greeks on the walls because they had to work to feed their families, or at least claimed as much. Leonardo was always biased against them and suspected that they claimed this as a pretext for cowardice. At some point in the siege, rations began to be issued to their families so that the men would not worry about feeding them and leave their posts.[28]

At a war council, Konstantinos, his officers (including Giustiniani), and the Italians collectively decided to hold the outer wall against the enemy, especially in the Mid-Wall sector, just as the Romans had done against Murad II in 1422.[29] This decision was criticized in retrospect by Leonardo, who later came to believe that they should have held the taller, inner wall instead, although its battlements were in a state of disrepair, for which he bitterly blames the Greeks. Yet he admits that, in the basileus' view, only the outer wall could realistically be defended.[30] The decision to hold the outer wall has been criticized by modern historians too as "unwise."[31] But the basileus was correct: there was no realistic alternative to holding the outer wall. Ideally, one would want to hold both walls simultaneously and they were built for precisely such a strategy: while the outer wall checked the enemy coming with ladders, archers on the inner wall could fire into the attacker's rear ranks. The outer wall, after all, was not insignificant. As Chrysoloras put it in 1411, it would suffice by itself for the defense of any other city.[32] And if it fell, which had never yet happened, then the defenders could fall back on the inner wall.

However, the defenders in 1453 did not have the numbers to properly man both walls. While they almost certainly did place some artillery on the inner wall to provide cover for defenders on the outer wall, it was the outer wall that they had to hold primarily. Not doing so would cede the moat and outer wall to the enemy. This could be potentially catastrophic because it would enable the enemy to shelter behind the outer wall, or even in the moat itself, and launch their assaults and possibly also artillery from a position of dangerous proximity to the defenders and the gates leading into the City.

It has also been suggested that the defenders chose to hold the outer wall to carry out sorties against the enemy.[33] It is true that holding the outer wall could enable sorties and that in the first days of the siege the defenders did mount a few. But, as explained previously, this is not why they chose to hold the outer wall. The sources do not support the sortie theory. Doukas, who mentions the sorties at the beginning of the siege, says that the defenders quickly realized that they were losing precious manpower in them and, even if they killed many more Turks, it was not worth the cost given the enormous disparity in the sizes of the two armies. So, an order was given, at the start of the siege, to cease the sorties and defend the outer wall.[34] Kritoboulos confirms this when he says that there was only one sortie at the very start of the siege but, because it suffered casualties, "they retreated to the City, shut the gates, and never came out again."[35]

We can now survey the positions on the walls taken by the defenders. However, our information comes overwhelmingly from our Italians informants, who were more interested in the positions of Latin defenders, rarely referring to the Romans, thereby giving the impression that the defense was almost entirely in the hands of their own people. This impression is certainly false. The majority of the defenders were Romans, although the command in certain sectors was in Latin hands, as it was in Giustiniani's overall.

The most vulnerable position was the section of the walls around the Fifth Gate (Pempton). This was assigned to the most formidable fighters among the defenders, Giustiniani and his company of heavily armored men, who were mostly Genoese from Chios. The sources number them between 300 and 400 men. Nestor-Iskander, who seems to have observed the siege at this location, says that the basileus augmented Giustiniani's company with 2,000 of his own men. It is likely that Giustiniani took up a position here even before the sultan arrived, in the expectation (which proved correct) that the main Ottoman force would attack at that point. "This was where the best part of the sultan's army would be focused, as well as the sultan's personal guard, his followers, and most of the cannon."[36] As the City's overall commander, he ensured that the land walls were equipped with catapults and other artillery. Drawing on his expertise of siege warfare, he positioned the defenders at the most advantageous positions.[37] Giustiniani "made a tour of the walls of the city and invigorated and even instructed the people so that they would not lose hope . . . all people admired and obeyed him in all things."[38]

The landmark nearest to the Fifth Gate was a church of St. Kyriake, who was believed to have been martyred in Diocletian's persecution in the early fourth century. There were many saints with this name. In the modern Orthodox Church, this saint is celebrated on July 7, but the calendar of saints' feast days compiled in tenth-century Constantinople—the *Synaxarion*—celebrates the most important saint Kyriake on May 19.[39] Thus, it is possible that just days before the final assault on May 29, Giustiniani and his men attended a service in honor of this martyr of the Christian faith and learned how she was struck with rods, hung, dismembered, and, while still clinging to life, thrown into the fire.[40] They knew that their fate could easily be similar. The Fifth Gate was haunted by Christian martyrdom.

While the main Ottoman attack would target the Fifth Gate, the sultan himself encamped on slightly higher ground to the south, opposite the Romanos Gate.[41] The walls to the north of this gate would be heavily targeted by cannon fire and it later came to be known as the Gate of the Cannon (or Top Kapi in Turkish). This sector of the defense was held by the basileus himself, although initially he established his headquarters inside the City by the Romanos Gate, to coordinate the defenses. The gate itself was guarded by two of the basileus' close associates, the cousins Ioannes and Andronikos Kantakouzenos, who were likely in their sixties.[42] Andronikos had long held the office of *megas domestikos*, which, in the past, designated the highest general in the Roman state.[43] Ioannes was a cousin of the basileus and one of his closest companions, from his days at Mystras.[44] Back in 1448, Ioannes governed Corinth, based in its lofty citadel, the Acrocorinth, where he was met by another old acquaintance, the Italian traveler, spy, and antiquarian Kyriacus of Ancona. Kyriacus had come up to Corinth from Mystras, where he had been spending time with the despot Konstantinos (later the basileus), the Platonist philosopher Georgios Gemistos Plethon, and a young student of Athenian origin, Nikolaos Chalkokondyles (who would later, under the name Laonikos, become one of the historians of the fall). Kyriacus calls Ioannes Kantakouzenos "an excellent and magnificent man of royal lineage."[45] His heroic death in the fighting on May 29, when the City fell, was recorded by none other than Laonikos (Nikolaos) Chalkokondyles, who likely knew him well from their days at Mystras.[46]

The landmark of the Romanos Gate was a church dedicated to the martyr Romanos who also died in the Diocletianic persecutions.[47] The feast-days celebrated in this church fell toward the end of the calendar year, but the naming of the adjacent gate after this saint would have cast an additional pall of martyrdom over the defense. That the martyr was named after the Roman people added additional poignancy to the location of the basileus' last stand.

A note is necessary on the names of these two gates. The name "Fifth Gate" is not attested after ca. 800 and is not used in the sources for the siege of 1453.[48] We do not know what this gate was called in 1453, if not St. Kyriake, after the nearby church. It is, however, reasonably clear that Giustiniani was posted in its vicinity, even if the sources do not use the name. He is said by all to have taken up the most dangerous position and this was by far the weakest point in the walls, being located in the dip caused by the valley of the Lykos stream. Moreover, the outer wall in this region has almost entirely disappeared because it suffered the most intense bombardment during the siege.[49] Yet the sources frequently refer to the area of the most intense bombardment as the Romanos Gate. This has led some scholars to conclude that, in 1453, both gates might have borne that name, or that they were confused.[50] What seems more likely is that the sources for 1453 refer to the entire stretch of the walls from the Romanos Gate to the Fifth Gate as "the St. Romanos Gate," and they do not have a separate name for what used to be called the Fifth Gate. Moreover, the sultan was positioned—and seems to have placed most of his cannons on—the higher ground of the Romanos Gate, from where he could fire down upon the Fifth Gate. This perhaps led the defenders to refer to the whole area of most intense bombardment as the Romanos Gate. It was the gate closest to the positions of both the basileus and the sultan.

Moving southward from the Mid-Wall, the Region Gate (also called Rousion or Myriandrion) was manned by the three Bocchiardi brothers (Paolo, Troilo, and Antonio), who were Latin natives of the City. They did so "in grave danger, at their own expense, and providing their own equipment, exercising the greatest vigilance by night and by day."[51] Paolo

Bocchiardi was a partner in a company that held a concession from the sultan to extract and trade in alum, a metallic chemical used in the dying of textiles.[52]

Next, the Pege ("Fountain") Gate was defended by the Roman Nikolaos Goudeles, the Venetian Battista Gritti, and their men.[53] Nikolaos Goudeles was about sixty years old. He had served Ioannes VIII as an ambassador to Russia, Germany, and Italy, and had governed Constantinople itself in the late 1440s. Gritti had previously spent much time in the City for trade. Posculo calls him a rather intimidating person ("*maximus*").[54] However, according to the Venetian diarist Barbaro, who was stationed with the ships in the harbor, the Pege Gate was held by the Venetian Nicolò Mocenigo.[55] Discrepant reports about who held which gate may reflect changes to their assignments during the siege, or else it reflects different perceptions among our authors about who was "in charge" of a given gate, with the Venetian Barbaro favoring information about Venetians, the Genoese Leonardo favoring the Genoese, and so on.

The Pege Gate was named after the famous church of the Virgin Zoodochos Pege, or "Life-Giving Spring," located just outside the walls. The church featured a healing fountain with a famous fish pond.[56] In the siege of 1422, the sultan Murad pitched his tent in the courtyard of that church.[57] In Ottoman times, the gate was called Selymbria/Silivri because it led out toward that city.

Close to the southern end of the land walls stood the Golden Gate fortress. The Golden Gate was a massive triumphal arch with three entrances that was built in the late fourth century. It was faced in marble and flanked by two huge adjacent projecting towers. By this time, the entrances had been built up and the whole had been turned into a fortress that had, in the fourteenth century, sheltered claimants to the imperial throne in the Palaiologan civil wars.[58] It was defended now by Andronikos Kantakouzenos (same name but different person from the *megas domestikos* stationed at the Romanos Gate) and the Venetian Catarino Contarini, with "a troop of young men under their command."[59] The Contarini were one of the most powerful and well-connected families of

Venice. Until his death in 1451, one Giovanni Contarini held the position of titular patriarch of Constantinople for the Catholic Church, although he does not appear to have traveled to the east, instead carrying out important diplomatic missions for the pope.[60] Our Catarino Contarini already had a long career of travel and trade in the east behind him. In 1436 and 1437, he had been part of a group of seven Venetian friends in Tana, at the head of the Sea of Azov, who got to wondering about some tomb-mounds in the area. They went so far as to hire over a hundred local workers and carried out two seasons of excavations, one of the first in history. Fifty years later, a member of the party, Giosafat Barbaro, wrote an account of their findings in meticulous detail, paying attention even to matters of stratigraphy.[61]

Looking northward now from the Mid-Wall, the next major gate was the Charisios Gate (or Charsiou) at the northern end of the Mid-Wall. This was the highest point in the circuit of the land walls (it was later called the Adrianople/Edirne Gate). This was guarded by the Roman Andronikos Leontares Bryennios and the Cretan Venetian Fabrizio Corner.[62] Bryennios had served the basileus as an envoy to Italy in 1451–1452.[63] Corner, who is called a "bold" or "brave" man, had been sent by the Venetian bailo of Constantinople on the embassy to Mehmed II back in late 1452, to plead for the life of Antonio Rizzo, the Venetian captain who had tried to sail past Rumeli Hisarı and was impaled by the sultan. As Corner was from Crete, he likely spoke Greek, too. He was to die in the fighting when the City fell.[64]

We then reach the Blachernai fortifications. The major gate here was the Kaligaria ("Bootmakers") in the wall of Manuel I Komnenos. There was no ditch here, but the walls were formidable.[65] This section of the defense was assigned to Theodoros Karystenos, a Roman who was old, pro-Union, and skilled with a bow. He had served the basileus Ioannes VIII as an ambassador, in which capacity, in 1443, he had astonished the knights at Chalon-sur-Saône in Burgundy with his ability to fire backward from a galloping horse, a "Parthian shot" that the Romans had likely learned from the Turks.[66] He was to die fighting when the City fell.[67] Also stationed at the Kaligaria was Theophilos Palaiologos, a scholar and kinsman of the basileus, also pro-Union, who died in the fighting on the May 29, struck down by an axe. The last words attributed to him later became famous: "If the City is lost, I do not wish to live." With him at the Kaligaria was also Johannes Grant, a German mercenary and military engineer,[68] and (according to a different source) Manuel Goudeles, brother of Nikolaos Goudeles who was stationed at the Pege Gate.[69]

The palace of Blachernai lay just to the north of the Kaligaria Gate and had a gate of its own. The basileus entrusted the defense of the palace to the Venetian bailo, Girolamo Minotto, and his secretary from Vincenza, Giovanni Giorgi, who had come to Constantinople possibly in order to study Greek.[70] The Palace Gate was guarded by Dolfino Dolfin, who is otherwise unknown.[71] Further north, the Xyloporta ("Wooden Gate"), located at the point where the Blachernai walls reached the Golden Horn, as well as the Anemas tower to the north of the palace, which was recently repaired with funds provided by the cardinal Isidoros, were entrusted to the Genoese Girolamo Italiano and Leonardo di Langasco, who were posted there "with numerous companions."[72] Another source puts the Xyloporta under the command of one Manuel Palaiologos, a kinsman of the basileus, but he is hard to identify.[73] It appears that Romans were paired with Italians all along the defense of the gates, although some Italian sources tend to mention only the Italians.

Apart from the palace, the major landmark in the Blachernai district was the church of the Virgin Blacherniotissa, which dated to the early days of the City's history. However, as previously mentioned, in 1434 it had burned down and was now a blackened ruin. Pero Tafur, the Spanish traveler who passed through the City four years later, says that "the church is so burned that it cannot be repaired."[74]

Turning the bend now to the sea walls along the Golden Horn, there was a potentially sensitive area at the Kynegos Gate, which could be reached either by land or by sea; this was why the basileus had the Venetian crews dig a ditch around it in late March. From here to the Phanarion Gate (modern Fener), a distance of about a kilometer, the walls were entrusted to the Venetian Gabriele Trevisan, captain of the two galleys, who led forty (or four hundred) of his compatriots. However, it seems that he was not posted there until May 9, and sources that put him there in their general overview of the defenders' positions are probably reflecting where everyone was by the end of the siege. Before May 9, Trevisan was active in naval operations in the harbor, which supports a later posting to the sea walls. Even from his later position there, he could presumably still call on naval assistance from the defense fleet in the harbor.[75]

The Phanarion Gate was held by Alexios Dishypatos. In 1444, he was known to have been the captain of the basileus' galley. Our source for that is none other than the antiquarian Kyriacus of Ancona, who sailed on that ship under Alexios Dishypatos' command from Constantinople to the island of Imbros. Kyriacus' letter about the journey gives us a wonderful sense of how interconnected this world was: it was addressed to none other than Georgios Scholarios, the later patriarch Gennadios who, in 1453, was leading the opposition against Union with Rome. In addition, the letter recounts Kyriacus' meeting on Imbros with Michael Kritoboulos, who, under the classicizing penname Kritoboulos, would become the historian of the fall and biographer of Mehmed II.[76]

From the Phanarion to the Imperial Gate, the defense was entrusted to the Venetian brothers Lodovico and Antonio Bembo, with 150 of their compatriots. The brothers are described as "exceptionally brave men" and were, incidentally, also creditors of the *megas doux* Loukas Notaras.[77] It is not clear where this "Imperial Gate" was located, although certainly along the Golden Horn, probably across from Pera; overall, then, a distance of 1.5 kilometers was assigned to this group.[78] They were so few because, so long as the enemy was barred from entering the Golden Horn, this zone was a low priority. Within that span of the sea walls, the Theodosia Gate was guarded by one Tzamplakon. The Eis Pegas Gate ("To the Fountains") was defended by Demetrios Palaiologos Metochites, a former diplomat, general, and now the City's (last) governor; he, too, was to die when the City fell on May 29. The Platea Gate was guarded by a Philanthropenos, possibly the young Manuel, who is known to have died on the day of the fall.[79]

Finally, the end of the harbor wall, at the northeastern tip of the City near where the chain blocking the Golden Horn was anchored, was guarded by the cardinal Isidoros, who was likely accompanied by his companion, Leonardo of Chios. The landmark church in this sector was dedicated to St. Demetrios, yet another martyr, this one being also a military saint, so doubly appropriate. The region was subsequently taken over by the Topkapi palace of the sultans.[80] Isidoros and Leonardo appear to have exchanged notes during the siege and, as both were learned scholars, they made classical comparisons to the astounding events that were unfolding around them.[81]

Inside Constantinople, but closer to the harbor district, the *megas doux* Loukas Notaras led a reserve force of 100 to 500 cavalry. "He patrolled the entire City, encouraging the defenders, inspecting the lookout-points and searching for those who abandoned their post. He did this every day."[82] "He was ready to bring help where needed, to protect the harbor."[83] This function was certainly more critical in the later phases of the siege, when the Ottomans had ships in the Golden Horn.

When the sources say that so-and-so with his men were posted to a certain gate, we understand that they were spread out along the adjacent lengths of the wall on either side, not simply concentrated at the gate itself. Civilians, including priests and monks, were also spread out thinly along the walls, especially the sea walls that were less vulnerable. All told, as Leonardo says, they were barely enough to watch over the entire circuit.[84] Additionally, there were two distinctive groups positioned by the sea walls on the Marmara side, about as far from any action as could be foreseen. Indeed, they saw none, although their leaders were executed by the sultan when the City fell. First, "the Catalan consul was assigned to the tower before the hippodrome." He has been identified as Joan de la Via, a merchant and captain from Gerona stationed in Constantinople since 1447.[85] And second, the Ottoman prince Orhan, whose upkeep money had possibly kicked off the entire war in the first place, "guarded one of the quarters of the City on the seaward side with the Turks in his pay, who had previously rebelled against their master [i.e., Murad II]."[86]

It is possible that Orhan's Turks were kept away from sensitive areas of the walls to prevent them from betraying the City to Mehmed and winning his favor. There was little chance that Orhan himself would do so as he knew that he was a dead man if he ever fell into the sultan's hands, but his followers did perhaps pose such a risk. Otherwise, there was little chance that any of the other defenders would betray the City. Their patriotism and religious dedication ensured that. Indeed, we hear of no treasonous activities during the siege. In the 1,123 years of Constantinople's existence, dissidents inside had betrayed the sitting basileus and opened the gates to allow in the armies of a *Roman* rebel seeking the throne in a civil war, but never—not once—had they opened the gates to let in a barbarian army, even when it was posing as the mercenary force of a Roman pretender. This is how "identity" functions as a historical force: it shapes the choices that people make between "us" and "them." Those lines were drawn starkly in 1453 for the Romans and Italians barricaded inside New Rome.

The City's second-most vulnerable point after the Mid-Wall was the Golden Horn harbor. Assaults could potentially be made here if the enemy controlled the sea, as the Venetians did in 1203 and 1204. In 1453, the defenders could not afford to divert the manpower necessary to properly guard the sea walls. If our numbers are correct, they spared fewer than a thousand men for this sector of the walls, plus the reserve force under Notaras. It was therefore vitally important to keep the Turkish fleet out of the harbor.

On April 2, the basileus ordered the Venetian Bartolamio Soligo to pull the chain (or "boom") across the entrance to the Golden Horn (see Color Plate 3). This was a series of blocks of wood joined together by thick iron bands, forming a floating chain that stretched across many hundreds of meters of water. We should not picture it as a continuous chain link, but as wooden blocks linked by iron bands. To make its ends more secure, they were attached to points inside the walls of Constantinople and Pera, probably in defensible towers.[87] This device, or rather its predecessor, was first attested in the last Arab siege of the City, in 717–718.[88] The links of an iron chain on display in the Istanbul Archaeological Museum that purport to be from 1453 may instead have been from Rhodes, dating to 1522.[89]

On April 9, nine or ten galleys took up positions next to the boom to protect it. Barbaro, who was in the harbor during most of the siege, says that they were nine but itemizes ten: five from Genoa, one from Ancona, one belonging to the basileus, and three from Venetian Crete (Candia); there were 27 other ships in the harbor, including five more galleys belonging to the basileus, but they were unarmed.[90] Leonardo says that the flotilla consisted of seven Genoese and three Venetian ships from Crete.[91] Tetaldi says that the harbor contained 30 ships plus the flotilla of nine galleys assigned to the boom. Of the nine, two were raiding ships belonging to "pirates"; three were Venetian merchant vessels; three belonged to the basileus; and one belonged to Giustiniani.[92] Why are there no Genoese ships in his list? It is likely that the "pirate" ships and two of the three ships of the basileus were in reality Genoese. The Genoese ships and Giustiniani had likely been corsairs before the siege and, moreover, the Genoese had an interest in denying that any of their ships were fighting for the basileus, as they were ostensibly at peace with the sultan. Thus, it could be maintained officially that there were no Genoese ships in the defensive flotilla.[93] This may explain the discrepancies in our lists, which concern primarily the "flag" of the ships, not their number or nature.

Everything that could be done to secure the City was done with careful planning, energy, and grim determination. The defenders could now change their strategy only if they received reinforcements from the West, for which they were hoping. They might also be forced to adapt if Mehmed managed to spring a surprise on them or if his cannons proved to be more effective than those of his father in 1422. Beyond that, Konstantinos XI could only pray, fight like hell, and hope that the siege followed the course of 1422 and not that of 1446 at the Hexamilion, where he had been soundly routed by Murad II. An eyewitness reported that he now:

> toured the City hourly, invigorating the generals, the soldiers, and in the same way all of the people so that they would not renounce hope nor slacken their resistance against the enemy but place their trust in the Almighty Lord: "For he is our helper and protector."[94]

5

Mehmed's Plan of Attack

Broadly speaking, the expansion of the Ottoman empire took place in two phases. The first lasted for just over a century, from the mid-fourteenth century to the later fifteenth, culminating in the conquests of Mehmed II. This phase was marked by a steady, if not explosive, trajectory of growth in Anatolia and the Balkans, resulting in a formidable state that could hold its own against any rivals. At that time, the Ottoman empire was roughly co-extensional with the lands ruled by the Roman emperor Manuel II Komnenos in the twelfth century. The more world-changing conquests came in the sixteenth century, with the acquisition of the entire Middle East, the north African coast, and further expansion in the Balkans and the Black Sea region. These transformed the Ottoman state into a massive empire of global significance. At that time, the empire was roughly similar in shape to that ruled by the Roman emperor Justinian in the sixth century, with the significant addition of Mesopotamia, Arabia, and parts of Hungary. Its ambitions were checked only by the emergence of peer empires during the early modern period, namely Spain, Austria, Russia, and Safavid Iran.[1]

In early 1453, Mehmed directly ruled territories in two regional commands, the Balkans (Rumeli) and Asia Minor (Anadolu), that amounted to some 575 square kilometers, so slightly larger than modern France. In addition, Mehmed commanded the nominal loyalty of a number of vassal states, specifically Serbia, Wallachia (north of the Danube), Karaman (southern Anatolia), and the Cadar dynasty of Sinop (on the Black Sea coast of northern Anatolia), but he could reliably expect obedience only from Serbia and Sinop (and had to wage war against Karaman as recently as 1452). Adding those two vassals, his empire amounted to some 670 square kilometers. The total population of the Ottoman empire at this time, including the vassal states that contributed military units, was around eight million people, considering historical norms for this territory and the impact of the plague.[2]

As a relatively new political formation, containing people who spoke many different languages, practiced different faiths, and had their own, local traditions of political independence, this empire was still unsettled. It required considerable skill and energy just to hold it together. The sultans had to carefully maintain countless relationships with local elites in every corner of the realm, even though the threat of overwhelming force gave them the upper hand. They preferred not to fall back on it in dealing with their subjects, but it did form the backbone of their power. That partly explains why they continued to wage ceaseless war along the frontier despite ruling a fractious empire inhabited by diverse and restless subjects: they needed a powerful, effective, and tested army to repel Christian threats from abroad and to suppress internal rebellions. The siege of Constantinople was, in this sense, both an external war, as it targeted a "foreign," non-vassal state, and an internal one, as it took place at the physical center of the growing Ottoman domain. It gave Mehmed the opportunity to marshal his resources on an unprecedented scale and to thereby further consolidate his hold over the empire.

Mehmed appears to have been an obsessive micromanager. Moreover, his eagerness to supervise operations in all their nitty-gritty detail and to study the technical aspects of his new technologies was coupled with an ability to grasp the big picture at the same time. We can accept Doukas' picture of the young sultan losing sleep by pouring over maps and diagrams of the City's layout, role-playing various scenarios for its conquest, and giving detailed instructions to his generals about where to position their men, cannons, and engines.[3] He had inspected the City himself in 1452 and was probably receiving detailed reports about the preparations of its defenders. During the winter of 1452–1453, he readied his fleet and cannons, as well as the arms, equipment, and supplies of his soldiers, recruiting sailors and soldiers, and was likely also supervising the logistics of what was to be a vast operation.[4]

Mehmed could reasonably expect that the City would not be surrendered or betrayed to him. The Romans had held out tenaciously in the face of famine and deprivation during the blockade of Constantinople by Bayezid in 1394–1402, and they had resisted Murad in 1422. He would have to break through their defenses by force. This he had in abundance. He could muster a vastly larger army than the defenders had, probably ten times larger; he was casting dozens of cannons, some of them huge weapons of destruction and intimidation the likes of which had never been seen on a battlefield; and he built a large armada with which the Ottomans could hopefully dominate the sea around the City. He could also draw resources from the empire and compel contributions from his vassals. Yet despite this disparity in strength, Mehmed knew that success was hardly assured. Some in his inner council even thought his odds were slim.

A frontal assault on the walls with ladders, as his father's men had tried in 1422,[5] would be costly. To be sure, Mehmed had lives to spare and was not averse to sacrificing them to get what he wanted. But that approach held little promise of success by itself. He needed the cannons to blow holes in the outer wall so that his men could pour into the breach and overwhelm the defenders with their greater numbers. This, in turn, would require a period of continual bombardment, which would be longer or shorter depending on how well the cannons performed when they were finally fired against the thousand-year-old Roman walls. This was a factor of uncertainty in Mehmed's planning, for slower progress carried risks. For one thing, his massive army and armada had to be supplied, fed, and paid for the duration of the siege, raising the cost of delays and the burden that the siege put on his subjects. Also, entrenched defenders had a tactical advantage. A small number could hold off a larger army of attackers who were climbing up ladders or crowded into a narrow breach in the walls. Only a few could fight in a tight place at one time. This could neutralize his greater numbers, unless he could wear the defenders down while replenishing his own men with reserves. Mehmed knew that the basileus had barely enough soldiers to man the walls, but perhaps he had just enough. How, then, could he offset the defenders' advantage?

First, Mehmed could deploy his army along more or less the entire length of the land walls to force the defenders to spread themselves thin, even while he concentrated his attack on the most vulnerable point, the Mid-Wall. Second, he had to prevent the arrival of reinforcements, for that would tilt the balance further against him. A delay caused by a potentially slow progress of the cannons against the walls might allow the Romans' overseas allies to send aid. A few more units like that of Giustiniani—whether mercenary or fired up to fight for the Christian cause—could shore up the defenses against his attack. The sultan would then face not only defeat and ruinous expense but humiliation, which stung more.

Thus, Mehmed's strategy depended on diplomacy. He had established peaceful relations with most powers that might be in a position to aid the Romans, including the Genoese colony at Pera. He did not need their active assistance, only for them to remain uninvolved. He gave assurances of friendship and dissembled his intentions until it would be too late for them to act. The impulsive and fiery young sultan, who was widely underestimated in the West, proved to be a skilled diplomat. Yet there were still too many wild cards, including the Venetians, whom he had not managed to seduce and with whom he was technically in a state of war. Even a small body of Venetian reinforcements could tip the balance against him both at sea and in the fighting on the walls, and his spies were reporting that the Senate was planning to send a relief force. There was, additionally, a large pool of western privateers, opportunists, mercenaries, and corsairs plying the Aegean and ready to take up service for pay, glory, and the faith. Giustiniani was one of them. The basileus might find more, buying their services in exchange for a fortress here or an island there.

Therefore, it was imperative for Mehmed to cut the City off from receiving reinforcements. That is why he needed the gunnery emplacement at Rumeli Hisarı, to choke off the Bosporos, and the large fleet to invest Constantinople. Kritoboulos claimed that Mehmed wanted to be more dominant on the sea with his fleet than he was on land with his army, and that he poured more of his effort into preparing the fleet.[6] This was hyperbole, but it reflected a valid concern: the Ottomans were still lagging far behind the Italians in naval skill and technology. In the fourteenth century, the former Roman basileus Ioannes Kantakouzenos noted that the Turks were formidable on land but inexperienced at sea and far easier to beat there.[7] During Bayezid's blockade of 1394–1402, it was relatively easy for western ships to break through and bring desperately needed supplies to the City—to be sold at exorbitant prices, of course.[8] Mehmed was determined to shift the balance of power at sea and prevent Constantinople from receiving assistance. That would shift the odds in his favor compared to his ancestors' attempts to take the City.[9] The new Ottoman fleet that he commissioned was, however, about more than just Constantinople. The empire now straddled two continents, and it was becoming increasingly absurd for the sultans' land armies to be unable to cross from one to the other without fear of attack from Italian ships. As recently as 1443–1444, during the Varna crusade, Murad II faced the prospect of being stranded on the Asian side of the empire while his enemies attacked him in Europe.[10]

While the primary strategic function of the new Ottoman fleet was to prevent aid from reaching Constantinople—explaining Mehmed's fury when it failed to do so on April 20—its logistical function was no less important. This was to provision his huge army with food and equipment. The scaling ladders and cannon emplacements required a lot of lumber, and the cannonballs had to be transported from afar, the hard stone possibly brought all the way from the Black Sea.[11] The fleet's primary mission was not to break through the boom or attack the sea walls. Eyewitnesses noted that it ferried supplies but otherwise stayed quiet at its base further up the Bosporos and did not seek to enter the fray, except when the Christian reinforcement ships arrived on April 20.[12] Barbaro, stationed in the harbor and possibly with the ships by the boom, marveled at this. The nearby presence of the Ottoman fleet, whose sailors made a great deal of noise, kept the Christians on edge and under arms, as they waited for an attack on the boom. "Yet their fleet never moved . . . but made us stand to our arms from fear of them, from April 12 until May 29, all day and all night."[13]

Thus, Mehmed's strategy was to use cannons and manpower to blast a way through the land walls, while forcing the defenders to spread themselves thin so that when his soldiers attacked, they would have the numerical advantage and the defenders could be worn down, as they would lack reserves. He would also use the fleet to prevent them from receiving reinforcements and provide his own army with supplies. Time, however, worked against him, not only because of the enormous cost of the operation, which drained his resources by the day, but the possibility that western powers, chiefly Venice, would come to the rescue. It helped Mehmed that most western powers did not believe the Greeks had done enough to fulfill the terms of Church Union. A protracted siege posed yet another problem; namely, it might give recently conquered provinces the opportunity to rebel.

In the end, the success of Mehmed's strategy hinged on his artillery. The Ottoman sultans were generally eager to give their armies every technological advantage. Their armies were early adopters of hand-held firearms and cannons, although the janissary corps was slow to equip itself with firearms, preferring the use of traditional bows.[14] Mehmed had dozens of cannons cast and tested during the winter of 1452–1453 by teams of engineers, consuming vast amounts of bronze, firewood, gunpowder, and stone. It is fascinating to read Greek authors such as Laonikos and Kritoboulos using their training in ancient rhetoric to describe this technological innovation, how it was cast in a deep pit using the lost-wax method in two massive pieces that were then fitted together, the deafening sound that cannons made when they were fired, and the terrifying impact of their cannonballs. Their rhetorical training proved equal to the task, and they proudly noted that no ancient writer had seen or described such a thing.[15] However, they seemed to be unaware that the cannons cast by Mehmed were, despite their gargantuan size, somewhat behind the times, compared to developments in western Europe. They were cast in bronze, not iron, which was lighter, cheaper, and more durable; also, they used stone shot, which was liable to shatter upon impact, rather than cast-iron balls.[16]

One of Mehmed's engineers was a Hungarian or Wallachian named Orban (Urban), who used to work for the basileus but was refused a raise and so offered his services to the sultan while the latter was building Rumeli Hisarı in 1452. This defection caused some consternation among the defenders during the siege, as after all they were being fired at by the handiwork of a Christian who was working for the enemy. The story was also emblematic of the problems caused by the basileus' lack of money.[17] However, we must be cautious with the tale of Orban. It is not the case that the defenders needed cannons and lost in Orban an engineer capable of making them. The defense did not need his massive cannons. The point of the story is that a lack of funds prevented Konstantinos from retaining Orban and thereby depriving Mehmed of his services. But all moralizing aside, that would have been a poor use of the basileus' scarce funds. If Mehmed wanted to hire expert cannon-makers, he could probably have found them elsewhere, whether Orban stayed in the City or not. Besides, Orban did not bring him the most cutting-edge cannon technology.

We should not treat Orban as the chief of Mehmed's engineers, as is often done. Nor should we assume that he built "The Big Cannon" for Mehmed or even accept that there was only One Big Cannon. This supposed item is one of the star attractions of many accounts of the siege, including some contemporary ones and all modern ones, but it is not clear that there was only One. Not all our sources assume that, and those that do give contradictory information about it: it either exploded while being fired (in 1460, James II of Scotland was killed when a cannon next to him exploded), or it was destroyed by a well-placed shot by Giustiniani, or it survived the siege and was still in use.[18] They also disagree about where "it" was positioned, while other authors speak of two or three Big Cannons. In reality, there were probably a number of big cannons, but a lore emerged during the siege about "the" Big One, which was probably the biggest one that each defender saw in his sector through the smoke clouds that the artillery produced. This lore about the One was then passed down to the historians of the siege who spoke with the survivors.

One of Mehmed's large cannons—or bombards, as they were also called—survives. It is called the Dardanelles Gun and was manufactured in 1464; currently it is kept in the United Kingdom (see Image 5.1). The inscription on its muzzle says "Allah, help sultan Mehmed Khan, the son of Murad. [This is] the work of Munir Ali, in the month of Rejeb, year 868 of the hijrah."[19] It weighs almost 17 tons, had a barrel length of five meters, and fires a rock 90 cm wide. When the predecessors of this beast were test-fired near Edirne during the winter of 1452–1453, the sultan's men warned inhabitants for miles around in advance, in order to prevent a panic. Such cannons required months to haul to the intended battle-site, so their long overland journey began before any other part of the sultan's army. Pulling them required 60 oxen apiece and 200 men

Image 5.1 The Dardanelles Gun, a bronze Ottoman cannon from 1464. It is currently in the Royal Armouries at Fort Nelson, Hampshire, UK. It was gifted to Queen Victoria in 1866 by Sultan Abdulaziz. Source: flickr/Tim Sheerman-Chase.

to keep it steady with ropes so it did not slip off the road. They also required teams of carpenters to smooth the road ahead with platforms and bridges, leading work crews of another 200. This was another way that the campaign consolidated and expanded Mehmed's control of his subjects' labor and resources.

The cannons' journey began in early February, with an estimated arrival time in early April. This could not be done in secret: the defenders knew exactly what was coming and when. The Romans sent out some light ships to raid Turkish territories along the coasts and took captives. But these attacks were a symbolic act of defiance and trivial compared to what was coming. At the same time, Mehmed's general for Rumeli, the *beylerbey* Karaca, swept through the remaining Roman territories in Thrace, slaughtering peasants and receiving the surrender of almost all the cities, except Selymbria.[20]

As the noose tightened around Constantinople, seven Venetian ships slipped out of the harbor on the night of February 26, one from Venice itself and another six from Crete. Their captains broke their oaths to the basileus to stay. They made it home safely, taking their cargos and 700 men, who would have been a valuable asset for the defense, had they stayed.[21]

We lack reliable information about the size of Mehmed's land army. A number of our sources, writing independently of each other, cite the figure of 300,000. Their agreement hardly means that the figure is accurate. It likely reflects a rumor that started among the defenders during the siege and then passed to the authors of our texts, some of whom were there to begin with. This is indicated by the fact that both Isidoros and Leonardo quote that figure in their letters to pope Nicholas V, even though they had not the opportunity to compare notes after the City's fall, during their subsequent flight. In their shared classical idiom, they also refer to the janissaries as "Myrmidons" (the elite corps of Achillles' fighters at Troy).[22] Thus, the inflated figure must have originated during the siege. Others report it too. The brief report by Benvenuto of Ancona states that the 300,000 soldiers of the sultan required 60,000 tents. Kritoboulos specifies that the figure of 300,000 included only fighters, not camp attendants and various other civilians, the addition of whom further inflated the total number.[23] The Athenian historian Laonikos gives Mehmed 400,000 soldiers and adds that:

> the number of pack animals in the sultan's camp would have been twice that [i.e., 800,000 animals]. For the sultan's armies bring into camp many more pack animals than men, to carry provisions sufficient for themselves and for the rest of the horses and men. The Turks are the only people we know who secure enough provisions for themselves, wherever they are campaigning, so as to be self-sufficient, and they bring as many camels and mules as they can for their supplies and even more mules for their convenience in other respects.[24]

In addition to camp attendants and civilian contractors, the pack animals had their own requirements for food, water, and other logistical needs. Laonikos adds that "large markets follow the sultan, supplying whatever is needed for the horses, slaves, and the army, so a great multitude of people is present there."[25]

Among the lowest estimates was Barbaro's, who gives Mehmed 160,000 soldiers on the landward side.[26] Two other sources, Tetaldi and Sphrantzes, give him 200,000 soldiers, with the former noting that only 60,000 were "trained for battle," whereas the rest were virtually unarmed, except for rudimentary military equipment. He adds that there were 35,000 or 40,000 cavalry soldiers, but he does not explain whether they were ranked among the 60,000 trained soldiers, the 140,000 "unarmed" ones, or were divided between both groups. There were also numerous "merchants and engineers . . . actors, sycophants [i.e., entertainers], moneychangers, and offensive individuals" (probably sex workers).[27] We may add blacksmiths and other craftsmen, cooks, pages, slaves, logistics officers, mule-drivers, messengers, medics, qadis (i.e., judges), Muslim holy figures, and various hangers-on who were just waiting to help loot the City.

Some members of these groups may have also been ranked among the combatants. In the end, there is no way to know reliably how many soldiers Mehmed assembled in 1453. The scale of hyperbole at work in our sources is revealed by Leonardo's estimate of the number of janissaries, a distinctive corps that could not be confused with another. He says that Mehmed brought 15,000 janissaries with them, but the total number of janissaries in the later fifteenth century, when the Ottoman empire was larger and the corps was expanding, did not exceed 8,000 (and they were never always in one place).[28] In 1453, Mehmed did not have more than 5,000 janissaries in total.[29] By historical standards, given the territories that Mehmed controlled, it would be extraordinary if his army was larger than 80,000, and he could bring only a part of that to the siege.[30] After all, his empire did not rest on consensus, and a prolonged absence of occupation forces from the provinces would likely spark rebellions, especially if the siege dragged on. One of Mehmed's former janissaries put it bluntly: at any time, the sultan "was afraid that all the Christian lands which he had conquered would oppose him."[31] Not just the Christian lands: the Muslim beyliks in Anatolia, especially Karaman, were also eager to throw off the Ottoman yoke. Garrisons and occupation forces could not be withdrawn empire-wide.

At the upper limit, therefore, Mehmed might have brought 60,000 soldiers to Constantinople, beyond which his camp also swelled with thousands of non-combatants and animals, making the army seem larger. In addition, he had just created a large armada whose crews added to the logistical stress and demographic footprint of the siege. Our sources give inflated figures for the number of ships too, most of them between 200 and 350 ships, although one low estimate, by Barbaro, has 145 ships, and he was closer to the naval action than any of our informants.[32] As he knew, ships came in a variety of shapes and sizes and performed different functions, so it would not have been easy to know what to count as part of the "fleet" proper. In addition to galleys that could fight, there were supply ships, transports, fishing vessels, and merchantmen that showed up to sell goods to the vast market represented by Mehmed's army.[33] It is more difficult to estimate the size of the combined crews of these ships. Only one of our witnesses tried to do so, Benvenuto of Ancona, and he says that there were 36,000 men at sea.[34]

Let us hypothesize, for heuristic reasons, that 100,000 people converged on the City as part of Mehmed's effort to capture it, almost all of them men between sixteen and forty-five years old. This means that slightly over 1% of the entire population of the empire (roughly 8 million) converged on the City in 1453, or over 2% of the entire male population. As about 40% of the male population would have been under sixteen, Mehmed's campaign drew in just under 5% of the adult male population. But those were just the people who were directly present. In premodern economies, the labor of eight or nine people working the land or with animals was required to support one person who did not. Therefore, the surplus production of a million people, or one-eighth of the empire, was diverted to support the army and its support personnel (craftsmen, sailors, and the like). And that was just for food. The economic impact of this army was greater if we factor in the cost of pay, equipment, ships, siege engines, and cannons. In other words, the siege of Constantinople was a massive logistical, demographic, and economic undertaking that, in one way or another, impacted most people and animals who lived in Mehmed's empire, Christians and Muslims alike. This partly explains the stress that he was under and his furious determination to win.

On the morning of Thursday, April 5, in the week after Easter, Mehmed's army appeared before the defenders at a distance of two and half miles from the walls of the City.[35] One scholar, possible residing in the Chora monastery near the land walls, made a note of this event on the title page of a book containing the poems of Theodoros Metochites. Metochites was a statesman and philosopher of the early decades of the fourteenth century and had renovated the Chora to the splendor that it has had ever since (subsequently as the Kariye mosque). In Chapter 1, we discussed his brilliant oration in praise of Constantinople. The note made on his poems by this scribe, in Greek, reads as follows:

> In the year 6961 [since Creation, i.e., 1453], on the 5th of April, in the fifth indiction, during the first week after Easter, the pious Mehmed [correct this to "impious"?] came against the Queen of Cities to besiege it by land and sea. He has with him a countless army and many siege-engines and towers. He also has a large fleet and has surrounded the City on all sides.[36]

This was likely written on April 5 itself, or soon after.

Mehmed had probably encamped at a position outside the line of sight of the City's residents during the previous night and marched the remaining distance on the morning of April 5.[37] His journey from Adrianople-Edirne had taken nine days,[38] suggesting a leisurely pace.[39] The City's inhabitants had been anticipating the sultan's arrival and had prayed to God that he not arrive before Easter, so that they could celebrate it in peace. This, at least, they had been granted.[40] It was now the week of Diakainesimos, or Bright Week, which follows Easter. Celebrations were held in the church of the Chora, near the palace, and the sacred icon of the Virgin Hodegetria was moved for that purpose from the palace to the Chora. It would remain there until the end.[41]

On Friday, April 6, no doubt watched closely by thousands of people on the walls, Mehmed advanced with half his force to within a mile of the walls.[42] On this day, the basileus left his palace in the Blachernai district and moved to the Mid-Wall, possibly initially to the Charisios Gate, entrusting the palace's defense to the Venetian bailo, Girolamo Minotto, and his compatriots.[43] The basileus also staged a spectacle on that day to bolster the defenders' morale and demonstrate their determination before the enemy. He had five Venetian galleys sail in battle order from the harbor to the Kynegos Gate, where their crews had recently dug the trench. Here, a thousand Venetians disembarked fully armed and marched under their respective banners along the entire length of the land walls and back, whereupon they retired to their ships and returned to their anchorage. This parade was a demonstration of sovereignty and defiance. It "appeared to give great comfort to those in the City and caused some surprise to the enemy."[44] It was the last time that the Christian forces would command the land outside the walls.

Kritoboulos reports that, before the siege began, the sultan sent envoys to the Romans pledging to guarantee the safety of all inhabitants of the City if they surrendered Constantinople to him. This last-minute offer was consistent with Islamic custom. Kritoboulos does not say when this took place exactly between Mehmed's arrival and the outbreak of fighting. The Romans rejected the terms. They said that they might agree to other terms, but surrendering the City was out of the question. The other terms they had in mind were likely the payment of tribute and accepting a Muslim qadi and representative of the sultan in the City. This was the standard Roman position. But for Mehmed, their refusal to surrender meant war.[45]

Doukas places this first diplomatic exchange after cannons had commenced their assault on the walls, which is less plausible. He reports the terms in a similar way to Kritoboulos—tribute offered by the Romans and surrender of the City demanded by the sultan. He then explains the considerations of honor that led the basileus to refuse the sultan's offer of safe passage to the Peloponnese. "It was simply impossible for the Romans to surrender the City to the Turks with their own hands. If that happened, they would be spat upon, reviled, and disgraced along every road, in every place, and in every Christian city to which they might emigrate. And not just by Christians: the Turks themselves and Jews would regard them as nobodies."[46] This sentiment was probably not a rhetorical invention by Doukas, who, admittedly, was prone to dramatic embellishment. It must be an idea that was expressed publicly in Constantinople by the basileus or his men, for it is also found in Nestor-Iskander, although he misunderstood its context. In Nestor-Iskander, the basileus is frequently pressured by his inner council to abandon the City and save himself. At one of these meetings, the basileus tells them that he cannot do that: "How can I leave the clergy, the churches of God, the empire, and all of the people? What will the world think of me? . . . No, my lords, no: I will die here with you." These words were most likely a public response to the sultan's terms than to any alleged pressure on the basileus from his advisors to abandon the City.[47] No other source suggests that the basileus was advised to leave.

The day after the Venetian parade, on Saturday, April 7, the Ottoman army moved forward to within a quarter mile of the walls. It deployed to its assigned positions, extending from the Golden Gate in the south to the Golden Horn in the north.[48] Bells rang out across the City to signal that a state of siege was in effect, and the basileus ordered everyone to take up their assigned posts on the walls.[49] The Ottoman forces were positioned as follows.[50] The sector from the Golden Gate to the Romanos Gate (i.e., to the Mid-Wall) was placed under Ishak Pasha, the *beylerbey* of Anatolia. His origins are unknown, but he was a close associate and second vizier of the former sultan Murad II. In 1444, he had escorted Murad to his temporary monastic retirement and later signed off as a witness and executor of his will, accompanying his body to Bursa for burial. He was confirmed in his position by Mehmed and made *beylerbey* of Anatolia, but he was also forced to marry Murad's widow when Mehmed murdered her infant son (i.e., his half-brother, a potential rival).[51]

The sultan himself, with Halil Pasha, Saraca Pasha, and the janissaries, who wore distinctive white hats, faced the Mid-Wall, the most critical point of the land walls. Kritoboulos places the sultan opposite the Romanos Gate, whereas Doukas places him opposite the Charisios Gate.[52] In reality, Mehmed must have moved across that span during the siege. Halil Pasha we have already met.[53] Saraca Pasha (or Saruca) was an older veteran with a long and distinguished career as a general and diplomat. He was possibly of Roman ethnic origin, enslaved as a child in the *devşirme*. He rose to the office of *beylerbey* of Rumeli and then became vizier to Murad II and Mehmed.[54]

Karaca Pasha, the current *beylerbey* of Rumeli, was assigned to attack the walls of the Blachernai district, from the Charisios Gate down to the Xyloporta at the Golden Horn, and for this he was given cannons too. Mehmed had married his sister, so they were brothers-in-law. Karaca Pasha had spent the winter reducing the remaining Roman forts in Thrace.

The districts across the Golden Horn, from the Xyloporta to Pera itself, were assigned to Zaganos Pasha. He was also of Christian origin and conscripted into the janissaries through the *devşirme*. He rose through the ranks, married a daughter of Murad II (so a half-sister of Mehmed), and was currently serving as the sultan's second vizier. He is remembered as being more hawkish and in favor of the war, in opposition to his rival Halil, but this may be propaganda that he himself put out, especially after Halil's disgrace later that year.[55] During the siege, Zaganos would supervise the most impressive engineering feats of the Ottoman attack, including the ship portage around Pera, a massive siege-tower placed up against the walls, and a pontoon bridge across the Golden Horn. He is described as a man who "commanded considerable power in military affairs and possessed true loyalty."[56]

The bombardment of the walls commenced on April 11, and continued, day and night, with terrifying regularity until the final assault in late May.[57] But the fighting, or rather skirmishing, had probably begun a few days earlier, on April 7, when the Ottoman infantry forces moved up to their positions by the walls. Their task was to prepare the ground for the mass assault that would take place when the cannons, which would be firing over their heads, finally brought down enough of the wall to allow a charge through the breach. The soldiers moved up to the moat where they entrenched their position behind protective screens and lattice-work. They also dug themselves in along the edge of the moat, with a ditch of their own and manholes, in an early form of trench warfare. From there they fired on the defenders with bows, crossbows, and guns. This was where blood was first spilled on the walls. These operations certainly took place in the Mid-Wall section, though we cannot rule out that they were also occurring elsewhere along the walls too. The Turks also began to excavate tunnels in the Blachernai district, where there was no defensive moat, but this was not discovered until later.[58]

The defenders on the outer wall fired back. They also mounted sorties against the attackers, although, as we saw, these proved too costly and were quickly discontinued. Even if Giustiniani's men killed many more Turks than they lost, the disparity in numbers between the two armies favored the attackers. The defense could not afford to lose *any* men. So, the sorties ceased, and the defenders were instructed to fire from the battlements with ballistae, bows, crossbows, and guns. The technical term for a fifteenth-century gun is "arquebus." They used stone shot from the Black Sea, about the size of a nut, which had such penetrative power that it could pass through armor and flesh and sometimes even kill the man standing behind. Doukas notes that the Turks had also learned to use such weapons and were better at using them.[59]

Meanwhile, the cannons were laboriously put in place and began their pounding cacophony on April 11. We do not know how many cannons Mehmed brought to the siege and we should stop trying to locate where the "Big One" was at any moment. As we saw earlier, our sources are confused about this spectacular specimen, if indeed there was only one.[60] Barbaro says that cannons were initially emplaced at four locations. Three cannons targeted the palace (i.e., the Blachernai district), two faced the Charisios Gate and its adjacent walls, four the Romanos Gate, and three the Pege Gate. The two biggest ones were among the four that faced the Romanos Gate and hurled rocks weighing approximately 480 kilograms (with a diameter of ca. 70–80 cm) and 320 kilograms (diameter ca. 50–60 cm).[61] These emplacements are generally confirmed by other sources, one of which adds that a cannon was deployed as far south as the Golden Gate.[62]

When Barbaro itemizes the cannons in this way, he is likely referring only to the "big" ones, each of which was supported by a number of smaller ones. A contemporary, but not eyewitness, source says that the sultan had a total of 37 cannons, including the Big One.[63] Leonardo says that "a terrible canon" was initially placed against the Kaligaria Gate (by the Blachernai district), where it brought down part of the wall by firing massive rocks that were "eleven of my hands in circumference." While the defenders rarely got a close look at the cannons themselves, they became well acquainted with their projectiles, which they saw up close, marveled at, and measured. This cannon was subsequently moved to fire at a tower near the Romanos Gate. By hurling balls weighing ca. 380 kilograms, it brought that tower down too eventually.[64]

The psychological impact of so much cannon fire on the defenders would have been severe, at least initially. No one had likely ever heard a sound as loud as this in their entire life. Although many had probably heard cannon fire in the past—the basileus had smaller cannon of his own and had certainly tested them in the City—this bombardment was on a different scale of volume, frequency, and duration. When the first shots were fired, the inhabitants of the City were struck speechless and cried out *Kyrie eleeson!*, "Lord, have mercy!"[65] Women allegedly fainted with shock.[66] "The bombard thundered suddenly . . . and disturbed the minds of those who were unfamiliar with it. It produced dense smoke through the air, over the walls and neighborhoods."[67] "Mothers shaking with fear throughout the City held tight their children to their breast."[68]

The bombardment continued day and night. However, the cannons had to cool down for hours after each use. The danger was that cold air would get into the pores of the superheated metal and cause it to shatter. Mehmed's engineers devised the following remedy. After each shot, they doused the metal with oil, preventing the cold air from getting in.[69] So there was a lot of downtime for each cannon. Referring to the larger cannons, Laonikos claims that they managed seven shots in the course of a day and one at night. Referring to the smaller ones, Tetaldi claims that they could fire 80 or 100 times per day.[70] This is a big discrepancy, and it is likely that the defenders could not accurately count how many times an individual cannon was firing because so many were active at once. The Ottoman artillery inevitably fired in a staggered sequence, given their different rates of fire. But the tremendous din that all this caused can be imagined. In addition to the explosion, there was the echo and reverberation, the hiss as the rock sliced through the air, and the devastating sound of its impact. "It is said that the sound was unbearable, and would cause the earth to shake . . . The Greeks were astonished and terrified."[71]

Yet no one fled in terror. Human beings adapt to loud noises, especially if they become routine. The background of constant booms would have quickly become unnerving rather than terrifying. What was less easy to cope with was the damage that the cannons were rapidly inflicting. Walls and towers gradually cracked until eventually some of them came tumbling down. Our sources often exaggerate the force of this impact. Kritoboulos says that "the rock was hurled with tremendous force and violence onto the wall, causing it to shake and immediately to collapse. It scattered debris everywhere and murdered anyone who happened to be there. Sometimes it would tear down an entire section of the wall, other times only half, and more or less of a tower or battlement." Yet it was not true, as he adds, that "nothing could withstand the rock's force and momentum."[72] A different account, just as rhetorical but written by someone who was present at the siege, the poet Posculo, notes that "at the first blow, the walls stood unmoved and only weakened . . . But after the bombard struck a second time, the immovable wall was unable to withstand a boulder of such a great weight; it yielded and, caving in, it makes a wide hole falling earthward in a dense mass."[73] It is likely that Posculo is referring to a specific incident here. Nestor-Iskander, who seems to have been at the Mid-Wall area of heavy bombardment, says that one of the two big cannons fired at Giustiniani's position, where the wall was in lower terrain and weaker (i.e., the Fifth Gate area). "As they struck at that spot, the wall began to sway and, on the second [assault], they destroyed and knocked off five *sazhen* from the top of the wall," or about eleven meters (although it is unclear whether this was measured vertically or horizontally).[74]

The walls could resist the cannonballs, but not repeated hits. Often the shots missed, or it was the ball that shattered instead. Nestor-Iskander recounts a shot by a big cannon that nicked the top of the battlements, snapping some of the teeth off, but then disintegrated upon impact with a church.[75]

The Ottoman gunners developed a special technique for bringing down the walls. Individual cannonballs were not as devastating to the ancient walls as Kritoboulos makes them seem, so the artillerymen would triangulate their fire to work in a synchronized fashion. "First, two smaller cannons on either side of the large one would fire a rock weighing about half a talent. These two rocks would strike the walls and crack them. Then they let fly the large one, weighing three talents, and it would knock down a large part of the walls."[76] Eventually, a tower and the walls on either side would come down, and the attackers could see the defenders clearly through the breach. This was all at the Romanos Gate.[77] Most of the towers there would lie in ruin by the siege's end.

During the initial bombardment, the Ottoman infantry by the moat did not directly assault the walls, although they kept up missile fire against the defenders on the battlements. Their primary task was different: while the cannons pounded the walls, Mehmed had ordered his soldiers to fill in the moat with rocks, wood, dirt, and sundry other materials so that they could cross it when a large enough breach had opened in the outer wall to enable a frontal charge.[78] Their proximity to the defenders inevitably led to skirmishing. Some of the janissaries were fired up for battle and would approach the outer wall to challenge the Christians. They were shot dead with guns or crossbows, at which point their comrades came to remove their bodies at the risk of being killed themselves as they carried them away. "They would rather die than suffer the shame of leaving a single Turkish corpse by the walls."[79] The siege was still young. Such scruples would vanish in the carnage to come.

The defenders frantically improvised techniques to lessen the damage caused by the cannonballs. First, they built a scaffold of wooden beams from which they suspended sacks filled with wool and similar material that would hopefully blunt the force and momentum of the rocks. But this had only a minimal effect and the walls and towers continued to crack and collapse. Then they barricaded the gaps that were emerging in the outer wall, blocking them with wooden poles, which they tied tightly together and used as a mold in which to pour debris, stones, more wood and branches, bails of vegetation, and other materials of that kind which they packed together with clay, to harden it. To protect this stockade from fire attacks, they hung hides and skins on the outside and shored it up on the inside with mounds of dirt so that the cannonballs would bury themselves in that and come to a halt. On top, they placed wooden boxes filled with dirt, or barrels tied together, to provide cover for the defenders.[80] They worked on these improvised defenses mostly at night, when the cannons fired less often.[81]

These stockades were certainly necessary in the Mid-Wall section, which was targeted intensively by the Ottoman artillery (see Image 5.2). We do not know if they were necessary elsewhere, north and south of there. We should assume that this was an ongoing process throughout the siege, not one-off events. The stockades themselves were certainly targeted by the cannons as well, and they would have to be repaired or rebuilt after each hit. Right up to the end of the siege we hear of "men

Image 5.2 Photograph taken in the 1920s of the ruined walls near the Charisios/Edirne/Adrianople gate of the Theodosian land walls (looking south). Source: Chronicle/Alamy Images.

and women, the old and the young and the priests, all working together at these repairs because of the urgency of the matter."[82]

The defenders had cannons too, although fewer and smaller ones, and they occasionally scored notable hits. What they were aiming at were the sultan's own cannons, and there is one report, unfortunately unconfirmed, that Giustiniani managed to hit the sultan's big cannon and destroy it.[83] However, the defense did not have enough gunpowder or shot to fire its cannons often, and the enemy were usually protected by their own stockades and trenches. Moreover, the defenders realized that they could not use the largest of their own cannons because the vibrations could damage the walls from the top of which it was being fired, so they stopped using it.[84] Laonikos recounts that the largest of the defense's cannons cracked upon its first use, whereupon they arrested the chief engineer and accused him of working secretly for the sultan, but no proof of this could be found and they let him go.[85]

The bombardment began, as mentioned, on April 11. On the following day, the Ottoman fleet arrived from its base in Gallipoli. It made no move to attack the chain protecting the Golden Horn or the sea walls of the City as that was not its purpose. It sailed up into the Bosporos and put in at the Diplokionion, or "Two Columns," just to the north of Pera (at modern Beşiktas). Those famous columns still stood (they would be destroyed by an earthquake in 1509). The Venetian fleet had also moored there just before its assault on the City in 1203.[86] The Ottoman armada was under the command of admiral Süleyman Baltaoğlu Bey. Possibly of Bulgarian origin, he was also a product of the *devşirme* and had worked his way up the ranks of the army. In 1449, he had led a naval attack on Mytilene, an island that was under the rule of the Genoese Gattilusi. Then, as governor of the district of Gallipoli, he was placed in command of the fleet assembled for the siege of Constantinople.[87]

The fleet gave the City a wide berth and sailed up along the Anatolian side, crossing over from there to the Two Columns. It announced its arrival by making a lot of noise through shouts, war cries, the coxswains yelling orders, and the crews competing with each other. Barbaro, who was present in the harbor, heard "their vehement cries, the sounding of castanets and tambourines, so that they filled our fleet and those in the City with fear." The Ottoman fleet had no intention of attacking, but the defenders in the harbor did not know this, so they remained armed and alert, day and night, after then. They positioned two lookouts on the walls of Pera to send word if they saw the fleet making any move. Every time an Ottoman ship sailed out, the commander in the harbor would sound the trumpet and everyone would take up their battle stations. "So each day we were in this difficulty, and in great fear, having by day and by night to stand to our arms, and yet their fleet never moved." Individual Turkish ships did head over to Anatolia or toward the Black Sea, probably to bring supplies or ferry men.[88]

Kritoboulos reports that, while he waited for the cannons to bring down the walls, Mehmed took a portion of his army, including janissaries and cannons, and marched to two forts in the region that had so far evaded capture, Therapeion and Stoudios. The first was halfway up the Bosporos, about two kilometers inland; the location of the second is unknown. After a brief but intense bombardment, the garrison of

Therapeion surrendered unconditionally and Mehmed impaled them then and there, 40 men all told. He captured the second fort in less than a day and force-marched its garrison, 36 men, to the City, where he also impaled them in sight of the walls. (However, a note written in real-time by the anti-Union writer Theodoros Agallianos says that Mehmed took Stoudios the year before, i.e., in 1452.) Meanwhile, Baltaoğlu took part of the fleet and attacked Prinkipo, the largest of the Princes' Islands in the Sea of Marmara. It had a fort with a garrison of 30 well-armed men. He demolished part of the walls with his cannons but was unable to take it by assault. So, he piled up flammable materials next to the walls, which he mixed with sulfur and tar, and set a fire in such a way that the smoke was driven inside by the wind. The resulting inferno killed many, while the rest surrendered unconditionally. He executed the garrison and sold the locals, who had sought refuge in the fort, into slavery.[89]

A week after the bombardment began, Mehmed determined that enough of the walls had been brought down to allow an infantry attack. The first general assault took place on April 18 or 19. Barbaro claims that it was a night attack, lasting for four hours, but Nestor-Iskander, who was likely present on the walls at the most critical section, says more plausibly that it was a daytime attack, and he describes it in greater detail. The Turks first chanted their prayers and played trumpets, pipes, and tambourines. The attack focused on the Mid-Wall and was preceded by a sustained and intense bombardment, forcing the defenders to seek cover, although some fired back with guns and cannons. Then, with a great shout, the Turks charged the walls, bringing fire, battering rams, and ladders. Cardinal Isidoros says that some of "these ladders had hooks attached on top so that, when they were placed against the walls, the hooks utilized their lower support and they could not be thrown off or be dislodged. Similarly, they were covered with planks, from top to bottom and all around, so that those who were climbing could not be thrown off."[90] Battle was joined on the parapets and in the breach. The basileus rode behind the line to encourage his men and ordered that bells ring throughout the City to call everyone out. In response, the Turks blared their trumpets and played their pipes and tambourines. Battle was fought under competing soundscapes.[91]

The janissaries crossed the moat, which in many places had by now been filled in. They tried to set fire to the improvised stockades, but the defenders quenched them. The attackers also took a different approach. With hooks attached to long poles, they tried to pull down the containers that were serving on top of the stockade as battlements to create a clear line of sight for their archers and small artillery. Others used nets to haul away cannonballs to reuse them. Another group tried to place ladders against the wall and climb them, and all the while the cannons continued to fire against the defenders. These attacks were resisted fiercely by Giustiniani, his men, and the Romans stationed there, who were mostly protected by their armor against small fire (see Image 3.3).[92] Unfortunately, we do not know what weapons janissaries used for hand-to-hand combat in this period, nor what forms of armor they wore, but it was probably not yet standardized. The defenders wore armor, and Giustiniani's men in particular wore heavy plate armor. This gave them a tremendous advantage over the attackers, who had to clamber up ladders or debris while protecting themselves against sustained fire from above.

Nestor-Iskander provides a vivid account of the chaotic fighting:

> The clatter of the cannons and arquebuses, the roar of the bells, the cracking of arms—like lightning flashing from both weapons—and the crying and sobbing of the people (the women and children of the city) made one believe that the sky and earth trembled; one could not hear another man's words. Weeping and screaming, the cries and sobs of the people, the roar of the cannons, and the pealing of bells combined into one din resembling great thunder. Again, rising from many fires and the explosions of the cannons and arquebuses, the smoke thickened on both sides and covered the city. The [opposing] armies were unable to see one another and did not know against whom they fought; many died from the fumes of the gunpowder. Slashed to pieces, they exhausted themselves on the walls until the nocturnal darkness separated them. The Turks even retreated to their own camps, without thought for their dead. The people of the city, however, collapsed from the struggle as if dead. Only the sentinels were left along the walls.[93]

The attack had been repulsed.

Widely different estimates are given for the casualties of this first battle, even by reporters who were present during the siege. Barbaro says that 200 Turks were killed and no defenders, which seems unlikely but not impossible. Nestor-Iskander says that on the following morning the basileus ordered the clergy to gather and bury the dead. The number of Roman dead was 1,740—an impossibly high figure—along with 700 Italians and Armenians. This is certainly mistaken, as Armenians are nowhere reported as present. Then, the basileus and his nobles set out along the walls to inspect the army and gaze upon the battlefield, which was littered with "broken corpses." The enemy had lost 18,000 men. According to one argument, Nestor-Iskander was likely assigned to burial duty or to counting the dead because he provides unique information about the disposition of the bodies. That may be true, but his figures are not credible.[94] The Anconitan consul Benvenuto says that, while Giustiniani defended the breach in the walls during the entire siege, only 40 defenders were killed as against 7,000 Turks.[95] These figures are too discrepant with each other for us to assess the casualties reliably.

Nestor-Iskander reports that the basileus then went to Hagia Sophia with his clergy and high officials to thank God and the Virgin for preserving the City. This must be taken with a grain of salt. It is likely that the basileus never left the front lines during the siege, not even to go to Hagia Sophia. (Nestor-Iskander is confused about many matters, such as the existence of an empress and patriarch.) He adds that on the next day, possibly April 21, Mehmed sent men to gather up his own dead and the basileus allowed it "so that the moat and breach would be cleared. Thus, they quietly took up their dead and burned them."[96] The sultan's delay in tending to his dead was likely caused by a shocking defeat inflicted on his fleet the previous day, April 20. Its repercussions changed the strategic calculus of the siege.

6

The Defenses Hold

On the afternoon of April 20, only a day or two after the first assault on the walls, four large Christian galleys were seen sailing toward the City at a good clip, driven by a favorable wind out of the south. They were bringing supplies, arms, and some soldiers. Three were Genoese, coming from Chios. Barbaro claims that they were attracted by a prior proclamation by the basileus: any ships that brought provisions and reinforcements to Constantinople would have the custom duties owed to him waived.[1] But Barbaro was a Venetian and perhaps wanted to make the Genoese seem mercenary. Kritoboulos says that these ships had been equipped at the pope's expense to support the defenders in the siege, although his version also cannot be corroborated.[2] Be that as it may, the ships had been loading cargos on Chios during March, but when April came around and they wanted to depart, they were hindered by winds out of the north. Finally, the winds turned and they were now hastening toward the City (see Color Plate 4).

The three Genoese ships were commanded by Maurizio Cattaneo, who also captained one. The other two were captained by Domenico di Novara and Battista di Felizzano. These two men are attested in notarial acts in Genoa from earlier in the year, in which they contracted to buy a ship, the Santa Maria, possibly one of the two that they were now captaining. They had accepted a commission by Genoa's "Romanía Office" to transport soldiers, weapons, and supplies to Pera, so they were not coming to aid Constantinople as such. After all, Genoa was officially neutral in the war.[3] The fourth ship belonged to the basileus; it was captained by the Genoese Francesco Lecavello and was bringing grain from Sicily or (more likely) the Peloponnese.[4] Each ship may have carried up to 200 men.[5]

One of the purposes for which the new Ottoman fleet had been created was to prevent reinforcements from reaching Constantinople. This was the moment of truth for it. The sultan galloped from his position before the land walls to the anchorage of his fleet at the Two Columns and ordered the admiral Baltaoğlu Bey to capture the incoming ships or destroy them, but at any rate to prevent them at all costs from entering the harbor. Baltaoğlu launched his ships, *all* of them if we believe the Christian accounts, "beating his drums and blowing his trumpets in a frenzy." With an overwhelming advantage in numbers and carrying well-armed men on board, the Turks were confident of victory. They intercepted the four Christian ships before the latter managed to reach the harbor entrance, just as they were rounding the acropolis cape. Thousands of observers crowded the walls of the City, Pera, and the hill above Pera, where the sultan himself stood to watch the battle in tense anticipation. All could hear the shouts of the rowers and marines on the ships, but none could do anything to help.

Warships in this period were beginning to be equipped with artillery, both hand-held firearms and small cannons.[6] After an initial exchange of gunfire from both sides, the larger Turkish ships, including Baltaoğlu's flagship, engaged with the basileus' galley, while the Genoese ships were surrounded by smaller Ottoman ships when they moved to protect it. Then the wind suddenly stopped. The crews now had to pick up oars and manually power their ships into battle. Lecavello steered the basileus' ship expertly, but soon the sea "was covered with armed boats, and the water could hardly been seen for the vessels." Soon the sea was covered with masts and decks crowded close to each other.

Cannons were fired at point blank range, the archers furiously loosed volley after volley, while catapults lobbed missiles. So many arrows were fired that the oars were churning them up in the water. Soon, however, the battle was fought hand-to-hand as the ships engaged at close quarters. But here the Christians had the advantage, even with four ships facing off against dozens or hundreds. Only a limited number of enemy ships could engage with them at a time, and the Christian crews were vastly more experienced at naval warfare; also, their ships were bigger, putting their decks higher out of the water. From there, as well as from their rigging and towers, they could fire down upon the crowded decks of the Ottoman ships, killing scores of the enemy. The Turks were trying to set fire to the galleys from below, or break through their hulls with their weapons. Others were trying to strike the Christian defenders from below with spears, arrows, and rocks. A few tried to swing over from the rigging of their own ships. But the defenders were well armored and held the higher ground. They had suspended water flasks above their decks to drop on any fires that threatened to spread. They also hurled rocks onto the decks of the enemy ships, crushing many. It was easier for them to strike down, with swords and clubs, upon anyone trying to climb onboard from below. Many right hands were chopped off. A vivid description of this close combat is provided by Kritoboulos, who was relying less on information given to him by participants or witnesses and more on his rhetorical training and imagination. "A great din of many voices arose, the clamor of people encouraging each other, striking, being struck, killing, being killed, pushing, shoved, cursing, insulting each other, threatening, groaning, and performing fell deeds."

The sultan could not believe that it was proving so difficult for his vast armada to defeat and capture four ships. He rode down to the edge of the water in a rage, shouting orders and obscenities at his crews, vainly trying to be heard over the din of battle. Seen by thousands of Christians in Pera and the City itself, he rode into the water, getting the hems of his robes wet in his fury to change the course of the battle through sheer willpower. It seemed to some as if he wanted to ride his horse over the waves and join the fighting.

The battle lasted for over two hours, at which point the two combatants disengaged, although it is not clear why or how. Kritoboulos and Doukas say that the wind picked up again, allowing the four ships to reach the harbor and leave the enemy behind. But how could they have even gotten under way if they were closely surrounded by enemy ships?

One possibility is that the Turkish ships disengaged after sustaining heavy losses to allow reinforcements to take their place and continue the fight, thereby creating gaps that the Genoese exploited to sail away when the wind picked up. With broken oars and reduced crews, it would have been hard for the closest Turkish ships to chase the larger vessels.

Barbaro, who was probably watching this scene from the harbor, does not explain why or how the battle ended, or why the enemy disengaged, but he does imply that the sea remained calm, and he explicitly says that the four galleys anchored outside the harbor, at least initially. He does not explain this decision. The answer may be that Baltaoğlu had adjusted his strategy, although none of our sources says so. Realizing that he could not overpower the Christians ships by boarding them, he decided to allow them to reach the boom to follow them into the harbor and force an entry when the chain was opened for them. That would explain why the four ships anchored outside, so as not to risk exposing the harbor, and this would have brought Baltaoğlu back to square one: attacking those invincible floating forts, an approach that had accomplished nothing the first time around. But anchoring outside the harbor exposed the Christian ships to a night attack. So, Barbaro continues, as soon as it was dark, captain Gabriele Trevisan left the harbor with his two galleys and the galley of Zaccaria Grioni, making a lot of noise with a superfluous number of trumpets "to give the impression to our enemy that it was a much larger fleet than really was there." The Genoese galleys were thus successfully escorted into the harbor while the Ottoman ships refrained from engaging. After all, fewer ships had defied them during the day and cost them greatly. Reasonably, they were reluctant to engage with an even greater number of Christian marines at night.[7]

The stunning victory against the odds bolstered the defenders' morale. It was a clear example that the enemy *could* be defeated and that the Christians were superior, in at least one arena of warfare. Their naval skill and technology were still more advanced than the Turks'.[8] Leonardo claims that not a single Christian had been killed in the battle, although some were wounded, whereas the Turks lost 10,000 men. The figures reported by Kritoboulos are more realistic, although perhaps designed to minimize Turkish losses for the sultan's ears: 22 dead on the Christian side, with half the crew wounded, and over a hundred Turkish dead, with 300 wounded. Kritoboulos also suppresses the sultan's unbecoming behavior at the water's edge.

Mehmed was bitterly stung by his armada's failure. It was not just a matter of ego. The defeat—for it amounted to that—meant that he could not effectively blockade the City, despite the enormous expense of creating a new fleet. What if an even larger flotilla with reinforcements arrived from the West? The defenders had managed, despite their small numbers, to repulse his assault on the walls only a few days ago. With more armored western soldiers at their side, the City might become effectively as impregnable to him as the Genoese ships had been at sea. Indeed, Maurizio Cattaneo, the captain of the lead ship, was subsequently posted to guard the southern stretch of the land walls, between the Golden Gate and the Pege Gate, with 200 crossbowmen, some of them native Romans.[9] (Incidentally, this indicates that there had been fighting in that sector of the walls, too, although our sources say little about it.) At any time, a random western knight seeking glory in a personal crusade against the Turks could show up with a few ships and tip the scales of the war. It had happened before, with Amadeo VI, the Green Count of Savoy, in 1366 and the French marshal Jean II le Mangre, known as Boucicaut, in 1399.

There was far more at stake than just strategy. The Ottomans had suffered two defeats in a row, one in the general assault on the walls and another now at sea. Tursun Bey, who was present in Mehmed's camp as a junior official, attests to a crisis in the Ottoman camp at this time. He was just over thirty years old, and he did not write a history of the sultan's reign until much later. Tursun came from a family of military officers and generals, but he had opted for an administrative and fiscal career himself. As he remembered it later, Baltaoğlu's failure threw the Muslims into dejection.[10] This is confirmed by an extraordinary document that appears to have been written at this time by the sheik, holy man, and Mehmed's spiritual advisor Ak Şemseddin, who was also in the Ottoman camp during the siege. Ak Şemseddin was among those who had previously encouraged Mehmed to attack Constantinople, and he wrote to the sultan now to shore up his resolve. The letter admits candidly that the naval battle was a disaster and that Muslim morale was low. More dangerously, it reveals that the prestige of the sultan was shaken and the Ottoman command's confidence in his leadership and decision to attack the City were in doubt. The sheik was concerned with his own standing, too, for he had prophesied that the City would fall on a date that apparently coincided with April 20. On that day, he had previously told Mehmed, the City would resound with the Muslim call to prayer.

Now, after this setback, Ak Şemseddin admits that many were doubting the sultan's leadership. He advises him to find the people responsible and punish them harshly. Otherwise, the soldiers may not obey when they are asked to fight in the moat. He insinuates that those responsible were not true Muslims but were only there for plunder. Perhaps this pointed to Baltaoğlu's non-Muslim origins.[11]

Mehmed probably needed little encouragement to punish the admiral. On the next day, April 21, he led his cavalry to the Two Columns and ordered that Baltaoğlu be brought before him. In full view of his army and many in the fleet, he dressed the admiral down and interrogated him about his failure. Baltaoğlu was deposed from his command, which was given over to Hamza Bey, an experienced officer. Some of our accounts claim that Mehmed wanted to execute Baltaoğlu but was moved by the man's pleas or by his officers, who begged the sultan to spare his life. Doukas paints a more vivid scene in which Baltaoğlu is held down by four soldiers while the sultan beats him a hundred times with a golden rod. This is unlikely. Many sources claim that Baltaoğlu lost an eye, although they disagree on how: perhaps it was in the battle, at the hands of one of his own men, or maybe a janissary struck him in the face with a stone after he was deposed.[12]

Meanwhile, the bombardment of the land walls had not abated. On the same day as Baltaoğlu's deposition, another tower was brought down by the Romanos Gate, along with a stretch of the adjacent wall. Barbaro says that this instilled great fear in the inhabitants, who remembered the prophesy that Constantinople would fall under the reign of a basileus named Konstantinos, the son of Helene, just as it had once been founded by one. This particular prophesy must have been discussed by the defenders during the siege itself, for it was mentioned by several of them afterward, when they independently wrote their accounts.[13] Barbaro opined that the City might well have fallen on that day had there not been so many brave Venetians present, men far superior to the Greeks who immediately began to repair the broken walls with barrels of stones and dirt. The fields outside were still full of Turkish soldiers, including janissaries with their white turbans and the light infantry, known as *'azab*, who wore red turbans.[14]

The defenders and the civilian population must have been so stressed and terrified that they saw omens and prophesies everywhere. Many scriptural passages happen to refer to God's anger or to the arrival of vast multitudes of foreigners. When these were read aloud in church, as inevitably they were at various times of the year during the liturgical calendar, they were taken to be prophesies that were already—or about to be—fulfilled.[15] Seeing the cannons bring down the walls prompted the cardinal Isidoros to think "that the ancient oracle preserved in our accounts had been fulfilled. It declared, 'Woe to you, City of the Seven Hills, when a young man lays siege to you, your mighty fortifications will be destroyed.'"[16]

The basileus did what he could to inspire and encourage his people, but the true hero of the defense was Giustiniani, who had chosen to bear the brunt of the sultan's attack at the Mid-Wall section. He faced this danger accompanied by his own men and the basileus' guard, as well as by many fighters from the Genoese of Pera, his compatriots. Pera was walking a fine line between the neutrality that it had pledged to Mehmed before hostilities began and its desire to assist the defense. The Genoese of Pera were hoping that no Turk would be able to pick them out from the Genoese in Giustiniani's company. So, on one day they would go to the Turks and sell them whatever supplies they needed, such as oil for cooling down the cannons, after which they would go to the Roman side at night and fight for them on the next day; meanwhile, other men from Pera would take their place in dealing with the Turks. They swapped places in turn so what they were doing would not be detected.[17] The harbor, after all, was still in Roman hands. At night there must have been much furtive traffic between Constantinople and Pera.

In later years the question of the blame for the fall of Constantinople was debated intensely in the West, and many accused the Genoese of not doing enough to save it; indeed, Pera preserved itself after the fall by surrendering to Mehmed. In that context, this double-dealing served to prove that the Genoese of Pera had not in fact remained neutral but had done all that they could to help. We should not doubt the reports that they helped both sides. This trickery is mentioned soon after the fall by Leonardo of Chios, who was Genoese himself and conflicted about this tactic. Pera provided men and weapons to the defense, he says, but only in secret. Pera should have declared open war on the sultan instead, but that was something that only the more heroic men of the past could have done, not the greedier, weaker Genoese of Leonardo's own day.[18] This admission confirms their double-dealing.

Pera was in a precarious position. On the south side, it faced the Roman-controlled harbor of the Golden Horn, where its own ships were moored alongside potentially hostile Venetian galleys. However, the Ottoman fleet was anchored just to Pera's north, at Two Columns. On that side, Pera was also completely surrounded by the Ottoman lines of communication that ran from Two Columns to the sultan's camp. The Ottoman general in command of that sector was Zaganos Pasha, who is represented in the sources as a war hawk. He was strengthening and expanding those communication lines in a way that effectively tightened the noose around Pera. The goal toward which he was working is presented in our narratives as a complete surprise to the Christians; however, in reality, they must have known what he was up to many days in advance, as he was doing it in plain sight. Specifically, he was clearing a portage over which to haul ships from Two Columns around Pera and down into the Golden Horn. Moreover, he was likely already assembling materials with which to construct a long pontoon bridge across the upper neck of the Golden Horn so that soldiers and supplies could move freely from his district to the armies investing the land walls. These two engineering feats are highlighted in our sources as momentous occasions that caused great fear in the defenders, and that much was true. In practice, however, they accomplished little.

Ancient and medieval armies rarely had to improvise ship portage during a military campaign, but it could be done. East Romans, Italians, and Turks all had experience of this practice. In 1097, when the Turkish-occupied city of Nikaia was besieged by the First Crusade, the emperor, Alexios I Komnenos, portaged ships into the lake next to the city, thereby cutting it off from access to forage and forcing it to surrender.[19] A more famous and recent incident had occurred in 1439, when the Venetians had portaged ships over the mountains between the Adige River and Lake Garda, in Lombardy, during the course of a war against Milan. Leonardo assumed that Mehmed was copying the example set by the Venetians at Lake Garda and that he was informed about it by a Christian traitor. In his mind, presumably, anything clever, imaginative, or spectacular done by a Muslim had to be copying Christian precedents.[20]

Later in the year, or early in 1454, the Italian humanist Antonio Ivana of Sarana wrote a brief account of the fall of Constantinople where he claimed that Mehmed portaged the ships around Pera in response to news that a Venetian relief fleet was on the way.[21] But almost the whole of Mehmed's strategy, including the speed with which he wanted things done and the extraordinary measures that he took to force the issue quickly was a response to the looming threat of a western intervention. Mehmed knew that a few units of knights armored and trained like Giustiniani's company could make the City impregnable, and a fleet of western galleys could easily break through his blockade.

In most modern accounts of the siege, the portage of the ships into the Golden Horn on April 22 is interpreted as a response by Mehmed to his naval defeat on April 20 and presented as a shock to the defenders. Suddenly, we are told, they saw a caravan of ships "sailing" around the hill behind Pera. In reality, work on this project must have begun well before the arrival of the Christian ships on April 20. Tursun Bey, the Ottoman historian present at the siege, says that the work crews were already busy on this project when the Christian ships arrived.[22] The work would have been obvious to the defenders for some time and did not come as a surprise when the parade of ships began on April 22, awesome though the sight of them floating across the land must have been, when it finally did take place.

Work crews consisting mostly of sailors had cleared and then smoothed a path about four kilometers long that ran around Pera from Two Columns to the northwest shore of the Golden Horn. Its exact route is unknown, but it likely passed through the area currently occupied by Taksim Square.[23] The ships were pulled along on wooden rollers greased with fat, probably held within frames that lay flat on the rollers. The first stretch of the route—up the hill behind Pera—was the most arduous, it being downhill after that. The method was first tested on a smaller vessel and, when that worked well, between 70 and 80 ships were portaged on April 22.[24] These were not among the larger ships in the Ottoman fleet. Their purpose was definitely *not* to engage in combat with the Venetian and Genoese galleys in the harbor, nor did they ever try to do so.

The overland parade of ships was spectacular and fired up the imagination of the historians. Doukas claimed that their sails were unfurled during their land journey and that they had a pilot at the prow giving directions and a captain at the helm. Drums were beaten to set the pace for the work crews, while trumpeters sounded out sailors' songs.[25] Kritoboulos reports that the crews stayed on board and had fun play-acting that they were at sea, calling out orders for the sails, rowing in the air, and giving the beat.[26] The ships were adorned with banners of every color,[27] and measures were taken to protect this stately parade: "cannons [were] placed along the shore to repel anyone who might attack in order to prevent them from dragging the ships to the sea."[28]

The sultan now had over 70 ships in the Golden Horn, although they kept to its northwestern reaches and did not seek to engage the flotilla protecting the chain. However, this development upset the delicate balance of power and caused consternation among the defenders. Barbaro, who was with the ships in the harbor, says that the defenders did fear an attack, whether a joint operation by the Ottoman fleet that was now both inside and outside the chain, possibly at night, or an attack with fire, and so they were extra vigilant and had henceforth to guard against both directions.[29] Nor, on the other hand, could it be ruled out that the Turks would attempt to scale the sea walls on the harbor side, or try to force its gates, which meant that scarce manpower had to be diverted from other locations to guard this section as well. This may well have been the chief aim of the ship portage; in sum, it was a distraction.[30]

Alarmed at this development, the Venetian Committee of Twelve met on April 23, in a church in Constantinople, to formulate a response. Giustiniani was present,[31] but Barbaro, our main source, omits to mention him, as he wanted to paint the Genoese as the villains and blame them for what had happened. In fact, it is likely that Giustiniani, as the head of the defenses, presided over the meeting.[32] The war council was resolved to attack the Ottoman fleet in the harbor, but they disagreed over how it should be done. Some wanted a frontal attack during the day, whereas others wanted to land marines on the opposite coast and attack the enemy crews in their tents. Giacomo Cocco, the captain of the Trebizond galley, argued that they should set fire to the Ottoman fleet, and this opinion eventually prevailed. So, on April 24, Cocco prepared his attack fleet, including two ships that were packed all around with wool and cotton to shield them from artillery. They were planning to sail out at midnight.

Barbaro then recounts the following controversial story. According to him, the attack was foiled by the Genoese of Pera, those "enemies of the Christian faith," and specifically by their podestà. The Genoese sabotaged the entire plan by, first, promising the Venetians that they would join in the venture if only it could be postponed for a day, while simultaneously sending a messenger named Faiuzo to the sultan to warn him about the attack. The sultan accordingly positioned men with guns and cannons to protect his fleet on both sides of the upper reaches of the Golden Horn shore, while the terrain around his men's encampments and the base of the fleet was studded with obstacles so that it could not be taken by surprise. This, then, was another (alleged) Genoese double-cross, only this time it favored the sultan.

Plate 1. Painting of the basileus Konstantinos XI Palaiologos in full regalia including a double-headed eagle, made during his reign in the Old Monastery of the Taxiarches in Aigialeia, in the northern Peloponnese. © Hellenic Ministry of Culture. A. Koumoussi, Ephor of Antiquities, Achaea.

Plate 2. Painting of the sultan Mehmed II by the Venetian portraitist Gentile Bellini, based on a visit to Constantinople in 1480, currently in the National Gallery of London. Source: Victoria and Albert Museum, Wikipedia.

Plate 3. Aerial view of the Golden Horn harbor looking west, showing the entrance (across which the chain was drawn during the siege) and the naval front of the siege that opened up once Mehmed moved his ships into the harbor. Galatas was on the northern side, where the bridge leads today. Source: Stoktur/Shutterstock.

Plate 4. Aerial view of Istanbul looking east, with the Asian side in the distance across the straits and Hagia Sophia in the center top (and slightly toward the right). The naval battle of April 20 was fought as the reinforcement ships rounded the cape, center top of the image. Source: murattellioglu/Shutterstock.

Plate 5. Hagia Sophia and the Marmara sea walls, viewed from the east. The minarets are a later addition. Source: The Byzantine Legacy/David Hendrix.

Plate 6. Interior of Hagia Sophia, where many frightened refugees fled on May 29, 1543. The medallions hanging on the walls are later Ottoman additions. Source: Artur Bogacki/Shutterstock.

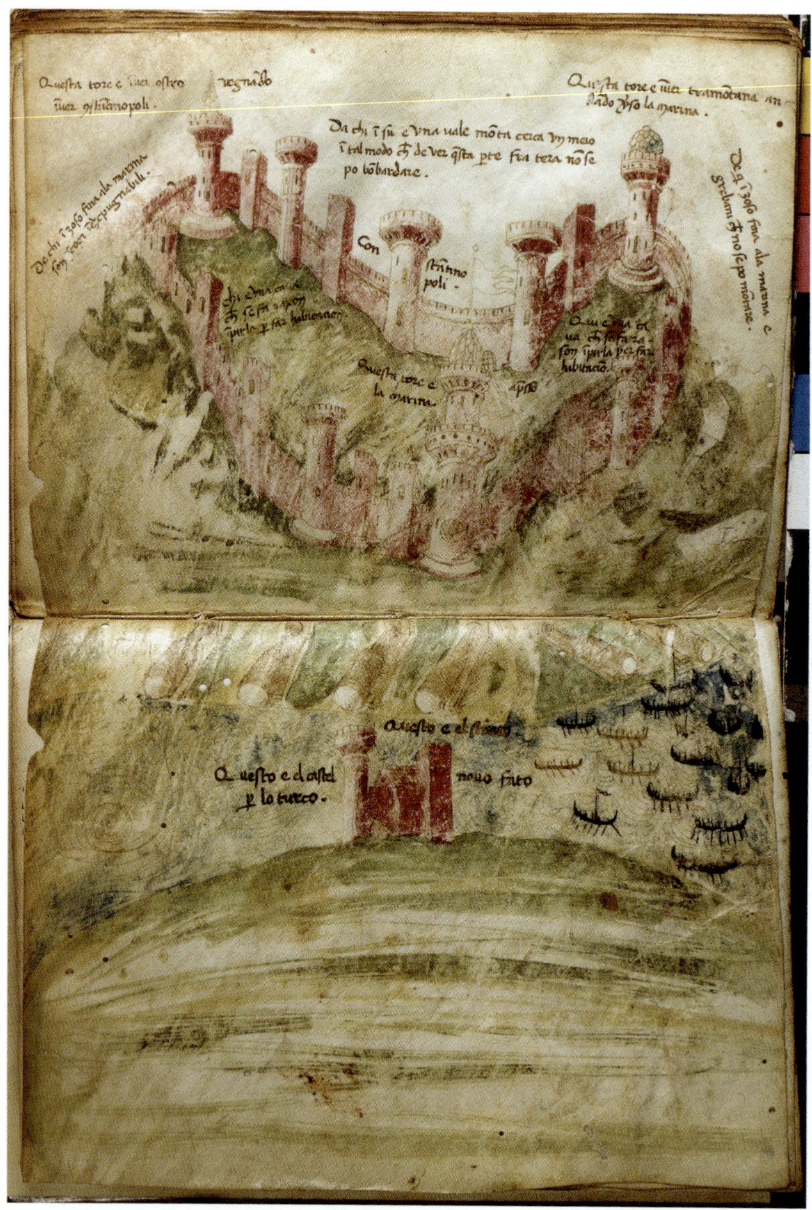

Plate 7. Venetian drawing of Rumeli Hisarı made soon after its construction in 1452. The Bosporos straits are visible at the bottom along with the facing fort of Anadolu Hisarı. The drawing survives at the end of Codex membranaceo 641, Biblioteca Trivulziana, Milan, an anthology of western sources about the fall of Constantinople. Source: Used by permission of the Archivio Storico Civico e Biblioteca Trivulziana, © Comune di Milano, all rights reserved.

Plate 8. Photograph (looking north) showing the ruined state of the walls in the Mid-Wall sector that was attacked intensively during the siege. The mostly filled-in moat in front of the walls is also visible. The Plate was published in A. Van Millingen, *Byzantine Constantinople: The Walls of the City and Adjoining Historical Sites* (Cambridge University Press, 1899), facing p. 87. Source: Alexander Van Millingen/ Wikipedia.

Plate 9. Modern restoration of the Theodosian land walls showing the three layers of defense, although the moat in the foreground is filled in. Source: The Byzantine Legacy/David Hendrix.

For unknown reasons, the attack was further delayed until April 28. On that day, two hours before dawn a flotilla set out to attack the Ottoman fleet. It consisted of the two ships enveloped in wool and cotton; the galley of Gabriele Trevisan and the galley of Zaccaria Grioni, both heavily armed ships; and three smaller ships captained by Silvestro Trevisan, Girolamo Morosini, and Giacomo Cocco. They brought with them small fireships, filled with pitch, brushwood, and gunpowder, which they intended to unleash on the enemy. (These were not armed with the incendiary compound known as Greek Fire, which had not been used in these parts since ca. 1200. They were just ships piled up with flammable material that would be set on fire and allowed to drift toward the enemy ships.) The wool-and-cotton ships were supposed to take the lead to absorb any cannon fire. But Cocco, who already held the distinction of evading the Turkish cannons at Rumeli Hisarı when he arrived at Constantinople, now rushed ahead, perhaps to claim greater glory by striking the first blow. Yet the Turks were prepared for a night attack. Posculo goes so far as to claim that they were treasonously signaled from a tower in Pera that the Christian ships had departed.[33] They targeted Cocco first. The first shot missed, but the second went through the middle of his ship, sinking it immediately along with its crew of 72 oarsmen, Cocco himself, and 17 mates and soldiers, the latter of whom Barbaro scrupulously names. "They all drowned, may God have mercy on them." Few medieval sailors knew how to swim. But they did not all die. Some were captured by the Turks.

The other ships in the Christian flotilla did not realize what had happened. They thought that Cocco was behind them, when in fact he had gone on ahead. Confusion was also caused by the smoke wafting out onto the water from the cannon fire, as well as by cries coming from all directions. Suddenly, Gabriele Trevisan's galley was also hit by two cannonballs that went through it, but some wounded men belowdecks managed to plug the holes with cloaks. Half-submerged, the ship limped back to its anchorage. At that point, the rest of the Christian ships withdrew as well, recognizing that the attack had been foiled. The Turks launched their own fleet of 70 smaller vessels, and they aimed their attack at the two padded, wool-and-cotton ships, which had become separated from their escorts in the retreat. These two ships were surrounded and a furious battle raged with arrows, guns, and cannon. Again, the Christian ships proved to be as invulnerable as they had during the battle at sea on April 20. After fighting for an hour and half, the Turks withdrew and returned to their base.[34]

In the morning, Mehmed gave orders that the captured sailors be executed before the eyes of the defenders on the walls, although we do not know where this took place. Tetaldi says that it was done in an especially cruel and gruesome way "to instill terror among the other Christians. They . . . slashed them from the lowest area of the belly to the highest point, and disemboweled them, with their entrails exposed, as if they were fish or sheep."[35] They were first forced to say exactly who they were, so that they could be recognized by their comrades on the walls.[36] The Christians then responded in kind: "Roused to anger by this, our men took the Turkish prisoners whom they had in captivity and slaughtered them cruelly on the walls in full view of their fellows. In this way the war was made more savage by a mixture of impiety and cruelty."[37]

It is entirely possible that there was no Genoese treason and that the Turks were instead just reasonably vigilant, posting men to watch the Christian ships and report any movement. It is easier to accept that Barbaro was biased against the Genoese than that the podestà of Pera, Angelo Giovanni Lomellino, personally sent a message to warn Mehmed of an impending night attack. But at the time, the defenders took perverse comfort in the narrative of treason. Even if it were true, Lomellino had nothing to do with it, as we know how invested he was personally in the defense of the City, even sending his own nephew to fight in the final battle.[38] It seems instead that, in the subsequent editing of Barbaro's diary, the podestà's name was confused with that of the alleged Genoese traitor, which is given by the poet Posculo as "the messenger Angelo Zaccaria."[39] Leonardo speaks of betrayal, but gives no names, nor does he directly implicate the Genoese, his own people. Yet his phrasing and embarrassment speak volumes: "Whom may I accuse? I must remain silent."[40] In other words, the treason narrative originated during the siege, likely soon after the naval battle in the harbor. It is not clear how quickly it was attached to the name Angelo Zaccaria.

Angelo Zaccaria was a real person and is mentioned, later that year, in a document regarding a loan made to the now-deceased basileus.[41] It is possible that he was sent as an envoy to the sultan by Lomellino, the podestà of Pera, around the time of the naval battle, which was how he came to be suspected.

But what about "Faiuzo," the man who, according to Barbaro, actually did reveal the defenders' plans to the sultan? It just so happens that we have a notarial act from Genoa, dated to April 1, 1457—four years after the siege—in which the former podestà Lomellino is recording the testimony of a merchant formerly active in Pera named Francesco Fazio. He was involved in a dispute with another man named Nicolò Pagliuzzo, and he wanted to go on the record that Pagliuzzo was a completely dishonest man who would do anything for money. The case concerned a cargo of silk that was lost when the City fell and a fourth person, one Girolamo di Franchi Giulia, who had allegedly lied about it. Be that as it may, the dishonest man, Pagliuzzo, is known from other documents where his name could be rendered as Paiuzo, which is almost identical to Barbaro's "Faiuzo." It appears that he was an interpreter occasionally employed in the communications between Pera and the sultan. This does not prove that he was the traitor—or, indeed, that any act of treason had in fact occurred—but it can explain the origin of the accusation. The notarial document that we have insists repeatedly that it was "common opinion" in Pera and Constantinople at the time of the siege that Paiuzo/Pagliuzzo was a dishonest scoundrel.[42]

The naval battle in the harbor did not tip the scales in the Ottomans' favor, despite the boost that it gave to their morale. The defenders did not concede the Golden Horn to the Turkish fleet, as is sometimes asserted.[43] On May 3, the defenders placed their own cannons inside the sea walls of the harbor and fired them against the Turkish cannons that had sunk Cocco's ship. They managed to sink a few Turkish vessels as well, and so the Turks began to fire their own cannons in return. This continued for ten straight days, day and night, "but neither side could be put out of action," as both batteries were protected by walls or earthworks. So this was an impasse.[44] The Romans also prevented the Turkish ships from moving freely about the harbor by firing catapults and ballistae at them from the walls, and their superior galleys attacked and harassed them whenever they moved out of their protective huddle. So, the Turkish fleet was limited to the firing range of the Turkish cannons in the northwest sector of the harbor. The Christian ships would chase their Turkish counterparts back to their anchorage, withdraw, and then the cycle would start again. These naval skirmishes took place thereafter on almost a daily basis.[45]

In other words, the two contestants had reached an equilibrium of forces in the harbor, one that lasted for a month *after* the portage of Ottoman ships, indeed down to the end of the siege. Given the strategies of the two sides, equilibrium favored the defenders. Mehmed had gained little of substance from the otherwise spectacular portage of his ships. The defenses held.

Mehmed had failed to break through in the harbor. Meanwhile, the bombardment of the land walls continued without break. Towers collapsed, stockades were built and patches made, and the fighting continued. Most of our sources lose sight of the individual events at this point, as the patterns became repetitive. "There were continual attacks on the walls by land, putting the city in perpetual danger, and we inside made good repairs with barrels and stakes and earth where needed, so that they were as strong as proper walls, as they had been at first, and cannon shots could not harm them." The defenders were, however, beginning to run short on necessities, such as wine and bread.[46]

Nestor-Iskander provides typically gruesome accounts of the fighting by the land walls, where he seems to have been positioned; indeed, he entirely ignores the naval aspect of the siege. However, it is impossible to date the assaults on the walls that he recounts, and in some respects his narrative is confused (e.g., he has the sultan deploy his cannons only after the first assault on the walls). Even so, Nestor-Iskander powerfully evokes the carnage that regularly took place on the walls, the barricades, and the moat. "Corpses fell on both sides like sheaves and blood ran from their visors . . . The Turks walked over the broken human corpses crammed to the top and fought on, for their dead resembled a bridge to the city . . . Thus, they butchered without restraint or mercy." At night the attackers would withdraw, and the defenders tried to get some rest, if their nerves allowed it. While the men were fighting, the women and children went in processions to the churches to praise and beseech the Mother of God.[47]

The carnage in the moat had revealed the wisdom of the basileus after the initial assault, when he allowed Mehmed to retrieve his own dead. Apparently, he did so again now, and so the sultan created vast funeral pyres for his men. Nestor-Iskander says that Mehmed wanted to catapult the bodies into the City as a form of biological warfare—a common tactic since ancient times—but his advisors explained to him that the City was too large for this to have any effect. However, we cannot put credence in reports about what the "faithless one" *would* have done but didn't. Mehmed could see for himself, after all, how large the City was. Even so, the blood and other putrefying liquids pooled in and around the moat, giving off a horrid stench that was carried by the wind.[48]

On May 3, the basileus prevailed upon the Venetians to send a ship out to search for the relief fleet that, he hoped, Venice had dispatched and was possibly on its way. All such a mission could do, assuming it found such a fleet, was to slightly speed it on its way or to reassure it that the Turkish fleet was not a serious threat and that its access to the harbor would not be impeded. A brigantine slipped out of the harbor in the middle of the night, with a crew of twelve dressed as Turks and flying the flag of the sultan, to look for a Venetian relief fleet.[49]

The stalemate in the harbor lasted for a week, until May 5, when Mehmed again displayed a penchant for improvisation. So far, he had managed to transport a fleet of smaller ships into the harbor but was unable to dominate it because of the presence of the larger and more powerful Christian ships. His cannons were positioned at the head of the Golden Horn and so, unless the defenders came too close (as Cocco had), he could not reach them. He could not fire at the defense flotilla directly at the mouth of the harbor where they were positioned, because the walls of Pera obstructed the direct line of fire. So, he or his engineers improvised a mortar technique for firing smaller cannons. They were fired up into the air but at an angle, so that the shot went over the obstacle between them and the target—in this case, the town of Pera. The ball was then pulled down by gravity to strike the target from above. The historian Laonikos Chalkokondyles called them "upturned cannons . . . they launch the rock up into the air, and as it descends it strikes at whatever position the artilleryman has directed it, having taken his aim; they are extraordinarily successful at hitting their mark with high trajectories." Both he and Kritoboulos—neither of whom were present at the siege of Constantinople—credit the invention of this technique to the sultan personally rather than his engineers, although this cannot be verified.[50] Mortars had been used by others before, but it is unclear whether this was known in Mehmed's camp.

On May 5, after having chosen the spot carefully, Mehmed's engineers positioned a cannon on the hill above Pera and fired it as a mortar. The rock fell into the harbor water, which allowed them to recalibrate the trajectory. They fired it again, at a slightly different angle, and on the third attempt it hit a ship and instantly sank it. Many of the crew onboard drowned, although others managed to swim to ships in the harbor. However, the ship was not part of the Christian flotilla defending the City. It was a private Genoese merchant ship, belonging to Barnaba Centurione, and it was loaded with silk, wax, and other precious commodities. According to the epic poet Posculo, Centurione had it coming, as he had sold oil to the Turks to use as a cannon coolant. The Genoese of Pera complained about this attack to the sultan's officers, who promised that they would be compensated when the siege was over.

This new development in the sultan's military capability greatly alarmed the defenders, at least at first. They repositioned their ships in the harbor, pulling them closer to the walls of Pera and sheltering them in the cover of the walls' shadow. The Turks continued to fire their mortars for a few more days, and they even managed to kill some men on the galleys—up to four at a time with one shot—but they did not sink more ships. Leonardo reports that they damaged many houses in Pera in the process. After all, the Turks were trying to hit ships that were hugging the walls. One Aron Maiavello, a merchant at Pera, was later recorded as saying to his partner, “I fear that we will lose the ship and the fish.” “What do you want me to do?,” the other man said. “Whatever you think is best.”[51] One townsperson was killed in the bombardment, a woman who was standing in a group of thirty people. Through all this, Pera was trying to preserve its neutrality, but was literally caught in the middle of the fighting. The defenders counted between 150 and 212 cannonballs fired from the top of the hill.

Eventually, on May 14, the Turks repositioned their cannon to fire at the sea walls of the City, specifically at the Kynegos Gate. But here, too, they caused little effective damage, so the cannons were taken back to join the bombardment of the land walls. The Christian ships left the shelter of Pera and returned to the boom.[52] So far, every time Mehmed contrived an ingenious way to circumvent or outflank the defenders, the latter regrouped and also found an effective way to neutralize his advantage, returning the siege to a stalemate. The siege dragged on, with both sides entrenched in their positions. In this situation, the arrival of reinforcements, for which the defenders fervently prayed, could tip the balance against the sultan.

7

Stalemate

The siege had reached a stalemate. Neither the portage of ships around Pera nor the mortar attacks over the town into the harbor changed that fact, despite the temporary alarm that those developments caused to the defenders. The sultan had displayed impressive ingenuity, adaptability, and an ambition for vast projects, leading the defenders to compare him to the ancient Persian king Xerxes. Yet all this sound and fury had faltered before the thousand-year walls of the ancient City. It was foiled also by the superior naval technology and skill of the Italians and the determination of the defenders. Despite his stratagems, the sultan's best chance for success was still what it had been at the start of the siege, specifically to bring down enough of the land walls with the cannons so his infantry could break through the breaches and swarm the defenders. This was an incremental process, and it too was slowed down by the improvised stockades and barricades that the Christians were putting up at night. They were repairing the walls as quickly as he was bringing them down. The race between the two sides had reached an impasse.

If he was to take the City by storming the breaches in the walls, Mehmed had to periodically send his soldiers to test the defenses. Barbaro records another mass attack on May 7, during the night, which was beaten back after three hours of intense fighting. This is likely the same attack recorded by Nestor-Iskander, who places it after a particularly fierce bombardment on May 6, which lasted throughout the day and following night. His account differs from that of Barbaro in that the fighting takes place during the day and stops at night. The two authors are likely referring to battles that took place on the same day but at different sectors of the wall. In Nestor-Iskander's account, on May 7, the Turks charged as soon as the wall and barricades were smashed by the cannon fire. "They jumped into that place and trampled one another. Similarly, the Greeks from the city fought face to face and roared like marvelous savages." A janissary named Murad rushed in and attacked Giustiniani, but a Greek jumped from the wall and cut his feet out from under him with an axe. Nestor-Iskander's writing is vague, but it appears that Giustiniani was drawn outside the stockade and was attacked, even surrounded, by the forces of one Ömer Bey, who is otherwise unknown. Just then, a Greek officer named Rangabes, also unknown, routed Ömer Bey, but was then cut down by the Turks in turn. "There was great slashing." It ended when night fell and the Turks withdrew.[1] Nestor-Iskander likes to report on episodes where Greeks, his Orthodox co-religionists, rescue (Catholic) Latin fighters, so these should be taken with a grain of salt.

In Barbaro's account of the fighting on May 7, the assault on the walls is paired with the naval front in the harbor. The sailors in the Ottoman fleet—he does not say whether he means that in the harbor or at Two Columns—shouted wildly and made a great din with castanets and tambourines, which forced the sailors of the Christian ships to take up their battle posts and remain vigilant. But no naval attack came. In his account, when the Turks withdrew from the Mid-Wall attack, they went to the Blachernai palace and threw fire at the gates there, but "our men ran there, and beat them back, and blocked up that gate in the wall." The reader may recall that the defense of the palace had, a month earlier when the siege began, been entrusted to the Venetian bailo, Girolamo Minotto. Another midnight attack on the palace, he says, was beaten off on May 12.

These kinds of attacks must have become routine after that point, and our sources do not pay attention to each one separately. Only Nestor-Iskander offers a detailed account of a battle that he places on May 8, although we cannot always trust his chronology. His narrative is again fuzzy, impressionistic, and imprecise. We do not need to repeat here all the back and forth of the battle as he tells it, or accept it as historically reliable.[2] What is interesting about his account is that he idolizes the basileus Konstantinos as a heroic warrior, something no other source does; he even comes to the rescue of the Latins and Giustiniani in particular on a couple of occasions. The basileus was "very large and a giant in strength." None of the Turks' weapons could harm him. "He alone, with sword in hand, slashed and rallied against them; they fled from him." However implausible, this is a welcome corrective to the pervasive bias in our Latin sources, which frequently insist that—as Barbaro put it—the critical point in the defenses was guarded exclusively by "foreigners, with not a Greek among them, because the Greeks were cowards."[3] In reality, the Latins were a minority among the defenders and surely much of the fighting was done by "Greeks," too, for all that the Latin sources are silent about them.

On the following morning, May 9, the eparch Nikolaos (likely Goudeles) supervised the cleanup. The bodies of the slain Turks—allegedly 16,000 of them, an impossible figure—were cast outside. Their co-religionists on the outside took them up and burned them. The breach was once again repaired with lumber and an improvised rampart.[4]

In the meantime, the Venetian leadership adjusted its command structure. On April 29, Alvise Diedo, the captain of the galleys from Tana, promoted Dolfino Dolfin to be captain of the galley from Trebizond in the place of Giacomo Cocco, who had died in the night attack on the Ottoman fleet the day before. Dolfin had, until that point, guarded the Palace Gate in Blachernai, and his post there was now taken up by Giovanni Loredan.[5]

On May 8, as battle was raging along the land walls in Nestor-Iskander's account, the Venetian Council of Twelve decided to unload the cargo from the galleys of Tana, store it in the City, and scupper the ships themselves. However, just as the unloading was about to begin, the crews of those ships drew their weapons and prevented it. "Where our property is, there our homes are also, and we also know that as soon as we have unloaded these galleys and sunk them, at once the Greeks will keep us in their city by force as their slaves, whereas now we are at liberty either to go or to stay." The protest worked and the plan was dropped. Diedo, the captain of these ships, took up residence onboard.[6]

It is not clear why the Twelve wanted to unload and sink the ships. I have been unable to find an explanation for this decision.[7] Perhaps they feared that, if the defense faltered, the crews might commandeer the ships, abandon the struggle, and flee, dooming the resistance when it still had a fighting chance. It made sense to unload the ships to make it more difficult for the crews to leave and incentivize them to fight. But why sink the ships as well? Even if, as unarmed cargo ships, they were militarily useless, they could still help people to escape in case the City did fall. The waters of the harbor are too deep for sunken ships to prevent the enemy from entering. Something was going on here behind the scenes that Barbaro does not tell us.

On the next day, May 9, the Twelve voted to assign Gabriele Trevisan, the captain of the two galleys, to the walls with forty men from his ships. He was to leave his galleys in the care of Alvise Diedo, the captain of the galleys from Tana that were almost scuppered the day before. However, Trevisan did not take up his post on the walls until May 13.[8] On May 10, the Twelve voted to place Alvise Diedo in command of the Venetian fleet in the harbor.

At the same time, during May, Mehmed was considering other stratagems for circumventing the defenses, or undermining them. On May 16, inhabitants of Constantinople in the vicinity of the Kaligaria Gate in the Blachernai district heard the sound of workmen—but this was at night and the sound seemed to be coming from the ground itself. They quickly realized that the Turks were digging a mine that had already passed under the foundations of the walls. That sector of the walls favored this kind of attack because here there was only a single wall and no moat. The latter was not necessary because the ground sloped away, putting attackers in a disadvantageous position, but such a terrain actually favored digging a mine directly into the City. The Turks had begun it about half a mile outside the walls, and so it was a long-term project. To be sure, with a vast supply of manpower, such as Mehmed had, works like these could be executed quickly, but a mine can fit only so many men at a time and men can dig only so fast. Mehmed had brought with him expert Serb miners and their specialized tools from Novo Brdo, one of the most important mining centers of medieval times.

The purpose of the mines was either to sneak men into the City through an underground passage or to hollow out the ground beneath the walls and towers, while supporting the excavated cavern on wooden props. Then, those supports would be set on fire and, when the hollowed-out chamber collapsed, it would bring down the tower above with it. Fundamentally, it was a method for bringing down the walls that complemented the cannons while also, of course, killing any soldiers who were stationed on top at the time. But it was difficult for the miners to know exactly when they had reached the point directly underneath their target, which they could sometimes overshoot. Moreover, the entire mine had to be supported with props along its entire length, which were liable to collapse if erected in haste or shoddily.

It is possible that we have eyewitness testimony from a Serb in Mehmed's army. Konstantin Mihailovič was captured at Novo Brdo, when Mehmed took that city in 1455. He was under twenty years of age at the time and forced to enroll in the janissary corps, or at least to accompany it thereafter, although he does not appear to have converted to Islam. At least, such was the impression that he wanted to give later in life, when he wrote his memoirs, whose purpose was to urge Christians to unite against the Turkish menace. He tells the history of the Ottoman dynasty and, when he reaches the fall of Constantinople, which took place two years before his own capture, he switches into the first-person, implying that he was there. He focuses on the contingent of soldiers that the despot of Serbia, Đurađ Branković, a vassal of the sultan, was required by treaty to provide to Mehmed in exchange for his own relative autonomy at home. He says that these soldiers were reluctant to take up arms against their fellow Orthodox Christians, but they had no choice: they were told that, if they tried to leave, the Turks would kill them. They were stationed across from the Charisios (Adrianople) Gate but apparently saw no action. "The City was not conquered by our help," he notes rather defensively. Konstantin does not mention the Serb miners, but they must have accompanied the same unit and were set to work only one gate up from the Charisios.[9]

According to Leonardo, it was the German mercenary Johannes Grant who first detected the sound of the mining. The defenders now became greatly alarmed and brought this to the attention of the *megas doux* Notaras, who, in turn, informed the basileus. A search was quickly made throughout the City for men who knew something about mining, and they were set to dig a counter-mine in search of the Turkish one. When the two met, the defenders threw fire into the Turkish mine, burning their joists and supports and causing the mine to collapse on the enemy, or else to suffocate in the smoke. As our accounts were not written by men who went on these counter-mining missions, they are thin on the details of what exactly transpired underground. They usually just say that fire was set to the mine, and it was destroyed. Presumably this means that fires were set inside the tunnels to smoke out the miners, after which the tunnels would be destroyed or collapsed by the defenders. In some cases, the miners were killed or chased away through hand-to-hand combat—in the suffocating dark tunnels, illuminated only by torchlight—and then the props holding up the tunnel leading out to their camp was fired and undermined, while the rest, the part under the walls, was filled in again to prevent it from collapsing. The defense quickly became adept at these grueling operations.

After the first mine was discovered, everyone in the Kaligaria district was placed on alert to listen for the sound of other mines, insofar as they could hear anything above the din of the cannons and the shouting that often filled the air. It was unnerving to know that the enemy might be crawling in the ground beneath one's feet, or that the foundations of the towers had been hollowed out. How many such mines had the Turks begun to dig? Moreover, having to divert precious manpower away from the defense of the walls was probably an intended, albeit secondary, goal of the mines.[10]

There were other distractions, too, probably purposefully arranged by Mehmed. On the same day as the first mine was discovered, a number of Turkish brigantines set out from Two Columns and approached the harbor entrance. The defenders there at first thought that these might be Christian crews seeking to defect from Ottoman service, but such hopes were dispelled when the ships began to fire on them. So, a number of Christian brigantines left the harbor to give chase, and they almost caught up with the Turks. At the last minute, the latter applied themselves furiously to their oars and returned safely to their anchorage.[11]

Another Ottoman reconnaissance fleet approached the boom on the next day, May 17, to spy on the condition and disposition of the Christian ships. The latter began to fire their cannons at them, about 70 shots all told, but they did not hit a single enemy ship. The Turks again withdrew to their base.[12]

At the same time, Mehmed was deploying siege towers against the land walls, apparently a number of them, some with wheels. They functioned chiefly as elevated platforms for firing at the defenders on the walls. However, it does not appear that they were brought right up to the walls or used as a bridge to storm the battlements. It might have been impossible to transport them across the uneven terrain of the filled-in moat, especially under fire by the defenders. Most of these siege towers go unmentioned in the sources. Nestor-Iskander recounts the highly memorable destruction of one of them, although his timeline is vague. Apparently, the Turks rolled one or several of these towers up to a breach in the walls, and they provided cover for a number of soldiers to approach as well. But the defenders had placed stores of gunpowder in the breach. When they set them on fire, "suddenly the earth roared like great thunder and lifted up the siege turrets and the men to the clouds, like a mighty storm. The siege turret was heard as it cracked and shook . . . People and logs fell from high—some into the City and others into the gates." Even after this explosion, the Turks charged into the now-ruined breach, but the defenders threw pitch and fire, burning them all. The sultan recalled the rest of his soldiers, while the Romans went out and killed all who survived in the breach. Then they made piles of them and set them on fire, along with the remains of their turrets.[13]

Only Nestor-Iskander describes that particular explosion. Our other sources focus on what must be a separate siege engine because it was not mobile and was destroyed in a different way. This one was erected in the southern sector of the walls, between the Golden Gate and the Pege Gate. This was the sector defended, among others, by Maurizio Cattaneo, the commander of the three Genoese ships that had arrived on April 20, and his 200 crossbowmen.[14] Barbaro claims that this tower was built during the course of a single night, May 17–18, so quickly that the men on the walls did not realize what was happening until the morning came and they saw the finished thing. It was perched on the edge of the moat and was taller than the outer wall. It consisted of a framework of wooden beams and was covered all around with camel skins. Earth had been heaped up all around its base and filled half of its interior, to make it immune to cannon fire. It was connected in the back to the Ottoman camp by a covered passageway that was itself protected with a double layer of obstacles and more camel skins, so that soldiers could move freely between the tower and the camp. Those inside the tower were throwing dirt into the moat and filling it up, creating a causeway from the tower to the outer wall. There were many ladders inside, which they hoped to use to scale the walls. Other soldiers inside fired from inside at the defenders.[15]

The basileus was immediately summoned and he rode down to inspect the situation, astonished at this new monstrosity that his men now had to face. For its eventual fate we are oddly reliant solely on the epic poet Posculo, whose reporting is largely trustworthy, although he embellishes it with Vergilian flourishes. Those flourishes affect his diction and imagery, rarely the substance of his narrative, but his account of the counterattack on the tower shines a spotlight on the heroism of the Venetian Battista Gritti, who helped to ransom the poet from captivity after the fall, so skepticism is warranted on this particular point.[16]

The local defenders in that sector, Posculo says, were the Venetian (Bernardo) Storlado and the Genoese Mollino, men about whom little is otherwise known. Storlado was to die in the fighting on May 29.[17] The initiative to destroy the tower was allegedly taken by Gritti, who had been assigned to the defense of this stretch of the walls at the beginning of the siege. With a band of Latins and Romans, he snuck outside the wall through one of the postern gates, crossed the moat, and approached the tower. His men chased away the Turks who happened to be there and set fire to its wooden framework. While the tower began to burn, they formed a perimeter around it to prevent the Turkish reinforcements, who were coming up from the Ottoman camp, from extinguishing it. When the fight became too unequal, the Latins and Romans performed a fighting retreat to the moat and slipped inside the wall. The extent of the damage done to the tower is unclear in Posculo's account. He implies that it was only partially devoured by the flames. It is possible that it continued in use, but it failed to give the attackers the advantage that they hoped for initially. It may have astonished the defenders because of the speed and manner in which it was built, but its military payoff was small. At any rate, it does not appear again in accounts of the siege.[18]

In a letter written from Crete soon after the City's fall, cardinal Isidoros describes a monstrous siege-engine that was possibly different from the one in the southern sector because it seems to have been mobile, unless he misunderstood its construction:

> Rectangular in shape and extremely thick but hollow in the interior, it resembled a house possessing an internal mechanism so it could move on wheels which rendered it mobile through superimposed ropes and other movable parts so that the entire structure could be directed; on top of it there were ladders . . . . as tall as our walls and towers and protected by timber planks all around so that the attackers who were to mount the walls could not be harmed.[19]

Unfortunately, Isidoros does not say how this tower was used or why it failed, as it surely did. The defenders on the walls somehow managed to neutralize or fight back against these mechanical terrors.

The towers astonished many people in the City. At just that moment, a Roman resident was reading the manuscript known today as Vaticanus graecus 163, a book with historical texts from the twelfth and thirteenth centuries, including the authors Konstantinos Manasses, who wrote a verse history of the Romans from antiquity to the twelfth century; Niketas Choniates, who recounted the fall of the City to the Fourth Crusade in 1204; Ioannes Kinnamos, who wrote about the glorious reign of Manuel I Komnenos (1143–1180); and Georgios Akropolites, who wrote about how the Romans regrouped after the Fourth Crusade and recovered Constantinople in 1261. Clearly, the ongoing siege had inspired this reader to read up on the history of past Roman greatness, the previous fall of the City, and the Romans' recovery. At the point in the text of Kinnamos, where the German ruler Konrad III beholds the walls of Constantinople in 1147 and decides that they are impregnable, our reader wrote this comment in the margins of the manuscript (see Image 7.1):

> Regarding the fortified City of Constantinople, what it was then and what it is now. Oh for this incomparable, incomprehensible, and unspeakable disaster! While I write these pitiable words, the Turks are laying siege to the City of Constantine, and they have brought their siege-towers so close to the walls that they are only about ten feet away. They are pounding the walls without cease with their so-called cannons, and they are hauling up rocks for this by the wagon-load. They have prepared towers and ladders and are expected to take the City any hour now. Oh, my beloved father-land, you have been brought into such danger and contempt by these

Image 7.1 Page of the Vaticanus Graecus 163 manuscript (f. 233r) with a scholion written during the siege of 1453 next to the historical work of Ioannes Kinnamos (twelfth century). Source: Biblioteca Apostolica Vaticana.

> infidels. Spare us, Lord! Let this pass us by, Lord! Show us compassion, you who alone love humanity! Spare us from these anticipated evils, for our hopes depend on you alone![20]

This reader was evidently struck by the contrast between how impregnable the City seemed to a powerful German ruler of the twelfth century and the determination with which Mehmed was now attempting to capture it.

It appears that this reader heard the same report about a great tower as had Barbaro, for the latter also says that it was built "ten paces" distant from the wall. Whether it was based on an oral report or the author's eyewitness, this marginal note could have been written only during the last days of the siege. It is in fact our *earliest* witness to the events it describes, for it was written as they were happening (even Barbaro's equally contemporary diary was later edited before it entered circulation). Interestingly, within two years or less this manuscript wound up in the Vatican collection, as its name implies, where it resides today.[21] It can only be hoped that our reader too escaped with it to Italy, where he likely had to sell this prized possession to obtain the means by which to live as a refugee in a foreign land.

A prior reader of the same manuscript was Ioannes Chortasmenos, who died in 1436–1437. He, too, scribbled in the margins of the same book some of his reactions to what he was reading. When he came to passages in the history of Niketas Choniates that described the use of Greek Fire and the former splendors of the Great Palace, he wrote, "Where is this Greek Fire now?" (referring to the incendiary, napalm-like weapon used by the Romans between the seventh and the twelfth centuries) and "How great the palace once was, and look at it now!"[22] Our later reader, in 1453, may well have come across Chortasmenos' notes when he, in turn, read the book. These late Romans were forced by the book's contents to contrast the former greatness of their state to its current sorry condition. The Romans were once powerful, rich, and respected; they were now on the verge of enslavement.

The historian Niketas Choniates, whose work is also contained in Vaticanus graecus 163, had experienced this feeling during his own lifetime, too. He was born and raised under Manuel I Komnenos and then experienced the fall of the City to the Latin soldiers of the Fourth Crusade, and he had to go into exile. In 1203–1204, when the army of the Fourth Crusade was encamped outside the City, Choniates also passed part of his time reading history. He read the ancient Greek historian Diodoros of Sicily and wrote epigrams and comments in the margins of the book, reflecting on his grim situation and uncertain future.[23] Other Romans sought comfort in prayer and in church, while some played the blame-game in the culture war over Union with Rome. Those who were interested in history turned to old books when the enemy was at the gates, seeking insight and understanding. How did their people, once so great, come to this?

Under May 19, Barbaro records in his diary that the Turks were constructing a long pontoon bridge that they intended to deploy across the Golden Horn in the next general attack. This engineering project was probably in the works for some time, under the direction of Zaganos Pasha,[24] and perhaps only now did the defenders, or at least Barbaro, become aware of it. This pontoon bridge has been misunderstood in the scholarship.

Judging from the accounts written by the survivors and Greek historians, this feat of engineering impressed and terrified the defenders no less than the ship portage of late April. It consisted of barrels fastened together, possibly with some small ships wedged in as well, on top of which were laid down platforms made of wooden planks, allowing infantry and cavalry to cross. It was supposed to bridge the Horn at the narrow point by the Kynegos Gate and would have enabled the Turks to bring soldiers directly up to the walls there, simplifying and securing the communication lines between the Ottoman land and naval forces. The classically educated defenders, which means probably Isidoros and Leonardo, compared this feat to that of the ancient Persian king Xerxes, who likewise built a pontoon bridge across the Hellespont during his invasion of Greece. The comparison stuck and is repeated in a number of our subsequent eyewitness accounts. Others transferred it to the ship portage, but the idea was the same: a tyrant of such immense arrogance and ambition will turn the sea into land, or vice versa, to achieve his goals.[25]

One argument about its function would link the pontoon bridge to the ship portage of late April on the assumption that these two projects were conceived, executed, and intended to work together. Thus, in this timeline of the siege, the bridge is dated to April 23. The purpose of the portage was, in fact, to enable the deployment of the pontoon bridge behind the cover provided by the Ottoman ships in the harbor, which would then defend the bridge.[26] However, no source puts the bridge that early in the siege. Barbaro is clear that it was first detected on May 19. Moreover, he clearly states that the Turks kept this bridge ready to use but that they never actually deployed it across the harbor. "It would have stretched to the Kynegos Gate, but it never was stretched across, because the Turks never needed to do so." Presumably, its function was to enable them to bring more soldiers up against the harbor walls and thus "to make our men spread themselves [thin] around the walls."[27] What Barbaro must mean is that it was not deployed before the final assault on May 29, because it is attested in use by other sources on that day. Leonardo says that the bridge was deployed and extended to the City side of the harbor on May 28, the day before the final assault.[28]

On May 21, two hours before sunrise, the entire Ottoman fleet sailed out of its anchorage at Two Columns and approached the harbor at full speed, making its usual racket with castanets and tambourines. The defense flotilla was armed and ready. But just as the attack fleet approached, the alarm bells rang out throughout the City, and everyone rushed to arms. The Turkish fleet withdrew, whether because they had second thoughts or because it was only a feint. At noon on the same day, a second mine was discovered near the Kaligaria Gate. Fire was thrown into this one, too, and it was abandoned by the Turks.[29]

A total of seven mines would be discovered before that week was out. The Turks had possibly dug even more, but none succeeded in its purpose. Two more were found on May 22, a fifth on May 23, a sixth on May 24, and the seventh on May 25. One of those discovered on May

22 collapsed on its own, killing the miners inside. From the one found on May 23, two Turks were pulled out alive. They were tortured to reveal the locations of other mines. Then they were decapitated and their bodies thrown over the walls so that their people could see them. In the sixth tunnel, discovered on May 24, the miners had already hollowed out the entire area beneath a tower and a stretch of wall and were preparing to set fire to it. The Romans secured it, filled it up, and walled it off, "making everything as strong as before, so that there was nothing more to be feared there." Barbaro says that the seventh mine was the most dangerous of all because it was dug under a crucial section of the wall by the Kaligaria and, had it been fired, the implosion would have brought it down and imperiled the defenses greatly.[30]

Among our sources, only the epic poet Posculo attempted to capture the experience of these underground battles.[31] The tunneling itself must have been a frightening experience, but fighting there was even worse, given the confined space, stale and suffocating air, uneven ground, the ever-present fear of a collapse, and the flickering torchlight. It is extraordinary that the Romans managed to prevail every time.

By this time, a month and a half after the siege began, the defenders had managed to neutralize, adapt to, or contain every one of Mehmed's lines of attack. They repaired the walls after every phase of bombardment and defended the breaches when the Turks charged. They had kept the Ottoman ships away from the sea walls in the harbor and prevented them from dominating the Golden Horn. The mortar attacks over Pera had done only minor damage. The chain blocking the harbor still held firm and the fleet guarding it was not only intact, but it was also confident that it could take on a much larger number of enemy ships in battle. The siege towers had proven ineffectual, and the mines had all been discovered and destroyed. And despite a solitary complaint from Barbaro, there was no sign that the City was critically running out of food and water, although it was always short on men, which was the real weakness. A few more galleys of reinforcements could tip the scales decisively in favor of the defense. There was no reason to think that a fall was imminent, even though everyone understood that it could happen at any time and could come from any direction. But vigilance had prevailed so far.

What would *not* be coming was help from the West, at least not anytime soon. On Wednesday, May 23, the brigantine that had been sent out three weeks earlier, on May 3, to search for the Venetian fleet and hasten it on its way, finally returned to Constantinople. It was sighted an hour before dawn, poorly disguised as a Turkish vessel, which did not fool the Turks. Their ships sailed out from Two Columns to intercept it, but the brigantine managed to enter the harbor before they could. Its crew of twelve told the following tale. They had reached the Aegean Sea but could find no evidence of a Venetian fleet or its passage. Some of them proposed that they sail on to some Christian land, for by the time that they returned the Turks would have taken Constantinople already, so soon did they expect the City to fall. But most of them were committed to completing their mission, and so they sailed back and reported to the basileus. This caused him to weep, for he realized that help was not coming from Venice. "The whole of Christendom has been unwilling to help me against this faithless Turk."[32]

That was not precisely true, although in the end it was effectively true. Back in February, the Venetian Senate had authorized the dispatch of significant forces, but assembling ships and their commanders from all the Republic's naval assets, which were scattered across the Aegean, took too long, especially given the communication lags and a distinct lack of urgency. The experienced politician, administrator, and naval commander Giacomo Loredan was placed in charge of this relief effort and given the position of Captain General of the Sea. But he never made it to the City, nor did the ships that pope Nicholas V outfitted at the last minute. Loredan was still on Euboia (Negroponte), and the papal ships were on Chios, when they were met by survivors and refugees from the fallen City, who brought their tales of woe.[33]

When the brigantine returned on May 23, it found the City in a state of heightened tension. Stress and fear, combined with prolonged vigilance and uncertainty, had led many defenders to ponder ancient prophesies or to discern omens in occurrences both mundane and uncommon.

Just the night before, on May 22, they had witnessed a partial eclipse of the moon. They expected the moon to be full, but as it rose after sunset it gradually disappeared until only a crescent sliver was left, like that of a three-day moon, even though the sky was cloudless and the air crisp and pure. Then its full volume returned, just as gradually. Barbaro says that the Greeks were afraid because of a prophesy that their City would not fall until the moon gave a sign. The Muslims, by contrast, rejoiced when they saw this, believing that victory was now theirs. The crescent moon, after all, was a symbol of Islam.[34]

While the eclipse can be astrologically confirmed, the other signs reported in the sources lack independent verification. All but one of them appear in only one account each, which makes them especially unreliable. Our authors had a dramatic incentive to presage the City's fall with portents and omens—this was not only conventional but expected in premodern historiography—and they clustered them together as the impending climax of their narrative approached. Thus, we cannot know which ones actually happened or, even if they did, whether they were interpreted as portents at the time—and therefore impacted the psychology of the moment—or were just seen as weather. The one event that is mentioned by two independent authors is a dark cloud that hung low over Constantinople at some point during the final days of the siege.[35]

It is especially difficult to believe Nestor-Iskander's report of a flame that encircled and illuminated the dome of Hagia Sophia on the outside, on the evening of Thursday, May 24. It then allegedly shot up toward the heavens, where a gate opened, received it, and closed again—a scene written for the end of a Hollywood movie. At first, people thought that the Turks had set fire to the church, but soon they realized that this was a miraculous occurrence that signified the flight of the Holy Spirit from Constantinople. It is hard to imagine that this happened and no one else recorded it. A special meeting of the basileus' council of advisors was supposedly convened on the following day, when yet again he was pressured to abandon the City and seek safety elsewhere. This pressure on the basileus to leave the City is a recurring motif in Nestor-Iskander's account, and equally hard to credit.[36] In all other sources, the basileus and his nobles are fully determined to stay and fight it out.

Konstantinos Palaiologos' resolve to stay and, if necessary, to die for his City is nowhere more forcefully expressed than in the responses that he allegedly gave to the sultan's diplomatic overtures. In many of our narratives, the sultan offers safe passage out of Constantinople to the basileus and his people if they surrender it to him. In response, the basileus counteroffers with alternative tokens of submission, such as tribute, but categorically refuses to surrender the City. Yet it is unclear how frequently such exchanges took place. Our sources recount a number of them, but they disagree about who initiated them and when they took place. Many of the sources, after all, do not report events in chronological sequence, and they may be telling only one side of an exchange, giving a misleading impression of who initiated it. It is theoretically possible that formal exchanges of envoys took place only twice, first upon Mehmed's arrival in early April and then right before the final assault, when the sultan offered his final terms.

Information about the final exchange of envoys and discussion of terms comes from the Greek historians, who were not present. Laonikos offers detailed information. He says that the initiative for the final round of diplomacy came from Ismail Isfendyaroğlu, the ruler of Sinop on the Black Sea (1443–1461), one of the last surviving beyliks of Anatolia. He was a vassal of the sultan and so was required to attend him on campaign; his principality would be annexed in 1461, right before the Roman state of Trebizond. According to Laonikos, Ismail offered to mediate between the sultan and the basileus to prevent the Romans from being enslaved or killed when the City fell. The basileus sent "a man of little note" to the sultan's camp, where Mehmed offered to lift the siege in exchange for an annual tribute of 100,000 gold coins. The basileus and his council allegedly rejected this offer and decided to risk battle, believing that their position was secure.[37]

We may or may not accept the role of Ismail Isfendyaroğlu in the final round of negotiations, but this account is otherwise impossible to believe. Even in Laonikos' own narrative, Mehmed is about to launch an all-out assault, with an intensity that had not yet been seen during the siege. He fully intended to conquer Constantinople—or at least make one final determined effort to do so—and he was not about to be bought off by a sum that would simultaneously be impossible for them to pay and trivial for him to receive. Even Laonikos admits that the offer was insincere and made only to test the Romans' resolve.

A more realistic narrative is found in Doukas. He has Mehmed send an embassy offering safety to Konstantinos and his people if they would but surrender the City. Konstantinos again refused to consider it. The sultan could keep all that he had conquered and even enjoy a tribute from the Romans on top of that. "But neither I nor any inhabitant of the City has the right to surrender the City to you. By a joint resolution we have all willingly decided to die and not spare our lives in its defense."[38]

8

The Final Assault

By late May 1453, Mehmed was running out of options. The cost of the siege was mounting, and he had little to show for it. Despite his impressive stratagems and engineering, he had scored no major victories, nothing that he could proclaim throughout his empire as a solid win. He had lost thousands of soldiers and burned their bodies on pyres before the walls. It literally looked as if he were sacrificing his men to the City, or to his dream of conquering it. His soldiers, officers, and allies were likely growing impatient and frustrated. They had no reason to think that the defenders were running out of arms, food, or the will to fight. Moreover, Mehmed was a young ruler whom many had considered too impulsive and unready to take on the responsibilities of governing a vast empire, far less a major war. His prolonged failure to take the City, despite the resources that he had poured into the siege, was reinforcing that humiliating narrative.

There were, moreover, mounting strategic anxieties. The longer the siege lasted, the likelier it was that aid would arrive from the West. Mehmed could ill-afford another setback like the one he suffered on April 20, when four Christian ships had shrugged his entire fleet aside. Other powers, chiefly Hungary, might also take advantage of the situation and attack from behind while he was pinned down at Constantinople. Unfortunately, the later Ottoman histories do not give us a realistic picture of conditions inside the Turkish camp, the morale of the soldiers, or the precarity and probably growing insecurity of Mehmed's own position as the siege dragged on. They were written in the aftermath of success and could depict the campaign as a foreordained victory for Islam, with Mehmed as a noble Muslim leader leading his people into a glorious new era of history. We should not follow them in projecting the outcome back onto the siege itself. The letter of the sheik Ak Şemseddin, written after the disaster of April 20, reveals a high state of disaffection in the Ottoman camp. A full month later, matters would have been considerably more dire.

Some of the Christians believed that the sultan's advisors were bitterly split between hawks, such as Zaganos Pasha, and doves, most prominently the vizier Çandarlı Halil Pasha, who, according to Leonardo, even shared sensitive military information with the basileus to slow down or undermine the siege.[1] That claim cannot be substantiated because at no point did the defenders appear to possess information that Mehmed wanted to keep secret. But the perception that the Ottoman leadership was divided over the war may well have been accurate. By late May, the sultan was surely under considerable pressure to rally his men or call the whole thing off. The Christian sources refer to a war council in the sultan's camp, one that possibly lasted for four days.[2]

There was, in fact, only one thing left for Mehmed to attempt. He had by now already used all his stratagems, diversions, and siege-technology. The defenders had countered them all or adapted to them successfully, but it had forced them to spread themselves thin along the walls. The only path forward for Mehmed at this point was to double-down on his core strategy, which was to demolish as much of the walls with his cannons as he could, storm the breaches with an all-out general assault, and hope that his men could prevail in the hand-to-hand fighting against the increasingly exhausted and thinned-out defenders. He had tried this before, but perhaps the cumulative damage to the walls from the cannon fire was beginning to change the balance of forces in the breaches. One more grand push might succeed where others had failed. There was not much that he could do to give this push extra momentum, but Mehmed was determined to try, for it would make or break the campaign. He would have to incentivize and threaten his soldiers just a bit more, create a charged atmosphere of anticipation in the camp, push everyone to their limits, and accept higher casualties by forcing everyone into the breach in waves. The margin between humiliation and glorious victory was razor thin.

Mehmed made a grand proclamation to his army on Saturday, May 26, designating Tuesday, May 29, as the day of the general attack. His plan was to let his soldiers rest, pray, and party for three days and nights, and then throw them all at the walls in a series of waves that would exhaust and overwhelm the defense. In the meantime, during those three days he would maintain a steady and intense bombardment so that the walls and improvised stockades would be as ruined as possible on the morning of the May 29 (see Color Plate 8). He personally delivered this proclamation to an assembly of officers and sent heralds to announce its terms throughout the encampment. The Christian sources report the content of this proclamation fairly consistently, and what they say matches the brief, one-sentence summary given by Tursun Bey, who was in the camp: "The sultan proclaimed a general assault and gave the troops permission to take booty in the city, for 'Glory comes only from Allah.'"[3]

Kritoboulos takes the opportunity to work the sultan's words up into a full-dress classical speech of the kind that is given to protagonists in ancient histories, which he was imitating in his narrative of Mehmed's reign. The other sources more realistically stick to the main points. Mehmed set the all-out assault for Tuesday and gave his soldiers three days to rest and prepare. He emphasized that he would allow them to plunder the City thoroughly after its fall, claiming only its physical infrastructure for himself. They could loot the inhabitants' belongings and enslave them for their own personal use or sell them for profit:

> The sultan swore by their immortal god, by the four thousand prophets, by Muhammad, by the soul of his father and by the sword with which he was girded that his warriors would be granted the right to sack everything, to take everyone, male or female, and all property or treasure which was in the city; and that under no circumstances would he break this oath.

Upon hearing this, his soldiers are said to have cheered wildly, all of it perfectly audible to the defenders on the walls. Leonardo says that they chanted, "There is no God but God and Muhammad is his Prophet." In the account of Kritoboulos, Mehmed highlights the pleasures that were to be had from enslaved women and from the houses and gardens of the City. The sultan would personally oversee the fighting to reward the brave and punish the timid.[4]

Mehmed's words must have been conveyed to the defenders inside the City almost immediately, which is why they are reported to us so consistently. He was not trying to hide his intentions. That something new was stirring was apparent, after all, in the markedly changed behavior of his army. For three days, from Saturday to Monday, they fasted and prayed during the day, while at night they were ordered to light as many fires as they could throughout the camp and keep them burning until midnight while they loudly chanted Muslim prayers, shouted war cries, played musical instruments, and sang songs. This was done as much to boost their own morale as to intimidate the defenders. It was not an uncommon practice in the Ottoman army. In describing the encampment of the sultan Bayezid in the late fourteenth century, Konstantinos XI's father, Manuel II, had referred to the fires that the Turks lit at night and the songs that they sung throughout the night, which sounded menacing to him.[5] Konstantinos might well have read this text, although he had ample first-hand experience of the Ottoman camps, for example that which attacked him at the Hexamilion wall in 1446.

Now, in 1453, the fires cast such a powerful blaze that some inhabitants of the City thought that the encampment had caught fire. They rushed to the edge of their battered walls only to see dancing, singing, and feasting. "Lord," they said, "spare us from your just chastisement and save us from the hands of our enemy." Knowing that the critical moment was upon them, when the City would either fall or be saved, the whole population was in a state of panic, and some even experienced stress-induced shortness of breath. For their part, the Turkish soldiers were joyfully greeting each other with kisses, embraces, and salutations.[6]

One Venetian fled. As dread gripped the City, Nicolò Giustiniani (not the general) hightailed it to Pera and, from there, slipped away to reach Venice in record time. This information comes from the epic poet

Posculo, and it is indirectly corroborated by independent evidence that Nicolò was in Constantinople during the defense and then in Venice shortly thereafter. It is unclear how he got his ship outside the harbor. At any rate, in Venice he claimed that the basileus' treasurer, Andronikos Koumouses—a Roman who held Venetian citizenship—had entrusted him with his deposits in Venice; possibly they were business partners. Of course, neither Nicolò nor the Venetians knew at that point that Constantinople had fallen or that Koumouses had died in the fighting. It seems that the latter had drawn up his will in anticipation of the final assault, indicating that he expected to die.[7]

During those three days, the sultan's cannons pummeled the "poor, ruined walls" in an intense bombardment, while Giustiniani and the defenders desperately tried to patch them however they could.[8] The clergy held prayers in the churches and religious processions around the City. A memorable, day-long procession in which icons were led along the length of the land walls is noted by Leonardo and Nestor-Iskander.[9] Crowds of men and women followed barefoot, beseeching Christ and the Virgin not to abandon them in the coming battle. This procession drew on centuries of Orthodox ritual practice in Constantinople. At times when the City was under foreign attack, the Romans had, since the eighth or ninth century, famously placed and paraded icons of the Virgin on the walls. By this point they probably believed that the practice dated back to Constantinople's very foundation.[10] Processions for the salvation of the City were famously associated with the emperor Theodosius II (408–450), who had walked barefoot from Constantinople to the parade grounds of the Hebdomon, seven miles away. He did this in the winter of 447, right after a devasting earthquake had destroyed many of the walls and towers of his recently built walls. Attila the Hun had just invaded the Balkans and was expected to reach the City itself, at the worst possible moment, so the emperor was seeking divine assistance.[11] This procession was commemorated in the liturgical cycle of the capital and even reenacted by later emperors. In 1453, there was, of course, no way to walk to the Hebdomon, so they processed along the Theodosian walls themselves, which were now ruined by cannon fire, not an earthquake.

Nestor-Iskander quotes the long penitent prayer spoken by the priests on that occasion (he is the kind of author who does not pass up a chance to sermonize in that vein). For his part, Leonardo quotes and probably invents a speech given by Konstantinos, asking the defenders to trust in God and not be afraid just because the walls were in ruin. He reminds them of the injustice of the sultan's actions and the glorious history of Constantinople. He addressed the Genoese, Venetians, and Romans by name as allies in this noble cause, speaking words of encouragement.

On Monday, May 28, as the Mid-Wall was relentlessly bombarded, Mehmed rode with his cavalry to Two Columns to inspect the navy and instruct it on its role in the next day's attack.[12] On that day, the pontoon bridge across the harbor was deployed and extended to the City gates to enable Zaganos to bring his soldiers up to the harbor walls during the general assault.[13] Mehmed also put his army along the walls in battle order. Soldiers were instructed by heralds and trumpets to go to their posts, so that they would be ready for the attack the next morning. About 2,000 long ladders and mobile siege-towers were brought up along with screens to shield those who would raise them up to the walls. The soldiers were in good cheer, praying and offering each other encouragement, thinking about the slaves and riches that would be theirs.[14]

There was not much that Mehmed could do at this point to improve his odds of success, but he did it all. The more ruined the walls at the time of the assault, the more he could bring his superior numbers to bear in the breaches that opened. Thus, he continued the bombardment during those three days. Tetaldi says that the outer wall in the Romanos sector had been leveled to the length of 200 paces, yet it had been filled in with "earth, containers, and logs."[15] Next, Mehmed would order his army and navy to attack along the entire length of the land *and* sea walls, to force the defenders to spread themselves out even more. Nestor-Iskander has him say that "we will bring the scaling ladders near the walls of the city at many places. We will divide the townspeople among all these places."[16]

The tip of the Ottoman spear would, of course, be the janissaries, whose task it was to storm the main breach in the Mid-Wall in the final wave of the assault. On Monday, Mehmed arrayed them in battle order, inspected them, and spoke separately to them as his most beloved soldiers. His battle plan was for them to fight in waves: as one group grew weary of the fighting, they would be relieved by a reserve line, and so on throughout the day. In this way they would wear down and exhaust the defenders, who, being far fewer, lacked rested reserves. Finally, the sultan incentivized his soldiers through inspections and rousing speeches in which he dangled the prospect of plunder and slaves before their eyes. He sent Muslim holy men, the *zahids*, throughout the lines to remind the men about their faith's view of the afterlife, the promises of Muhammad, and their duty to fight for the glory of Islam. Mehmed made great promises to those who scaled the barricades first, and he threatened any who ran away with a "horrible death."[17]

The defenders prepared, too, as best they could. Bells sounded throughout the City, calling men, women, and children to their assigned duties. They carried stones to the battlements and barricades to throw down upon the Turks who were scaling the ladders; a slightly later source refers to vats of scalding oil. Everyone took his assigned post and waited anxiously. There was not much more that they could do. Many were weeping and shaking in terror.[18]

Our main Italian sources, Barbaro and Leonardo, criticize the Greeks for the inadequacy of the preparations and make their own people look better, in an effort to shift the blame in the later recriminations. These accusations need to be read with caution. Specifically, Barbaro says that "we Christians" made seven cartloads of mantlelets for the battlements to shield the defenders. The Venetian bailo ordered the Greeks to position them there, but the Greeks refused unless they were paid, leading to an argument. The Venetians were willing to pay for this labor while the Greeks were not, meaning presumably the notable Greeks, such as Notaras. By the time that it was done, it was dark and the mantlelets could not be positioned correctly, so they were not used during the fight, all because of "the greed of the Greeks." Be that as it may, the bailo ordered all Venetians to take up positions on the land walls or in the harbor fleet guarding the chain.[19]

Leonardo says that Giustiniani requested cannons for the defense of the walls from Notaras, who refused him in an insulting way, leading to an argument between the two. As a result, Notaras allegedly withheld supplies from the wall defense.[20] This incident, assuming it even happened, cannot be dated precisely, but it is yet another way of blaming the Greeks, and especially the conveniently dead scapegoat Notaras, who became a polarizing figure afterward. Leonardo goes on to say that the Greeks were jealous of the Latins "because the glory of saving the City had been given to them." As both authors tell stories that conveniently shift the blame for the defeat onto the Greeks while simultaneously casting their own people—the Venetians and Genoese respectively—in a good light, we must be skeptical.

That night the Turks lit their fires again, more of them than on the previous nights, and made a tremendous amount of noise, which was compounded by the cannon fire, further unsettling the defenders. The Muslims prayed to Allah and his Prophet, while the Christians prayed to their God and his Mother and the saints. "And when each side had prayed for victory, they to their God and we to ours, our God in Heaven determined with His Mother which of us should be successful in this battle, which was to be so fierce."[21] As one survivor reported, the defenders may well have believed that "if they proved able to survive this attack, without doubt the enemy would lift the siege and depart."[22]

On Tuesday, May 29, the quality of our first-hand reporting suddenly declines, as our authors who were present during the siege were suddenly transformed into fleeing refugees with no access to reliable information, especially about what had happened in the fighting at the Mid-Wall. Until that day, or until the very hour when they began to flee or were captured, even if they were not stationed near the action in any given sector, our eyewitnesses were able to access information that circulated among the defenders. Word spread along the walls and across the different groups that had banded together to defend Constantinople. There had been pauses in the fighting, briefings, and war councils from which reports and orders filtered down to the rank and file. But on May 29, most of the people who were close to the fighting died, making it difficult for our authors, who by definition were among the survivors, to ascertain what happened. A generally consistent picture does emerge, but most reports contain a dose of rumor passing as fact, guesswork, flat-out lies, rhetorical fiction, dramatization, or recrimination. Also, everyone was so focused on what had happened at the Mid-Wall where the defenses failed that they paid little attention to the rest of the circuit, even though the fighting appears to have been intense elsewhere too. As a result, there is some uncertainty about the events of that Tuesday morning.

The Ottoman sources are unhelpful in this regard. To be sure, their authors did not face these challenges, but their accounts of the siege are either brief or dominated by poetic, religious, and panegyrical themes, with little attention paid to the granular detail of operations on that fateful day.

The common view in modern scholarship is that Mehmed gave the order for the assault somewhere between midnight and three hours before dawn on Tuesday morning. The attack came in three waves, the first two of which were defeated by the defenders but wore them down, whereupon the third wave, consisting of the elite janissaries, who were rested and spoiling for a fight, finally broke through.[23] This reconstruction is plausible but not certain. It is based primarily on Barbaro, who was with the Venetian ships in the harbor, far from the Mid-Wall section, although when he escaped from the falling City he was likely in the company of Venetians who had fought on the walls and could tell him what had happened. According to him, the first group came up three hours before dawn. It consisted of expendable (and, in some cases, even involuntary) Christian irregulars whose job it was to raise the ladders up to the walls and improvised stockades in the Romanos sector. They were slaughtered en masse by the defenders' projectiles. When some tried to flee, they were killed by Turkish soldiers behind them. The second wave consisted of the lower quality Turkish soldiers, who were also cut down in large numbers. The defenders' artillery and cannons were firing into the massed Turkish ranks, causing great casualties, while the Turks' own cannons were also firing upon the defenses. The area was therefore filled with smoke, making it hard for anyone to see, especially as the sun had not yet risen. Turkish archers fired so many arrows from behind that the *peribolos* walkway between the walls was littered with thousands of them. Finally, the dreaded white-hat janissaries came up to find the defenders exhausted.[24]

The attack may have been broadly structured in that way, although no other source says so. Moreover, Barbaro's account of the actual fall is wildly incorrect, as we will see. It is also unclear when the fighting began. The Turkish breakthrough certainly took place at or soon before dawn: on that all are agreed and knew well, because it was when they began to run for their lives. But a number of sources state that fighting was taking place all night between May 28 and 29, at least at the critical sections of the Mid-Wall. It would have made sense for Mehmed to harass the defenders with skirmishing all night to deprive them of sleep before the main assault. The cardinal Isidoros contradicts himself on this point. In his letter to the pope he says that the sultan "gained entry early in the morning after an all-night attack, with our forces exhausted," but in his letter to Bessarion, written just ten days earlier, he had said that the attack began "a little after the break of dawn, while the sun's rays were blinding our side."[25] This, of course, is impossible, as the sunrise faced the Turks, not the Romans. Kritoboulos features the same motif, but he flips it around. He says that the battle began as night fell, when the light was in the eyes of the defenders. That gets the orientation right, but his sense of strategy is lame. The light of the sunset is hardly blinding, and the effect would not last long, so this was no reason to start the assault then.[26] We cannot rely on Kritoboulos' testimony here, and his account of the last day of fighting generally contains much rhetorical invention.

Nestor-Iskander, who was possibly somewhere in the Mid-Wall sector, is the most difficult source to understand. On top of his many confusions and errors, he was incapable of describing anything precisely and had little or no sense of chronology. In his narrative, there is no three-day pause in the fighting before the final assault, only a series of daily attacks. It is almost impossible to follow the ebb and flow of battle in his blurry account. Between the wounding of Giustiniani and the entry of the Turks into the City, he places too much time and too many battles starring Konstantinos XI for his account to be credible. He wants to heighten the basileus' heroics and is not afraid of fictionalizing events to achieve this. Yet he does get one thing right: "as there were multitudes of Turks, they alternated in the battle. The townspeople were always as one [i.e., alone] and became weak from too much labor . . . no aid could be expected from anywhere."[27] The epic poet Posculo put it as follows: for the Turks, "others take the place of those who are exhausted. But for the citizens there is no pause, nor are they granted any rest.[28]

We can imagine the carnage and chaos of the fighting by the improvised outer stockade. Both sides were firing guns, bows, and possibly cannons at each other, the defenders from the high inner wall and the Turks from behind their front ranks. Beneath this hail of artillery, furious combat raged as the attackers sought to scale the wall, climbing over the bodies of their fallen comrades, and without being able to dodge the rocks and flaming pitch thrown down on them by the defenders. And when they reached the top, they were cut down by axes and swords. Smoke filled the air, along with the sounds of rage, pain, death, gunpower, and the drums beaten by both sides. Bells rang throughout the City. Most people could see little and hear too much, a dangerous and volatile combination.

The Romans and Italians were holding their ground until shortly before dawn, when suddenly Giustiniani was injured and fell back. Our sources disagree about the type of weapon that struck him—an arrow or gunshot—and where on his body he was struck, whether through the arm or on his chest. But fall back he did. And that is when confusion, and possibly also panic, spread through the Roman ranks and our sources begin to diverge in their reporting. Least reliable here is our otherwise trusty Barbaro, who wants to defame Giustiniani, the Genoese hero of the war. He presents a fictional scenario where a single cannon blast destroys the wall and allows 70,000 Turks to enter the *peribolos*, from the sea to the Golden Horn, at which point—with no mention of a wounding!—the coward Giustiniani flees to his ship in the harbor shouting "The Turks are in the City!" the whole way. Everyone else thereupon abandons his post and flees, even though there was still some fierce fighting to be done as the Turks tried to force their way through the Romanos Gate (i.e., the Fifth Gate).[29]

Barbaro was not only ignorant of the sequence of events, but he allowed partisanship and prejudice to get the better of him here. It is clear from all other sources that Giustiniani was in fact wounded and fell back to seek treatment, and this turned the tide of the battle, allowing the Turks to pour into the *peribolos*. Tursun Bey, on the Ottoman side, was also clear about it: "When they saw that their commander had been wounded, the enemy troops were overcome. They tried to escape by fleeing into the inner fortress, but the defenders had barred the gate. Left trapped between the walls, they were all put to the sword. The Ottoman troops immediately stormed the inner walls and pushed back the defenders."[30]

There can be no doubt that Giustiniani was grievously wounded, likely mortally. He was carried to his ship and died on Chios a month later, on August 1.[31] There was even a version of events, attested by two independent sources, that he was wounded twice. The first is Nestor-Iskander, who has the Genoese captain struck by a fragment of a cannonball on the day or night before the final battle. He was taken away, treated, and then insisted on returning to the battlefield, where he received his second, fatal wound.[32] The second author who says that Giustiniani was wounded twice, albeit without providing any detail, was the Greco-Venetian scholar, diplomat, spy, and interpreter Nikolaos Sekoundinos (or Sagundinus), one of the most extraordinary figures of the fifteenth century.[33] Sekoundinos wrote this in early 1454, after visiting Edirne and Constantinople and speaking to survivors, therefore long before Nestor-Iskander wrote his account; it is unlikely that either account depended on the other.

Be that as it may, Giustiniani's withdrawal from the battle at the critical moment immediately became controversial as the debate raged among survivors over whom to blame for the catastrophe that Christendom suffered on that day. Cardinal Isidoros, who had barely managed to escape from the City with his life, already hinted at these debates in a letter he sent soon afterward from Crete, but clearly felt the matter was too painful or too controversial to discuss. "Many hold him to be the primary cause of that enormous destruction and resulting captivity; but let me omit this matter."[34] In his letter to pope Nicholas V, written in mid-August, Leonardo of Chios was more explicit. The defenders were winning until Giustiniani was wounded. He left secretly to find a doctor without appointing a deputy to take his place. Had he done so, the City would not have fallen. People saw that he was missing, and they began to withdraw. Their officers did not keep them informed about what was going on, perhaps because they themselves did not know. The basileus tried but failed to persuade Giustiniani to stay. Leonardo levels a direct accusation of cowardice against his fellow Genoese man: "like a boy unused to war, he trembled at the sight of his own blood and feared for his life." "Showing a great cowardice," Giustiniani insisted that the gate through the inner wall be opened so that he could retreat, causing a stampede behind him, as others sought to pass, too, and so he abandoned the basileus to his fate.[35]

Surprisingly, Leonardo is almost as critical of Giustiniani, a fellow Genoese, as the Venetian Barbaro was. Interestingly, he wrote his letter on August 16, 1453, on his native island of Chios, the very place where Giustiniani had sought refuge and lay dying until August 1. We do not know when Leonardo arrived on Chios from Pera, but inevitably one wonders whether he spoke with the man himself or his guard, and whether his verdict was based on their version of events, which may indeed have been excessively self-critical and contrite. Not everyone is engaged in public relations and self-promotion all the time, especially when they are expecting to die. This does not mean, however, that we should accept his version of events or blame Giustiniani for what happened.

Giustiniani was hardly "a boy unused to war." Upon receiving his wound, he may have been in excruciating pain or only semi-conscious; he did not imagine that his search for aid would lead to a rout. Tetaldi states that, as he was leaving, Giustiniani entrusted the defense to two other Genoese nobles, just before dawn.[36] Sudden panic in the rank and file is an unpredictable and irrational reaction that can happen with no known cause. It likely occurred that Tuesday morning when the defenders saw their commander missing or taken away and interpreted it as a retreat. It was then easy, in the dark and violent cacophony of the Mid-Wall, to imagine that the Turks had broken through somewhere out of sight. Having drawn this conclusion, a few no doubt did flee to save themselves. Others then saw them and did the same, setting off a chain reaction that led to a stampede and mass death at the gate.

After the warlord's departure, the fog of uncertainty settled even more thickly on the Mid-Wall sector, as even fewer people were likely to escape from the killing grounds of the *peribolos* walkway and so be in a position to report later what had happened. A rare nugget of possibly authentic information occurs in Leonardo's letter. As the defenders were stampeding the gate and dying in large numbers, the Turks climbed up onto the outer wall and fired upon those inside. (Posculo adds that they planted their red flags upon the battered outer walls.) At that moment, the brothers Paolo and Troilo Bocchiardi, Latin natives of Constantinople who had been posted to the Myriandrion Gate just to the south, saw the stream of defenders fleeing, so they rushed north on their horses to bring help, accompanied by both Roman and Latin soldiers. They managed to push some Turks back, but they soon realized that the City was lost, and so they abandoned the walls and retreated toward Pera.[37] We know from other documents that they were in fact captured on the way there but quickly ransomed.[38] It was likely at Pera that Leonardo heard their testimony because he was there in June as well, after his own brief captivity. Their account may well be our last authentic glimpse into the *peribolos* as the Turks were breaking through.

No one really knew what happened to the basileus Konstantinos. All stories told about his fate are likely inventions, including that he begged his men to kill him so that he would not be taken alive, that he removed his insignia and died fighting as a common soldier, that he returned into the City and was hunted down by Turkish soldiers, or that he fought heroic battles before finally meeting his end. These stories filled the painful gap left by ignorance about his fate. The basileus' tragic tale called out for closure, whether ennobling or bathetic. Even if one of these versions is true, we will never know which one. In later times, it was believed that he had turned to stone and still awaits the day when he will return to life and lead his people to victory. Into that same category we can put the tale that his head was cut off by his killers, or by those who later searched for his body, and brought it to Mehmed, who, in one version, put it on display.[39]

It is certain that Konstantinos XI Palaiologos died in the fighting, although we cannot say where or how. His body was likely never found. Thus, the basileus did exactly what he had pledged, which was to die rather than surrender his City. He died as a warrior, even though he had never been an exceptional general in life.[40] It was wise of him to entrust the defense of the City to an experienced commander such as Giustiniani and to allow the Venetians to defend his harbor, as he lacked the skills, manpower, and resources with which to do either as well they had. But, at the end, he could not—or did not—flee, as they did.

On that note, it is possible that we can attribute a final action to Konstantinos XI in the moments before he died. Independent sources claim that he tried to persuade the wounded Giustiniani not to leave, precisely to avoid a panic, or simply so as not to draw his desperately needed fighters away from the defense. This suggests that the basileus was fighting in Giustiniani's vicinity in the Mid-Wall section or rushed over to him when he was informed about his decision to leave. "Stay, captain, I beg you, for your flight will encourage others to do the same."[41] But it is possible that this story too was a dramatic fiction that filled the void at the end of the two men's tragic relationship.

Once the walls were stormed, our reports become even more chaotic and unreliable. Even the few people who survived the carnage of the *peribolos* were running for their lives and not looking back to see exactly where and how the Turks scaled or got past the inner wall into the City. Some reports are hopelessly vague on this point, failing to distinguish clearly between the inner and outer walls. The Ottoman sources are also vague. Even if, in the aftermath of their victory, Ottoman officials had tried to piece together what happened just before their army started to fan out throughout Constantinople, they would likely have heard many contradictory boasts on the part of their soldiers.

The first Turkish soldiers likely entered through the Fifth Gate, once they had cut their way through the stampeding press of fleeing defenders. This is what the poet Posculo says.[42] After all, it did later come to be called the Gate of the Assault (Hücum Kapı).[43] Alternately, some sources state or imply that the *inner* wall, too, had been demolished at that point by cannon fire, just enough to enable the attackers to climb over the rubble or walk through the cracks.[44] The defenders had put all their effort into patching the outer wall, so it is possible that the inner one had also been ruined by the bombardment and was no longer a solid defensible line. Another possibility is that the Turks, having overcome the obstacle of the outer wall and with the defenders now in flight, brought their ladders up to the inner wall, too, although this would require some improvisation as the inner wall was taller.

A story unlikely to be true was told by the historian Doukas, writing a few years later from the island of Lesbos, which was ruled by the Genoese family of the Gattilusi. His story has become a standard talking point about the fall of the City in the national Greek consciousness. Its focal point, an alleged postern gate called the Kerkoporta has even become an expression in Greek for a small unguarded entranceway, usually to the side or at the back, through which an enemy might sneak in due to the negligence of the defenders. Doukas' account, however, is both unverifiable and incoherent. In an earlier part of his narrative, he introduces this door and situates it in the walls of the palace in the Blachernai district, as a door by which the defenders could get outside the walls and attack the Turks in sorties. He links it closely to Giustiniani's efforts to repair the ruined outer wall at that spot. He implies that it was a door in the outer wall, but he is not clear on this point. Later, in his account of the fall, he has the Turks fighting against Giustiniani notice this door, which had carelessly been left open, and they sneak fifty men inside. They climb to the top of the wall, killing the defenders and enabling their comrades below to scale the walls with ladders.[45]

However, the palace and Blachernai district were far from the Mid-Wall where the intense fighting took place. From the moment when he introduces the Kerkoporta, Doukas' sense of topography is confused. The Blachernai district did not have an outer wall, which was what Giustiniani was trying to repair in his account, so the Kerkoporta would have been useless to him, nor could it have even existed, if Doukas means that it was a postern in the outer wall. He is unclear on this point, which is another sign of his general confusion, but if it was a postern in the outer wall of the Mid-Wall sector, then his narrative still leaves unexplained how the Turks passed through the inner wall.

Kritoboulos offers a variation on this story, although it occurs in his highly fictionalized account of the final battle (which features, for example, the sultan leading the charge). He says that earlier in the siege Giustiniani had opened a postern gate in the *inner* wall so that the defenders could gain easy access to the *peribolos* and repair the outer wall; presumably he did this because, when they exited the inner wall via the regular gates they could easily be targeted by Turkish archers and artillery.[46] Be that as it may, no door matching either Doukas or Kritoboulos' description has been found nor can its existence be verified.[47] It is possible that this secret postern through which the Turks entered—whether through the outer or the inner walls—was one of the many legends that began to be told about the fall of Constantinople soon after.

With so much attention paid to the Mid-Wall sector, we are left almost entirely in the dark about the course of the final assault along the rest of the City's perimeter. It was a core part of Mehmed's plan to overwhelm the defenders by throwing everything at them at once, so that they would have to spread themselves thin. Yet while fighting certainly occurred in sectors other than the Mid-Wall, it does not appear that the Turkish forces broke through anywhere else. The defenders there must have fled only when they realized that the City had already been lost, at which point Turkish soldiers began to enter Constantinople from elsewhere, too.

Another point of attack were the harbor walls at the location where Zaganos' pontoon bridge crossed the Golden Horn. This is the only moment during the siege when we hear of this bridge being used; recall Barbaro's testimony that it had not in fact been unfurled before that day. The poet Posculo says that soldiers crossed the bridge with ladders with which to scale the harbor walls, where there was no moat and no outer wall, but they were resisted by the Venetian captain Gabriele Trevisano. Kritoboulos adds that the Turkish attack was supported by artillery fire from the Ottoman ships in the harbor.[48] This information is generally credible and consistent with what we know from Barbaro about Trevisano's posting after May 9. At any rate, it does not appear that the attackers broke through there.

An extended front was opened by the Ottoman navy, which, on the day of the assault, deployed along the entire length of the sea walls. The ships already in the harbor spread out while the fleet at Two Columns enveloped the entire City along the southern sea walls. As might be expected, it is Barbaro who provides the most information about these activities. As for the ships in the harbor, in addition to providing covering fire for Zaganos' soldiers approaching via the bridge, they also attacked the Phanarion location—Barbaro does not say exactly how—but were driven back. The rest of the fleet decided not to attack the defense flotilla by the boom and instead encircled the City on the southern side. They had ladders with them and presumably their intention was to land soldiers beneath the walls and attempt to scale them. This much is confirmed by numerous independent sources, including Ottoman texts.[49]

If the Ottoman sailors had this capability, it is curious that they had not tried it already, as those sea walls were the least well defended part of the circuit. At any rate, they did not have to fight their way up because they saw the sultan's banner flying above a tower in the City and realized that it had already fallen. Only Barbaro then recounts what they did: they landed beneath the walls, left their ships unattended, and entered the City to join in the plunder. It was precisely for that reason that some of them had approached the Jewish quarter that was situated there, on the assumption that its homes would be full of money and jewels. It is also likely that Barbaro is projecting his own Christian-Italian biases onto to the Turks at this point.[50] Unfortunately, he does not explain how they entered the City, even in the absence of resistance, which had by that point collapsed.

Superficially, it may appear that Constantinople fell because of an accidental or contingent event: the random wounding of one man, whose departure sparked a panic that gave the attackers the opening that they needed to overrun the walls. The story so far suggests that the defenses might have held, but for that twist of fate, just as they had held for almost two months at the Mid-Wall and still did everywhere else along the perimeter. This points to a narrative whose ending was governed by unpredictable, random events, with the fate of empires hanging on the wild trajectory of an arrow or the decision made by one man in distress. Some may find this view of history satisfying, others not.

Accidents like that happen all the time, but their impact on the broader course of events is not random. Probabilities of risk increase or decrease depending on structural factors. For example, are there redundancies and backup systems to fall back on in case something goes wrong? These parameters shape the potential for a fluke event to cause a rout. That probability was high because the defenders were too few to man the walls properly and were too tired, having no reserves. The defense of this crucial sector was also too dependent on one man's leadership, and it had been for months. The razor-thin margins for error or accident, the lack of redundancies, meant that the defense was operating at a high risk-level. One strike could spell the difference between success and defeat. This is not a philosophical statement about history in general but a structural analysis of the imbalance of forces between these two combatants at that specific moment. Mehmed could afford thousands of casualties; the defenders could not, and they especially could not afford *that* one. Mehmed knew this and so he did everything that he could to increase the defense's exposure to risk. He could do this by hurling everything at them all at once. Their margin of error was so thin on all sides, especially at the Mid-Wall, that this strategy paid off for him in the end.

The causality behind the fall of Constantinople, therefore, consists of the factors that created those thin margins of error. These are potentially infinite, of course, and include the state of the walls, the weather, human morale, and so on. But as historians we are interested in the human decisions that shaped those margins. A large responsibility, for instance, is born by Venice, which dragged its feet for months and did not expedite its relief fleet. The out-of-touch leadership of its octogenarian doge Francesco Foscari has been faulted on this point. If Venice had sent just two ships of well-armed knights and experienced commanders, thereby *doubling* the size of the force that Giustiniani had brought in January, it would have made a world of difference. It might well have forced Mehmed to withdraw. A solid argument has been made that the events of May 29 could easily have been avoided but for Venetian short-sightedness.[51] It is not as if Venice was incapable of doing this. In 1452, they sent Trevisan with two galleys post haste, but only to protect a trade convoy. It was largely against the spirit of the Senate's orders that Trevisan was caught up in the siege.

To be sure, Konstantinos had offended Venice back when he was despot in the Peloponnese by encroaching on some of its territories and again as basileus by imposing minor taxes on its citizens in the City. This perhaps made the Venetian Senate reluctant to help him, so some blame bounces back on him for alienating a potential ally. However, if this was the case, Venice was cutting off its nose to spite its face, for it lost far more in the fall of Constantinople than it gained by blocking the basileus' efforts to tax their taverns. Its trading position in the east was fatally compromised, to say nothing of the death of its bailo and many citizens in the siege and aftermath and the loss of their properties, amounting to a total of about half a million ducats. These losses cascaded into the failure of a major bank and turned into a general economic crisis.[52] Venice would go on to fight a series of long and costly wars against the Ottomans anyway, without the benefit of Constantinople as a base or the ability to disrupt Ottoman communications between Asia and Europe by holding the Bosporos. The Republic found itself in this situation in part because it prioritized short-term financial interests over long-term planning and failed to help potential allies decisively before they were conquered by the Ottomans. It thus found itself alone and exposed to them at the end.[53]

Another factor that increased the defenders' exposure to risk was the cannons used by Mehmed. Their importance has recently been downplayed, in fact denied, by recent scholarship. According to this argument, the cannons failed to accomplish anything and the fall of the City came down to hand-to-hand combat. At most, the cannons had a psychological impact on the defenders, although, as we have seen, even that wore off after the first volleys. Otherwise, they were a bust, a strategic failure.[54] This view is now passing into the work of other historians and is becoming mainstream.[55]

However, we must disagree with this verdict, as would all our eyewitness sources. Had the cannons not brought down so much of the outer wall, there would not have been so much close combat in the breaches on that morning in the first place. Giustiniani would not have been as exposed to random shots had the walls been intact. The demolition of the walls had, then, increased his exposure to risk by increasing the breadth and depth of combat in that sector. It was far easier for the Turks to scale or pull down improvised barricades than it was to climb ladders to the battlements, only to have their heads and arms quickly cut off. Revisionist scholars claim that "rubble was just as serious an obstacle to the assailants as the walls themselves,"[56] but if that were true then Mehmed would not have spent two months trying so hard to reduce the walls to rubble. Indeed, premodern cities would not have spent so much on walls to begin with if rubble could protect them just as well.

There is a reason why the most intense fighting was concentrated at the Mid-Wall and why Mehmed poured his manpower into that sector: it was because the walls there had been extensively damaged by cannon fire. The cardinal Isidoros explained this precisely: "Overrunning the walls was not a difficult undertaking in that sector because the whole sector had been under incessant bombardment; that is why the enemy easily broke into the City."[57] The same verdict was expressed independently by Kritoboulos, who observed that the tunnels dug by the sultan's miners "turned out in retrospect to be a pointless and wasted effort, for it was the cannons that accomplished everything."[58] The chief goal of the mines, we recall, was to demolish the walls and towers above them.

In sum, it was only because of the cannons that Mehmed was able to take the City. Without them, he would have had almost no chance of storming the walls and would have had to starve it out, as his great-grandfather Bayezid had tried to do over fifty years earlier. On the other hand, cannons did not guarantee victory. They only gave his forces a better chance by shifting the balance from siege warfare to open warfare on uneven ground, literally leveling the field a bit in his favor. That was why his forces made little progress in all the other sectors, even when they erected massive siege-towers against the outer walls. In those other locations, the cannons had not done as much damage to the walls. Without cannons, the siege would have failed, as had every attack on Constantinople by land in its thousand-year history. In the early fourteenth century, the Roman philosopher and statesman Theodoros Metochites had boasted that the walls of the City seemed immune from the passage of time, which caused everything else to wither and decay. Somehow, time itself had flowed around the Theodosian walls for a thousand years.[59] When Mehmed brought up his cannons, however, time caught up with the ancient walls.

There were many factors that gave the defenders a slight edge, such as the fact that they were holding a fortified wall and their superiority in naval warfare. But these advantages were severely compromised by their small numbers, and this is where Christian religious divisions possibly favored the Ottomans. To be sure, religious and other divisions *among the defenders themselves* did not significantly impact the course of the siege. The defense consisted of both Orthodox Romans and Catholic Latins, who had long histories of mutual suspicion, resentment, and negative stereotyping behind them. Moreover, the Romans were divided between pro- and anti-Unionists while the Italians were divided between Venetians and Genoese, who hated each other for non-religious reasons. Nevertheless, there is no evidence that these groups came to blows, refused to cooperate, or failed to contribute to their joint defense of the City. The Ottoman historian Tursun Bey was simply wrong when he claimed that the Romans became bitterly resentful when the basileus entrusted the defense of the critical area to the Latins, causing disunity and hard feelings among the defenders.[60] The Romans appear to have been genuinely grateful for all the assistance provided by the Italians, and egos, identities, and ideologies did not get in the way.

The defenders might have been terrified by the prospect and consequences of failure, but they were relatively unified and confident that they could meet each challenge as it arose. The aura of doom and gloom that our sources project onto the last days of the defense was written in part with the benefit of grim hindsight. But when we look at the broader Christian world *outside* Constantinople, we do notice a striking lack of interest in the fate of the City. To be sure, there was a general willingness to help, a loose ideological alignment with the City's survival, and "genuine" feelings of sadness when it fell. The question rather concerns the willingness to provide *effective help*. This the broader Christian world did not send, at least not in time or with the requisite urgency. Konstantinos XI had done everything within his power to enforce Union on his reluctant people, as the pope had demanded, but papal assistance was scant and most of it did not arrive in time. No help came from the Romans' supposed Orthodox brothers in the Balkans and beyond.

An eloquent witness to this failure is Georgios Sphrantzes, the basileus' advisor. He devotes four entire pages of his otherwise terse memoirs to a stinging indictment of other Christian powers whose inaction he blamed on pettiness, fear, religious bigotry, and indifference. Hungary, the Catalans, the Genoese, and the pope all demanded that Konstantinos make territorial or ideological concessions, and they did not help. Serbia sent soldiers to help the sultan but did not secretly send men or money to Constantinople as well. The Turks had even taunted the defenders by shouting to them, "See, even the Serbs are on our side!" No move to help was made by the Orthodox Wallachians, Trapezuntines, and Georgians, or, for that matter, by the basileus' brothers in the Peloponnese, his rivals in the vicious cycle of Palaiologan dynastic infighting.[61] To a great degree, this inaction was due to the sultan's astute diplomacy, which, through subtle threats and false assurances, had neutralized the basileus' efforts to find allies, perhaps even within his own extended family. Yet realistically, only the West could have sent effective help. A few boatloads of western mercenaries in full armor could have dramatically reduced the risk exposure of the defenders on May 29. That they did not come was largely due to the on-again, off-again schism of the Churches that had made most westerners deeply doubt that the Greeks would ever submit to the pope and renounce their religious traditions. And in this they were right.

9
Conquerors and Slaves

The Ottoman army was designed to do two things and do them exceedingly well: to defeat other armies in battle and enrich itself by plundering the lands that it overran, especially by taking captives for sale into slavery. It was highly practiced at methodically stripping towns and cities bare and rounding up prisoners, who were often sold off to the slave traders who accompanied most expeditions. Constantinople was the largest city that an Ottoman army had ever entered, indeed the largest that its soldiers had ever seen. Tursun Bey, the Ottoman writer, called it "greater than the space contained in the imagination."[1] Even so, they had not bitten off more than they could chew. They stripped the City down to its bones within hours and rounded up and enslaved its entire population before the day was out. The sack of Constantinople lasted for barely a day, not the three that the sultan promised in accordance with Islamic tradition. That day began with the fighting at the Mid-Wall and the collapse of the defenses, and by the end of it the City was denuded of inhabitants. They were forcibly rounded up into the slave pens of the camps outside the walls or on the ships in the harbor. Constantinople momentarily became a ghost town, an eerily quiet museum, or tomb, marking the end of a thousand years of Roman history. Its historical fate would hinge upon this fulcrum. After a period of uncertainty lasting a few years, it then embarked upon a different phase of its career, this time as the Ottoman imperial capital.

The fighting did not end at the walls. It continued sporadically for another three hours as the Ottoman soldiers fanned out through the

City and encountered resistance in the streets and in homes. Many inhabitants refused to surrender. Tursun Bey says that some fled, while others resisted. The Ottoman armies of Rumeli, Anatolia, and the fleet left a trail of bodies in their wake as they streaked through the streets.[2] Laonikos cast this more patriotically. "Many Greek men who were brave fought and died on behalf of their country rather than witness their own wives and children taken captive."[3] Even monks took up swords to defend their monasteries when the enemy approached, and they fell fighting.[4] Most monks, after all, had secular backgrounds, and some had fought before. Doukas claims that he spoke to Turkish soldiers after the war who told him that "we killed everyone we found because we were afraid that there were others behind them. If we knew that there were so few people in the City, we would have sold them all off like sheep." Not realizing that the defense force was so small, they killed another 2,000 after breaking through, fearing the presence of reserves.[5] But there was no reserve force.

The resistance continued most fiercely at the harbor walls and gates, where the defense forces had successfully repelled the attackers, who were trying to prop up ladders. Then, suddenly, their fellow Romans started streaming toward them from the inside, pursued by Turkish soldiers. According to one report, the guards at some gates refused to open them and let their own people *out* to the ships; they wanted to force them to turn back and fight the Turks. An oracle had circulated widely according to which the enemy would make it only as far as the forum of Constantine, whereupon they would meet mass resistance and be pushed back (more on this oracle in a moment). So, the guards threw the keys of the gates away to motivate the people to fight.[6] In other parts of the harbor walls, the guards were attacked from both within and outside, allowing the Turks from the fleet to set their ladders, climb up, and break down the gates from the inside to let their comrades in. Eventually, the defenders scattered and were captured piecemeal. Some rushed home only to find that their women and children had already been taken and their goods plundered. Then they too were captured.[7] More people were killed whether they resisted or not, as the Turks also wanted to terrorize the population into submission.[8] Our sources invoke the rhetoric of streets running red with rivers of blood, a literary trope of the ancient *urbs capta* motif; this was the tragedy of the "captured city" narrated in ancient histories, whose archetype was the fall of Troy.[9] Barbaro says that the slaughter lasted until midday,[10] so for about three hours.

The plundering could now begin in earnest. The work of looting and enslaving the population was efficient, swift, and thorough, and was carried out by experienced professionals. "When they went into a house, at once they raised up a flag with their emblem on it, and when other Turks saw this flag flying, they left this house alone and went in search of another house without a flag, and so they put their flags everywhere, even on the monasteries and churches."[11] These flags must have corresponded to units, not individuals, for any one soldier could gather up only so much booty and so many slaves before having to take them back to the camp. Working in teams, with men designated to watch over the mounting loot and slaves, allowed soldiers to plunder while knowing that their gains were being securely watched for them. I have found only one reference to soldiers fighting among themselves over the spoils. It is in Doukas, who, as we saw, claimed to have spoken to some soldiers who participated in the sack.[12]

Women were raped on a mass scale and continued to be raped while they were held as captives in the camp or ships. For many, that ordeal then continued into their subsequent enslavement. The *urbs capta* motif in our literary sources focuses on their plight, dwelling on the violation of nuns, married women, and virgins to heighten the reader's outrage. Respectable matrons were dragged out into the streets, while women who had lived decorously indoors were put on display and humiliated before crowds of strangers. Some authors, especially Kritoboulos, rely on ancient rhetorical templates to bring out the pathos of those moments.[13] Nor were women alone the target of sexual violence and attention. For two whole pages, Tursun Bey waxes erotic about the beauty of the young boys and girls who were captured.[14] In fact, he sees the entire conquest as an act of sexual subjugation of a reluctant "bride" (Constantinople) by her ardent "groom" (Mehmed, representing Islam generally).

Churches and monasteries were targeted for plunder, and their precious vessels and dedications were looted regardless of their religious value. Books and icons had their covers ripped off if they contained gold, silver, or gems. Christian writers saw this as a deliberate desecration of their religion,[15] but greed was the likeliest motive. The saint commemorated on that day, at least as far back as the tenth century, was the Christian martyr Theodosia. A number of people had just come out of an all-night vigil in her honor—no doubt praying for the salvation of the City—and many women, adorned and holding candles, were heading to the church where her relics were kept when a band of Turkish soldiers took them all captive.[16] A second-hand account says that the attackers "dismembered the body of saint Theodosia, which was famous for many miracles, and threw the pieces to dogs."[17] In one of his letters from Crete, the cardinal Isidoros later lamented that Saint Theodosia's festival day would henceforth be tarnished by the memory of "such a great disaster visited upon the Christians."[18]

Panic spread quickly among the inhabitants. Some rushed to the harbor, hoping for passage on Genoese or Venetian ships. They were to be disappointed. Few of those ships were anchored at the docks on the southern coast of the Golden Horn to begin with. Some embarked on the small boats that they found there, which sank under the sheer numbers of people who piled onto them.[19] Scenes of chaos and confusion ensued, while most of those who made it to the docks were captured by the sailors of the fleet anyway. Other refugees converged on the City's focal points, such as the forum of Constantine, which many in those days called the Column of the Cross (see Image 1.2). There, frantic, bedraggled, and even wounded inhabitants shared the terrible news among each other.[20] Then they moved to Hagia Sophia, where a large part of the populace was converging (see Color Plate 6). Some, perhaps even a majority, had boycotted the Great Church in protest of the mass of Union with Rome that was celebrated back in December, but it was still the most obvious assembly point for solidarity and mutual comfort. Throughout the City's history, it had served as a place of asylum, although the inhabitants knew that the Muslim invader was not bound by the rules of the Church and the emperors. Huge crowds kept pouring in regardless. Hagia Sophia, after all, could fit about 16,000 people,[21] just under half the current population of the City.

Doukas says that many flocked to Hagia Sophia due to the oracle that was mentioned above, and he discloses more of its contents. Most of the oracles that circulated in the City during the siege predicted its fall. But, tragically, this was the only one that predicted a Roman victory. The City would fall to the Turks, it said, but they would reach only as far as the forum of Constantine. At that point, an angel would descend from the heavens and bestow a sword along with a crown on a commoner standing by the column. The tide of battle would then turn, and the Romans would expel the Turks from both the Balkans and Asia Minor, as far as the borders of Persia, to a place called the Solitary Tree. Thus, many believed that if they put the forum of Constantine behind them by going to Hagia Sophia, they would be saved. Doukas uses this opportunity to push his pro-Union agenda and scold the Romans for boycotting the Great Church because it had been stained by Catholicism. Just a few days ago, he says, the Romans claimed that they would rather be ruled by Turks than by Franks.[22] There was some truth to that, perhaps, but history had played out differently: the Romans had in fact entrusted the defense of their City to the Italians and had fought side-by-side with them against the Turks.

When the attackers reached the forum of Constantine, they took down the banners of the basileus and St. Mark (Venice) that were flying there and raised up the banner of the sultan.[23] As they closed on Hagia Sophia, they were essentially tightening a circle of conquest that had begun long ago, hundreds of miles away on the frontier. It was fitting that Hagia Sophia, the symbolic center of the capital of the Roman state, was the last place to fall. The first groups arrived there about an hour after dawn.[24] They broke down the doors of the church and rushed in, grabbing captives and dragging them out. They tied them up in groups, and then went back for more while their comrades guarded the growing slave harvest. There was no resistance but much sobbing and wailing as families and friends were broken up, many never to see each other again.

Some soldiers began to plunder the church, stripping away its valuables and engaging in some gratuitous smashing.[25] Eyes on icons were gouged out, anticipating the building's conversion to Muslim use.[26] Isidoros was captured at Hagia Sophia and later lamented its "desecration," which was accompanied by Muslim prayers. The soldiers placed precious altar clothes on their dogs and horses and stomped on the Gospels and ecclesiastical books.[27] Romans who during the siege had read the history of Niketas Choniates would remember that the Catholic warriors of the Fourth Crusade had engaged in similar outrages when they took the City in 1204.[28]

Emptying out the Great Church and securing the captives must have taken up a good part of the day. The captives and plunder were then laboriously transported out of Constantinople to two destinations, the camps of the land army outside the walls and the ships of the fleet in the harbor. Everyone who was captured was led away, tied up like livestock, and the City gradually emptied out.[29] The captives would either be ransomed, which only a few could hope for at this point, as there was hardly anyone left to ransom common Romans; or they would be sold, at bargain prices, to the slave merchants who accompanied the Ottoman armies; or else they would be taken away by the soldiers to their homes to work as domestic servants or agricultural workers. This was all a realistic logistical operation. If the population of the City was ca. 35,000, it was half the size of Mehmed's army, so about one slave for every two soldiers. Some soldiers—especially the officers—would have seized more than one slave for themselves. As Tursun Bey put it, many people got rich that day, their tents full of silver and gold, boys and girls.[30] The ships of the Ottoman fleet were loaded with prisoners and booty, too.[31] Kritoboulos says that 4,000 Romans were killed overall and 50,000 taken captive. The first figure is plausible, especially if we include the fighting during the siege, but the second is probably too high.[32]

Mehmed made his triumphant entry around midday, accompanied by the officers and religious figures of his court. It was the first and only time in the City's history when its population was leaving as its new ruler was entering. The moment was more gruesome than glorious. Columns of bound prisoners were being led out, and in some places they had to pick their way around the bodies that were strewn about. A sixteenth-century Greek chronicle preserves a memory of this or plausibly reconstructs the scene: "The Charisios and Romanos Gates were congested up to the arches with dead bodies. The captives, women and children, could not be brought out but had to be lowered by rope from the walls."[33]

As he advanced through the conquered City, Mehmed gazed upon its ancient monuments, broad boulevards, churches, manors, and artwork. He longed to see Hagia Sophia, a temple that Muslims had dreamed of conquering for eight centuries. The effect was somewhat spoiled when he reached it, for he encountered there the multitudes of grieving captives being prepared for departure and heaps of plunder that his soldiers had amassed. That was the deal that he had struck with them, and he would honor it. The buildings would be his, yet some of his men were smashing and desecrating the place. Doukas tells a memorable story. The sultan came across one of his own soldiers who was breaking parts of the church. When asked why, the man replied, "For the faith." Mehmed struck him and reminded him that the buildings belonged to him now. The soldier was dragged and dumped outside half-dead.[34]

Tursun Bey, a junior official at that time, was in the sultan's retinue and wrote an evocative description of the majestic church's architecture and aesthetics. "What a dome, which claims to rival the nine spheres of the heavens . . . If you looked at the ceiling from the floor, it appeared as the starry sky, and if you looked at the floor from above, it appeared like a stormy sea" (probably due to the undulations and glistening of its marble pavement). He scrupulously avoids naming the divine figure represented in the dome. What is fascinating about his description of the Great Church is that it follows Greek rhetorical templates for ekphrasis, or vivid description, meaning that he probably consulted with educated Romans on how to praise the building.[35]

After gazing upon the complex art and images of the church, Mehmed, the *padishah* of the world, climbed up and went out onto the dome. As he gazed upon the ruin of the surrounding buildings, especially the Great Palace, he spoke verses that evoked the faded glory of past empires.

Tursun recorded them for posterity: "The spider weaves its web in the towers of Khusrow [in Persia] / The owl makes its rounds on the fortress of Afrasiyab [in Samarkand]." Mehmed ordered one of his imams to call out a Muslim prayer from the ambo of the Great Church, and then he too entered the sanctuary and performed his own prayer, thanking Allah for granting him a momentous victory.[36]

Unlike the Romans, who were losing their homeland, many Venetians and Genoese had the option of leaving, if only they could get to their ships in time. A number of Venetians were already manning the defense flotilla and so were well positioned to leave, but others had put themselves at considerable risk by agreeing to fight on the walls. Some Genoese who were involved in the fighting might have been able to simply cross over to Pera and blend in with the rest of their countrymen, as the colony was technically at peace with the sultan. Obviously, Giustiniani and his men did not have that option, and so they were among the first to reach their ships, seeing as they were the first to abandon the fighting along the walls.[37]

However, sailing out of the harbor presented several difficulties. First, the chain was still drawn across its entrance and it was anchored in Constantinople, which was now dangerous territory, and Pera. Second, many of the captains and crews of the ships had fallen in the fighting, had been taken captive, or were still missing. And third, the harbor was filling up with crowds of Romans who wanted to be taken away, "a pitiful sight: men, women, monks and nuns, wailing horribly, striking their breasts and begging to be taken onboard . . . But even if the ships had wanted to take them on, they could not do so." On the positive side, the crews of the Turkish fleet had abandoned their ships to join in sacking the City. When they returned, it was to fill their holds with captives and plunder, not to attack the formidable Italian vessels that were desperate to get away and would fight fiercely to do so, with little left to lose. The Ottomans wisely gave the galleys wide berth. Some of the residents of Pera were also caught up in the dash to escape, as they did not know what the sultan intended for them, their neutrality notwithstanding. They began to load their belongings onto their ships and crowd their own dock, in some cases dropping cargos into the depths in their haste.[38]

The Venetian commander of the harbor, Alvise Diedo, went to Pera and conferred with its podestà, Angelo Giovanni Lomellino, about whether he should try to escape or fight, and whether they would be doing either together. Barbaro was present at this meeting—he was probably a distant kinsman of Diedo—and says that Lomellino asked them to wait while he sent an envoy to the sultan to inquire whether his intentions toward the Genoese and Venetians were warlike or peaceful. According to Barbaro, this was a trap. Lomellino did not dispatch an envoy but instead locked the gates of Pera. If this account is true and not the product of Venetian bias, the podestà may have been trying to position Pera on the sultan's good side by delivering to him the leader of his Venetian enemies. After all, the Genoese colony hoped to survive and continue doing business in the Ottoman empire.

The Venetian ships in the harbor were meanwhile preparing to depart even without their commander. Eventually Diedo managed to persuade Lomellino to let him go and so the convoy set sail under his command. Before it could leave, it had to somehow break through the chain. Two brave men leaped down onto one of the wooden floats that made up the boom and laboriously chopped through it with axes. Free to leave, the Venetian fleet now decided to wait in case survivors managed to reach it. They were not, at least not yet, being pursued by the Turks, who were still preoccupied in the City. So, they waited at the Two Columns anchorage. The Venetian and Ottoman fleets had essentially swapped places.[39]

All this took place in the morning hours. Barbaro says that the fleet waited at Two Columns until midday, "to see if any of our merchants could reach the galleys, but none of them were able to do so, because they had all been captured." However, the Florentine Giacomo Tetaldi says that about 400 refugees managed to reach the Venetian fleet at anchor. Tetaldi oddly calls himself a Venetian nobleman who bravely continued to fight at the walls for two hours after the Turks entered the City. Then he went down to the shore, removed his clothes, and swam to the galleys; he was accompanied by Valentino, his twelve-year-old Russian slave. They boarded the ship of the Cretan Antonios Hyalinas. Eventually, the fleet sailed off. Following the galleys of Alvise Diedo and Girolamo Morosini, Dolfino Dolfin's galley (from Trebizond) had difficulty in raising its sails because 164 of its crew were missing, but slowly it too limped off. There followed the galley of Gabriele Trevisan, although he had been taken captive, and the four Cretan galleys under Giovanni Venier, Antonios Philomates, Antonios Hyalinas, and Sgouros. The galley of Grioni was captured by the Turks (it is unclear how), as were the ships left behind in the harbor, including the five galleys of the basileus, which were plundered.[40]

The Cretan ships reached home exactly a month later, on June 29, bringing the sad news of the fall of Constantinople. A scribe at a local monastery recorded his reaction immediately: "This caused tremendous grief and great mourning on Crete, on account of the depressing news that came. Nothing as bad as this has ever happened, nor will it ever happen again."[41] Diedo led the rest of the ships to Venice, where he died in 1466. His tombstone inscription remembered his role in that fateful drama: "When Byzantium was captured and his son, born of Britannia [his mother's name], was left behind a chained captive for the sake of the Republic, he [Diedo] led the Venetian fleet back home through the midst of the enemy."[42]

In the wake of the Venetian departure, a number of Genoese ships from Pera, between five and seven, also abandoned their now-imperiled colony, in addition to the ships of Giustiniani. This flight from Pera was so frantic and chaotic that families were separated when the Turks eventually moved their own ships to block off the escape route. Properties were dropped into the water and jewels were scattered about the quay.[43] One of the Genoese ships that made it out that day belonged to Giorgo Doria. When it reached Candia on Crete, the Venetian bureaucracy made a list of its passengers: among various Italians, there were also five Palaiologoi, two Kantakouzenoi, two Laskarides, two Kalaphates, two Komnenoi, and others, each of them "with his men."[44] For these Romans to have embarked on that ship, they must have been at Pera on the morning of the May 29, but how they arrived there, before or even while the final battle for Constantinople was being fought across the Golden Horn, is unclear. Perhaps they were men with preexisting ties to the Italian communities and possibly held Venetian or Genoese citizenship.[45]

As for Giustiniani, we can trace his journey to Chios via the inventories taken by a notary onboard his ship.[46] Giustiniani would die not long after his arrival on that island. But even as he was leaving Constantinople, he must have known that his name would forever be associated with its fall, and his erstwhile heroic role in that terrible defeat would quickly become a point of contention and debate. It still is.

Meanwhile, after enjoying the views and experiencing the raptures of Hagia Sophia, Mehmed turned to the less savory work of regime change. Tursun Bey is briefer and utterly unpoetic when he recounts Mehmed's execution of his political prisoners. The sultan, he says, returned to his camp, held a meeting of his divan (council of advisors), and decided to execute a number of high-ranking Romans and Italians, although he kept some alive and under guard.[47] These executions, however, did not take place immediately. Tursun Bey has compressed the narrative, sending Mehmed back to Edirne within a few lines, even though that departure occurred over three weeks later, on June 22.[48]

Mehmed had clearly been keeping a list of "persons of interest" who were to be arrested and brought to him to decide their fate. In the Christian sources, this part of the story focuses (briefly) on the Ottoman prince Orhan and (at far greater length) on the *megas doux* Loukas Notaras. Both knew that they would be hunted down, and Orhan, in particular, knew that he would be executed. So, he disguised himself, either as a monk or a common soldier, and tried to escape. Even if he were captured, he might still not be recognized and thereby would avoid falling into the pitiless hands of his kinsman the sultan. The sources give different versions of his fate, but it seems that he died or killed himself before Mehmed arrested him. His head was likely brought to the sultan, who wanted him dead or alive.[49] The sultan would not have forgotten that the Romans had tried to use Orhan to meddle in the Ottoman succession.

Notaras took the opposite approach. He went home to find his household staff resisting the Turks, whereupon he, his retinue, and his family were arrested, or else he surrendered at a tower where he and Orhan were holed up, while the latter tried to sneak off in disguise. The sultan knew that Notaras was the highest-ranking Roman left alive and had given special orders that he be secured; he even paid the soldiers who captured him, thereby effectively ransoming him. Notaras now belonged to the sultan, as did his family. Mehmed placed them all under his protective custody.[50]

Another person who disguised himself was the cardinal Isidoros, suspecting that he was also on the sultan's shortlist. He was, after all, the main link between Constantinople and the papacy, the source of potential reinforcements and anti-Turkish crusades. During the chaos of the City's fall, he reached Hagia Sophia on horseback but was wounded in the head by an arrow. He was captured but, in what he later regarded as a miracle, was not recognized. According to some stories, the sultan was shown a head by someone who claimed that it was the cardinal's and so interest in finding him waned. In fact, many heads must have been brought to Mehmed by soldiers who claimed to have found Konstantinos XI, Orhan, Isidoros, and others, and were seeking a bounty. The sultan likely acquired a collection of the basileus' heads, which is possibly how the stories started about the latter's death: everyone who brought a head had a different tale to tell about how the basileus had supposedly died. "As for the basileus, some janissary later brought his head to the sultan, for which he received gifts and a command."[51] That head, in particular, was valuable, even if it came in multiples.

Isidoros spent two or three days in the misery of the prison camps outside the walls, after which he was ransomed relatively cheaply. Possibly his disguise fooled his captors but not his liberators, who were able to identify and ransom him. His story was reconstructed later that year by one Henry of Sommern, who had access to more of the cardinal's letters than we do. It tells a fascinating tale of the escape of a fugitive on the run, who was relying on his ability to pass as an ethnic Roman:

> What preserved him was the rumor that he had been killed. Finally, he was ransomed for 100 ducats and conveyed to Pera; he remained hidden for eight days, as he secretly fled from house to house. But after he heard that Pera would surrender to the Turks [this actually happened immediately after the fall of Constantinople], he concluded that it would not be safe for him to stay any longer . . . he boarded a Turkish galley and stayed on board for three days; he was not recognized, as his head was covered with bandages because he had been wounded by an arrow in the face. The galley of the Turks brought him to Prousa [Bursa]; he pretended to be an impoverished man who had been captured and then ransomed, seeking to ransom his sons who were captured in Constantinople. Gradually, he attached himself firmly to a Turk, with whom he reached a place called Phocaea. Then . . . certain Genoese recognized him and inadvertently revealed his identity. He became anxious, because this region belonged to the Turks, and so he boarded a very small boat which brought him to Chios; next he went to Crete, where he was still in residence, trying to recover somewhat, as of last July 8.[52]

A Greek source, Laonikos, adds that "if the sultan had identified him . . . he would certainly have killed him and not let him get away."[53]

In the days after the fall, Mehmed executed a number of high-ranking Romans and Italians. In some cases, he may have personally ransomed them from their captors to do so. Specifically, he executed the *megas doux* Loukas Notaras, after first making him watch the execution of two of his sons. The youngest, Iakobos, was enrolled in the sultan's service staff, the serai, where he converted to Islam, likely under pressure as a child. He later escaped and joined his sister Anna in Rome. Other victims included the *megas domestikos* Andronikos Kantakouzenos (who had fought at the Romanos Gate) and his three sons; the eparch of the City Nikolaos Goudeles (who had fought at the Pege Gate); and a number of other leading Romans.[54] Mehmed was expunging the roster of high-ranking Romans in order to decapitate not only them but their entire political culture, to leave the Romans without leadership cadres of their own.

Mehmed also executed a number of the Romans' Latin allies, including the Venetian bailo Girolamo Minotto (who had defended the Blachernai palace), his son Giorgio, seven other leading Venetians, the Catalan consul Joan de la Via, and two, five, or six other Catalans.[55] The sultan allegedly intended to execute six additional Venetians, including Catarino Contarini, who had defended the Golden Gate, but in the end they bought their lives for huge sums of up to 7,000 gold coins (i.e., ca. 2,000 Venetian ducats).[56] The Genoese generally got off lightly, as Mehmed was technically not at war with their colony at Pera.

One person whom he would not forgive, however, was Maurizio Cattaneo, who had led the four ships that arrived on April 20 and humiliated the sultan's fleet. The Genoese podestà at Pera, Lomellino, says in his letter to his brother that the sultan was searching intensely for Cattaneo, who was in hiding. He was also searching for Paolo Bocchiardi. He had defended the Myriandrion Gate and was, as we saw, among the last to make it out alive from the killing grounds of the Mid-Wall as the defenses were failing. But that was not why the sultan wanted him. Bocchiardi was a partner in the concessions for the mining of alum, which, in the eyes of the Ottoman court, carried expectations of loyalty; therefore, his actions during the siege were treasonous.[57] As it happens, Bocchiardi and his brothers were taken captive but managed to ransom themselves quickly; possibly they were not recognized by their captors. While in captivity, they vowed, if released, to go on pilgrimage, but later they petitioned the pope to convert that into contributions to ransom other prisoners, which they duly paid.[58]

When they discuss the executions, our sources focus especially on Notaras. The truth behind his demise will likely never be known, enveloped as it is behind layers of polemic and fictionalization. In particular, we can never know what was said between Mehmed and Notaras (on the one hand) and between the sultan and his advisors (on the other), although our sources confidently reveal the contents of those otherwise private conversations and the political intrigues at the Ottoman court. It does not help that some of our sources are biased against Notaras, with Catholics such as Leonardo and Posculo casting him erroneously as an anti-Union ally of Gennadios. In reality, he followed the basileus' pro-Union policy, albeit with the pragmatism of a politician. Leonardo also accused Notaras of hoarding wealth and not contributing it to the common cause, the point of this charge being to suggest that he got exactly what he deserved: subjection to the sultan (i.e., slavery and death).[59]

Mehmed and Notaras did meet, possibly twice: first after the sultan's visit to Hagia Sophia on May 29, and then again on the following day, when the sultan returned to tour the empty City. "The whole place was now uninhabited, without a single person in it, or beast of burden, or bird chirping or singing, except for a few Turks who had been unable to plunder anything [the day before] on account of their low status." Soldiers were picking through the leftovers on the second day. According to some of our sources, Mehmed reassured Notaras that he would have a brilliant future in Ottoman Constantinople and would even be put in charge of the City. For his part, Notaras allegedly gave to the sultan lists of high-ranking Romans and their families, presumably so that they could be sought out and freed. Notaras was probably not ratting them out. According to these accounts, however, he did reveal that the vizier Halil Pasha had betrayed the sultan during the siege.[60]

We do not know for certain whether Halil was helping the Christians during the siege or whether Notaras betrayed him to ingratiate himself with the sultan. It is even possible that Notaras said nothing about Halil. What we do know is that Halil was arrested by the sultan, probably on the day after the fall of the City, and his property was confiscated. He was sent to Edirne, where he was executed a few days later. This *may* have been because of Notaras' revelations, but it seems unlikely. Mehmed and Halil had a tense relationship, dating back to the reign of Murad II. When Mehmed had first occupied the throne as a teenager (1444–1446), the vizier had orchestrated his deposition and the return of Murad. Halil was known to be opposed to the attack on Constantinople and was tight with the janissaries, with whom Mehmed also had a tense relationship. The sultan probably wanted to rid himself of this thorn in his side and the best time to strike was as soon as the City fell, when he was flush with victory and the janissaries were glutted with loot and slaves. If Notaras added anything to this, it was only a pretext, not the motive, desire, or opportunity.

But the budding partnership between Mehmed and Notaras soured quickly. According to a story that began to circulate within a year, right after their meeting the sultan requested one of Notaras' sons, Iakobos, who was twelve or fourteen, to be enrolled in his palace service, the serai. There are a number of ways to interpret this demand. Some Christian accounts equate it to sexual slavery to the sultan; in other words, that he wanted the boy for his harem (narrowly understood). Notaras balked at this request, and as a result he and his sons were publicly executed, on May 31 or June 1. Iakobos was then placed in the sultan's serai anyway, although, as we saw above, he later rejoined his sister Anna in Italy. In the sources that recount Notaras' execution, this story is meant to highlight Ottoman depravity and, in some cases, to cast Notaras as a kind of martyr for the faith. This more favorable account of his death was sponsored by his daughter Anna in Italy, possibly to counter the slander that was already circulating about her father. According to this version, Notaras asked for his sons to be executed first, before his eyes, to ensure that they did not convert to Islam at the last minute to save themselves.[61]

This was a highly moralized drama that we should not take at face value. Enrollment in the serai did not automatically entail servicing the sultan's sexual desires; it was also a form of hostage-taking to ensure the loyalty of Notaras and his kind. Mehmed regularly took young boys and girls from captured lands into his personal service to be trained as pages at his court. Some rose to hold important positions in his administration. However, it did mean that Notaras was not a fully free person, as the sultan had perhaps promised, with power over his own family. It was common for children who entered the serai to convert to Islam, and this was an affront to the religion and identity of the *megas doux*. So, there might have been a tragic clash of political and religious values behind the abrupt ending of this budding political relationship.[62] Nor should we entirely dismiss the sexual angle. Pages at the serai were not entirely free persons and they could be required to perform sexual services for the sultan. When the sultan toured the soldiers' camps after the City's fall, he picked out the best-looking boys and girls for himself, purchasing them from their captors.[63] It would be naïve to believe that such power was exercised innocently. These children may or may not have been required to service him sexually, but it was an ambiguity that Notaras was unwilling to accept.

A Wallachian prince who was taken into the sultan's serai in later years tried to murder Mehmed for attempting to assault him sexually.[64] Another who also tried to kill the sultan, possibly for the same reason, was a son of Georgios Sphrantzes, the basileus' advisor. Sphrantzes himself was captured and ransomed (he does not say by whom), and made his way to the Peloponnese, although his wife and children remained in captivity. At first, they belonged to "elderly and good Turks," but then they were sold to Ilyas Bey, the chief of the sultan's stables, who was "making good money from them," possibly through sex work. "As the beauty and charms of my children could not be kept secret," they were purchased by the sultan for his own use, leaving the mother alone with one daughter. But, in December 1453, the sultan personally executed Sphrantzes' beloved son Ioannes, who was fourteen, on the grounds that the child had attempted to kill him.[65]

Even if there was a kernel of truth behind the salacious rumors spread by the Christian sources, there was certainly more going on in the background of Notaras' execution than a tragedy about sexual tyranny. Mehmed did not turn from reconciliation to wrath only because Notaras refused to surrender his son to his pleasure, although that may have been part of the story. Kritoboulos points to a general shakeup in the upper echelons of the Ottoman regime, reflecting an initial uncertainty about what to do with Constantinople. He says that Mehmed's initial plan was to entrust post-conquest Constantinople to a mostly Roman leadership, with Notaras at the head of the reconstruction. But he was persuaded to abandon that plan by unnamed courtiers who believed that the Romans were unreliable. It was easy to suspect, on May 30, that if the Romans rebelled and brought the Latins back, Constantinople would have to be conquered all over again. Also, existing Ottoman elites were bound to want to profit from the new opportunities and not relinquish them to members of a conquered nation.

According to Kritoboulos, Mehmed yielded to the lobbying of his advisors and executed the top tiers of the Roman political class. This does not make him look like a strong ruler, which was Kritoboulos' panegyrical purpose, but it does deflect responsibility for the killings away from him, which is what he probably intended through this lame explanation. Yet he adds that Mehmed later turned against his Muslim advisors, executing, or exiling some of them, although we do not know why. Possibly this group included his long-time ally, Zaganos Pasha, who we know fell into disfavor after the siege. Unfortunately, our sources for these policy changes and court intrigues are poor, but the overall picture that they paint is plausible. Mehmed was a young ruler who was just finding his feet and did not know whom to trust among the ambitious men surrounding him. Frequent purges are one way for insecure rulers to cope with complexity. Eventually, Mehmed appointed Karışdıran Süleyman Bey to govern the City and inaugurate its Ottoman phase.[66]

One group did not fit neatly into the distinction between conquerors and slaves: the Genoese of Pera. Their neutrality during the siege could easily be exposed as a fiction. In his victory letter to the Mamluk sultan of Egypt, Mehmed spoke quite clearly about the fact that Genoese of Pera had been found among the dead and that this violated their ostensible neutrality.[67] So, he could now choose whether or not to respect that fiction. Many Genoese who had fought for Constantinople were missing, presumed dead or captured, including the nephew of the podestà Angelo Giovanni Lomellino. This uncertainty and precarity led many residents of Pera to flee on the May 29, before the Turkish fleet could block them in. Zaganos Pasha, who had overseen this sector of the assault, moved his forces to surround Pera and prevent anyone from leaving. He ordered the townspeople to sit tight and not make rash moves.[68]

Under such circumstances, the leadership of Pera decided to surrender and fall on the sultan's mercy. As his ambassador to the sultan, Lomellino sent the aristocrat Babilano Pallavicino, who was accompanied by Marchisio di Franci and an interpreter, the notorious Nicolò Pagliuzzo.

"Full of terror," they passed through Zaganos' guards, delivered the keys of their gates, and pledged obedience. A number of embassies must have been exchanged before the two sides came to an agreement.[69] In an affidavit submitted many years later, in 1467, Pallavicino claimed that he had to spend 1,346 gold coins of his own money in order to bribe the sultan's officers to guarantee the safety of Pera, although in fact this money played a small role in the resolution of the standoff. However, he was asking to be reimbursed for part of it, which is why he highlighted its importance. Accordingly, he stressed the terrors and "perils to my life" of the journey to the sultan's camp, "when all around them there were the sounds of murder and fear."[70] Presumably the group had to pass by or through the vast slave camps where the Romans were being held.

In the end, Pera did receive assurances of safety in the form of an *aman-name*, a unilateral declaration of Pera's security by the sultan, an original copy of which exists in the British Museum. It was issued in demotic Greek, which was an official language of the Ottoman chancery and still a widely used lingua franca in the territories of the former east Roman empire. It was, after all, the main or only language in which Turks and Genoese could communicate, as many of them were bilingual with Greek, seeing as they lived, and many were raised, in majority Roman lands. The text says that Genoese representatives came to the sultan and, bowing before him, asked to be allowed to live as they had before and retain their walls, property, families, and freedom of movement and trade. They recognized him as their lord and would pay the tax levied by the Ottomans on their Christian subjects, but their children would never be drafted into the janissary corps. They would worship freely but would not ring church bells. However, they would no longer be governed by a podestà dispatched from Genoa but by a local "chief elder," a *protogeros*, chosen locally and watched over by a servant of the sultan. The *protogeros*, a Greek term, was an Ottoman institution, referring to a person who was expected to be loyal to the sultan and appointed to govern his own people in a particular locale on the sultan's behalf. Mehmed swore to uphold these terms and put them in writing, on June 1. Zaganos Pasha signed this pledge, too, in Arabic. Lomellino would be the last podestà of Pera, but he survived the transition, unlike his Venetian and Catalan counterparts.[71]

Zaganos Pasha entered Pera and installed the governor, Karaca, designated by Mehmed.[72] As the Genoese had voluntarily surrendered, they were given the concession of choosing their own *protogeros* (something that, as we will see, was not allowed to the Romans of Constantinople). At the same time, however, agents of the sultan began to comb Pera for wanted men. We infer this from the fact that Isidoros, who had been ransomed and moved to Pera, had to go into hiding and move from house to house before he left the region for good. In apparent contravention of the *aman-name*, Pera was ordered to tear down long stretches of its land walls to make future rebellions impossible, especially if it received reinforcements from the West. Mehmed preferred that the city not have walls at all than that he have its keys. The harbor walls were left intact, but the city's cannons were confiscated. On June 2, Mehmed personally visited Pera and commissioned an inventory of the properties of all who had fled. If they returned within three months, they could claim it, otherwise it would be confiscated to his treasury. Couriers were sent out, chiefly to Chios, to give notice of this order, and a number did return, such as the notary who had accompanied Giustiniani on his final voyage to Chios.[73]

The Genoese landed on their feet, at least compared to their former neighbors, the Romans. Even the captains of the ships that arrived on April 20 and broke through the blockade—Battista di Felizzano and Domenico di Novara—got to go home and continue trading in the east in later years.[74] There were some losses, however. The sultan took away with him the podestà's nephew Imperiale, as a hostage and page at his court, and would not allow him to be ransomed. Imperiale had fought on the Roman side. Lomellino was pained by this loss, and for good reason. Later that summer, news arrived in Italy that Imperiale had converted to Islam and had received a post at the sultan's court, but the report of his conversion might be an unreliable inference made at a time when a great deal of confusion prevailed about the fate of captives.[75] The sultan also took away for his "pleasure" the daughters of Barnaba

Centurione, the Genoese merchant whose ship Mehmed had sunk with his mortar experiments in the harbor during the siege. It is not clear why the girls were taken away or on what legal pretext.[76]

This raises the question of who was likely to be ransomed and freed in the aftermath of the fall of Constantinople, and who was not. Wealthy Latins had an overwhelming advantage, especially if they could access funds or loans via the Genoese of Pera. This appears to be how Isidoros was ransomed: although he was an ethnic Roman, as a cardinal he was also the highest-ranking representative of the Catholic Church in the region. His friend, Leonardo of Chios, the archbishop of Mytilene, was also captured, bound, beaten, and later ransomed, although again we do not know exactly how. This process—which reduced them to chattel—was not something that they wanted to talk about in detail afterward. It was easier to talk about the captivity itself than the ransom, because the latter created uncomfortable relationships of dependence on the Christians who had "bought" them back from captivity.

Leonardo later accused two alleged partisans of Gennadios Scholarios, the Orthodox enemy of Church Union whom Mehmed subsequently appointed to be patriarch of Constantinople, of harassing him while he was in captivity. After his ransom, Leonardo aided in the effort to liberate other Catholic priests and monks from captivity, but he also took the opportunity to buy up their books, which the Turks had plundered when they sacked a Franciscan monastery in Constantinople and were now selling at low prices. Their owners, now liberated, were demanding the books back and sought an injunction against Leonardo from the pope, who had banned such practices. Meanwhile, Leonardo had made it back to Chios.[77] He might have also purchased Greek books, which the Turks had plundered in huge quantities, piling them onto carts and selling them off at discount prices. "For a single coin you could buy ten books, Aristotle, Plato, the theologians, and anything else at all."[78]

The dispersal of Constantinople's books is illustrated by a manuscript of the ancient mathematician Pappos. It contains a note which recounts the book's tale:

> This book came from poor Constantinople. After its fall, it was purchased by a man named Zonaras who was from the wretched island of Lesbos, which has suffered so much, and he practiced the profession of *tabellio* [notary] for quite a few years, until that island too fell, at which time it [the book] fell into the hands of Sophianos, who was from Rome. After him, it quite unexpectedly fell into my hands. I am determined that it not leave my hands henceforth.[79]

A copy of Prokopios' *Wars*, formerly kept in Constantinople, was bought by Alexios Sphrantzes, the bishop of Sebastopolis. In January 1455, he lent it to one Demetrios Leontares, who read it in Edirne as he awaited the release of his wife from captivity. Leontares was the scion of a prominent political and military east Roman family, but he was now a refugee. He recorded the book's fate in a comment that he wrote in the margin as he read, noting that it "had come from the wretched megalopolis."[80] Unfortunately, he did not record his reactions to the text itself, which described how a Roman emperor of Constantinople had long ago fought off the Persians and reconquered North Africa.

The Turks did not set fires in 1453, unlike the Latins in 1203 and 1204, who had set several fires to gain a tactical advantage in the fighting, only to see the blazes consume large parts of Constantinople.[81] So, it is unlikely that many books were destroyed in 1453, at least not unique copies, although the humanist Lauro Quirini on Crete claimed that Isidoros had told him that 120,000 volumes were destroyed.[82] Surely that was an exaggeration, if not an invention, as no refugee in flight could have known the truth. Many western humanists were left with the impression that several Greek classics that had not yet reached Italy were lost forever. Typically, they cared more about the potential loss to their own intellectual interests than to Greek intellectual life.[83] Still, we cannot discount the possibility that rare books were irretrievably lost in the violence of that day and in what followed. A complete text of the historian Diodoros of Sicily was allegedly seen in the palace library in 1453, although only parts of his work survive today.[84]

Captive Latins could hope for help from overseas. Venice sent envoys to the sultan to negotiate on behalf of its citizens. To accompany the envoy who was sent to Edirne right after the City's fall, the Senate chose the Greek scholar Nikolaos Sekoundinos. He was one of the most interesting men of the fifteenth century. We may say a few words about him here because he shaped perceptions of the City's conquest in a lasting way, especially in the West. Sekoundinos was an ethnic Greek from Chalkis on the island of Euboia, which was under Venetian rule.[85] Born in 1402, he and his wife and children were captured by the Turks in the fall of Thessalonike in 1430 (that city had been under Venetian rule for seven years by that time). He was held hostage for thirteen months, which possibly means that he was not fully enslaved and that the Republic redeemed him. In addition to his other qualities, this experience made him an excellent choice to negotiate for the redemption of captives after 1453.

Sekoundinos served Venice in various postings, also some of the popes. He was fluent in Italian, Latin, and Greek, and had an excellent humanistic education. On April 4, 1436, he met Kyriacus of Ancona at Chalkis and wrote some Homeric verses in the latter's notebook, with a dated personalized dedication to his "friend" Kyriacus. In 1438–1439, Sekoundinos worked as a chief translator at the Council of Ferrara-Florence. He was praised and trusted by both sides for his skill and impartiality, no small feat, especially when he had to provide rapid simultaneous translation of heated arguments. At that gathering, he had the opportunity to work with pope Eugenius and Ioannes VIII Palaiologos, in addition to leading humanists and philosophers, such as Leonardo Bruni (Florence's chancellor), Bessarion, Plethon, and Scholarios. He subsequently stayed in contact with some of them, especially Bessarion and Plethon.

In July 1453, Sekoundinos was ordered to accompany the patrician Venetian Bartolomeo Marcello to the court of Mehmed II and negotiate over the release of his captives. Sekoundinos likely reached Edirne via Ainos, on the coast of Thrace, but returned to Italy via Constantinople, which gave him the opportunity to see the site of the battle. Upon his return, he reported to Venice, the pope, and the Aragonese king, Alfonso V the Magnanimous, at Naples, all in late 1453 and early 1454. These reports, especially his speech to Alfonso, which was published and widely disseminated, formed the basis of many subsequent reactions to the fall of Constantinople and its aftermath. It was he, for example, who began to publicize the "martyric" account of Notaras' death, which also made it across the Aegean and into the account of the fall written in Greek by Doukas on the island of Mytilene. Sekoundinos had not only first-hand experience of Turkish captivity, but he actually met Mehmed, whose habits and dispositions he describes in detail.[86]

In 1464, Sekoundinos wrote his most influential work, a treatise on *The Origin of the Ottoman Family, namely the Turks*, dedicating it to the bishop of Siena, Enea Silvio Piccolomini, who later, as pope Pius II (1458–1464), tried to launch a major crusading expedition against the Turks. For a century or more, this treatise was a popular source of information in the West about Ottoman origins and objectives; in 1556, it was published together with Laonikos Chalkokondyles' history.[87]

Sekoundinos' life is an extreme version of the imbrication of Greek, Italian, and Turkish lives in the fifteenth century. History was not finished with him yet. In 1460, he sent his family by ship to Crete, where he was about to take up a new post, but the ship sank soon after leaving Venice's harbor. His pregnant wife drowned (presumably a second wife) along with two of their sons, a daughter, and all their property. He still had one son and five other daughters, and the Senate made provision to compensate them financially. In the year after this tragedy, he was sent back to negotiate with the sultan, but the latter was on campaign in Asia Minor, so Sekoundinos had to follow him there. As a result, he was present at the siege and capture of Trebizond, about which he again briefed the Senate on his return to Venice.

Thanks to the efforts of Marcello, Sekoundinos, and others, many noble Venetians were ransomed and had returned home within a year, having paid between 800 and 2,000 ducats for the wealthiest among them. The typical ransom was much smaller.[88] But others had to wait longer for the Republic to find them and negotiate a ransom. The poet Posculo, who was originally from Brescia, spent a year in captivity, as the war caught him in his studies in Constantinople: "I became barbarian war plunder." His ransom was processed by the deputy bailo of the

Venetians in the City, Battista Gritti, to whom he assigns heroic actions during the siege, actions that are not attested elsewhere. He then resided at Pera for a while, writing a book on ancient prophesies that foretold the fall of Constantinople.[89] Beyond ransoming prisoners, the Republic of Venice provided financial support to the families of men who had died during the war, including the crew of Giacomo Cocco, whose ship sank in the Golden Horn in the night attack of April 28. The Republic even set up a process for reimbursing citizens who had incurred financial losses during the siege, for example by paying their crews or losing cargos.[90]

In comparison to the Italian captives, the Romans were in a much more difficult situation, especially non-elite Romans who did not enjoy foreign citizenship. As the entire population of the City had been enslaved and their property forfeit to the enemy soldiers or the sultan, there was no one left in the vicinity to ransom them, unless they happened to have wealthy Genoese friends at Galatas. Paradoxically, the largest number of captured Romans were freed by the sultan himself. According to Islamic tradition, he was entitled to one-fifth of the movable property plundered by his soldiers during the sack of a city, which included slaves. After his first tour of Constantinople, Mehmed then went to his soldiers' camps to inspect the slaves. The scene was a stark combination of exultant partying on the one side and abject misery on the other. It was a scene that had played out in other cities the Turks had conquered, with captives crying out in the camp for their parents, wives, and husbands. After picking out the best-looking boys and girls for himself, the sultan sent forty handsome lads and pretty girls as a gift to the Mamluk sultan of Egypt and resettled the rest along the shoreline of the City's harbor.[91] For them, this was a dizzying change of fortune: forced out of their homes in one part of the City on one day, enslaved and then set free, they were now resettled, in a matter of days, in another part of their own City where they were forced to mix with foreign people, many of them "infidels" brought in by the sultan.

The anti-Union Church official Theodoros Agallianos called the new City a "tower of Babel" where no one knew his neighbor anymore.

Some people returned from captivity with their own wives, some with the wives of others, and some were utterly alone. Families were broken up and spouses lost, with survivors eventually forming new unions only to have husbands and wives show up unexpectedly and throw their new lives back into chaos. The rules of marriage had been destroyed in the violent upheaval, and Agallianos found it impossible to restore order according to Church rules.[92]

To help these new Constantinopolitans restart their lives as his subjects in the conquered city, the sultan granted them homes—the infrastructure of the City belonged to him now—along with tax exemptions for a fixed number of years. He offered similar terms to all captives who managed to ransom themselves and wanted to settle in the City. He also gave manors, gardens, and churches to his officials to incentivize them to move there.[93] Those who took him up on this generous offer presumably brought their newly acquired slaves with them, the former residents of Constantinople, who now found themselves living in different homes in their native city. Thus, the first new Constantinopolitans after the great "reset" of May 29 consisted in part of repurposed former Constantinopolitans.

The Roman community of Constantinople would have its own chief official, a *protogeros* (or "chief elder"), as would the Genoese at Pera. Presumably, the original plan was for Notaras to serve this function, but it now fell to one Laskaris Kanabes, an ethnic Roman from the Ottoman empire, who was almost certainly from the sultan's entourage.[94] He and Michael Kantakouzenos (the son of Ioannes Palaiologos Kantakouzenos, who had died fighting at the side of Konstantinos XI) apparently helped to liberate captive Venetians and so were granted free and safe passage throughout all Venetian territories—an extraordinary concession—via a letter written by the vice-bailo of the Venetian community in Constantinople. This was a rare case of Romans helping Italians, albeit these were Romans with pull at the Ottoman court.[95] The *protogeros* would be the leading official of the Roman community of Constantinople, presumably subordinate to the governor of the City as a whole, a position that (as we saw) was assigned to Karışdıran Süleyman

Bey. However, Kanabes seems to have also been the last *protogeros* of Constantinople, as his political role eventually passed to the patriarch of the City, once Mehmed decided to appoint one (see below).

As for the majority of the Roman captives, their fate was sealed when Mehmed disbanded his army and fleet only a few days after the sack of the City, allowing his soldiers to return to their homes across the Ottoman empire with their captives in tow; or else they sold them to slave merchants who dispersed them through their networks across the Mediterranean and beyond. Many families were broken up, never to see each other again, like that of Georgios Sphrantzes, and few managed to return to their native land. Noting this tragedy, Leonardo does not hesitate to score more points against the Greeks: "You did not want the Latins, so now you got the Turks."[96]

Only a small number of Romans could have been ransomed in the few days between their capture and the army's dispersal. To be sure, some might have hidden themselves somewhere in Constantinople and tried to ride out the storm without being detected, although none are attested. Some Venetian merchants tried that, but they were found and enslaved. We are told of a certain citizen of Perugia who hid for a number of days "in a cavern" and managed to escape.[97] But even if some Romans had done this—and they would have known the best hiding-places—it is hard to see how they could have gone into the army camps during those days to ransom their family members and friends, assuming they even had the funds. Some Romans, as we saw, moved to Pera before the end of the siege from where they escaped to Crete on the Genoese ships, although others may have stayed behind there to ransom their kin, hiding among the Genoese.[98]

Most enslaved Romans simply had to endure their lot. They were taken to foreign lands and set to whatever work suited their new owners. Few would ever be liberated, and even that was only after long periods of anguish, uncertainty, and despair. Some managed to be liberated after a few weeks. The scholar Michael Apostoles was sent from the slave camps to the hold of a ship sailing to the Black Sea, where he spent 37 days in chains.[99] He was liberated—he does not say how—and sought refuge on

Crete, where he eked out a living by copying books on commission from Italian patrons, including the cardinal Bessarion. He signed some of his books as "Michael Apostolios, a Constantinopolitan, captured in war by the Huns [Turks], living in poverty, copied this book for money."[100]

A few wealthy Romans had Latin friends who searched for them. The Italian humanist Francesco Filelfo had studied in Constantinople and had married Theodora, the daughter of his Greek teacher, Ioannes Chrysoloras. Even though Theodora had died before 1453, Filelfo made an effort to locate her mother and sisters and obtain their release from slavery. They seem to have passed into the ownership of a Jewish family. Filelfo even wrote a flattering letter to the sultan on the matter, offering to pay the women's ransom, and he also appealed to other monied westerners to ransom captive Greeks.[101] Such appeals tapped into the guilt felt by western Europeans for not doing enough to save one of the greatest cities in Christendom. But some Italians had more pragmatic reasons for seeking to liberate captured Romans. The banks in Genoa and Venice where the Notaras family had parked its huge fortune needed to find their heirs to continue making their interest payments and thus discharge their fiduciary obligations. In addition, the Notaras family had acquired both Venetian and Genoese citizenship, entitling them to special attention. Thus, with the support of their respective Republics, the banks used the earnings of the accounts to initiate a process of finding and liberating Notaras' children, which entailed diplomacy with the sultan.[102] The same was done with the funds of Andronikos Koumouses, the basileus' treasurer, also a Venetian citizen. His executors in Venice requested permission to use the funds to liberate his heirs (three sons), to the tune of 700 ducats.[103]

Such initiatives, of course, benefited only elite Romans. For the majority of people, the effort to locate and redeem their enslaved family and friends was much more difficult. Churches traditionally played a major role in collecting funds for this purpose. They had likely stepped up their efforts in this grim age of mass slave-raiding and slave-trading that plagued the Aegean world after the Roman state had been carved up among predatory Latin and Turkish principalities. The touching figure of a distressed father, husband, or son going around from town to town and begging for help to ransom his children, wife, or parents was familiar, and explains why Isidoros chose to act that way as he escaped from Pera to Crete. Some people had barely enough resources to travel to Italy to beg for funds, but not enough to ransom relatives on their own.[104] Such itinerant beggars often secured documents called *aichmalotika* (a term formed from the Greek word for captivity). These were provided by Church officials who stated that the bearer was a relative of someone in captivity and should be helped by pious Christians. These documents enhanced their prospects of success and limited the scope for scammers and grifters.[105]

One refugee from Constantinople was Demetrios Leontares, scion of a leading Roman political family, who had been trained as a scribe. We do not know where he was during the siege. Immediately after, he was trying to obtain the release of his wife, Euphrosyne, who had been captured and enslaved in the fall. In early 1455, Leontares was in Edirne because Euphrosyne was being held there. Euphrosyne was the daughter of the City's last governor, Demetrios Palaiologos Metochites, so it is likely that she was held by the sultan as a political prisoner. We met Leontares earlier in this chapter, as a reader of a copy of Prokopios' *Wars*. On March 30, 1455, he wrote a comment in another book, one containing a Psalm commentary, that his wife had died and was buried at Edirne only two weeks after her release there (see Image 9.1). Leontares pitied his evil fate and entrusted himself to God. He would eventually emigrate to the West, begging for assistance and working as a copyist of Greek works.[106]

Networks of influential Romans outside Constantinople, or Orthodox elites more broadly, tried to ransom captives on the grounds of kinship, ethnicity, shared religion, or just compassion. Some Roman merchants of Constantinople happened to be abroad at the time of the siege, and they could ransom their families when they heard the news and returned.[107] There were also Roman officials in the service of the sultan who became contact points for those seeking to find and liberate their relatives. One such person was Nikolaos Isidoros, an ethnic Roman who had served the sultan as an administrator for some time and possibly

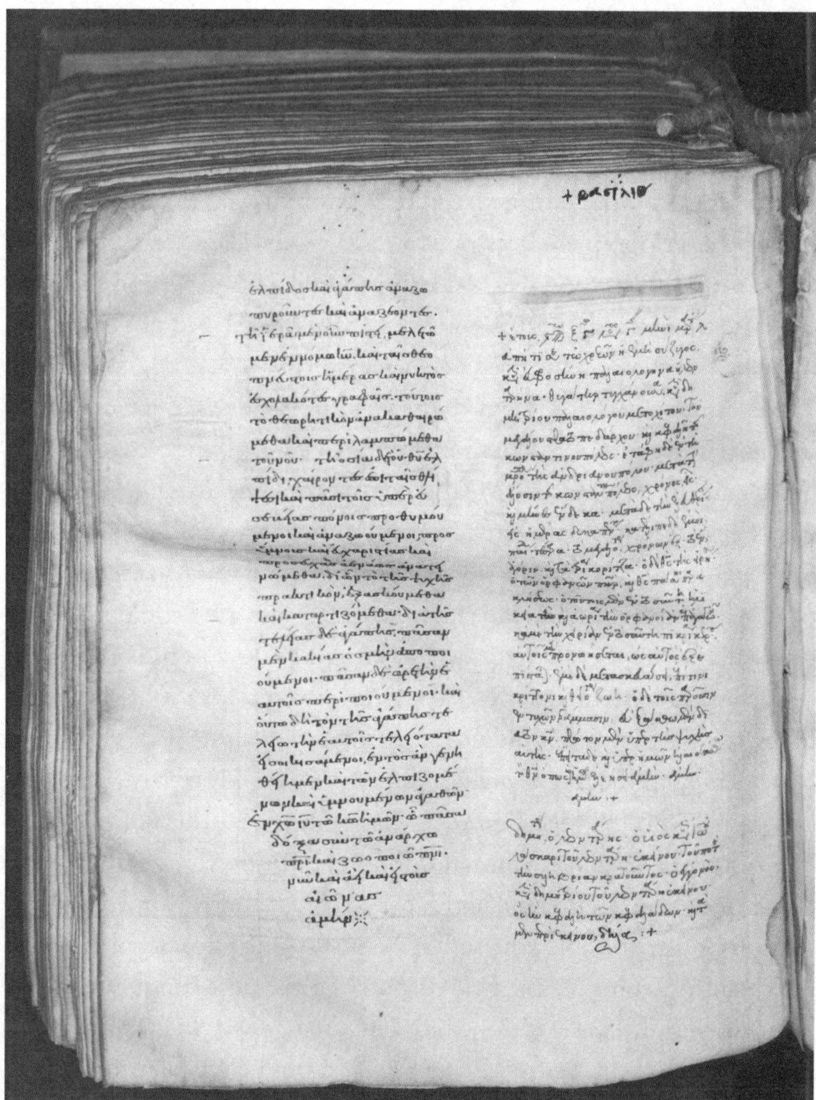

Image 9.1 Personal notice written at Edirne by the scribe Demetrios Leontares in the manuscript Vossianus graecus 42, f. 312v, recording the death of his wife soon after her release from captivity. Source: Rijksuniversiteit Bibliotheek, Leiden.

had never lived in a Roman-run state. He was one of the sultan's closest confidants and had pull and access to resources. Letters survive that were addressed to him by co-religionists hoping that he would intervene on behalf of their relatives.[108]

Yet captives who returned could face suspicion. Dionysios, a native of the Peloponnese, was put forth as a candidate for patriarch of Constantinople in 1466. He was required to lift his robes and show his genitals to an ecclesiastical assembly to prove that he had not converted to Islam and been circumcised while in captivity.[109]

We cannot assess how many of the victims of May 29 were ransomed. It is likely that most of the population of the City was scattered across the Ottoman empire, the Mediterranean, and the Middle East. The City's history had essentially paused and had to be reset. For a few days, it stood empty, apart from the sultan's garrisons, and was regarded as "deserted, lying there dead, stripped naked, mute, distorted and ugly."[110] Its repopulation by the sultan proved to be a difficult and prolonged process. As we saw, Mehmed offered generous incentives for subjects willing to resettle there, but this did not work out as well as he had hoped, and so he turned to the forcible relocation of people, only to have them slip away and return to their homes, or die in new outbreaks of plague.[111] The history of Ottoman Constantinople got off to a rocky start.

Mehmed took a different approach to the Orthodox Roman population of Constantinople when he appointed Gennadios Scholarios, the opponent of Union, as the first patriarch of the post-conquest city. As Gennadios II, he was enthroned on January 6, 1454. He had managed to avoid capture on the first day of the sack, but he was captured on the following and taken to Edirne.[112] A controversial figure, embattled and defensive, he described how he ascended to the patriarchate in a sermon that also tried to explain why he was stepping down from it just over a year later. After his capture, he says, while others were being ransomed, he was allowed to languish, although he was of no real use to his captors. They did not mistreat him, but he feared that his friends had abandoned him to his fate. In fact, they were lobbying the sultan on his behalf, saying that he would make an excellent Church leader. Reading between the lines, this means that he would be pro-Ottoman. Eventually, he was escorted back to the City, "which was in a more decrepit state that I could describe," and placed in charge of a monastery that had been thoroughly sacked. Without access to funds, he was expected to ransom its monks while dealing with the "barbarians" who kept demanding bribes and praising their own virtues to the skies, by which they signaled that everyone should obey them.[113] In his mind, this was a punishment sent by God for the chastisement and edification of the souls of Christians. It was fully merited, especially by those who had flirted with Union. But Gennadios also intimates that some were blaming *him* for the fall, for fostering opposition to the basileus before the siege.[114]

Gennadios was sweeping many uncomfortable facts under the rug. Chief among them was the extent to which his appointment as patriarch was approved by Mehmed because Gennadios' own anti-Latin politics served Ottoman strategic interests. Just a year earlier, the alliance of a nominally pro-Union basileus with a handful of Venetians and Genoese had almost delivered a stinging defeat to the sultan. Mehmed now had an interest in driving a wedge between the City and the West. He therefore fostered a long-standing alliance of anti-Latin Orthodoxy, represented by Gennadios, and Ottoman paternalism. The patriarchs would henceforth be appointed and sometimes hand-picked by the sultans, making their election by the Church often a formality. This was, in effect, a continuation of east Roman practice, when the basileus had often selected the patriarch.

This alliance is obfuscated by Gennadios in his sermon. The "friends" who rescued him—in fact, who lobbied Mehmed to appoint him as patriarch—were a consortium of Roman Orthodox businessmen and court officials, which included none other than Ioannes Basilikos and Thomas Pyropoulos. These two men had been condemned by the basileus for their apparently treasonous dealings with the sultan right before the siege and their homes had been demolished. They had removed to Pera and, after the fall of Constantinople, swooped in to assume the leadership of the Roman community, leaning on their connections at the court. Another backer of Gennadios—in fact, it would more accurate to call him the new patriarch's patron—was the sultan's agent, Nikolaos Isidoros.[115] Gennadios had been in close contact with these men before the siege and possibly, through them, with the Ottoman court too. Gennadios also turned for support to the anti-Union Synaxis, entrenching it in power in the Church of Constantinople. This Ottoman-sponsored patriarchate backed anti-Union agitation among the Orthodox, and not only those who lived in the Ottoman empire. Its propaganda reached Venetian Crete, rupturing relations between the Latin colonial states and their Orthodox subjects. Henceforth, and for centuries to come, the patriarchate was an instrument of Ottoman policy and its Orthodox monied interests, both anti-Latin. This alliance was, if not forged, then at least consolidated by the revolution that was the fall of Constantinople.[116]

10

Aftermath and Legacy

Initial reports of the fall of Constantinople were brought to the Aegean islands by survivors who managed to flee on the ships that got away on May 29. They knew only *that* the City had fallen and nothing about what happened later that fateful day. The imagination inevitably filled in the gaps, resulting in a great deal of exaggeration, confusion, outright fiction, and fears presented as facts—although many of those fears did in fact come to pass. As the news traveled along with the survivors, groans and lamentations for the fallen City rippled out throughout the islands, the rest of Romanía, and then reached Italy.[1] The ships sent by Venice and the pope to assist the City learned of the City's fall in the Aegean, at Euboia (Negroponte) and Chios respectively. Eventually, additional information began to arrive with the first ransomed captives, such as Isidoros on Crete and Leonardo on Chios. Official reports began to be drafted and letters were sent to interested western rulers, even as Mehmed announced his glorious victory to fellow Muslim rulers. Many of the sources that we rely on for the events of the siege were written during the next two months. But in Italy confusion reigned throughout the summer, as contradictory reports could be not reconciled and horrific atrocities could neither be confirmed nor ruled out.[2]

The experience of first hearing the news provided authors of laments for the fall of Constantinople with a powerfully dramatic framing device. The genre of the lament proliferated in the decades and centuries to come, with some taking the form of elaborate compositions that followed the rules of classical rhetoric while others were more vernacular poems that echoed the ritual laments of the Greek funerary tradition. One of the most famous specimens, the *Anakalema*, movingly evokes the suffering of the captives who were dispersed across the Ottoman empire:

> Now they will be taken to Turkey to be sold as slaves,
> and scattered from East to West
> naked and barefoot, beaten, hungry,
> to tend oxen, sheep, horses, and buffaloes,
> little ducks, geese, and suchlike . . .
> and in the evening they will stay with Muslims,
> who will defile them, and they will give birth to bastards,
> who will become Muslims and bloodthirsty dogs
> and make war on Christians and annihilate them!
> Sky, don't endure this, and earth, don't bear it!

The lament takes the form of a conversation between a boat coming from the fallen City bearing the grim news and a galley that it encounters off the island of Tenedos, an encounter that was historical as survivors fled (minus the talking boats, of course).[3]

Laments were written in other languages, too, including Latin, Italian, Armenian, and Hebrew (on Venetian Crete).[4] Those in Greek channeled a Roman national sentiment, mourning as they did the loss of the Roman people's principle and symbolic homeland. Prophecies began to circulate during the period of Ottoman rule that the Romans would one day reclaim it and drive the Turks out. As we have seen, these had begun to circulate already before the City's fall, anticipating its conquest by the enemy. A folklore developed around the figure of Konstantinos XI Palaiologos, as he passed into legend. In the *Anakalema*, he is called "the glory of the Romans." Some Romans viewed him as a tragic martyr, whereas others claimed that he had not died on that fateful day but rather turned to marble and that he would return one day to liberate his City. This repurposed the common idea, shared across cultures, of the Sleeping King who is waiting to save his people.[5] One way of coping with loss was to pretend that the battle for the City had merely paused and would resume again in the future. That idea died only in 1922, but it died then for good.[6]

By contrast, many westerners made sense of the disaster, even normalized the loss, by arguing that the Greeks deserved it because of their "disobedience" to the pope and their general moral failings. A number of our eyewitness sources made that argument, including Leonardo, a philosophically educated bishop, and Posculo, a young student of the classics.

There were other ways of symbolically "canceling" the fall of the City. Soon after the event itself, the Valencian Johannot Martorell (d. 1468) wrote a novel in Catalan, *Tirant lo Blanch* (*Tirant the White*), whose protagonist, a brave knight, is summoned to Constantinople by the emperor to defend it against the Turks. He is given the rank of *megas doux* (the office that Notaras held in reality) and manages to save the City, accomplishing what Giustiniani failed to do. He thereby rewrote history, at least in this early experiment in speculative fiction.[7]

The conquest of Constantinople changed the conqueror, too, in part by upgrading the standing of the Ottoman state in the eyes of both Muslims and Christians. Romanía had blocked the expansion of Islam into Europe for six centuries, making Constantinople the apple in the eye of Muslim imperialism. The Prophet himself had supposedly proclaimed that his people would conquer it. However, again and again that dream had been indefinitely deferred, as the City resisted capture and Romanía rebounded after every disaster. It was Mehmed II who finally made that dream a reality. Immediately after the conquest, in his victory letter to the sultan of Egypt and other Muslim rulers he appealed to the hadith traditions—those reported sayings of the Prophet—to portray himself as a supreme Muslim commander.[8]

The conquest of Constantinople changed the emerging Ottoman empire in more tangible ways as well, and it had an impact that was far out of proportion to the small territory and few people who were conquered in 1453. It is not clear when Mehmed decided that Constantinople would become the capital of his empire, a decision with consequences more far-reaching than even he imagined at the time. Tursun Bey and Kritoboulos imply that it was his plan from the start, but they are almost certainly projecting later developments back onto the conquest. For a few years after 1453, it is not certain that Mehmed planned to make Constantinople the imperial capital that it later became. It is likely that his plans evolved during those years. It was not until 1458 that he first spent the winter there, signaling through his personal presence, building projects, and efforts to repopulate the City after the desolation of May 29 that he had great things in store for it.[9]

In the 1460s, after a few years of vacillating on the issue, Mehmed appealed to Muslim traditions again to justify treating Constantinople as the center of Ottoman power. He razed the church of the Holy Apostles and erected over its ruins his New Mosque (i.e., the Fatih or "Conquest" Mosque) (see Image 10.1). In the dedicatory inscription above the portal he referred to himself as "the greatest sultan . . . who conquered with his sword this city whose like has not been created . . . which had not been conquered by caliphs and sultans and emirs." Above this, a plate bore the Prophet's saying, "They will conquer Konstantiniyye. Hail to the prince

Image 10.1 Fatih Mosque built by Mehmed II, in part as his mausoleum, on the site of the church of the Holy Apostles, which he demolished.
Source: Turkey Photo/Shutterstock.

and the army to whom this is given."[10] The creation of the Eyüp complex for religious pilgrims, where the burial of the early Arab warrior Abu Ayyub was discovered soon after the conquest, was another way to forge links to the origins of Islam. Abu Ayyub was believed to be a companion of the Prophet who had died in the seventh-century siege of the City.

Yet even as Mehmed remade the City in his own image, it also drew him into its own matrices and, at least partially, diverted his planning into preexisting Roman channels. Initially, Mehmed wanted to build his palace in the middle of the City, around the site of the forum of Theodosius, whose column it would enclose, but he later abandoned this idea and built it on the acropolis, just north of the ruin of the old Great Palace and Hagia Sophia, on a site from which he could view the City, the lands, and the waterways around it.[11]

The Fatih mosque also hosted Mehmed's tomb. In conception, then, it followed Roman precedents, for the Holy Apostles was the church adjoining the imperial mausoleum where the rulers of Constantinople were buried between the fourth and the eleventh centuries. The conqueror's mosque replicated those very functions, on the same spot no less; moreover, in architectural form it emulated and aspired to surpass Hagia Sophia. Tursun Bey claimed that the "great mosque [was] based on the design of Ayasofya, and not only encompassed all the arts of Ayasofya but moreover incorporated modern features constituting a fresh new idiom."[12] Yet the mosque turned out smaller than Hagia Sophia, allegedly causing Mehmed to execute his chief architect. Be that as it may, through his own mosque-mausoleum Mehmed strove to appropriate the symbolic significance of both the Holy Apostles and Hagia Sophia. Hagia Sophia became a touchstone and reference point for Ottoman architecture after 1453, emulated again and again in subsequent mosque construction.[13]

The early Ottomans were not merely imitating the Roman past: we should not downplay the "new idiom" of their art and culture, as Tursun Bey evocatively called it. Quite the contrary, theirs was a distinct culture that only partially poured itself into the old wineskins of east Rome. Contrary to a common misconception, the Ottoman empire was not in its own self-conception an extension of its Roman predecessor. Scholars have ascribed far too much significance to the limited ways and the rare occasions on which the sultans cast themselves as heirs to the Roman emperors. Mehmed was addressed that way by a handful of Roman intellectuals who were desperately trying to make sense of their new predicament in the first years after the conquest. It was not a tradition that would last. Moreover, the sultans themselves rarely used Roman titles, usually only to troll their Habsburg rivals. In truth, there was little continuity of governance and institutions between the Roman and Ottoman systems, and almost none of identity and ideology. This makes it all the more fascinating to see how the City exerted its own gravitational pull on its conquerors after 1453.

Constantinople changed the Ottomans as much as they changed it. It catalyzed and accelerated their conversion from nomadic warriors expanding the frontiers of Islam to a centralized state with a sedentary capital. Before 1453, the sultans were warriors who spent most of their reign on campaign. Edirne was more of an operating base in the Balkans than an imperial capital, as Bursa had been in Asia Minor. But Constantinople would not allow itself to be treated as a site of convenience, and it sucked Mehmed into the vacuum that he himself had created there. The City called for palatial organization on a grand scale, for investment in monumentality, and for a large population to act as a sounding-board for the performance of imperial majesty. Constantinople effectively de-nomadized the Ottoman regime.[14] Mehmed heeded its call, and his heirs became increasingly sedentary, palace-based distant rulers. Some still accompanied expeditions, but few were hands-on generals in the field as all had been before 1453. Interestingly, the City had had a similar effect on the Roman emperors of late antiquity. Between the late second and late fourth centuries, the emperors were mostly itinerant warlords, residing in temporary capitals along the frontier when they were not actively on the march. When Constantinople lured them in, they also became palace-based civilian rulers focusing on law, piety, and administration. In this sense, Constantinople conquered the Ottoman empire too.

This transformation was not uncontested after 1453. There were elements within the Ottoman system who regarded the City with suspicion and opposed its elevation to a centralized administrative capital. They are usually identified with the semi-independent frontier-warlords who had a looser conception of the project of Ottoman expansion, which was now being tightened up, micromanaged, and placed firmly under sultanic control. They loved the idea that Hagia Sophia had been turned into a mosque and that Muslim dreams were realized, but they hated Constantinople. It was the first place, some believed, where the Devil had set his foot on earth. It had fallen into ruin, they allegedly told the sultan, because of "adultery, sodomy, lewdness, and debauchery, and black waters emerged from its ground at night . . . It is not a place of serenity and joy . . . If you rebuild this city, it will destroy the world."[15]

And yet the City prevailed, and even managed to preserve its identity. In the aftermath of its fall, the cardinal Isidoros had groaned that it would henceforth be known as Turcopolis.[16] That did not happen. Its name remained Constantinople down to the early twentieth century, and it was only when the Ottoman empire itself fell that it was formally renamed Istanbul. The latter was an unofficial name, also of Greek origin. It derived from the expression *eis ten Polin*, "in the City."[17] Likewise, Hagia Sophia retained its name as a mosque: Ayasofya, the only church-mosque in Constantinople to do so. This likely happened because both the City and the church were valuable to the new regime only so long as they retained their names and identities that would broadcast the conquest narrative that lay at the heart of the new order. But thinking of your city and its greatest monument as objects of conquest can produce some odd results, such as the annual reenactments of The Conquest that occur in Istanbul today. In their own way, like the legend of the Marbled King who will return to liberate the City, these celebrations also treat 1453 as a perpetually unsettled issue, an "open question" that must be periodically resettled through ritual reenactment.

Pockets of free Roman life did survive for a few years after 1453, especially in Trebizond, where a parallel, splinter Roman state had existed since 1204, and also in the Peloponnese, which was ruled by the basileus' rival brothers, Thomas and Demetrios. Mehmed quickly put an end to them. The Morea was conquered in 1460. Thomas fled to Italy and became a dependent of the pope. Demetrios, who had long been pro-Ottoman and anti-Union, was granted lands in Thrace, where he retired. The brothers' divergent fortunes illustrate the contradictions that had long been pulling Roman society in different directions. In 1461, Mehmed also conquered Trebizond. The city surrendered instead of fighting to the death, and its rulers were deported. Many of them were subsequently executed. Surrender had not saved their lives. In contrast to Constantinople, Trebizond went out with a whimper, not a bang. Part of its population was forcibly resettled to the new capital. The next year, 1462, Mehmed conquered Lesbos, which had been ruled for over a century by the Genoese Gattilusi, in theory as vassals of the Roman basileus, but they had done nothing to help him at the end.

These episodes were mere epilogues, mopping-up operations. The main story had ended in 1453. Without a basileus, the despots in the Peloponnese were petty regional lords whose polity lacked an identity, and they made no move to proclaim themselves basileis. As for Trebizond, it has a valid claim to the Roman tradition and to continuity from antiquity, as its scion Bessarion stressed in an oration in praise of his native city.[18] Yet Trebizond, too, had long since accepted a subordinate status to the Seljuks, Constantinople, the Mongols, and the Ottomans in turn, for all that it was de facto autonomous behind its mountain ranges. It was not a place that could internationally project east Roman claims, as Constantinople had done to the end.

It was, then, 1453 that marked the end of the Roman imperial monarchy, which began with the reign of Caesar Augustus a millennium and a half earlier. That monarchy had emerged from the civil wars of the Republic, which was the earlier version of the polity of the Roman people. By the time of its fall in 1453, this polity was by far the oldest in the world, with a continuous history of culture and institutions that stretched back to antiquity. Its people traced that history even further back, to the fall of Troy and the flight of Aeneas to Italy. Arguably, no state in human history can match the sheer longevity, resilience, adaptability, and institutional continuity of the Roman *res publica*, which had gone by the name Romanía since ca. 300 AD. Its east Roman phase alone had survived for over a millennium. All empires fall, but this one merits a special place in the annals of history. Kritoboulos was right to observe that the fall of Constantinople marked the end of "the greatest and oldest state of all that we know."[19]

The fall of Constantinople greatly affected how the east Roman tradition would be remembered by posterity, in both east and west. Even at the end, in its impoverished state, Constantinople was still a free city, with its own native rulers, where east Roman traditions were preserved as its people saw fit. Roman voices still had a state, albeit a weak one, to preserve and project their claims to history, culture, identity, and religion. But without a center of their own, their lands and monuments fell under Ottoman power, most of their institutions were dismantled, and their memory was taken up by western European scholars. Neither the Ottomans nor the western Europeans had an interest in keeping them alive. Each selected, suppressed, and appropriated them in ways that suited their own interests instead.

As recently as the twelfth century, the east Romans and Constantinople had the most sophisticated, wealthy, glamorous, and prestigious culture in the entire Christian world, respected in many parts of the Muslim world, too. That culture was backed by armies, resources, and robust institutions. Roman leadership, court titles, protocols, and insignia were coveted and emulated internationally, as were the Romans' cuisine, dress, sacred music, architecture, and direct access to classical traditions. Traces of this admiration survived even in the fifteenth century, which is why western scholars still traveled to Constantinople to study Greek, and Russian pilgrims came to venerate relics and icons. The basileus Manuel II Palaiologos knew how to use soft power to impress peers from Paris to Muscovy with gifts that showcased the Romans' unparalleled access to classical, Christian, and Roman traditions.[20] Before 1453, Constantinople was home to a Roman aristocracy and was a center of trade, Orthodoxy, and education. It still maintained a diplomatic presence on an international scale.

The City's fall ended most of these traditions, allowing only Orthodoxy to survive. What remained of the Roman aristocracy was killed in the siege, executed soon afterward by the sultan, or assimilated into the servant elites of the Ottoman court, treated as secretaries and middlemen through whom the sultan governed Orthodox subjects. This had negative, long-term consequences for the memory of east Roman traditions that the survival of Constantinople, even as an impoverished capital, had held at bay. It matters to the history of a people, whether it has an independent political center of its own, even if only a weak one. The difference between zero and something, no matter how small, is infinite.

In other empires of that time, especially Christian ones on the European mainland, many native aristocracies did manage to survive, even if subordinated to foreign courts. In part this was because those empires, being looser in structure than the Ottoman, consisted of smaller principalities that retained their local laws and cultures, and were united only insofar as they recognized the same monarch; the latter, in turn, recognized local rights (although this was not to be the case in the overseas colonial empires that were soon to be established by the Christian states). In this way, local aristocracies kept native traditions alive, endowed cultural institutions and centers of learning, and wrote proto-national literatures. When nation-states later formed around these nuclei, they drew on these endowments, resources, and living cultural patrimonies. For a fleeting two days after May 29, Mehmed perhaps considered allowing the native Roman aristocracy to survive and perhaps govern their City in his name. This possibility vanished when he decided to execute Notaras and his fellow notables instead.

Ultimately, the Ottoman empire was not one in which the various ethnic aristocracies—Roman, Serb, Bulgarian, and other—retained local quasi-autonomy and flourished. As a result, within a few years after 1453 Roman culture was reduced largely to a vernacular and impoverished version of itself, mostly whatever could survive at the village level, with very few exceptions. As a result, when the Christian populations of the Ottoman empire eventually attained independence, they found themselves lagging far behind their western counterparts in the realms of high culture. They had to start anew in conditions not only of material but also cultural poverty, lacking credible leadership cadres with historical depth or links to a prestige, imperial past. They had few cadres with experience of running a state.

One casualty of 1453 was the tradition of Roman higher education and the production of classical scholarship and literary composition in the elite registers of ancient Greek. Until 1453, the City continued to host schools and libraries for the advanced study of Greek. Italian scholars traveled there to hone philological skills that were still unavailable in Italy. Higher education in Greek was, after all, one of the marks of elite status in Roman society since the days of the ancient Republic. In 1453, this tradition came to an end. To be sure, the court of Mehmed was not entirely uninterested in the Greek tradition, and some of its members made efforts to keep parts of it alive and package it for elite Ottoman consumption.[21] But this effort did not amount to much, far less than what a mid-sized Italian town would be producing within a few years in terms of classical education. This weak showing is especially noteworthy, given the resources that the Ottoman regime *could* have drawn on had it seriously wanted to promote Hellenic studies. What we see instead are the activities of a handful of men who were educated before the fall. However, the education that they received was largely unavailable after 1453 and so it could not reproduce itself beyond the reign of Mehmed II. Whoever was educated before 1453 continued to write in the high style for another generation, after which Greek writing in the Ottoman empire was largely restricted to demotic, utilitarian, and administrative registers. The sultans and their court were invested mostly in Islamic learning and did nothing to promote Roman and Hellenic traditions.

Thus, after 1453, the supply of native Greek scholars gradually dried up. Italian and other western cities and courts subsequently had to rely on their own talent for Hellenic philology, the first generations of which had been trained by Greek scholars such as Manuel Chrysoloras, Ioannes Argyropoulos, and Demetrios Chalkokondyles. In the long term, this enabled western European scholars to reinvent the history of classical scholarship in Eurocentric terms. Even today, most such histories focus on the West as if only that mattered and are indifferent to the east Romans, seeing them as mere vessels who passively preserved the classical texts for the benefit of western scholars. Specialists know that their contribution to the shaping, transmission, and study of classical texts entailed more than passive preservation. The east Romans never lost touch with ancient traditions and so never required a "Renaissance." However, the Eurocentric narrative dies hard among non-specialists, in school curricula, and among the general public. That narrative even sees a silver lining in 1453. Yes, what happened to the "Greeks" was tragic, but it forced their scholars to flee as refugees to the West, bringing their knowledge and manuscripts with them, transplanting Hellenist scholarship to Italy and eventually the rest of Europe. This is always seen as a positive development, as the West is generally seen as the true and destined "heir" of the classics. Western scholars were now able to grasp the "inner spirit" of the classical texts, which had supposedly lain dormant for a millennium and for which "the Byzantines" had never cared. This encounter led to democracy, science, capitalism, and the like.

In reality, the actual impact of 1453 was quite different. Greek scholars had been moving to Italy long before the fall of Constantinople. To be sure, they may have emigrated in part because of the growth of Ottoman power, but most of them had been trained in the east, if not in Constantinople itself, and their practice of philology was rooted in east Roman traditions. Greek manuscripts had also been making their way west by the hundreds before 1453. Giovanni Aurispa, who had served Manuel II Palaiologos (d. 1425) as a secretary, took at least 238 books with him back to Italy in 1423. Filelfo brought back another forty when he returned.[22] An industry of copying ancient texts for the Italian market had already emerged. The fall of Constantinople did not enrich those trends at all. No scholar survived that experience with his library intact, nor did it open doors and positions for him in the West that were not already open before. What it did for most of them was plunge them into family tragedy and poverty. Refugee scribes, such as Demetrios Leontares and Michael Apostoles, had to beg for scraps from western patrons in exchange for copying Greek books for them. They would likely have continued to engage in that work in Constantinople, had it survived the siege, only under far better circumstances.

In fact, the fall of Constantinople was detrimental to the study of ancient literature in *both* east *and* west. In the east, as mentioned, the secular schools did not recover from the shock of 1453, so no more great scholars were trained. For the West, 1453 meant that classical studies in Greek could depend on the expertise of native speakers for only about a generation, after which the tradition had to be carried on by their western students. After 1500, Hellenist scholarship in western Europe evolved with little input from native Greek-speakers, which had a number of detrimental consequences. In general, it entailed the loss of a vital voice in the preservation, study, and formation of the classical tradition, one, moreover, that had a native relationship to the language in question. The study of any tradition or body of literature would today be deemed seriously impaired if it lost access to the contribution of native speakers. But in the western tradition of classical scholarship, this led to specific distortions, which can in part be put down to 1453 and the end of Roman contributions. I gesture here to the botched experiment that is known as the "Erasmian" pronunciation of ancient Greek, one that was riddled with anti-Greek bias from the start and intended to create a distinct sociolect for western classicists that protected their work from contamination by actual Greeks.[23]

The fall of Constantinople caused other distortions too. To claim the classical tradition as their own exclusive heritage, western humanists began to disparage contemporary "Greece" as a land that had fallen into barbarism under the tyranny of the Ottoman yoke. The Greeks had supposedly become unworthy of their own traditions, as they were ignorant, indifferent, and even hostile to them. The only literate people left there were priests, who were regarded with increasing contempt by Enlightened European scholars.[24] This meant that manuscripts of ancient texts and classical artworks could legitimately be removed from the Greek lands. The natives did not understand their value, after all, and did not care for them, or believed that they were haunted by wrathful demons and allegedly begged western travelers, scholars, and diplomats to take them off their hands. This is in part how western museums and libraries came to acquire their books and art. The arrogance of this appropriation climaxed in the atrocities perpetrated by Lord Elgin on the Parthenon, an act of western supremacy carried out in the belief that the European nations literally owned the classical tradition, even the parts of it that were rooted in the Attic bedrock.

A glimpse into an alternative history—the way things *could* have gone were it not for 1453—is offered by the travels and letters of the first western European to explore ancient ruins in Greece, Kyriacus of Ancona. In his journeys through the Peloponnese and the Aegean islands, which took place in the years before 1453, he sought out learned Greeks to guide him, to help him read the inscriptions, and to tell him the relevant ancient histories. For example, he was guided around the ruins of Sparta by a young Nikolaos Chalkokondyles (later the Thucydidean historian Laonikos), who was studying with the famous philosopher Plethon under the rule of the despot Konstantinos Palaiologos. Kyriacus met and spoke with all of them, praising his Greek contacts for their learning, scholarship, and refined manners.[25] Other Italian scholars who studied under teachers trained in Constantinople, such as Argyropoulos and Laonikos' kinsman Demetrios Chalkokondyles, also praised them for preserving in their learning and character the virtues of antiquity.[26] Yet after 1453 and the extinction of the few remaining Roman homelands, there would be no more men like Plethon, Chalkokondyles, and Argyropoulos. Greek voices would fade away in the western engagement with Greek antiquity.

It was not only their perspective that was lost. So was the medieval culture that they preserved and represented alongside the classical texts that the westerners wanted. East Roman scholars were usually trained in both Hellenic and Christian traditions, which they called respectively "the outside" wisdom and "our wisdom." The latter was not limited to the Church Fathers but included works written by Christian east Romans down to the present. But western humanists had little or no interest in that yet. They reached with both hands for classical and some patristic texts, and discarded the rest, everything that would later be branded as Byzantine. This was an act of violence in its own way. The Greek literary tradition that had been preserved and curated by the scholars of Constantinople was a complex and diachronic whole, at least in their mind, with symmetrical and interlocking pagan and Christian components. Plato and Aristotle had been preserved because of the proximity of Middle- and Neo-Platonism to early Christian theology. Classical and Christian oratory were part of the same tradition. Histories of ancient Rome were preserved because of their direct relevance to later east Roman history. And the epigram and novel had both ancient pagan and Christian expressions that were often preserved together and read in tandem.[27]

However, the western humanists of the fifteenth century were interested exclusively in classical and some early Christian texts. Over time these two foci of interest gradually drifted apart, too. The process of ripping the classics out of their context was already underway in the fifteenth century, as reflected in the selection of texts that Michael Apostoles, a survivor of the fall, was commissioned to copy by his western patrons. These are almost exclusively ancients texts and exclude ecclesiastical works, theology, and anything to do with the history and culture of the eastern Roman empire.[28] Likewise, only classical Greek works were translated at the court of Alfonso V (of Aragon) at Naples, nothing pertaining to the history of Constantinople,[29] although early patristic works that reinforced Catholic thought were sometimes sought as well. Alfonso's scholars were far more eager to obtain such manuscripts than the king was to send military aid. His court thanked Gennadios for sending them a work by Cyril of Alexandria and promised that ships with aid were on their way—the letter is tragically dated May 27, 1453.[30] Be that as it may, a premium was placed on classical works, and "later" texts were sought only by scholars with specialized interests. A direct line runs from that narrow focus to the curricula of classics departments today and the institutionally conditioned aversion of many classicists to "later" and "Byzantine" literature.

When western scholars did finally become interested in the history of the eastern empire, in the sixteenth century, they were already hugely prejudiced against it, as their thinking was immersed in stereotypes and misconceptions that had proliferated since medieval times. In real time, they identified contemporary "Greek" culture with the supposedly barbarous Greece of the Ottoman empire, poor, ignorant, and mired in "monkish superstition." Thus, when scholarship on the eastern empire began, because of 1453 and the extinction of the rump Roman polity in the east, western scholars would never be given the chance to be informed about it from a native scholar of the caliber of Nikephoros Gregoras, Manuel II Palaiologos, or Ioannes Chortasmenos, to say nothing of a Plethon. Even in its diminished state, Constantinople had still been able to produce scholars of such impressive intellect and erudition. They would have been able to explain that what we understand today as "classical Greek literature" was only one half of an east Roman archive that was selectively preserved to complement its Orthodox counterpart and its east Roman extensions, which continued down to the fifteenth century. As Michael Apostoles had to admit to one of his Latin patrons, we Greeks are now "mere remnants" of a once great people, and enslaved to boot, at the end of our story, whereas you Italians are free and embarking on your historical trajectory.[31]

The fall of Constantinople meant that no educated Roman aristocracy or learned elite existed after 1453 to counter the nonsense that would be written by western historians about the eastern empire, its culture, and its history. They may not have prevailed against western biases, but, again, the difference between having no say and having even a small say is infinite. Had such voices survived past 1500 AD, it would have been much more difficult to cast Byzantium as the antithesis of classical values, as western scholarship was to do, or to erect walls of separation between "Classics" and "Byzantine Studies."

It was not only western Europeans who reinvented Byzantium to suit themselves. The fall of Constantinople also enabled the Ottomans to rewrite the story of east Roman culture and shape how it would be perceived by posterity, even western posterity. This was the result of both policy and the cumulative impact of selective pressures.

To start with the obvious, Ottoman policy delivered the Orthodox Church over to its most anti-Union elements. The Synaxis, headed by Gennadios, went from being quasi-schismatic, in opposition to the imperial Church, to leading the official Church into the Ottoman era. The sultans had a vital security interest in ensuring that the leadership of the Church would not make deals with western powers. The sole purpose of those deals in the past, after all, had been to secure western aid against Ottoman imperialism. To be sure, those deals and the project of Union in general had been unpopular among the majority of Romans, who had long resented the imposition of Catholicism on them. The fall of Constantinople made that project pointless. Anti-Union forces in the Church had long been more open to dealing with the Turks, prioritizing the survival of their religious identity over political independence. It was natural for the sultans to place them in power and require that the Church leadership henceforth reject Catholicism. As a result, the two Churches settled into a prolonged state of alienation. Orthodox hardliners were (and are) not wrong in believing that Ottoman rule saved the Church from Catholicism. Orthodox fundamentalists who dread the "corruption" of western modernity still pine for neo-Ottoman solutions, when they are not fantasizing about Orthodox Russian imperialism.

At the same time, the Ottomans dismantled most secular institutions of Roman life, especially the political ones and generally anything that might pose a challenge to their hegemony, just as they had eliminated, downgraded, or absorbed Roman elites. To manage their Orthodox subjects, they relied instead on churches and monasteries, which became, by default, the only surviving representatives of the conquered civilization. This interposed a selective filter on the preservation of its culture. Over time, secular buildings, architecture, manuscripts, archives, and even social practices and memory were lost, when they were not actively destroyed, as the institutions that had once sustained them were now no more. On the other hand, Orthodox buildings, books, archives, practices, and memories had a greater chance of survival, resulting in a differential skew toward the religious in the survival of materials for study today. This process was already well advanced by the time that modern western travelers began to visit the lands of the former empire: they saw only its religious aspects, and those in a state of ruination to boot. Thus "Byzantium" was gradually identified with its Church and religion, as these, after 1453, became the only surviving representatives of an otherwise lost civilization. This bias continues to be perpetuated today. To a considerable degree, it was the indirect result of Ottoman policy and the religiously oriented mode of its imperial governance, which organized and classified its subjects by religion. There is a reason most books published today about Byzantium have religious images on the cover, even when they are otherwise about secular topics. It is the same reason why the term "Orthodox" would loom so large in the word cloud of Byzantine Studies.

The same process of differential, selective survival shaped the physical remains of Constantinople itself. Churches were vastly more likely to survive than secular and imperial buildings. Many churches were converted into mosques with minimal architectural alteration and so survive that way. Some remained in use as churches, but in time most of them were converted into mosques too (only one remained in continual Christian use). Other churches were converted to secular purposes, such as schools, menageries, commercial centers, or incorporated into the estates of Ottoman lords.[32] By contrast, few secular or imperial buildings survive, such as palaces, manors, praetoria, archives, imperial forums, colonnades, paved streets, senate houses, arches, tetrapyla, and the like. These were either demolished due to their ideological associations, such as the statues of emperors, for example the equestrian statue of Justinian;[33] pulled down or built over because they were in the way of other projects; or used as quarries for construction materials, as happened to the hippodrome. Thus, the surviving art and architecture of Roman Constantinople is mostly religious. We know about the rest mostly from literary descriptions, which are themselves rare, because they too were subject to the selective pressures that, after 1453, prioritized the survival of Orthodox texts in the Ottoman empire and ancient texts in the book markets of western Europe.

The direct impact of the fall of Constantinople was, therefore, not limited to the people who happened to live there when the sultan's armies arrived. Beyond its direct impact, moreover, the fall acquired symbolic importance too, and historians have connected it to transformations in global history that were underway in the fifteenth century, even if the event itself did not materially contribute to them.

For example, 1453 emerged as a significant marker in the schemes that were proposed by early modern scholars for the periodization of history. In 1688, one Christoph Keller (Cellarius) defined "the Middle Age" as the era between Constantine the Great and the storming of Constantinople in 1453. The Middle Age(s) was a category that made sense only for western European societies, but, still, Cellarius interestingly demarcated it via the history of the *eastern* emperors. This was in part because he regarded the Middle Age negatively, so it was convenient for him to associate it with the decadent and un-Roman eastern empire. For him, 1453 stood for a series of developments that collectively ended the dreadful Middle Age and ushered in modernity, even if the fall of Constantinople itself was not causally linked to them. They included the flight of Greek scholars to Italy and transplantation of Hellenic studies, which supposedly kicked off the Renaissance; the discovery of the New World (1492), the introduction of the printing press (1440s), and the Reformation (Cellarius was a Protestant).[34] Thus, his Middle Age, a dark period for mankind, was linked to the history of Constantinople, whereas modernity kicked off with a set of (for him) positive western developments.

The fall of Constantinople is still used by some historians and in school curricula to mark the end of the Middle Ages and the start of modernity, although the specific developments for which it stands vary. They include both western and eastern developments. 1453 marked the maturation of the Ottoman empire, which transitioned from a frontier, nomadic emirate to a settled administrative state. This process marked the rise of the so-called Islamic gunpowder empires, a term coined for the Ottoman, Safavid (Iran), and Mughal (India) empires that dominated south Asia from the fifteenth to the eighteenth centuries.[35] Mehmed's spectacular use of cannons to demolish the walls of Constantinople and accomplish what no foreign invader had been able to do vividly proclaimed the dawn of a new era of warfare and weaponry. Looking to the West, in addition to the developments flagged by Cellarius, 1453 also coincided with the end of the Hundred Years War between England and France. One scholar has recently claimed that "the year 1453 marked the start of modern European geopolitics, with the collapse of the Byzantine Empire in the east, followed shortly afterward by that of the English empire in France. These two events had profound consequences for Europe as a whole, and especially for the Holy Roman Empire of the German Nation . . . which lay at its heart."[36] This is because it fell to the German emperors to defend central Europe against the Ottoman advance. Thus, 1453 coincided with the emergence of a modern geopolitical paradigm, and even contributed to it.

For the first time in history, a major Muslim power was entrenched in southeastern Europe, and it was still expanding. The crusades of Nicopolis (1396) and Varna (1444) had failed to dislodge it, and 1453 confirmed that it was here to stay. Ottoman expansion affected not only the peoples who were conquered by it. It rolled back the western European colonization of Greece, the Aegean Sea, and eastern Mediterranean generally. Eventually, only the Ionian islands would remain in western hands, the sole lasting territorial legacy of European colonialism (commonly known as the crusades) in the region.

It has also been argued that 1453 finally ended "the ideal of the crusade, which simply withered away" as attention focused on the Ottoman threat.[37] It seems, however, that crusading ideals were enjoying a Renaissance in the fifteenth century as the humanists endorsed them powerfully through their newly revived brand of classical rhetoric. The fall of Constantinople inspired many of them to call for and enthuse about future crusades that would reclaim the "eastern empire" for Christianity.[38] To be sure, these calls were defensive. The Ottoman advance had indeed put Europe on a defensive footing. More than any other single event, the fall of Constantinople instilled fears that the Ottomans, aspiring to world dominion, would march into the heart of western Christendom and take Rome too, not just New Rome. This apprehension took on apocalyptic aspects, as if Ottoman expansion was about to bring about the End Times. Countless pamphlets and proposals for action against the Turkish menace were written after 1453, many of them echoing the language of crusade against the infidel.[39] In fact, a number of our sources for the siege were meant to sound the alarm in precisely this way.

A defensive tone, however, does not signal the withering away of crusading ideals. Crusading ideology had been "defensive" from the start, as its purpose was to reclaim Christian lands that had been conquered by Muslims. Christians always saw themselves as victims defending against an aggressor. It is possible that, rather than laying medieval crusading ideology to rest, 1453 extended its life into the modern period. As a way of marshaling and channeling the surplus aggression of Christian societies, crusading ideology proved to be remarkably adaptable and resilient. In the sixteenth century, it became a prime vehicle for intra-Christian warfare and also provided the framework for grand coalitions aimed against the Ottomans. Calls for crusades to liberate Constantinople continued to be issued well into the sixteenth century, and actual wars against the Turks were cast in the language of the crusades.[40] The campaign of Lepanto (1571) that was waged by the Holy League against the Ottomans was essentially a crusade. Crusades did not wither away: they metastasized into inter-state or inter-imperial warfare. In fact, they had always been mutating in such ways, ever since they first began in the eleventh century. First, they were directed against the Holy Land, then against North Africa, Constantinople, the Baltics, southern France, the Ottomans, and so on.

Crusading attitudes were also channeled into the Christian Reconquista of Spain. A case can even be made that proto-crusades took place in Spain and Sicily *before* pope Urban called for the liberation of the Holy Land in the 1090s.[41] And through a striking coincidence, the Christian conquest of Spain and the expulsion or conversion of its Muslim population reached its culmination around the same time as Constantinople fell to the Ottomans. One can even speak of a balance of conquest at this time between Christians and Muslims, with the former taking Spain and the latter the Balkans. 1453 thus stands for the emergence of two major empires of early modernity, the Ottoman and Spanish, at opposite ends of the Mediterranean.[42] In the course of their expansion, both empires destroyed a major city, the capital of a preexisting empire: Constantinople and the Aztec capital of Tenochtitlan. This was done in ways so spectacular that parallel traditions of lament evolved to mourn their loss by the conquered populations.[43] The cusp of modernity was thus marked by the destruction of the oldest state in history, paired with the conquest of the New World that was opened by European expansion.

The fortunes of these two expansionist empires, the Ottoman and the Spanish, were closely interlinked beyond the wars that they fought against each other, such as the Lepanto campaign. The Ottomans' assertion of control over trade networks, especially through the Bosporos straits, made eastern routes less profitable to western merchants and cost them many of their colonial outposts. The sultans were not as easy to push around as the basileis of Constantinople. Venice opted to fight a series of costly wars against the Ottomans to maintain its eastern position, though these were mostly ineffectual. By contrast, the Genoese secured terms from the sultan, and some remained active in Ottoman Pera after 1453, though on a reduced scale. Soon many of them found it hard to get ahead and so they abandoned the east as Turkish pressure increased. Genoa's presence in the east collapsed rapidly after 1453 and Pera dwindled. This incentivized Genoese navigators, such as Columbus, and their royal sponsors in Spain to seek alternative routes to the Far East, such as via the Atlantic. The fall of Constantinople was one among many factors that pushed European explorers in that direction. As a free city down to 1453, even while surrounded by the Ottoman empire, Constantinople had still functioned as a tax-free hub for transit and trade between the Black Sea and the Mediterranean. But after its fall, many Genoese merchants began to look to the Atlantic. Antonio Salvago, the son of one of Konstantinos XI's Genoese creditors in 1453, shifted operations from Pera to Seville and engaged in trade between Portugal and Madeira. In the story that he exemplifies, the fall of Constantinople and the discovery of the New World were linked.[44]

It has often been observed that Columbus' first voyage occurred in the very year, 1492 AD, that east Roman divines of this period had fixed for the end of the world and the Second Coming of Christ, an event that they conflated with the fall of their City. Constantinople had been predicted to fall many times in the past but had always outlived the forecasts of its demise. That prophesy had to be periodically updated. Disregarding explicit warnings in the New Testament that man shall not know the date of the End,[45] exegetes in the fifteenth century assumed that the world would endure for a cosmic "week," in which each day was like a thousand years.[46] East Roman tradition had long fixed the date of Creation in what we would call 5509 BC, so 7,000 years yields a date for the End in 1492 AD. One theologian even specified that it would happen on a Sunday, during the seventh hour of the night, to match the Resurrection of the Christ.[47] Gennadios Scholarios devoted entire texts to this tradition of thought, although he struggled to explain why the world had not ended when the City fell in 1453.[48] Unfortunately none of the exponents of this tradition lived until 1492 or reflected on the significance of the discovery of the New World.

Constantinople was also the last autonomous Orthodox state in Europe. All others had either been liquidated, such as Bulgaria, or recognized Muslim overlordship, as did Serbia and increasingly Wallachia. Even Muscovy was still nominally subject to the Mongols. Thus, after 1453, for the first and last time in history, all independent Christian states in Europe were Catholic. But this high point of Catholic power proved transient. The popes held little sway over their spiritual sons, the Christian kings, and their hegemony was soon shattered by the Reformation. Moreover, by 1480 Muscovy had shaken off Mongol overlordship and embarked upon its own career as an Orthodox empire.

It is common to view Russia as the heir to Constantinople, with a baton of continuity passing between them in 1453. This notion has been repeated so often that it seems almost intuitive, but it is highly misleading. Apart from the Orthodox faith, there were no lines of continuity between east Rome and Russia, and to insist on religion to such an extent is to fall into the trap of "Byzantinism." These were profoundly different polities in their political ideology and institutions, laws, social organization, culture and traditions, and historical imagination. The evidence for a Russian sense of continuity from Constantinople is meager, ambiguous, and late. Apart from the text of Nestor-Iskander, there is little proof that 1453 impacted Russian culture or awareness. The later notion of Moscow as a "Third Rome" was marginal to Russia's political culture and limited to small circles of churchmen, some of whom were theorizing about the Apocalypse. It has, however, become a required talking point in *modern* discussions of Russian absolutism or imperialism, as a shorthand formula: somehow the Byzantine matrix is supposed to "explain" Russia, whether tsarist or Soviet. Popular though this idea may be on the internet, among both critics and defenders of Russian goals, scholars struggle to document any connection between the two in the fifteenth and sixteenth centuries.[49]

The idea that Russia and Byzantium belong together has become intuitive, but largely through repetition. This notion is largely of western European origin and emerged during the nineteenth and twentieth centuries. In the period before this, during the Enlightenment, many in the West hoped that the Russia of Peter and Catherine the Great would emerge as a properly Enlightened European state. Those hopes were dashed, and the failure was widely explained by postulating that Russia emerged from the matrix of the despotic and nefarious Byzantium, itself a fiction of western imagination. But this link is an ideological trap. It projects Russian absolutism back onto Constantinople, thereby misreading and distorting east Roman political culture, and then finds the origin of Russian dysfunction in Byzantium. In other words, in many of these discussions Byzantium has already been reverse-engineered to look like Russia in advance, and so Russia can easily be postulated as its heir.

It makes more sense to see the Russian appropriation of Byzantine symbols during the early modern period in the context of similar *western* practices. Russian rulers and their spokesmen were emulating what their western counterparts had been doing for centuries, albeit belatedly. This included marrying princesses from Constantinople; using imperial regalia, titles, and symbols such as the eagle; calling their imperial capitals New Romes; imitating Constantine the Great; and developing theories of a "transfer of imperial authority" (*translatio imperii*) from Rome via Constantinople to Aachen, Paris, Moscow, or wherever. The Russian "Third Rome" was just a variation on an old western medieval idea. There was nothing especially original or distinctive about the Russian version. These links—nearly all of them fictional—do not demonstrate that Russia inherited the mantle of Byzantium any more than medieval Germany or France did. What they show is that Russia was following western modes of imperial self-fashioning, which had always mixed appropriated Byzantine motifs with native traditions.[50]

Russia had drawn much of its religious culture from Constantinople and was aware that it was now the only Orthodox empire left in the world. Yet it still kept "the Greeks" at arm's length. Many Russian religious writers believed that the Greeks had betrayed their faith at the end, were justly punished by God, and were generally disreputable. In other words, Russians did not defend the Greeks against western polemic. They held many of the same stereotypes about them as western Europeans did. They, like western Europeans, called them Greeks, a polemical term meant to diminish them. They assumed that they themselves, rather than the Greeks, were God's chosen people and that their state was his designated Christian empire. Western powers had been saying much the same with their own theories of *translatio imperii* for centuries. Rather than draw a genealogical link, mediated by 1453, between Byzantium and Russia, it is probably best to see imperial Russia as engaged in a synchronic dialogue with its western peers: all were repurposing an imaginary Byzantium, among other cultural assets, to suit their current ideological needs.

The fall of Constantinople instantly became a matter of interest and concern around the world, if not globally then at least wherever Christians and Muslims lived. Many sensed that, beyond the magnitude of the event itself, the conquest of the City signaled important transformations. It is no accident that eyewitness accounts were written soon in Latin, Italian, Greek, Turkish, and Russian, and dozens of secondhand accounts appeared soon in these and other languages as well. Possibly no prior siege, except that of Troy, had yet produced such a rich body of narrative and debate. It still has a way of galvanizing attention through popular histories, novels, films, and official commemorations. Christian rulers continued to plan the City's reconquest down to the early twentieth century, perpetuating the idea that the matter of the conquest was still an open question. The first rulers to step forward as the City's potential liberators were Catholic, including popes, French kings, and German emperors. The Russians were again late to this game, but they are more closely associated with it today because of their proximity to us. Tsars from Catherine the Great (in the late eighteenth century) to Nicholas II during World War I contemplated and planned the City's reconquest. The imperial army even tasked an officer of Greek descent with the charge to replace the cross on top of the dome of Hagia Sophia, were the City to fall into Christian hands during the Great War.[51]

But for those who experienced it, the siege of Constantinople was not an abstract idea or symbol. It was a material reality shaped by stone, iron, their own bodies, ships, gunpowder smoke, the thunder of cannons. Insofar as it reflected a meeting point and clash of cultures, those were Roman, Italian, and Turkish. The siege pushed their encounter to its limits. They were capable of living at peace with each other, though always in a state of tension, given their incompatible objectives: of the sultans, to conquer; of the Italian merchants, to profit; and of the Romans, to survive. These asymmetries collided during the siege, framed by experiences of imperialism and conquest, enslavement and captivity, migration and assimilation, cultural exchange, booming trade, classical studies, new technologies, and ancient religious disputes. That was the context of the siege. Its basic script, however, was written by a few thousand men who, for months, fought furiously amidst the ruins of ancient walls under the booming echo of massive cannons firing massive stone rocks. No theories were on their mind as they climbed, dodged, thrust, shouted, hacked, slipped, fell, bled, and died.

Glossary of Terms and Places

akçe: Turkish silver coins worth about 1/10 of an hyperpyron or 1/30 of a ducat.

Anadolu: Turkish for Anatolia (i.e., Asia Minor), one of the two principal administrative divisions of the Ottoman empire in 1453 (the other being Rumeli).

Anadolu Hisarı: fortress built on the Asian side of the Bosporos by the sultan Bayezid I in connection with his blockade of Constantinople (1394–1402).

bailo: governor of the Venetian community of Constantinople (the word is etymologically related to English "bailiff"), dispatched by the Senate.

basileus of the Romans (pl. basileis): official Greek title of the ruler of Constantinople. It is conventionally translated as "emperor," but that can be misleading, especially for periods when there was no empire.

beylerbey: "general of generals," title of the two highest-ranked generals of the Ottoman empire, one for Rumeli and one for Anadolu.

beylik: territory under the command of a bey, a quasi-independent Muslim general or warlord; something less than a state, something more than the territory of a brigand chief.

Blachernai: district in the northwest corner of Constantinople where the palace of the Palaiologoi was located along with the manors of many leading Romans and an important church of the Virgin.

demarchs: "mayors" of the various neighborhoods of Constantinople.

devşirme: "collection" of Christian children by the Ottoman authorities. They were then prepared for a career of service to the sultan, often as janissaries, and typically converted to Islam.

ducats: Venetian gold coins worth roughly 3 hyperpyra or 33 Turkish akçes.

emirate: conventional name given to the dynastic Muslim statelets that emerged in Anatolia after the collapse of Seljuk power in the late thirteenth century, such as Germiyan, Menteşe, Aydın, Karaman, and the Ottomans.

eparch: magistrate presiding over the administration of the city of Constantinople (prefect in Latin).

Fatih: "conqueror" in Turkish (i.e., Mehmed II).

Fetih: "conquest" in Turkish (i.e., of Constantinople in 1453).

Galatas: see Pera.

Gallipoli: naval base of the Ottoman fleet.

gazi/gaza: holy warriors and holy war waged to expand the territories of Islam's hegemony.

Hospitaller Knights: the Order of the Knights of St John of Jerusalem was a military monastic order founded in the twelfth century to promote crusading plans in the eastern Mediterranean. Since the early fourteenth century, it was based on the island of Rhodes.

hyperpyra: late Roman gold coin. These had ceased to be issued in practice since the fourteenth century but were still used in notional calculations of value. They were worth 1/3 of a Venetian ducat or 10 to 11 Turkish akçe coins.

janissaries: elite military corps of the Ottoman empire that reported directly to the sultan. Many of its soldiers were the product of the *devşirme* system.

Karaman: powerful emirate in southern Anatolia that had accepted vassal status in the Ottoman empire but was in practice autonomous and often rebellious.

megas domestikos: high-ranking Roman military title.

megas doux: high-ranking Roman military title.

Mamluks: generically a mamluk was a non-Arab soldier in the slave armies of certain Islamic states. One such army took over Egypt and was ruling it at this time, so "the Mamluks" refers to this phase of Egyptian history.

mesazon: a prime minister or chief-of-staff of the Roman basileus.

Morea: alternate name of the Peloponnese in southern Greece.

patriarch: honorific title given to the bishop of Constantinople.

Pera (Galatas): Genoese city across the Golden Horn from Constantinople, established with permission by the basileus Michael VIII Palaiologos in the 1260s. By 1453 it was a fortified community and de facto independent, a center of Genoese trade governed by a podestà sent from Genoa.

podestà: meaning or "power-holder," this was the governor of the Genoese community of Constantinople, dispatched from Genoa.

Rumeli: the collective Turkish name for the Balkan provinces of the Ottoman empire in 1453, meaning something like "Romanland" (from Rum). The other principle division of the empire was Anadolu (i.e., Anatolia).

Rumeli Hisarı: fortress built by Mehmed II in 1452 preparation for the attack on Constantinople.

Trebizond: independent Roman state in northwestern Anatolia, founded by the Komnenoi dynasty in 1204, in the chaos that followed the Fourth Crusade. It lasted until 1461.

Union of the Churches: effort to establish communion between the Catholic Church of Rome and the Orthodox Church of Constantinople and repair the Schism between them. Both sides were, in theory, in favor of Union, but as a technical term in 1453 this referred to the terms worked out at the Council of Florence in 1439, which made significant concessions to Rome.

vizier: high-ranking court advisor of the Ottoman sultans, their prime ministers or chiefs-of-staff. Sultans in the fifteenth century often had three viziers, of whom the lead was the grand vizier.

1453: A Who's Who

This prosopography does not include everyone mentioned in connection with the siege of Constantinople, only figures who were important or who occur in several places in the book. Authors of the main sources for the siege are designated with the letters **AU** after their name.

Apostoles, Michael: a student of Ioannes Argyropoulos, he was in Constantinople during the siege. Captured in the fall and held captive for just over month, he then emigrated to Crete where he worked as a teacher and scribe on commission, producing important copies of classical authors for the Italian book market.

Argyropoulos, Ioannes (d. 1489): philosopher and medical expert who had studied in Italy, then returned to Constantinople. He was there during the siege, after which he returned to Italy where he enjoyed a distinguished career as a teacher and classical scholar.

Baltaoğlu Bey (Süleyman): until April 21, he was the admiral of the Ottoman fleet at Gallipoli and then at Two Columns by Constantinople.

Barbaro, Nicolò (**AU**, present during the siege): young Venetian of middling nobility, serving as a crossbowman and/or medic on the eastern trade convey under Alvise Diedo. He was stationed mostly in the harbor during the siege and kept a diary account in Venetian dialect; he was biased against the Greeks and the Genoese.

Bayezid I: bellicose Ottoman sultan (1389–1402) who expanded the empire and blockaded Constantinople for many years (1394–1402). In 1402, at the battle of Ankara, he was defeated by the Mongol conqueror Timur (Tamerlane).

Benvenuto of Ancona (**AU**, present during the siege): consul of the city of Ancona in Constantinople who wrote two-page report about the siege in Latin right afterward.

Bessarion (d. 1472): a native of Trebizond, he acquired a classical education and participated at the Council of Florence on the Greek side, after which he joined the Catholic clergy and rose to the position of cardinal. He sponsored Greek scholars who emigrated to Italy and collected manuscripts of Greek works to preserve his people's heritage after the fall.

Bocchiardi brothers (Paolo, Troilo, Antonio): Latin natives of Constantinople who helped man the walls during the defense. Paolo held a concession from the sultan for the extraction and export of alum. They were captured during the fall of the City and subsequently released.

Cattaneo, Maurizio: commander of three Genoese relief ships that arrived at Constantinople on April 20 and broke through the naval blockade. He was subsequently posted to defend the southern sector of the land walls.

Chrysoloras, Manuel (d. 1415): leading Greek scholar of his generation, he was employed by Manuel II Palaiologos in diplomatic missions to the West. He emigrated to Italy, accepted Catholicism, and became one of the first expert teachers of Greek there.

Cocco, Giacomo (d. 1453): Venetian captain of the galley from Trebizond, he played an active role in the defense of Constantinople, especially in the fighting in the harbor.

Cyriac of Ancona: see Kyriacus of Ancona.

Demetrios Palaiologos (d. 1470): brother of the basileus Konstantinos XI Palaiologos and despot in the Morea at the time of the siege. A troublemaker, he sided with anti-Union factions and accepted Turkish help for attacks on other members of his dynasty.

Diedo, Alvise (d. 1466): commander of a Venetian trade convoy that was in Constantinople at the time of the siege. He took an active role in the defense of the harbor.

Doukas (**AU**, not present during the siege): pro-Union, ethnic Roman historian working for the Gattilusi rulers of the island of Lesbos. In the late 1450s and early 1460s, he wrote a history of the rise of the Ottomans and fall of the Roman polity in accessible Greek prose. He interviewed survivors and Ottoman soldiers and was biased against anti-Union Romans and Turks.

Gattilusi: extended Genoese family that had acquired significant holdings in the Aegean via concessions from the basileis of Constantinople, including the islands of Lesbos and Lemnos and the city of Ainos in Thrace.

Gennadios Scholarios (d. ca. 1472): the scholar Georgios Kourteses took the penname Scholarios and then the monastic name Gennadios, which he also used as the first patriarch of Constantinople after the fall. Even though he seems to have accepted to the terms of Union at Florence in 1439, he later repudiated that position and became the leader of the anti-Union Synaxis.

Giustiniani, Giovanni Longo (d. 1453): Genoese mercenary who was hired by the basileus Konstantinos XI to lead the defense of Constantinople during the siege. He fought in the most critical Mid-Wall sector of the land walls and was critically wounded there.

Goudeles, Nikolaos (d. 1453): scion of a Roman family that had risen to political prominence through trade. He was eparch of Constantinople at the time of the siege and posted to defend the Pege Gate.

Halil Pasha (d. 1453): grand vizier of Mehmed II at the time of the siege, he came from a prominent aristocratic Muslim family (the Çandarlı), who had produced several viziers. He was allegedly against the war and tried to steer Mehmed away from it.

Hamza Bey: replaced Baltaoğlu Bey as admiral of the Ottoman fleet after April 21.

Ioannes VIII Palaiologos (1425–1448): basileus of the Romans and elder brother of Konstantinos XI. He led Roman recovery efforts in the Peloponnese and pushed for Union with the Church of Rome at the Council of Ferrara-Florence in 1438–1439.

Ishak Pasha: Mehmed's *beylerbey* of Anatolia during the siege.

Isidoros ("Isidore of Kiev") (**AU**, present during the siege): ethnic Roman scholar who accepted Catholicism and was appointed a bishop and then cardinal by the pope. He had attended the Council of Florence (1438–1439) but his mission to convert Moscow to Union failed. He was sent to Constantinople in 1452 to promote Union. He brought reinforcements and joined in the defense. He wrote letters about the siege while on Crete immediately after making his escape.

Karaca Bey: Mehmed's *beylerbey* of Rumeli during the siege.

Konstantinos XI Palaiologos (1448–1453): the last basileus of the Romans, a son of Manuel II and brother of Ioannes VIII. Before moving to Constantinople in early 1449, he was despot in the Peloponnese, based at Mystras.

Kritoboulos of Imbros (**AU**, not present during the siege): governor of the island of Imbros, who, in the later 1460s, wrote a panegyrical account of Mehmed's conquest of Constantinople in classical Greek. The work contains biting criticisms of the sultan, if read between the lines.

Kyriacus of Ancona (d. 1452): antiquarian, scholar, diplomat, and spy, he traveled widely throughout the Aegean collecting information for Italian patrons along with notes about classical antiquities and inscriptions.

Laonikos Chalkokondyles (**AU**, not present during the siege): a native Athenian who grew up at Mystras in the Peloponnese while Konstantinos Palaiologos was despot there, and studied under the philosopher Georgios Gemistos Plethon. In the 1460s, he wrote a history of the rise of the Ottoman empire in difficult classical Greek. He was the least biased Greek historian to date.

Leonardo of Chios (**AU**, present during the siege): Genoese from Chios who joined the Dominican order and was appointed (Catholic) archbishop of Mytilene. He was brought to Constantinople by his associate Isidoros to promote the cause of Union and wrote an important account of the siege, in Latin, for the pope afterward; he is heavily biased against the Greeks.

Lomellino, Angelo Giovanni (**AU**, present during the siege): merchant and podestà of the Genoese colony of Pera whose letter to his brother after the siege contains valuable information.

Manuel II Palaiologos (1391–1425): basileus of the Romans who was forced to serve as a vassal of the Ottoman sultan Bayezid, then rebelled against him and traveled to the West to seek aid for Constantinople during the sultan's blockade of the City; he was also an accomplished author who wrote in many genres of literature.

Minotto, Girolamo (d. 1453): bailo of the Venetians in Constantinople during the siege, he was entrusted with the defense of the palace of Blachernai.

Morosini, Girolamo: commander of two Venetian galleys from Caffa in the Black Sea, who took an active role in the defense of the harbor during the siege.

Nestor-Iskander (**AU**, present during the siege?): putative author of a confusing account of the siege in Russian. The text we have was embellished later but contains a core that likely came from someone present, almost certainly inside the City. It is the only such source we have with an Orthodox bias, although it is not anti-Latin.

Notaras, Loukas (d. 1453): possibly the wealthiest Roman of his generation, he was the chief minister (*mesazon*) and *megas doux* of Konstantinos XI. His role in the defense of the siege became a contentious matter after the fall of the City (almost certainly unfairly).

Orban: Hungarian or Wallachian engineer specializing in cannon design, who allegedly sold his services to Mehmed II when Konstantinos XI could not pay him the salary for which he was asking. His story should probably not be taken at face value.

Orhan (d. 1453): Ottoman prince living in Constantinople and supported by funds provided by the sultan; he can be seen as a Roman hostage, kept in reserve as a potential diplomatic bargaining chip.

Posculo, Ubertino (**AU**, present during the siege): student from Brescia (Italy), who was in Constantinople when the siege began. He was captured and enslaved for a year, after which he wrote an epic Latin poem on the siege in the manner of Vergil. His information is often wrong about events to which he had no access, such as diplomacy and leadership decisions, but it is vitally important for other aspects of the siege. He is biased against the Greeks, especially for not adhering to the Union.

Saraca Pasha: a former *beylerbey* of Rumeli, he served as vizier to Murad II and Mehmed II, including during the siege.

Sekoundinos, Nikolaos (**AU**, not present at the siege, d. 1464): ethnic Greek with a classical education from Euboia (Venetian Negroponte) who took up a series of posts in the service of Venice and became one of its most trusted agents. He was the official translator at the Council of Florence (1438–1439), networked with many prominent intellectuals of the time (both Greek and Latin), and was sent by Venice to negotiate over the release of Venetian captives after the fall of Constantinople. He wrote (in Latin) one of the most influential accounts of the rise of the Ottoman empire.

Sphrantzes, Georgios (**AU**, present during the siege): confidant of Konstantinos XI and one of his chief diplomats. He wrote a series of notes about his own life, a sort of memoir, although he says little about the siege. He was captured and ransomed afterward. He should not be confused with the author of the "longer" (*Maius*) version of his memoirs, which is a sixteenth-century forgery ("pseudo-Sphrantzes"; in reality, written by Makarios Melissourgos).

Tafur, Pero: Spanish gentleman from Andalusia who traveled throughout the Mediterranean, visiting Constantinople in 1438, and wrote an account of his journeys and experiences.

Tetaldi, Giacomo (**AU**, present during the siege): obscure Florentine who claimed to be a Venetian when he escaped during the fall. He wrote a brief Latin account of the siege with valuable, although not always reliable, information.

Timur (Tamerlane) (d. 1405): terrifying Mongol conqueror who, among his many victories, defeated the Ottoman sultan Bayezid I at the battle of Ankara in 1402, throwing the Ottoman empire into chaos.

Trevisan, Gabriele (d. ca. 1470): Venetian admiral sent by the Senate to help in the defense of Constantinople if it came under Ottoman attack. At first, he commanded the defense fleet of the harbor, then he was posted to the sea walls of the harbor.

Tursun Bey (**AU**, probably present during the siege): the main Ottoman historian of the siege and fall, he came from a military family but opted for a bureaucratic career. His account is invaluable as it reflects an Ottoman perspective, even though it contains poetic interludes and theological digressions.

Urban: see Orban.

Zaganos Pasha: general and vizier of Mehmed II during the siege, he was regarded as the leading war hawk at the Ottoman court.

Notes

INTRODUCTION

1. Gennadios Scholarios, *Pastoral Letter on the Fall of Constantinople*, in *Oeuvres*, v. 4, 213–214.
2. G. D. Brockett, 'When Ottomans Become Turks: Commemorating the Conquest of Constantinople and Its Contribution to World History,' *The American Historical Review* 119 (2014) 399–433.
3. S. Runciman, *The Fall of Constantinople, 1453* (Cambridge 1965), cited by, e.g., Angold, *Fall*, vi, 1; and G. Saint-Guillain and N. Vatin in Déroche-Vatin 13 n. 1.
4. The best among the older popular narratives is E. Pears, *The Destruction of the Greek Empire and the Story of the Capture of Constantinople by the Turks* (London 1903); among the more recent, it is R. Crowley, *Constantinople: The Last Great Siege, 1453* (New York 2005). S. Gouguenheim's *Constantinople 1453: "La Ville est tombée!"* (Paris 2024) is disappointing. It covers events before 1400 in a hundred pages drawn mostly from modern general scholarship, skips the crucial years from 1402 to 1452, and then covers the siege in fewer than 60, large-print pages, sticking mostly to the conventional picture.
5. Leonardo in Belgrano 233 = Melville-Jones 12 = Déroche-Vatin 692.
6. Emecen, *Fetih ve Kyamet*, 65–80.
7. A. Kaldellis, *The Case for East Roman Studies* (Leeds 2024).

CHAPTER I

1. Tafur, *Travels*, pp. 115–126.
2. E. Fenster, *Laudes Constantinopolitanae* (Munich 1968).
3. Made to rule: Metochites, *Byzantios* 52 (p. 476); ruins: 66 (p. 487); cosmos: 80 (pp. 500–502). For close readings, see Polemis, *Theodore Metochites*, 131–146; P. Magdalino, *Roman Constantinople in Byzantine Perspective:*

The Memorial and Aesthetic Rediscovery of Constantine's Beautiful City, from Late Antiquity to the Renaissance (Leiden 2024) 109–140.

4. Tafur, *Travels*, pp. 123, 145–146.
5. Metochites, *Byzantios* 95–98 (pp. 514–518); location: 9–10 (pp. 436–437), 13–14 (pp. 439–440), 19 (pp. 444–445), 22–23 (pp. 448–450).
6. Clavijo, *Embassy*, p. 90; also, Bertrandon, *Voyage*, pp. 88–89; Tafur, *Travels*, p. 115; Scalamonti, *Life of Cyriac of Ancona* 37.
7. Jacoby, 'Constantinople,' esp. 203–204 for slaves; and see the following chapter.
8. Tafur, *Travels*, p. 149.
9. Bibliothèque nationale de France, mss. fr. 9097, f. 207v.
10. Schiltberger, *Bondage*, p. 81.
11. Necipoğlu, *Byzantium*, 138–139, 201–202.
12. Necipoğlu, 'Ottoman Merchants'; *Byzantium*, 201–202.
13. Doukas 20.4; Sphrantzes 3.1.
14. Scalamonti, *Life of Cyriac of Ancona* 42; for libraries and schools, see E. P. Petrou, *Ἡ παιδεία στὴν Κωνσταντινούπολη τὸν 15ο αἰ.* (PhD dissertation, University of Ioannina 2017).
15. Dolphins: Kyriacos of Ancona, *Letter* 40.2.
16. In Pertusi, *Caduta*, v. 2, 52.
17. Metochites, *Byzantios* 93 (p. 512).
18. Ioannes Chortasmenos, *Letter* 44, ed. Hunger, *Chortasmenos*, 200.
19. T. Ganchou, 'Les ultimae voluntates de Manuel et Iòannès Chrysolôras et le séjour de Francesco Filelfo à Constantinople,' *Byzantinistica: Rivista di studi bizantini e slavi* 7 (2005) 195–285.
20. H. Lamers, 'Hellenism and Cultural Unease in Italian Humanism: The Case of Francesco Filelfo,' in J. De Keyser, ed., *Francesco Filelfo, Man of Letters* (Leiden 2019) 22–42, here 37, 40.
21. Metochites, *Byzantios* 88 (p. 508), 90–91 (pp. 509–510).
22. Polemis, *Theodore Metochites*, 37, 39–40, 139–140.
23. Clavijo, *Embassy*, p. 76; Schiltberger, *Bondage*, p. 80; Tafur, *Travels*, p. 139.
24. Janin, *Les églises et les monastères*, xiv.
25. Majeska, *Russian Travelers*, 164.
26. E.g., T. Ganchou, 'Géôrgios Scholarios, «Secrétaire» du Patriarche Unioniste Grègorios III Mammas? Le Mystère Résolu,' in P. Odorico, ed., *Le Patriarcat oecuménique de Constantinople aux XIVe–XVIe siècles: rupture et continuité* (Paris 2007) 117–194, here 117, 162 n. 97.
27. S. Brock, 'A Medieval Armenian Pilgrim's Description of Constantinople,' *Revue des études arméniennes* n.s. 4 (1967) 81–102.

28. S. H. Cross and O. P. Sherbowitz-Wetzor, *The Russian Primary Chronicle: Laurentian Text* (Cambridge, MA 1953) 111.
29. M. Angold, 'The Decline of Byzantium Seen through the Eyes of Western Travellers,' in R. Macrides, ed., *Travel in the Byzantine World* (Burlington, VT 2002) 213–233.
30. Majeska, *Russian Travelers*, 44-46. I suspect that a number of texts studied today under the *Patria* rubric originate in the milieu of Constantinopolitan tour guides.
31. Wright, *Gattilusio Lordships*.
32. Scalamonti, *Life of Cyriac of Ancona* 85; more in Necipoğlu, *Byzantium*, 201.
33. Moustakas, 'Μεθοδολογικά ζητήματα.' Past estimates: Necipoğlu, *Byzantium*, 222.
34. Madden, 'Fires.'
35. A. Kontogiannopoulou, 'Εσωτερικές μεταναστεύσεις στο ύστερο Βυζάντιο,' *Byzantina Symmeikta* 27 (2017) 211–238.
36. Doukas 5.5.
37. H.-M. Congourdeau, 'La peste noire à Constantinople de 1348 à 1466,' *Medicina nei secoli* 11.2 (1999) 377–389.
38. Mergiali-Sahas, 'Οι Βυζαντινοί'; Grant, *Greek Captives*.
39. Necipoğlu, *Byzantium*, ch. 7.
40. Manuel Chrysoloras, *Comparison of Old Rome and New Rome* 6 (p. 8); tr. Smith p. 200.
41. Gennadios Scholarios, *Lamentation* 4, in *Oeuvres*, v. 1, 287.
42. Buondelmonti, *Description*, pp. 147, 150; for the different surviving versions, see I. R. Manners, 'Constructing the Image of a City: The Representation of Constantinople in Christopher Buondelmonti's Liber Insularum Archipelagi,' *Annals of the Association of American Geographers* 87 (1997) 72–102.
43. A.-M. Talbot, 'Agricultural Properties in Palaiologan Constantinople,' in A. Berger et al., eds., *Koinotaton Doron: Das späte Byzanz* (Berlin 2016) 185–195.
44. Clavijo, *Embassy*, pp. 87–89 (modified); also, among others, Buondelmonti, *Description*, p. 150; Bertrandon, *Voyage*, pp. 98–99; Tafur, *Travels*, p. 146; for more, including ibn Battuta, see J. P. A. Van Der Vin, *Travellers to Greece and Constantinople: Ancient Monuments and Old Traditions in Medieval Travellers' Tales* (Istanbul 1980) 254.
45. Kritoboulos 1.14.13.
46. K.-P. Matschke, 'Rolle und Aufgaben des Demarchen in der spätbyzantinischen Hauptstadt,' in idem, *Das spätbyzantinische Konstantinopel:*

Alt und neue Beiträge zur Stadtgeschichte zwischen 1261 und 1453 (Kovač 2008) 153–187; for the early fourteenth century, see Agoritsas, *Κωνσταντινούπολη*, 231–232. Protocol: K. Sathas, *Μεσαιωνική Βιβλιοθήκη*, v. 6 (Venice 1877) 643–644; lists: Sphrantzes 35.6–8.

47. Schiltberger, *Bondage*, p. 79; Tafur, *Travels*, p. 145.
48. Bertrandon, *Voyage*, p. 101; also Clavijo, *Embassy*, p. 69; Buondelmonti, *Description*, p. 148; Tafur, *Travels*, p. 143; Scalamonti, *Life of Cyriac of Ancona* 41; for more and later sources, see T. Koutsogiannes, 'The Hippodrome of Constantinople in the Renaissance,' in *Constantinopla*, v. 3, 43–66.
49. F. Miklosich and I. Müller, *Acta et diplomata graeca medii aevi sacra et profana*, v. 2 (Vienna 1862) 495–496.
50. H. Hunger et al., eds., *Das Register des Patriarchats von Konstantinopel* (Vienna 1981–2001) v. 3, 68. Forum market: Oikonomidès, *Hommes d'affaires*, 101–102.
51. Tafur, *Travels*, p. 141.
52. Clavijo, *Embassy*, p. 84; Tafur, *Travels*, pp. 141–142; see Majeska, *Russian Travelers*, 365; Agoritsas, *Κωνσταντινούπολη*, 79–80.
53. R. Macrides et al., *Pseudo-Kodinos and the Constantinopolitan Offices and Ceremonies* (Burlington, VT 2013). The historians are Nikephoros Gregoras and Ioannes Kantakouzenos.
54. Burning: Sphrantzes 21.14; Isidoros: G. Mercati, *Opere minori* (Vatican City 1937 = *Studi e testi* 79) v. 4, 188–192; Tafur, *Travels*, p. 142.
55. Clavijo, *Embassy*, pp. 63, 79; also Tafur, *Travels*, pp. 118, 124; Sphrantzes 31.8.
56. Kyriacus of Ancona, *Letter* 12.
57. M. C. Bartusis, *The Late Byzantine Army: Arms and Society, 1204–1453* (Philadephia 1992), esp. 217–221 for the Peloponnese, 286 for the lack of palace guards in 1453; S. Kyriakides, *Warfare in Late Byzantium, 1204–1453* (Leiden 2011). There is no evidence that *pronoia* grants were used in the final decades. Estangüi Gómez, *Byzance*, offers a detailed study of the institutional means of governance, but does not discuss the army.
58. Oikonomidès, *Hommes d'affaires*; A. E. Laiou, *Gender, Society, and Economic Life in Byzantium* (Variorum 1992) VII and VIII; Necipoğlu, *Byzantium*, 210–218; Estangüi Gómez, *Byzance*, 196–201. For the Notarades, see K.-P. Matschke, 'The Notaras Family and Its Italian Connections,' *Dumbarton Oaks Papers* 49 (1995) 59–72; Ganchou, 'Le rachat des Notaras,' 158–167; and 'L'ultime testament de Géôrgios Goudélès, homme d'affaires, *mésazôn* de Jean V et *ktètôr* (Constantinople, 4 mars 1421),' *Travaux et mémoires* 16 (2010) 277–358.

59. J. Chrysostomides, 'Venetian Commercial Privileges under the Palaiologoi,' *Studi veneziani* 12 (1970) 267–356, esp. 286; D. Jacoby, 'Between the Imperial Court and the Western Maritime Powers: The Impact of Naturalizations on the Economy of Late Byzantine Constantinople,' in A. Ödekan et al., eds., *The Byzantine Court: Source of Power and Culture* (Istanbul 2013) 95–103.
60. N. B. Tomadakis, 'Ἰωσὴφ Βρυεννίου Δημηγορία περὶ τοῦ τῆς Πόλεως ἀνακτίσματος (1415 μ.Χ.), *Ἐπετηρὶς Ἑταιρείας Βυζαντινῶν Σπουδῶν* 36 (1968) 3–12, here 9–10. See also Gennadios Scholarios, *Defense Speech Addressed to Konstantinos Palaiologos*, in *ΠΠ*, v. 2, 96.
61. Ioannes Chortasmenos, *Poems* b, d, g, ed. Hunger, *Chortasmenos*, 190–195; see Necipoğlu, *Byzantium*, 197–198.
62. Ganchou, '"La tour d'Irène"'; P. Magdalino, 'The sebastokrator Isaac at home,' in V. F. Lovato, ed., *Isaac Komnenos Porphyrogennetos: Walking the Line in Twelfth-Century Byzantium* (London 2024) 63–78, here 68–69.
63. U. Dorini and T. Bertelè, eds., *Il libro dei conti di Giacomo Badoer* (Rome 1956), with G. Bartelé, *Il libro dei conti di Giacomo Badoer (Constantinopoli 1436-1440): Complemento e indici* (Padova 2002); analyses: Necipoğlu, *Byzantium*, 191–193; Angold, *Fall*, 35–36.
64. Ganchou, 'La famille Koumousès,' 49–50; 'La *fraterna societas*'; and 'Sujets grecs crétois.'
65. Ganchou, 'La *fraterna societas*,' 117–118.
66. M. Vassilaki, *The Painter Angelos and Icon-Painting in Venetian Crete* (Variorum 2009) I.
67. 200,000 vs. 30,000 hyperpyra: Gregoras, *Roman History* 17.1β (v. 2, 841–842); see N. Oikonomides, 'The Role of the Byzantine State in the Economy,' in A. E. Laiou, ed., *The Economic History of Byzantium* (Washington, DC 2002) 973–1058, here 1054–1055.
68. Jacoby, 'Constantinople,' 209–210.
69. Tafur, *Travels*, pp. 146, 149 (I have changed the translation to match the Spanish more accurately: *e así son todos ricos*).
70. N. Necipoğlu, 'Byzantines and Italians in Fifteenth-Century Constantinople: Commercial Cooperation and Conflict,' *New Perspectives on Turkey* 12 (1995) 129–143, here 133–135.
71. E.g., G. Morgan, 'The Venetian Claims Commission of 1278,' *Byzantinische Zeitschrift* 69 (1976) 411–438; Nicol, *Byzantium and Venice*, 197–206.
72. Tafur, *Travels*, pp. 146–147.
73. Oikonomidès, *Hommes d'affaires*, 101–103; Angold, *Fall*, 38.

74. Later fourteenth century: A. Laiou, 'Women in the Marketplace of Constantinople (10th-14th Centuries),' in N. Necipoğlu, ed., *Byzantine Constantinople: Monuments, Topography, and Everyday Life* (Leiden 2001) 261–273.
75. P. Canivet and N. Oikonomidès, '(Jean Argyropoulos) La Comédie de Katablattas,' *Δίπτυχα* 3 (1982–1983) 5–79, here 55–57.
76. For the claim and context, see Shukurov, *Byzantine Turks*, 359–380.
77. Makarios Makres in Necipoğlu, *Byzantium*, 199–200, 209; Symeon of Thessalonike in S. Vryonis, 'Crises and Anxieties in Fifteenth Century Byzantium,' in R. Olson, ed., *Islamic and Middle Eastern Societies: A Festschrift in Honor of Professor Wadie Jwaideh* (Brattleboro, VT 1987) 100–125, here 101–102, 107.
78. See pp. 74 and 249 below.

CHAPTER 2

1. A. Kaldellis and S. Kennedy, 'Thucydides in Byzantium,' in P. Low, ed., *The Cambridge Companion to Thucydides* (Cambridge 2023) 249–264; Kaldellis, *New Herodotos*, esp. 30–38.
2. E.g., Manuel Chrysoloras, *Comparison of Old Rome and New Rome* 36 (p. 17); Kantakouzenos, *History* 3.87 (v. 2, 537). See Chapter 4 for the moat.
3. For the context of the emergence of the emirates, see D. Korobeinikov, *Byzantium and the Turks in the Thirteenth Century* (Oxford 2014).
4. These processes are reconstructed by C. Foss, *The Beginnings of the Ottoman Empire* (Oxford 2022), and Lowry, *Nature*.
5. Laonikos Chalkokondyles 2.47–49, 4.62, 5.50; Mihailović, *Memoirs*, pp. 89–91, 96; see Fodor, 'Ottoman Warfare,' 205; Kaldellis, *New Herodotos*, 147–153; Imber, *Ottoman Empire*, 131–133. The study by A. Gheorghe, *The Metamorphoses of Power: Violence, Warlords, Akıncıs and the Early Ottomans (1300–1450)* (Leiden 2023) reached me after I had finished writing this book.
6. Lowry, *Nature*, 54.
7. Isidoros Glabas, *Homily* 4.1, ed. V. Christophorides, *Ἰσιδώρου Γλαβᾶ περιστασιακὲς ὁμιλίες* (Thessalonike 1981) 37–67; Doukas 23.2, 23.9; in general, see Imber, *Ottoman Empire*, 134–141.
8. D. Pipes, *Slave Soldiers and Islam: The Genesis of a Military System* (New Haven 1981).
9. Babinger, *Mehmed the Conqueror*, 64–65.
10. E.g., Angold, *Fall*, 30.

11. Necipoğlu, *Byzantium*, 202–203; sources regarding his pro-Roman stance are cited by eadem, 'Ottoman Merchants,' 162; Philippides and Hanak, *Siege*, 484–485 n. 37.
12. E.g., Doukas 35.5.
13. H. Inalcık, 'Greeks in the Ottoman Economy and Finances 1453–1500,' in J. Stanojevich Allen et al., eds., *το ελληνικον: Studies in Honor of Speros Bryonis, Jr.*, v. 2 (New Rochelle, NY 1993) 307–319.
14. For his career, see Déroche-Vatin 1312–1313.
15. Babinger, *Mehmed the Conqueror*, 8, 14–15.
16. Settlements: Kolovos, *Στους καιρούς των σουλτάνων*, 121; army structures: Fodor, 'Ottoman Warfare,' and 199 for Christians; Imber, *Ottoman Empire*, 257–267.
17. Tafur, *Travels*, pp. 127–128.
18. For this tension, see Kafescioğlu, *Constantinopolis/Istanbul*, 2, 174, citing previous studies.
19. K. Şahin, 'Constantinople and the End Time: The Ottoman Conquest as a Portent of the Last Hour,' *Journal of Early Modern History* 14 (2010) 317–354, here 327 (contrary to its intention, this article persuaded me that the apocalyptic overtones of the conquest were marginal and weak on the Ottoman side). For Muslim predictions about the conquest of Constantinople, see, in general, L. Massignon, 'Textes prémonitoires et commentaries mystiques relatifs à la prise de Constantinople par les Turcs in 1453,' *Oriens* 6 (1953) 10–17; S. Bashear, 'Apocalyptic and Other Materials on Early Muslim-Byzantine Wars,' *Journal of the Royal Asiatic Society* ser. 3, 1 (1991) 173–207; N. M. El Cheikh, *Byzantium Viewed by the Arabs* (Cambridge, MA 2004) 25–28, 65–67.
20. Mehmed II, *Fetihname to the Sultan of Egypt*, in Déroche-Vatin 750. This is a major theme in Emecen, *Fetih ve Kyamet*, esp. 52–55, who presents these traditions in detail, but relies too much on suppositions about Mehmed's psychology.
21. Biography: The *Menakıbname of Ak Şemseddin* in Déroche-Vatin 1052–1059; letter: see pp. 138–139 below.
22. C. Imber, 'The Ottoman Dynastic Myth,' *Turcica* 19 (1987) 7–27. Some of these elements are on display in the early Ottoman chronicle translated by Kastritsis, *An Early Ottoman History*.
23. Tafur, *Travels*, p. 137.
24. Sphrantzes 23.10–11; also Doukas 31.8.
25. Sphrantzes 23.5–6.
26. J. Gill, *The Council of Florence* (Cambridge 1959) 349–355; M.-H. Blanchet, 'L'église byzantine à la suite de l'union de Florence (1439–1445):

de la contestation à la scission,' *Byzantinische Forschungen* 29 (2007) 79–123.

27. *The Holy Wars of Sultan Murad*, in C. Imber, *The Crusade of Varna, 1443–1445* (Aldershot, UK 2006) 42–44.
28. For a history of these western perceptions, see Kaldellis, *Phantom Byzantium*.
29. Necipoğlu, *Byzantium*, 210–218.
30. Sphrantzes 23.2–3 (condensed).
31. Aeneas Silvius Piccolomini, *Europe (c. 1400–1458)*, tr. R. Brown (Washington, DC 2013) 80.
32. Kiousopoulou, *Βασιλεύς ή οικονόμος*, 58–77.
33. Blanchet, *Georges-Gennadios Scholarios*, 383–450.
34. References in Necipoğlu, *Byzantium*, 217.
35. Burial: Gennadios Scholarios, *Defense of the Antiunionists* 13, in *Oeuvres*, v. 3, 100. Unless he means that anti-Union rites were not "real" rites at all. Coronation: see below.
36. J. Harris, 'The Patriarch of Constantinople and the Last Days of Byzantium,' in C. Gastgeber et al., eds., *The Patriarchate of Constantinople in Context and Comparison* (Vienna 2017) 10–16.
37. Indicative statements in Gennadius Scholarios, *Oeuvres*, v. 3, 96–97, 147, 158–163.
38. Ioannes Eugenikos, *Letter to Notaras*, in *ΠΠ*, v. 1, 142. The sentiment was old. The pro-Union author Manuel Kalekas had claimed that his enemies would rather convert to Islam than Catholicism: *Against the Errors of the Greeks*, in *PG* 152: 239B–C.
39. Doukas 37.10, 39.19.
40. Doukas 37.10. A similar view of Notaras in Posculo: Whitchurch, *The Constantinopolis*, 11. For the meaning of his words, see D. R. Reinsch, 'Lieber den Turban als was? Bemerkungen zum Dichtum des Lukas Notaras,' in C. N. Constantinides et al., eds., *Φιλέλλην: Studies in Honour of Robert Browning* (Venice 1996) 377–389.
41. Philippides, *Constantine XI*, 246; T. Kiousopoulou, 'Λουκάς Νοταράς: Ψήγματα μιάς βιογραφίας,' in F. Euaggelatou-Notara and T. Maniati-Kokkini, eds., *Κλητόριον εἰς μνήμην Νίκου Οἰκονομίδη* (Athens 2005) 161–176, here 170–171. For his links to Gregorios III, see Ganchou, 'Le rachat des Notaras,' 184.
42. T. Ganchou, 'Nikolaos Notaras, *mésengyos tôn Ausonôn*, et le *mésastikion* à Byzance au XVe siècle,' *Bizantinistica* ser. 2, 14 (2012) 151–181, here 152.
43. It is a tiny number of modern crusades historians who fantasize that "the Greeks" wanted to be ruled by manly western knights, while, on the other

side, it is only fringe neo-Ottoman ideologues who believe that the Greeks sought shelter under the protective embrace of the Ottoman empire.

44. Meletios, *Against the Italians* 228–231, in V. Laurent and J. Darrouzès, *Dossier grec de l'Union de Lyon* (Paris 1976) 562.
45. Gennadios Scholarios, *On the Rarity of Miracles at the Present Time* 13, in *Oeuvres*, v. 3, 387.
46. Manuel II Palaiologos, *Funeral Oration on his Brother Theodoros*, p. 129; Gennadios Scholarios, *Panegyric of the Holy Apostles* 6–8, in *Oeuvres*, v. 1, 178–181; *Lament on the Misfortunes of His Life* 3, in *Oeuvres*, v. 1, 285–286; *Pastoral Letter on the Fall of Constantinople* 7, 10, in *Oeuvres*, v. 4, 219, 225. For conversion to Islam, see S. Vryonis, *The Decline of Medieval Hellenism in Asia Minor and the Process of Islamization from the Eleventh through the Fifteenth Century* (Berkeley 1971).
47. E. A. Zachariadou, 'Mount Athos and the Ottomans *c.*1350-1550,' in M. Angold, ed., *The Cambridge History of Christianity*, v. 5: *Eastern Christianity* (Cambridge 2006) 154–168; for bishops in conquered territories, see T. Papademetriou, 'The Turkish Conquests and Decline of the Church Reconsidered, in D. Angelov, ed., *Church and Society in Late Byzantium* (Kalamazoo, MI 2009) 183–200. In general, see M. Balivet, *Byzantins et Ottomans: Relations, Interaction, Sucession* (Istanbul 1999) 31–47.
48. See pp. 82, 225–226 below.
49. Demetrios and anti-Unionists: Gennadios Scholarios, *Letter to Demetrios Palaiologos against Union*, in *Oeuvres*, v. 3, 117–136 (1450 AD), esp. 119–121 on the events of 1442; and *Letter to Demetrios Palaiologos against Union*, in *Oeuvres*, v. 3, 174–178 (December 25, 1452). Coup with Turkish support: Sphrantzes 25.3; Laonikos Chalkokondyles 6.32. Same contacts: Ganchou, 'La *fraterna societas*,' 136–138.
50. Kritoboulos 1.16.13 (in the mouth of Mehmed), and, e.g., Philippides and Hanak, *Siege*, 533.
51. A. Koumousi, 'Παλαιά Μονή Ταξιαρχών Αιγιαλείας: η αναχρονολόγηση της ίδρυσης στους μεσοβυζαντινούς χρόνους και η προσωπογραφία του τελευταίου βυζαντινού αυτοκράτορα,' in M. Xanthopoulou et al., eds., *Το αρχαιολογικό έργο στην Πελοπόννησο 3* (Kalamata 2024) 747–759.
52. Consensus: A. Kaldellis, *The Byzantine Republic: People and Power in New Rome* (Cambridge, MA 2015); no crown and writers: Philippides, *Constantine XI*, 221–223 (exaggerating the extent of the contemporary controversy over this); and Philippides and Hanak, *Cardinal Isidore*, 149–150.

53. Ioannes Argyropoulos, *Address to Konstantinos XI*, in S. Lambros, *Ἀργυροπούλεια* (Athens 1910) 45–47.
54. Kiousopoulou, *Βασιλεύς ή οικονόμος*, 149.
55. Nicol, *Byzantium and Venice*, 390–391.
56. Sphrantzes 32.7, 34.9.
57. Leonardo in Belgrano 247 = Melville-Jones 29 = Déroche-Vatin 715.
58. Sphrantzes 12.3.
59. Philippides, *Constantine XI*, 54–58, 60, 106–121, who is perhaps too negative about Konstantinos; a narrative survey in J. Harris, *The End of Byzantium* (New Haven 2010) 112–126.
60. Philippides, *Constantine XI*, 139–146.
61. Philippides, *Constantine XI*, 177–190.
62. F. Thiriet, *La Romanie vénitienne au Moyen Age: le développement et l'exploitation du domaine colonial* (Paris 1959).
63. Wright, *Gattilusio Lordships*. For the Genoese in the east, see Balard, *Romanie génoise*, esp. ch. 3 for a geographical overview. For alum, see Fleet, *European and Islamic Trade*, ch. 7.
64. P. Argenti, *The Occupation of Chios by the Genoese* (Cambridge 1958).
65. Balard, *Romanie génoise*, 289–310, 785–833; Fleet, *European and Islamic Trade*, ch. 4; Mergiali-Sahas, 'Οι Βυζαντινοί'; Grant, *Greek Captives*.
66. Ch. Maltezou, *Ὁ θεσμὸς τοῦ ἐν Κωνσταντινουπόλει Βενετοῦ βαΐλου (1268–1453)* (Athens 1970).
67. Lane, *Venice*, 127–138; D. Stöckly, *Le système de l'incanto des galées du marché à Venise (fin XIIIe–milieu XVe siècle)* (Leiden 1995).
68. M. Angar, '*Pera Ianuensium pulcherrima civitas est*: Creating a Genoese Identity on the Golden Horn,' in N. Bakirtzis and L. Zavagno, eds., *The Routledge Handbook of the Byzantine City* (London 2024) 451–477; for its urban evolution, see Balard, *Romanie génoise*, 179–198.
69. Tetaldi 19.1, in Philippides 198–199; Tafur, *Travels*, p. 149.
70. C. Delacroix-Besnier, *Les Dominicains et la chrétienté grecque aux XIVe et XVe siècles* (Rome 1997) 187–197; N. I. Tsougarakis, *The Latin Religious Orders in Medieval Greece, 1204–1500* (Turnhout 2012).
71. Nicol, *Byzantium and Venice*, 390–391; Philippides and Hanak, *Siege*, 362–362; Philippides, *Constantine XI*, 240–241.
72. Necipoğlu, *Byzantium*, 188–189, 205.
73. Full sources for these episodes in Rohan, *Transforming Empire*, 228–229; for Genoese trade with the Ottomans, see Fleet, *European and Islamic Trade*.
74. Nicol, *Byzantium and Venice*, 394.
75. Tafur, *Travels*, p. 127.

76. Balivet, *Byzantins et Ottomans*; R. Shukurov, *The Byzantine Turks, 1204–1461* (Leiden 2016) esp. 306–387.
77. Barbaro in Cornet 14 = Jones 23.

CHAPTER 3

1. Civil war: D. Kastritsis, *The Sons of Bayezid: Empire Building and Representation in the Ottoman Civil War of 1402–1413* (Leiden 2007); treaty: G. T. Dennis, 'The Byzantine-Turkish Treaty of 1403,' *Orientalia Christiana periodica* 33 (1967) 72–88.
2. Doukas 22.5 (the equivalent of 10,000 Venetian ducats).
3. Terms: Doukas 29.1; envoys: Sphrantzes 12.4; 1422 siege of Constantinople: Kananos, *The Siege of Constantinople*; Thessalonike: Necipoğlu, *Byzantium*, ch. 4–5; context of 1424 treaty: ibid. 34–36 (the figure of 100,000 ducats in Sanudo must be an error); pretender instigated in Asia Minor in 1422: Doukas 28.6–8.
4. Sphrantzes 23.7.
5. Doukas 31.8.
6. Sphrantzes 29.2; Laonikos Chalkokondyles 7.61; for Demetrios, see Ganchou, 'La *fraterna societas*,' 136–138.
7. Doukas 33.1; Sphrantzes 29.3.
8. E.g., Doukas 33.6; for more, see Philippides and Hanak, *Siege*, 360–361.
9. Doukas 33.12–34.1 (the terms are given only here); Sphrantzes 30.4; Kritoboulos 1.5.3. If Doukas is right, Laonikos Chalkokondyles 7.65 gets this wrong: the lands were not in Asia Minor and the basileus was not given them, only their revenue. Posculo, *Constantinople*, book 2, claims that Murad II removed Herakleia (on the Sea of Marmara) from the Romans and that the latter requested, and received, it back from Mehmed II upon the latter's accession. This story appears to be wholly erroneous. For Herakleia in this period, see Külzer, *Ostthrakien*, 404.
10. Doukas 33.12; Laonikos Chalkokondyles 7.66.
11. Doukas 33.11; Mihailović, *Memoirs*, p. 49.
12. Kritoboulos 1.15.
13. Sphrantzes 30.4–6. This record was likely colored by later events.
14. E.g., F. Dölger and P. Wirth, *Regesten der Kaiserurkunden des oströmischen Reiches von 565–1453*, v. 5: *Regesten von 1341–1453* (Munich 1965) 134–136, with an itemized list of embassies, citing the relevant sources; also Philippides and Hanak, *Siege*, 361 ("alarmed"); iidem, *Cardinal Isidore*, 124.
15. Setton, *Papacy*, v. 2, 108.

16. Gennadios Scholarios, *Letter to Konstantinos XI Palaiologos*, in *Oeuvres*, v. 3, 152–153.
17. His letter can be found in F. Cerrone, 'La politica orientale di Alfonso di Aragona [cont.],' *Archivio storico per le province napoletane* 27 (1902), here 592–593.
18. W. Hanak, 'Pope Nicholas V and the Aborted Crusade of 1452–1453 to Rescue Constantinople from the Turks,' *Byzantinoslavica* 65 (2007) 337–359.
19. Doukas 34.2–4.
20. Sphrantzes 33.1.
21. Nicol, *Byzantium and Venice*, 393.
22. Kastritsis, *An Early Ottoman History*, 176; Laonikos Chalkokondyles 7.64, 7.67; Tursun Bey in Déroche-Vatin 193.
23. See Chapter 5.
24. Mehmed II, *Fetihname to the Sultan of Egypt*, in Déroche-Vatin 745–753; *Fetihname-i Sultan Mehmed*, in Déroche-Vatin 1069.
25. Laonikos Chalkokondyles 6.53, 6.55, 6.59; Doukas 32.4, 34.6; Kastritsis, *An Early Ottoman History*, 166.
26. Kritoboulos 1.14.16–1.16.6.
27. Aşikpaşazade in Déroche-Vatin 346; Babinger, *Mehmed the Conqueror*, 72 (where the source is not cited, costing me a few hours of my life to track it down).
28. Tursun Bey in Déroche-Vatin 196–197.
29. Many sources in several languages describe the building of Rumeli Hisarı. Church: Doukas 34.8; cannons: Kritoboulos 1.11.6–7; "dragons" and "bird": Tursun Bey in Déroche-Vatin 199.
30. F. Babinger, 'Ein venedischer Lageplan der Feste Rümeli Hisâry (2. Hälfte des XV. Jhdts.),' *La bibliofilia* 57 (1955) 188–195.
31. Doukas 34.6; Kritoboulos 1.7–8.
32. Barbaro in Cornet 1–2 = Jones 9 = Déroche-Vatin 465.
33. Sphrantzes 35.2; Doukas 34.9–10; Tursun Bey in Inalcik-Murphey 34 = Déroche-Vatin 200.
34. Doukas 34.11; Tursun Bey in Inalcik-Murphey 34 = Déroche-Vatin 200; Posculo 3.243–250 = Ellisen 46–47; see Philippides and Hanak, *Siege*, 408.
35. Barbaro in Cornet 2 = Jones 9 = Déroche-Vatin 465; Posculo 3.291–296 = Ellisen 47–48; Doukas 34.11; Kritoboulos 1.17.3–1.18.1; Kastritsis, *An Early Ottoman History*, 177. Tursun Bey in Inalcik-Murphey 34 = Déroche-Vatin 200 implies that Mehmed gave Konstantinos the option to surrender the City at this point, but that is unlikely.
36. Laonikos Chalkokondyles 8.1.

37. Theodoros Agallianos in Schreiner, *Byzantinischen Kleinchroniken*, App. 6 (2:636). I have slightly compressed and paraphrased the text.
38. S. Eustratiades, 'Ἐκ τοῦ κώδικος τοῦ Νικολάου Καρατζᾶ,' *Ἐκκλησιαστικὸς Φάρος* 6 (1910) 200–206, here 205.
39. Doukas 34.5; Kritoboulos 1.7.1; Posculo 3.204–207 = Ellisen 46 and 3.300–307 = Ellisen 48.
40. A. Rigo, 'Lo *Horismòs* di Sinân Pacià, la presa di Ioannina (1430) e le "lettera" del sultano Murâd II,' *Thesaurismata* 28 (1998) 57–78, here 62.
41. Necipoğlu, *Byzantium*, ch. 5; and Kolovos, *Στους καιρούς των σουλτάνων*, 29–37.
42. Ioannes Anagnostes, *History of the Final Fall of Thessalonike* 14, 18.
43. Grant, *Greek Captives*, 187–188.
44. Kananos, *Siege of Constantinople*, pp. 28–29.
45. Doukas 34.6; Kritoboulos 1.18.2.
46. See p. 249 below.
47. Philippides and Hanak, *Siege*, 214–231.
48. G. Dennis, *The Reign of Manuel II Palaeologus in Thessalonica* (Rome 1960).
49. P. Gautier, 'Action de grâces de Démétrius Chrysoloras,' *Revue des études byzantines* 19 (1961) 340–357.
50. J. W. Barker, *Manuel II Palaeologus, 1391–1425: A Study in Late Byzantine Statesmanship* (New Brunswick 1969) 146–147.
51. Manuel II, *Funeral Oration for Theodoros Palaiologos*, pp. 175–211, esp. 185 for opposition; Laonikos Chalkokondyles 2.45.
52. Necipoğlu, *Byzantium*, 44, 53, 59–83.
53. Barbaro in Cornet 16 = Jones 25 = Déroche-Vatin 473.
54. Nicol, *Byzantium and Venice*, 394; Trevisan: Barbaro in Cornet 3 = Jones 10-11 = Déroche-Vatin 467; July 1452 knowledge: Halff, 'Nicolò Barbaro,' 27 n. 100. Doge: D. Romano, *The Likeness of Venice: A Life of Doge Francesco Foscari, 1373–1457* (New Haven 2007) ch. 4.
55. Philippides and Hanak, *Cardinal Isidore*, 127–130, 168–170; idem, *Siege*, 374–375; for Leonardo, see also Déroche-Vatin 681–691 (against Scholarios: ibid. 687).
56. Barbaro in Cornet 2–4 = Jones 10–12 = Déroche-Vatin 466–468 (truncated); Doukas 35.2.
57. For these missions, see R. Guilland, *Études byzantines* (Paris 1959) 135–176.
58. Sphrantzes 36.2–14; commentary in Philippides and Hanak, *Siege*, 365–373.

59. Laonikos Chalkokondyles 8.2; Sphrantzes 35.4. Help requested: Kritoboulos 1.19.1.
60. Doukas 36.2–6; "pinned to his door": see Gennadios in *ΠΠ*, v. 2, 120–121; aid from the West: Gennadios in *ΠΠ*, v. 2, 125–126; for reconstructions citing more sources, see Philippides and Hanak, *Cardinal Isidore*, 135–156; Blanchet, *Georges-Gennadios Scholarios*, 437–444.
61. Leonardo in Belgrano 234–235, 239–240 = Melville-Jones 12, 19–20 = Déroche-Vatin 692–693, 702; Sphrantzes 36.6.
62. Posculo: analysis in Philippides and Hanak, *Cardinal Isidore*, 152–154; "fiction": Leonardo in Belgrano 236 = Melville-Jones 15 = Déroche-Vatin 696; see also Doukas 36.2, 36.5, 37.5–6, 37.9–10.
63. Isidoros, *Letter to Pope Nicholas V* 1, in Philippides and Hanak, *Cardinal Isidore*, 208, 210. Barbaro also says that the people did attend: Cornet 5 = Jones 12 = Déroche-Vatin 468.
64. Gennadios Scholarios, *Letter to the Megas Doux against the Union* 5, in *Oeuvres*, v. 3, 145.
65. Philippides and Hanak, *Cardinal Isidore*, 157.
66. Philippides and Hanak, *Cardinal Isidore*, 163.
67. Barbaro in Cornet 5–11 = Jones 12-20 = Déroche-Vatin 468-469 (truncated); also Posculo 3.748–770 = Ellisen 57; and Doukas 38.1; Kritoboulos 1.24.3; for Barbaro, see Halff, 'Nicolò Barbaro,' 7–11.
68. Doukas 36.7.
69. Doukas 38.1 (500 men), 38.5; Balletto, 'Battista di Felizzano e Domenico di Novara,' 36–37. Lomellino in Pertusi 42–45 = Melville-Jones 132 = Déroche-Vatin 527.
70. Posculo 3.629–634 = Ellissen 54.
71. Ganchou, 'La *fraterna societas*,' 132–134, 154, 180–181; and 'Sujets grecs crétois,' 366 n. 75.
72. Barbaro in Cornet 13 = Jones 22 = Déroche-Vatin 470–471. Brief biography: Déroche-Vatin 1298–1299; longer study (partly outdated): M. Philippides, 'Giovanni Guglielmo Longo Giustiniani, the Genoese *Condottiere* of Constantinople in 1453,' *Byzantine Studies* 3 (1998) 13–54; Lemnos: Doukas 38.2; Kritoboulos 1.25.1; armor: ibid. 1.36.1; and Philippides and Hanak, *Siege*, 493 and n. 63.
73. Ganchou, 'Le rachat des Notaras,' 188, and 164; and the notarial act in Déroche-Vatin 657–665. Coins: C. Morrisson and S. Bendall, 'Monnaies de la fin de l'empire byzantin,' *Revue numismatique* 157 (2002) 471–494, here 491; Philippides, *Constantine XI*, 242.
74. Necipoğlu, *Byzantium*, 225–228, citing the relevant sources (not only about Notaras).

75. For Orban, see p. 115 below.
76. Philippides, *Constantine XI*, 242; S. Bendall, 'The Coinage of Constantine XI,' *Revue numismatique* ser. 6, 33 (1991) 134–142.
77. Notaras in *ΠΠ*, v. 2, 198.

CHAPTER 4

1. P. Rance, 'The Last Byzantine Military Manuscript,' *Byzantina Symmeikta* 34 (2024) 251–291; for the family and its books, see idem, 'Finding the Right Words: A Letter to the Emperor (Laur. Plut. 55.4, f. 197v),' *Parekbolai* 12 (2022) 27–56.
2. For the cannons, see Chapter 5.
3. Geoffroi de Villehardouin, *Conquest of Constantinople* 239 in Faral v. 2, 41 = Shaw 89. For the currents by the southern walls, see (implicitly) Laonikos Chalkokondyles 8.5; Kritoboulos 1.24.2.
4. For the chain, see p. 107 below.
5. Nikephoros Gregoras, *Roman History* 14.9 (v. 2, 727). See also the German emperor Konrad in 1147, in Ioannes Kinnamos, *History* 2.14 (p. 75, Bonn ed.).
6. Geoffroi de Villehardouin, *Conquest of Constantinople* 128 in Faral v. 1, 131 = Shaw 58–59 (modified).
7. Konstantinos of Rhodes, *On Constantinople and the Church of the Holy Apostles* 330–348, ed. and tr. I. Vassis, ed. L. James (Farnham, UK 2012) 43 (modified).
8. Niketas Choniates, *History* 591.
9. Philippides and Hanak, *Siege*, 306–308. For the Theodosian walls in detail, see also Asutay-Effenberger, *Landmauer*. Van Millingen, *Byzantine Constantinople*, is outdated in some respects but still useful.
10. For a brief, near-contemporary description of the moat, said to run from sea to sea, see [Isidoros], *Panegyric for Manuel II and Ioannes VIII Palaiologos*, in *ΠΠ*, v. 3, 147.
11. Andronikos Kallistos (a Greek philologist and who subsequently worked in the West), *Monody for Suffering Constantinople*, in S. Lampros, 'Μονῳδίαι καὶ θρῆνοι ἐπὶ τῇ ἁλώσει τῆς Κωνσταντινουπόλεως,' *Νέος Ἑλληνομνήμων* 5 (1908) 190–269, here 208 (the text is 203–218).
12. Manuel Chrysoloras, *Comparison of Old Rome and New Rome* 36 (p. 17). See Van Millingen, *Byzantine Constantinople*, 55–58 for the possibility of water in the moat.
13. Andronikos Kallistos (see n. 11 above): ποταμὸς τις ἄλλος τοῖς παριοῦσι δοκοῦσα.

14. Buondelmonti's text refers to the moat as *vallum aquarum surgentium* (p. 121 von Sinner). A more recent edition (p. 50 Bayer) interprets this as a reference to springs or fountains near the wall (which surely did exist): "Springbrunnen." But Buondelmonti's map (in all versions) shows water in the moat.
15. Philippides and Hanak, *Siege*, 344–350; Asutay-Effenberger, *Landmauer*, 118–146.
16. Van Millingen, *Byzantine Constantinople*, 104–108.
17. Anonymous, *Encomium for Ioannes VIII Palaiologos*, in *ΠΠ*, v. 3, 296–297.
18. Kananos, *The Siege of Constantinople*, pp. 10–12.
19. Leonardo in Belgrano 248 = Melville-Jones 30 = Déroche-Vatin 716. For Neophytos, see also Sphrantzes 33.5; Doukas 37.6.
20. Philippides and Hanak, *Siege*, 306, 364–365.
21. Leonardo in Belgrano 246 = Melville-Jones 27 = Déroche-Vatin 713.
22. Barbaro in Cornet 14–15 = Jones 23–24 = Déroche-Vatin 472 (with conversion rates in n. 71).
23. Doukas 37.2–4.
24. Benvenuto in Philippides 199 = Déroche-Vatin 567.
25. Leonardo in Belgrano 244–245 = Melville-Jones 25 = Déroche-Vatin 709.
26. Tetaldi 5.1, in Philippides 154–155 (and see n. 8 for contemporary and modern estimates of the defenders). Population estimate: Moustakas, 'Μεθοδολογικά ζητήματα.'
27. Sphrantzes 35.6–8.
28. Leonardo in Belgrano 244–245 = Melville-Jones 25–26, 28–29 = Déroche-Vatin 710, 714–715; Kritoboulos 1.18.9; for 1422, see Kananos, *The Siege of Constantinople*, pp. 34–37.
29. Laonikos Chalkokondyles 8.5 mentions only the Greeks at this council, but Giustiniani and the Venetians were certainly there for they would be manning the most dangerous sectors of the walls: Doukas 38.2; for 1422, see Laonikos Chalkokondyles 5.15–17; Kananos, *The Siege of Constantinople*, pp. 36, 40.
30. Leonardo in Belgrano 245, 247–248 = Melville-Jones 26, 30 = Déroche-Vatin 716–717.
31. Philippides and Hanak, *Siege*, 308.
32. Manuel Chrysoloras, *Comparison of Old Rome and New Rome* 36 (p. 17).
33. Philippides and Hanak, *Siege*, 492–501.
34. Doukas 38.3. Philippides and Hanak, *Siege*, 497 n. 74 and 500, therefore need to claim that this order must have been given "toward the end of the siege," but Doukas obviously puts it at the start and confirms this in the

next section (38.4) when he uses it explain the course of the siege during the first part of April.

35. Kritoboulos 1.25.5. Nestor-Iskander 13 (pp. 32–33) strongly implies the same, as does Leonardo in Belgrano 237 = Melville-Jones 17 = Déroche-Vatin 698. Philippides and Hanak, *Siege*, 498–499, point to passages in Nestor-Iskander that refer to hand-to-hand combat, arguing that these were sorties, but if we read these passages in their narrative context it becomes clear that this combat was taking place in the breaches created in the outer walls by the cannons, which the defenders were struggling to refortify in makeshift ways and hold against Turkish assaults.
36. Kritoboulos 1.25.4; also Leonardo in Belgrano 245 = Melville-Jones 26 = Déroche-Vatin 709–710. Almost all the sources place Giustiniani there. Philippides and Hanak, *Siege*, 338, 327, claim that the outer wall in the vicinity of the Fifth Gate was in such disrepair that the defenders built a wooden stockade to fill in the gap in anticipation of the sultan's arrival. This is a mistake. The sources make it clear that the stockade was erected *during* the siege, after the cannons had brought down stretches of the outer wall, which had to be hastily repaired in makeshift ways. At the time when the siege began, the outer wall was reasonably intact and defensible. Philippides and Hanak get it right at 126, 396, 502, 505.
37. Kritoboulos 1.25.3.
38. Nestor-Iskander 23 (pp. 40–41).
39. For the church of St. Kyriake, see Philippides and Hanak, *Siege*, 338–342, who (at 338) follow the modern liturgical calendar. The church is attested in Kananos, *The Siege of Constantinople*, pp. 12–13.
40. *Synaxarion of Constantinople*, May 19 (col. 696).
41. Nestor-Iskander 52 (pp. 68–69); Kritoboulos 1.23.1, and more vaguely "at the Mid-Wall" in 1.26.1. I accept the identification of this gate in Philippides and Hanak, *Siege*, 323–330, 333–337, which is the traditional identification, against that of Asutay-Effenberger, *Landmauer*, 83–94.
42. Posculo 4.165–167 = Ellisen 65 = Déroche-Vatin 369 (see n. 48 there).
43. For Andronikos, see Nicol, *Byzantine Family*, 179–181.
44. For Ioannes, see Nicol, *Byzantine Family*, 196–198.
45. Bodnar, *Cyriac of Ancona*, 329–343.
46. Laonikos Chalkokondyles 8.18.
47. Janin, *Les églises et les monastères*, 448–449; Philippides and Hanak, *Siege*, 323–327.
48. In a non-antiquarian source, the name is last attested in the *Life of Philaretos the Merciful*, line 787, ed. L. Rydén, *The Life of St Philaretos the Merciful Written by his Grandson Niketas* (Uppsala 2002) 108.

49. Philippides and Hanak, *Siege*, 491.
50. See the discussion in Philippides and Hanak, *Siege*, 338, 341–343. I am not entirely sure what their argument is. They seem to be arguing that there was no confusion in the sources, but there definitely is, if not confusion then at least a very broad use of the term "Romanos Gate."
51. Leonardo in Belgrano 245 = Melville-Jones 27 = Déroche-Vatin 711 and 724 (and n. 114 for their family background). For the gate, see Asutay-Effenberger, *Landmauer*, 106–110.
52. Ganchou, 'Le rachat des Notaras,' 189–190.
53. Posculo 4.157–161 = Ellisen 65 = Déroche-Vatin 368.
54. Posculo 4.579–580 = Ellisen 72 = Déroche-Vatin 381.
55. Barbaro in Cornet 16 = Jones 25 = Déroche-Vatin 473.
56. Anonymous Russian pilgrim in Majeska, *Russian Travelers*, 148, commentary at 325–326. In general, see I. Kimmelfield, 'The Shrine of the Theotokos at the Pege,' in B. Shilling and P. Stephenson, eds., *Fountains and Water Culture in Byzantium* (Cambridge 2016) 299–313.
57. Doukas 28.3.
58. Philippides and Hanak, *Siege*, 315–320.
59. Posculo 4.151–161 = Ellisen 65 = Déroche-Vatin 368; Barbaro (Cornet 16 = Jones 25 = Déroche-Vatin 473) and Leonardo (Belgrano 246 = Melville-Jones 27 = Déroche-Vatin 712) mention only Contarini. For this otherwise unknown Andronikos Kantakouzenos, see T. Ganchou, 'Le Mésazon Démétrius Paléologue Cantacuzène a-t-il figuré parmi des défenseurs du siège de Constantinople (19 Mai 1453)?' *Revue des études byzantines* 52 (1994) 245–272, here 263 and 271–272.
60. D. Mureșan, 'Le patriarcat latin de Constantinople comme paradoxe ecclésiologique,' in H.-M. Blanchet and F. Gabriel, eds., *Réduire le schisme? Ecclésiologies et politiques de l'Union entre Orient et Occident* (Paris 2013) 277–302, here 295.
61. Brown, *Venice and Antiquity*, 150–154.
62. Posculo 4.169–172 = Ellisen 64 = Déroche-Vatin 369 (and see the notes there). Barbaro mentions only Corner at that gate: Cornet 16 = Jones 25 = Déroche-Vatin 473.
63. Philippides and Hanak, *Siege*, 125, 361–362, 372.
64. Bold: Posculo 4.951 = Ellisen 80 = Déroche-Vatin 391 (his death: 369 n. 50). Embassy: Barbaro in Cornet 2 = Jones 10, and see p. 77 above.
65. Leonardo in Belgrano 237 = Melville-Jones 16 = Déroche-Vatin 697–698.
66. *Mémoires d'Olivier de la Marche, maître d'hôtel et capitaine des gardes de Charles le téméraire*, ed. H. Beaune and J. D'Arbaumont, v. 1 (Paris 1883) 288.

67. Isidoros, *Letter to Bessarion* 7, in Philippides and Hanak, *Cardinal Isidore*, 200, 204.
68. Leonardo in Belgrano 246 = Melville-Jones 27 = Déroche-Vatin 712; Theophilos' death: Leonardo in Belgrano 253–254 = Melville-Jones 37 = Déroche-Vatin 724; Laonikos Chalkokondyles 8.22. There is no evidence that Grant was Scottish.
69. Posculo 4.177–178 = Ellisen 64 = Déroche-Vatin 369.
70. Leonardo in Belgrano 246 = Melville-Jones 27 = Déroche-Vatin 712; Posculo 4.169–176 = Ellisen 64 = Déroche-Vatin 369 (with n. 52 on Giorgi); and Barbaro in Cornet 19 = Jones 28 = Déroche-Vatin 474.
71. Barbaro in Cornet 16 = Jones 25 = Déroche-Vatin 473.
72. Leonardo in Belgrano 246 = Melville-Jones 27 = Déroche-Vatin 713.
73. Posculo 4.179–181 = Ellisen 64 = Déroche-Vatin 370 (see n. 54 there).
74. Tafur, *Travels*, p. 142.
75. Trevisan's activities and postings are more reliably reported by Barbaro in Cornet 38-39 = Jones 47–48, 49, and see pp. 137 and 145 below for his naval operations in the harbor before May 9. Some sources put him on the walls seemingly at the start of the siege.
76. Bodnar, *Cyriac of Ancona*, 94–97 (= *Letter* 17); for the defenders of the sea walls mentioned previously, see the following note.
77. Leonardo in Belgrano 246 = Melville-Jones 27–28 = Déroche-Vatin 713 (and see notes there); and Posculo 4.181–190 = Ellisen 64 = Déroche-Vatin 370; for the Venetians in this sector, see Doukas 38.16; Ganchou, 'Le rachat des Notaras,' 183.
78. Asutay-Effenberger, *Landmauer*, 208; Ganchou, '"La tour d'Irène",' 173–180.
79. Posculo 4.190–192 = Ellisen 64 = Déroche-Vatin 370, with n. 59 on the restoration of Tzamplakon's name, and n. 62 on Manuel Philanthropenos (for whose death see also Déroche-Vatin 848–850; Necipoğlu, *Byzantium*, 214). For Palaiologos Metochites, see V. Laurent, 'Le dernier gouverneur byzantin de Constantinople: Démétrius Paléologue, Grand Stratopédarque († 1453),' *Revue des études byzantines* 15 (1957) 196–206.
80. Leonardo in Belgrano 246 = Melville-Jones 27 = Déroche-Vatin 712, where the position of Isidoros is correctly identified. For the church and the location, see Janin, *Les églises et les monastères*, 89; also Gregoras, *Roman History* 17.6α (v. 2, 860) and Doukas 38.7 who explicitly refer to the acropolis at the point of Saint Demetrios where ships sailed around the City. Philippides and Hanak, *Siege*, 501, wrongly place him by the Blachernai district.

81. M. Philippides, 'The Fall of Constantinople 1453: Classical Comparisons and the Circle of Cardinal Isidore,' *Viator* 38 (2007) 349–383.
82. Doukas 38.17 (500 cavalry).
83. Leonardo in Belgrano 246 = Melville-Jones 27 = Déroche-Vatin 712–713; also Barbaro in Cornet 19 = Jones 28 = Déroche-Vatin 474–475 (100 cavalry). By contrast, Posculo 4.192–194 = Ellisen 64–65 = Déroche-Vatin 370, assigns Notaras specifically to guard the Imperial Gate of the harbor.
84. Civilians: Leonardo in Belgrano 245 = Melville-Jones 26–27 = Déroche-Vatin 712–713; and Barbaro in Cornet 19 = Jones 28 = Déroche-Vatin 475.
85. Leonardo in Belgrano 246 = Melville-Jones 27 = Déroche-Vatin 712 (see n. 127 there for his identity).
86. Barbaro in Cornet 19 = Jones 28 = Déroche-Vatin 475.
87. Barbaro in Cornet 15–16 = Jones 24–25, 30 (towers) = Déroche-Vatin 472–473, 475 (towers); and Doukas 38.6; Laonikos Chalkokondyles 8.5.
88. J. and Y. Takeno, 'The Mystery of the Defense Chain Mechanism of Constantinople,' in T. Koetsier and M. Ceccarelli, eds., *Explorations in the History of Machines and Mechanisms* (New York 2012) 199–211, which is, however, based on the assumption that the links in the Istanbul Archaeological Museum are from the chain used in 1453.
89. Philippides and Hanak, *Siege*, 432 n. 9.
90. Barbaro in Cornet 20 = Jones 29–30; the list is not in Déroche-Vatin 475. For an attempt to tally the ships coming and going from the harbor during those months, see Setton, *Papacy*, v. 2, 111–112 n. 9, although one must disregard the testimony of pseudo-Sphrantzes.
91. Leonardo in Belgrano 240 = Melville-Jones 20 = Déroche-Vatin 702–703.
92. Tetaldi 5.1, in Philippides 154–155.
93. Philippides and Hanak, *Siege*, 381–383.
94. Nestor-Iskander 16 (pp. 34–35).

CHAPTER 5

1. In general, see now G. Ágoston, *The Last Muslim Conquest: The Ottoman Empire and Its Wars in Europe* (Princeton 2021).
2. B. Frier, 'The Demography of the Early Roman Empire,' in *The Cambridge Ancient History, v. 11: A.D. 70–192* (Cambridge 2000) 787–816; D. Stathakopoulos, 'Population, Demography, and Disease,' in E. Jeffreys, ed., *The Oxford Handbook of Byzantine Studies* (Oxford 2008) 309–316; and C. Behar, ed., *Osmanlı Imparatorluğu'nun ve Türkiye'nin nüfusu, 1500–1927* (Ankara: State Institute of Statistics, Prime Ministry,

Republic of Turkey, 1996) 4, extrapolating backwards from the data for 1520.

3. Doukas 35.6.
4. Laonikos Chalkokondyles 8.3; Kritoboulos 1.20.2, 1.21.1–2.
5. Kananos, *The Siege of Constantinople*, pp. 26–27.
6. Kritoboulos 1.21.2.
7. Kantakouzenos, *History* 3.38 (v. 1, 539).
8. For conditions during the blockade, see Necipoğlu, *Byzantium*, ch. 7; D. Hatzopoulos, *Ἡ πρώτη πολιορκία τῆς Κωνσταντινουπόλεως από τούς Ὀθωμανούς* (Athens 2004).
9. Kritoboulos 1.22.4.
10. Laonikos Chalkokondyles 6.53, 6.55, 6.59; Doukas 32.4, 34.6; Kastritsis, *An Early Ottoman History*, 166. For Ottoman fleets at this time, see Fodor, 'Ottoman Warfare,' 224–225; for the slow growth of Ottoman naval power, see C. Imber, 'Before the Kapudan Pasha: Sea Power and the Emergence of the Ottoman Empire,' in E. Zachariadou, ed., *The Kapudan Pasha: His Office and His Domain* (Rethymnon 2022) 49–59.
11. Barbaro in Cornet 21 = Jones 31 = Déroche-Vatin 477; Laonikos Chalkokondyles 8.6.
12. Leonardo in Belgrano 240 = Melville-Jones 20 = Déroche-Vatin 703. Ships bringing ladders during the final assault: Doukas 39.6.
13. Barbaro in Cornet 22 = Jones 31-32 = Déroche-Vatin 477–478. He repeatedly notes that the Ottoman fleet did not engage the ships guarding the chain: e.g., in Jones 46 = Déroche-Vatin 488 (truncated). Barbaro's eyewitness testimony, corroborated by the other sources (usually implicitly, through their silence), refutes Kritoboulos' solitary claim that the Ottoman fleet "daily" fought against the ships stationed by the chain to break into the harbor: *History* 1.28.2, 1.37.3–4; see also Philippides and Hanak, *Siege*, 431 n. 7.
14. G. Ágoston, *Guns for the Sultan: Military Power and the Weapons Industry in the Ottoman Empire* (Cambridge 2005) 19–23, 88; for 68 mortars in 1453; D. Petrović, 'Fire-Arms in the Balkans on the Eve of and after the Ottoman Conquests of the Fourteenth and Fifteenth Centuries,' in V. J. Parry and M. E. Yapp, eds., *War, Technology and Society in the Middle East* (London 1975) 164–194.
15. Laonikos Chalkokondyles 5.15–16 and esp. Kritoboulos 1.29–30.
16. Cf. C. Allmand, *The Hundred Years War: England and France at War c. 1300–c. 1450*, rev. ed. (Cambridge 2001) 81.
17. As seen in Leonardo in Belgrano 242 = Melville-Jones 22 = Déroche-Vatin 706. For more on him, see Doukas 35.1; and Laonikos Chalkokondyles

8.6 (the only source that gives his name); see Philippides and Hanak, *Siege*, 389–396.

18. Nestor-Iskander 25 (p. 43) and 33 (p. 49); Leonardo in Belgrano 237 = Melville-Jones 16 = Déroche-Vatin 697–698; Barbaro in Cornet 21 = Jones 21 = Déroche-Vatin 476 (two to four large cannons, in gradation); Isidoros, *Letter to Bessarion* 6, in Philippides and Hanak, *Cardinal Isidore*, 199–200, 204 (three, in gradation); Kritoboulos 1.29.1 (one) but 1.31.1 (three); Doukas 35.1, 35.3, 38.11 (one); Laonikos Chalkokondyles 8.3 (one) but 8.6 (two). See, in general, Philippides and Hanak, *Siege*, 481–485, who don't follow their logic to the end, but come close, though at 413–425 they uphold the One Big Cannon narrative (and cite more sources that refer to it).
19. Philippides and Hanak, *Siege*, 414 n. 67.
20. Doukas 37.1–2, 37.4; Barbaro in Cornet 3 = Jones 10 = Déroche-Vatin 466; Laonikos Chalkokondyles 8.3. Cannons escorted by *yaya* soldiers: Tursun Bey in Déroche-Vatin 202; in general, see Philippides and Hanak, *Siege*, 424–425, 475–476.
21. Barbaro in Cornet 13 = Jones 22-23 = Déroche-Vatin 471 (truncated).
22. Leonardo (16 August 1453, from Chios) in Belgrano 236 = Melville-Jones 15 = Déroche-Vatin 696–697; and Isidoros (15 July 1453, from Candia, Crete) in Déroche-Vatin 615; Philippides and Hanak, *Cardinal Isidore*, 208 and 211; for the significance of "Myrmidons," see Philippides, *Mehmed II*, 141 n. 2.
23. Benvenuto of Ancona in Philippides 198 (tents) = Déroche-Vatin 566; and Kritoboulos 1.23.3 (attendants).
24. Laonikos Chalkokondyles 8.4, see also 7.22.
25. Laonikos Chalkokondyles 7.22.
26. Barbaro in Cornet 18 = Jones 27 = Déroche-Vatin 474.
27. Tetaldi 1.1–2, in Philippides 138–139; Sphrantzes 35.6. For the variety of soldiers in the Ottoman armies at this time, see Fodor, 'Ottoman Warfare.'
28. G. Ágoston, 'Firearms and Military Adaptation: The Ottomans and the European Military Revolution, 1450–1800,' *Journal of World History* 25 (2014) 85–124, here 113.
29. G. Ágoston, 'Janissaries,' in idem and B. Masters, eds., *Encyclopedia of the Ottoman Empire* (New York 2009) 296; Fodor, 'Ottoman Warfare,' 208.
30. A reasonable estimate made by Babinger, *Mehmed the Conqueror*, 84; for roughly consistent estimates for succeeding eras, see R. Murphey, *Ottoman Warfare, 1500–1700* (London 1999) ch. 3.
31. Mihailović, *Memoirs*, p. 73.

32. Barbaro in Cornet 21 = Jones 30–31 = Déroche-Vatin 477. For some of the other numbers cited, see Philippides and Hanak, *Siege*, 430–431.
33. Kritoboulos 1.22.1–2; Tetaldi 3.1, in Philippides 142–145.
34. Benvenuto of Ancona in Philippides 198 = Déroche-Vatin 566.
35. Barbaro in Cornet 18 = Jones 27 = Déroche-Vatin 474; and Leonardo in Belgrano 236 = Melville-Jones 15 = Déroche-Vatin 696–697.
36. The scholion is published by J. M. Featherstone, *Theodore Metochites's Poems 'To Himself'* (Vienna 2000) 13; for the history of this manuscript, see C. Förstel, 'Metochites and his Books between the Chora and the Renaissance,' in H. A. Klein et al., eds., *The Kariye Camii Reconsidered* (Istanbul 2011) 257–266.
37. Arrival on April 4: Sphrantzes 35.6; Tetaldi 1.1, in Philippides 136–137, with deployment on the next day. Benvenuto of Ancona in Philippides 198 = Déroche-Vatin 566, says that he arrived on the night of April 4, but that his land forces were assembled on the next day.
38. Kritoboulos 1.23.1.
39. Leonardo in Belgrano 236 = Melville-Jones 15 = Déroche-Vatin 697.
40. Doukas 37.8.
41. Doukas 38.10.
42. Barbaro in Cornet 18 = Jones 27 = Déroche-Vatin 474.
43. Barbaro in Cornet 18–19 = Jones 28 = Déroche-Vatin 474.
44. Barbaro in Cornet 19–20 = Jones 28–29.
45. Kritoboulos 1.26. For the Romans' counter-terms, see, from before the siege began, Kastritsis, *An Early Ottoman History*, 179. Nestor-Iskander 12 (pp. 32–33) offers a less plausible account of this exchange. He has the basileus send his own envoys upon the sultan's arrival to inquire what his intentions were. The sultan dismisses them and initiates hostilities. This appears to be a narrative told by someone who knew that a diplomatic exchange had taken place but did not know what was said by either side.
46. Doukas 38.18. Passage to the Peloponnese: Nestor-Iskander 36 (pp. 52–53).
47. Nestor-Iskander 31 (pp. 48–49).
48. Barbaro in Cornet 18 = Jones 27 = Déroche-Vatin 474.
49. Nestor-Iskander 13 (p. 33).
50. Kritoboulos 1.27 and Laonikos Chalkokondyles 8.4 give the most concise and comprehensive survey of the Ottoman deployment; parts of it are confirmed by Tursun Bey in Inalcik-Murphey 34–35 = Déroche-Vatin 205, who was in the Ottoman camp; see also Nestor-Iskander 52 (pp. 68–69). The position of the Ottoman generals was the same in the final assault in

late May, excepting only the change in the admiralty: Kritoboulos 1.51, 1.56; and Lauro Quirini, *Letter to Pope Nicholas V*, in Pertusi, *Testi inediti*, 70–73 = Déroche-Vatin 629–630.

51. Babinger, *Mehmed the Conqueror*, 41, 45–47, 65–66; for his campaigns in Anatolia, see 70–71. Kritoboulos 1.27.4, 1.51.4, pairs Ishak Pasha with Mahmud Pasha, but he seems to have projected Mahmud's later prominence (at the time when Kritoboulos was writing) back onto the siege itself. There is no other sign that Mahmud was an important figure before or during the siege.
52. Kritoboulos 1.23.1; Doukas 37.8.
53. See pp. 41–42 above.
54. For his career, see Déroche-Vatin 1310–1311.
55. For his career, see Déroche-Vatin 1312–1313.
56. Tetaldi 3.2, in Philippides 144–145.
57. Barbaro in Cornet 21 = Jones 30 = Déroche-Vatin 476.
58. Leonardo (on the third day, i.e., April 7) in Belgrano 236–237 = Melville-Jones 15–16 = Déroche-Vatin 697–698; Laonikos Chalkokondyles 8.8.
59. Doukas 30.7, 38.3; Laonikos Chalkokondyles 7.23; for the sorties, see also Kritoboulos 1.25.5; Nestor-Iskander 12 (pp. 32–33); and Leonardo in Belgrano 238 = Melville-Jones 17 = Déroche-Vatin 698.
60. See pp. 115–116 above.
61. Barbaro in Cornet 21 = Jones 30 = Déroche-Vatin 476 (who explain the measurement units).
62. Kritoboulos 1.27.3 gives cannons to Karaca (at Blachernai) and says, at 1.31.1, that the three largest ones faced the Mid-Wall. Laonikos Chalkokondyles 8.6 says that one of the two "big" cannons faced the palace and the other the Romanos Gate, with smaller ones planted everywhere. Doukas 38.2 places cannons against the palace (but is confused about Giustiniani's position); then, at 38.9, he focuses on "the" big cannon, which he places against the Romanos Gate. Posculo 4.251–255 = Ellisen 66 = Déroche-Vatin 372, has cannons at the Pege Gate, Golden Gate, and Kaligaria (which seems to get three cannons all to itself). See Philippides and Hanak, *Siege*, 477–481, 486–487.
63. Antonio Ivani de Sarzana, *The Fall of Constantinople* 23, in Pontari and Marcucci 262 = Pertusi 156; translated and discussed in Philippides and Hanak, *Siege*, 486.
64. Leonardo in Belgrano 237–239 = Melville-Jones 16, 18 = Déroche-Vatin 697–698. For the move, see Philippides and Hanak, *Siege*, 329–330, 349.
65. Doukas 38.9.
66. Barbaro in Cornet 44 = Jones 54.

67. Posculo 4.488–490 = Ellisen 70 = Déroche-Vatin 378, and in Philippides and Hanak, *Siege*, 486, referring to a later attack on Pera.
68. Posculo 4.259 = Ellisen 66 = Déroche-Vatin 372; translation from Whitchurch 97.
69. Doukas 38.11; Posculo 4.509–514 = Ellisen 71 = Déroche-Vatin 378.
70. Laonikos Chalkokondyles 8.7; Tetaldi 2.2, in Philippides 140–141.
71. Laonikos Chalkokondyles 8.7.
72. Kritoboulos 1.30.4–5.
73. Posculo 4.261–270 = Ellisen 66 = Déroche-Vatin 372; translation from Whitchurch 97.
74. Nestor-Iskander 24 (pp. 42–43).
75. Nestor-Iskander 24 (pp. 42–43).
76. Laonikos Chalkokondyles 8.7. Philippides and Hanak, *Siege*, 370–371 are correct that no credence should be put in Doukas 38.12 that a Hungarian ambassador to the camp of Mehmed revealed to his gunners this triangulating trick (because of some prophesy, etc.). For triangulation, see also probably Benvenuto of Ancona in Philippides 198 = Déroche-Vatin 566
77. Doukas 38.14.
78. Kritoboulos 1.31.2, 1.35.1.
79. Barbaro in Cornet 22 = Jones 32 (modified).
80. Kritoboulos 1.34; Leonardo in Belgrano 238 = Melville-Jones 17 = Déroche-Vatin 699; and Nestor-Iskander 24 (pp. 42–43).
81. Nestor-Iskander 32 (pp. 48–49); Laonikos Chalkokondyles 8.11.
82. Barbaro in Cornet 44 = Jones 54.
83. Nestor-Iskander 25 (pp. 42–43); aiming at the Ottoman cannons: Laonikos Chalkokondyles 8.11.
84. Leonardo in Belgrano 237–238 = Melville-Jones 16–17 = Déroche-Vatin 698.
85. Laonikos Chalkokondyles 8.11.
86. F. Barry, '*Disiecta membra*: Ranieri Zeno, the Imitation of Constantinople, the *Spolia* Style, and Justice at San Marco,' in H. Maguire and R. S. Nelson, eds., *San Marco, Byzantium, and the Myths of Venice* (Washington, DC 2010) 7–62, here 11; for the location, see Külzer, *Ostthrakien*, 335–336.
87. For his career, see Déroche-Vatin 1311.
88. Barbaro in Cornet 22 = Jones 31 (modified) = Déroche-Vatin 476–477; also Kritoboulos 1.22.1–2. For the fictional attacks on the boom reported by Kritoboulos, see p. 285 n. 13 above.
89. Kritoboulos 1.32–33. For Therapeion ("Therapeia"), see Külzer, *Ostthrakien*, 673–674; for "Studiu," see ibid. 663. Agallianos: Schreiner, *Die byzantinischen Kleinchroniken*, v. 2, 635–636.

90. Isidoros, *Letter to Pope Nicholas V* 5, in Philippides and Hanak, *Cardinal Isidore*, 209, 211.
91. Barbaro in Cornet 23 = Jones 32-33 = Déroche-Vatin 478; and Nestor-Iskander 18–19 (pp. 36–39), who dates it to the seventeenth day (after April 4). The date is roughly confirmed by Doukas 38.4, who says that two-thirds of April passed before any heavy fighting began.
92. Kritoboulos 1.35; Leonardo in Belgrano 246–247 = Melville-Jones 29 = Déroche-Vatin 714–715.
93. Nestor-Iskander 19 (pp. 36–39, modified).
94. Barbaro in Cornet 23–24 = Jones 32–33 = Déroche-Vatin 478; Nestor-Iskander 20 (pp. 38–39), with Philippides and Hanak, *Siege*, 115.
95. Benvenuto of Ancona in Philippides 198 (tents) = Déroche-Vatin 566–567.
96. Nestor-Iskander 20–21 (pp. 38–39).

CHAPTER 6

1. Barbaro in Cornet 23 = Jones 33 = Déroche-Vatin 478–479.
2. Kritoboulos 1.39.1.
3. Captains' names: Leonardo in Belgrano 241 = Melville-Jones 21 = Déroche-Vatin 704; for Cattaneo, see G. Olgiati, 'Genovesi alla difesa di Costantinopoli,' *Atti dell'Accademia Ligure di Scienze e Lettere* 46 (1989) 492–503, here 497–498; for Novara and Felizzano, see Balletto, 'Battista di Felizzano e Domenico di Novara,' esp. 36–38. For the nature of their ships, see Déroche-Vatin 704–705 n. 92.
4. For his name, see Déroche-Vatin 705 n. 93; Sicily: Leonardo in the previous note; Peloponnese: Doukas 38.7.
5. Posculo 4.359 = Ellisen 68 = Déroche-Vatin 374.
6. J. F. Guilmartin, 'The Early Provision of Artillery Armament on Mediterranean War Galleys,' *The Mariner's Mirror* 59.3 (1973) 257–280; and K. R. DeVries, 'A 1445 Reference to Shipboard Artillery,' *Technology and Culture* 31.4 (1990) 818–829.
7. This composite account of the battle draws from (in order of reliability) Barbaro in Cornet 24 = Jones 33–34 ("sea covered": 33) = Déroche-Vatin 478–479 (truncated); Leonardo in Belgrano 241–242 = Melville-Jones 21–22 ("beating drums": 21) = Déroche-Vatin 704–705; Posculo 4.353–471 = Ellisen 68–70 = Déroche-Vatin 374–377; Doukas 38.7 ("ride over the waves"); and Kritoboulos 1.39–40 ("din of voices": 1.40.5).
8. Philippides and Hanak, *Siege*, 429–434.

9. Leonardo in Belgrano 245–246 = Melville-Jones 26–27 = Déroche-Vatin 711.
10. Tursun Bey in Inalcik-Murphey 35 = Déroche-Vatin 207–208.
11. Ak Şemseddin, *Letter to Mehmed*, in Déroche-Vatin 503–507; for Ak Şemseddin's prior predictions that the City would fall, see p. 44 above.
12. Barbaro in Cornet 24–25 = Jones 34–35 = Déroche-Vatin 479–481; Leonardo in Belgrano 242 = Melville-Jones 22 = Déroche-Vatin 706; Doukas 38.7; Kritoboulos 1.41.4; Laonikos Chalkokondyles 8.12.
13. References in Philippides and Hanak, *Siege*, 219–220; for Barbaro, see the following note.
14. Barbaro in Cornet 27 = Jones 36–37 = Déroche-Vatin 481–482.
15. Doukas 38.10 on readings from Jeremiah; Leonardo in Belgrano 234 = Melville-Jones 13 = Déroche-Vatin 693, on readings from Isaiah.
16. Isidoros, *Letter to Bessarion* 6, ed. and tr. Philippides and Hanak, *Cardinal Isidore*, 200, 204.
17. Isidoros in Pertusi, *Caduta*, v. 1, 108–109 (the entire letter), defending the Genoese; the key passage ed. and tr. in Philippides and Hanak, *Cardinal Isidore*, 219–220; the scheme is explained by Doukas 38.15.
18. Leonardo in Belgrano 239 = Melville-Jones 18–19 = Déroche-Vatin 700–701.
19. A. Kaldellis, *Streams of Gold, Rivers of Blood: The Rise and Fall of Byzantium, 955 A.D. to the First Crusade* (Oxford 2017) 296. Ancient precedents: D. K. Pettegrew, *The Isthmus of Corinth: Crossroads of the Mediterranean World* (Ann Arbor, MI 2016) ch. 5. Accounts of portage across the medieval Isthmos of Corinth are probably legendary.
20. Leonardo in Belgrano 240–241 = Melville-Jones 20–21 = Déroche-Vatin 703. A note on Barbaro's text (Jones 37) also claimed that it was a Christian who showed him how to do it. For the trope of treason in these sources, see Philippides and Hanak, *Siege*, 443.
21. Antonio Ivani da Sarzana, *The Fall of Constantinople* 19–21, in Pontari and Marcucci 260–261 = Pertusi 154–155.
22. Tursun Bey in Inalcik-Murphey 35 = Déroche-Vatin 207.
23. Philippides and Hanak, *Siege*, 439–440.
24. For various reported numbers, see Philippides and Hanak, *Siege*, 438–439 n. 25.
25. Doukas 38.8.
26. Kritoboulos 1.42.5.
27. Tursun Bey in Inalcik-Murphey 35 = Déroche-Vatin 207.
28. Laonikos Chalkokondyles 8.9.

29. Barbaro in Cornet 27–28 = Jones 37–38 = Déroche-Vatin 482–483 (truncated).
30. Kritoboulos 1.43.2.
31. He is specifically said to have been present by Posculo 4.574–584 = Ellisen 72 = Déroche-Vatin 380–381; for the rest of the information presented here, see Barbaro in Cornet 29–30 = Jones 39–40 = Déroche-Vatin 483–484.
32. Leonardo in Belgrano 243 = Melville-Jones 24 = Déroche-Vatin 707–708. See also Doukas 38.19 and Kritoboulos 1.44.1, who erroneously has Giustiniani lead the ensuing naval attack, which may only reflect his overall command. I don't believe that this represents an echo of an otherwise unattested naval attack by Giustiniani, as Philippides and Hanak, *Siege*, 458–460, suggest.
33. Posculo 4.610–613 = Ellisen 73 = Déroche-Vatin 381–382.
34. Barbaro in Cornet 30–32 = Jones 40–42; Kritoboulos 1.44.1–2.
35. Tetaldi 7.2, in Philippides 158–159.
36. Posculo 4.673 = Ellisen 74 = Déroche-Vatin 383.
37. Leonardo in Belgrano 244 = Melville-Jones 24 = Déroche-Vatin 707–708; and Laonikos Chalkokondyles 8.9.
38. For Lomellino's position, see, among many sources, his own report in his *Letter to Antonio Lomellino*; see also Philippides and Hanak, *Siege*, 13–14, 452.
39. Posculo 4.587–588 = Ellisen 72 = Déroche-Vatin 381.
40. Leonardo in Belgrano 243 = Melville-Jones 24 = Déroche-Vatin 707–708. Doukas 38.20 accuses the Genoese of Pera of treason but gives no names.
41. Déroche-Vatin 663.
42. See the discussion and translation of the document in Déroche-Vatin 837–845.
43. Philippides, *Mehmed II*, 159 n. 10.
44. Barbaro in Cornet 34 = Jones 43.
45. Kritoboulos 1.44.3.
46. Barbaro in Cornet 33–34 = Jones 43.
47. Nestor-Iskander 26 (pp. 44–45) and 29 (pp. 46–47).
48. Nestor-Iskander 30 (pp. 46–47).
49. Barbaro in Cornet 34–35 = Jones 44 = Déroche-Vatin 485–486.
50. Laonikos Chalkokondyles 8.44 (at the siege of Novo Brdo in 1455); Kritoboulos 1.38.2 (misplaced chronologically in the history of the siege).
51. A. Roccatagliata, *Notai genovesi in Oltremare: Atti rogati a Chio (1453–1454, 1470–1471)* (Genoa 1982) doc. 65, p. 101, recorded later that year on Chios.

52. Kritoboulos 1.38.3–5; Barbaro (who gives the date) in Cornet 35–40 = Jones 45, 46–47, 49–50 = Déroche-Vatin 486–487 (truncated); Posculo 4.472–531 = Ellisen 70–71 = Déroche-Vatin 378–379; Leonardo in Belgrano 242 = Melville-Jones 22 (chronologically disordered) = Déroche-Vatin 706; Doukas 38.20 (also disordered).

CHAPTER 7

1. Barbaro in Cornet 36–37 = Jones 46 = Déroche-Vatin 488; and Nestor-Iskander 38–40 (pp. 54–57); for these fighters, see Philippides and Hanak, *Siege*, 128–129.
2. Nestor-Iskander 41–45 (pp. 56–61); for the individuals and officials mentioned in this section of the narrative, see the notes by Hanak and Philippides; also Philippides and Hanak, *Siege*, 122–128.
3. Barbaro in Cornet 40 = Jones 50.
4. Nestor-Iskander 46 (pp. 60–61).
5. Barbaro in Cornet 33 = Jones 43.
6. Barbaro in Cornet 37–38 = Jones 47.
7. Nicol, *Byzantium and Venice*, 402–403, merely reports it from Barbaro.
8. Barbaro in Cornet 38–39 = Jones 47–48, 49.
9. Mihailović, *Memoirs*, pp. 46–47 = Déroche-Vatin 446.
10. Barbaro in Cornet 41 = Jones 50–51 = Déroche-Vatin 489–490; Leonardo in Belgrano 238 = Melville-Jones 17–18 (Serbs and Grant) = Déroche-Vatin 699–700; Laonikos Chalkokondyles 8.8; Kritoboulos 1.33.3. Tetaldi 7.1, in Philippides 160–165, puts the mining project under the direction of Zaganos Pasha, but is confused about many aspects of it. In general, and for more sources, see Philippides and Hanak, *Siege*, 505–512.
11. See Barbaro in the previous note.
12. Barbaro in Cornet 41–42 = Jones 51–52.
13. Nestor-Iskander 33–34 (pp. 50–51).
14. Posculo 4.697 = Ellisen 75 = Déroche-Vatin 384; Leonardo in Belgrano 245 = Melville-Jones 26–27 = Déroche-Vatin 711.
15. Barbaro in Cornet 42–43 = Jones 52–53 = Déroche-Vatin 490–491 (truncated). Ladders: Leonardo in Belgrano 238 = Melville-Jones 18 = Déroche-Vatin 700; and Laonikos Chalkokondyles 8.8. Many other sources refer briefly to this tower.
16. Whitchurch, *The Constantinopolis*, 4, 51.
17. For them, see Déroche-Vatin 384 n. 90–91.
18. Posculo 4.694–742 = Ellisen 75–76 = Déroche-Vatin 384–385.

19. Isidoros, *Letter to Bessarion* 10, ed. and tr. in Philippides and Hanak, *Cardinal Isidore*, 200, 205 (modified).
20. S. Lampros, 'Μονῳδίαι καὶ θρῆνοι ἐπὶ τῇ ἁλώσει τῆς Κωνσταντινουπόλεως,' *Νέος Ἑλληνομνήμων* 5 (1908) 190–270, here 260–261 (f. 233r); it was written next to the text of Ioannes Kinnamos, *History* 2.14 (p. 75, Bonn ed.).
21. A. Manfredi and F. Potenza, *I codici greci di Niccolò V. Edizione dell'inventario del 1455 e identificazione dei manoscritti. Con approfondimenti sulle vicende iniziali del fondo Vaticano greco della Biblioteca Apostolica Vaticana* (Vatican City 2022) 789–792.
22. I. Ševčenko, 'The Decline of Byzantium Seen through the Eyes of its Intellectuals,' *Dumbarton Oaks Papers* 15 (1961) 167–186, here 173 n. 23. For Chortasmenos, see H. Hunger, *Johannes Chortasmenos (ca. 1370–ca. 1436/37): Briefe, Gedichte und kleine Schriften* (Vienna 1969).
23. A. Kaldellis, *Byzantine Readings of Ancient Historians: Text in Translation, with Introductions and Notes* (London 2015) ch. 5.
24. Kritoboulos 1.27.2, implies that it had been planned from the start, but he might be projecting later developments.
25. For the main sources, see Philippides and Hanak, *Siege*, 165 n. 102, 444–447.
26. Philippides and Hanak, *Siege*, 439–440, also 444, 447, 575 (timeline).
27. Barbaro in Cornet 44 = Jones 53 = Déroche-Vatin 491 (truncated).
28. Leonardo in Belgrano 252 = Melville-Jones 35 = Déroche-Vatin 722.
29. Barbaro in Cornet 45 = Jones 54–55.
30. Barbaro in Cornet 45–48 = Jones 55–58. Leonardo in Belgrano 238 = Melville-Jones 17 = Déroche-Vatin 699–700, must be referring to the sixth tunnel.
31. Posculo 4.743–811 = Ellisen 76–77 = Déroche-Vatin 385–387.
32. Barbaro in Cornet 47, and 35 = Jones 57, and 44–45.
33. Nicol, *Byzantium and Venice*, 397–399, 406.
34. Barbaro in Cornet 46 = Jones 56 = Déroche-Vatin 491–492. Hanak and Philippides, *Nestor-Iskander*, 128 n. 74 (as well as Philippides and Hanak, *Siege*, 226 n. 99) assert that the eclipse happened on May 24, and that Barbaro got the date wrong or changed it later (but why?). Yet the correct date is May 22, as a number of scientific-astronomical websites confirm, including that by NASA: https://eclipse.gsfc.nasa.gov/5MCLE/5MCLE-Figs-09.pdf. In a separate article, Philippides cites this website in support of his May 24 date, but it clearly says May 22 (on Plate 417): 'The Date of the Conquest of Constantinople: 29 May, 1453?' *YILLIK: Annual of Istanbul Studies* 2 (2020) 197–199. The eclipse might in fact be what

Nestor-Iskander is referring to when he says that, on May 21, "there was, for our sins, a frightful sign in the city," although he does not tell us what it was before moving on to another portent that occurred "on the eve of Friday": Nestor-Iskander 47 (pp. 62–63).

35. Kritoboulos 1.46.1 (all day); Nestor-Iskander 68–70 (pp. 80–81: in the evening only), whose chronology here is confusing.
36. Nestor-Iskander 47–50 (pp. 62–65), although the chronology of this episode is consistent, as the religious procession on the walls is placed "on the second day" after it, namely on Saturday, when we know from other sources that a procession took place (see below).
37. Laonikos Chalkokondyles 8.13–14.
38. Doukas 39.1.

CHAPTER 8

1. Leonardo in Belgrano 237, 249–250 = Melville-Jones 16, 31–33 = Déroche-Vatin 698, 717–719; and (not named) Tetaldi 9.1, in Philippides 168–171 (and n. 14 there).
2. Tetaldi 9–10, in Philippides 168–179.
3. Tursun Bey in Inalcik-Murphey 36 = Déroche-Vatin 209, quoting Koran 3:126.
4. Quotation: Leonardo in Belgrano 250 = Melville-Jones 33 = Déroche-Vatin 719; see also Doukas 38.2; Laonikos Chalkokondyles 8.13 (wrongly implies that the proclamation was on Sunday); Kritoboulos 1.47–51 (wrongly implies that it was on Monday, 1.50.4). The campfires began on Saturday, so the proclamation must have been on that day. Barbaro in Cornet 48 = Jones 58 has the fires and festivities in the Ottoman camp begin on Friday night, "because they knew that they were soon going to make a general attack," but this is surely one day too early.
5. Manuel II Palaiologos, *Funeral Oration on his Brother Theodoros*, p. 151.
6. Doukas 39.3; Leonardo in Belgrano 250 = Melville-Jones 33 = Déroche-Vatin 719; and Barbaro in Cornet 48 = Jones 58.
7. Ganchou, 'La famille Koumousès,' 64–67.
8. Doukas 39.4. The sorry state of the walls at this time is stressed by Barbaro.
9. Leonardo in Belgrano 250–251 = Melville-Jones 33–34 = Déroche-Vatin 719–721; Nestor-Iskander 50–51 (pp. 64–69).
10. B. V. Pentcheva, *Icons and Power: The Mother of God in Byzantium* (University Park, PA 2006).

11. C. Kelly, 'Stooping to Conquer: The Power of Imperial Humility,' in idem, ed., *Theodosius II: Rethinking the Roman Empire in Late Antiquity* (Cambridge 2013) 221–243.
12. Barbaro in Cornet 50 = Jones 60 = Déroche-Vatin 494.
13. Leonardo in Belgrano 252 = Melville-Jones 35 = Déroche-Vatin 722.
14. Barbaro in Cornet 49–50 = Jones 59–60 = Déroche-Vatin 494.
15. Tetaldi 16.1, in Philippides 182–185.
16. Nestor-Iskander 46 (pp. 60–61).
17. Kritoboulos 1.52.3; Laonikos Chalkokondyles 8.15–17.
18. Barbaro in Cornet 50–51 = Jones 60–61 = Déroche-Vatin 494; Leonardo in Belgrano 252 = Melville-Jones 35 = Déroche-Vatin 721–722. Antonio Ivani da Sarzana, *The Fall of Constantinople* 29, in Pontari and Marcucci 264 = Pertusi 158–159.
19. Barbaro in Cornet 50 = Jones 60 = Déroche-Vatin 493–494.
20. Leonardo in Belgrano 247 = Melville-Jones 29–30 = Déroche-Vatin 715; for Leonardo's bias against Notaras, see Philippides and Hanak, *Siege*, 250–252.
21. Barbaro in Cornet 51 = Jones 61 = Déroche-Vatin 494.
22. Tetaldi 13.1, in Philippides 178–179.
23. E.g., Philippides and Hanak, *Siege*, 520.
24. Barbaro in Cornet 52–53 = Jones 62–63 = Déroche-Vatin 495–496 (truncated). Philippides and Hanak, *Siege*, 36, claim that the first source to refer to the three-part structure of the assault was the Venetian humanist (and colonial landowner on Crete) Lauro Quirini, who wrote a letter to pope Nicholas V soon after the City's fall, based on information that he received from refugees on Crete, including the cardinal Isidoros. But that is not what Quirini says: he is instead talking about the left-center-right division of the Ottoman armies along the walls, among their three commanders; see his letter in Pertusi, *Testi inediti*, 70–73 (Latin and Italian tr.) = Déroche-Vatin 629–630 (French tr.).
25. Cf. Isidoros, *Letter to Pope Nicholas V* 6, in Philippides and Hanak, *Cardinal Isidore*, 209, 211, with his *Letter to Bessarion* 11, in ibid. 201, 206. The podestà of Pera, Lomellino, also says that the attack lasted all night before the morning of May 29: Pertusi 42–43 = Melville-Jones 132 = Déroche-Vatin 527.
26. Kritoboulos 1.54.1.
27. Nestor-Iskander 73 (pp. 84–85); for the bracketed phase, see also the French tr. in Déroche-Vatin 433.
28. Posculo 4.922–923 = Ellisen 79 = Déroche-Vatin 390 = Whitchurch 171 (whose translation I quote).

29. Barbaro in Cornet 53–55 = Jones 64–65 = Déroche-Vatin 496–498 (truncated).
30. Tursun Bey in Inalcik-Murphey 36 = Déroche-Vatin 211–212.
31. Déroche-Vatin 730.
32. Nestor-Iskander 60–64 (pp. 74–79).
33. Nikolaos Sekoundinos (Sagundini), *Oration for King Alfonso of Aragon*, in Pertusi, *Caduta*, v. 2, 134–135 (*duobus acceptis vulneribus*) = Déroche-Vatin 793; for these two versions, see Philippides and Hanak, *Siege*, 120–122, 528–529; for Sekoundinos, see pp. 216–217 below.
34. Isidoros, *Letter to Bessarion* 12, in Philippides and Hanak, *Cardinal Isidore*, 201, 206.
35. Leonardo in Belgrano 253 = Melville-Jones 36–37 = Déroche-Vatin 722–723; for most versions of what happened to Giustiniani, see Philippides and Hanak, *Siege*, 523–538.
36. Tetaldi 18.1, in Philippides 184–185.
37. Leonardo in Belgrano 254–255 = Melville-Jones 38 = Déroche-Vatin 724. Flags: Posculo 4.1037–1038 = Ellisen 82 = Déroche-Vatin 393.
38. Déroche-Vatin 724–725 n. 168. There is no reason to think that Leonardo invented this episode, whereas it is easy to see why he suppressed the brothers' brief captivity, for the purposes of both narrative flow and discretion.
39. These versions are discussed by Philippides and Hanak, *Siege*, 40, 89–90, 100 n. 32, 147, 232–237. For the heads that were brought to Mehmed, see p. 205 below.
40. For this last point, see Philippides, *Constantine XI*.
41. Leonardo in Belgrano 253 = Melville-Jones 37 (quotation) = Déroche-Vatin 723; Nestor-Iskander 66 (pp. 78–79); Kritoboulos 1.57.3. Doukas 39.9 even has the two men fighting side-by-side.
42. Posculo 4.1041–1048 = Ellisen 82 = Déroche-Vatin 393–394.
43. Philippides and Hanak, *Siege*, 337, for this and its other names.
44. Laonikos Chalkokondyles 8.20. Implied by Barbaro in Cornet 54–55 = Jones 65 = Déroche-Vatin 497–498 (truncated); Tursun Bey in Inalcik-Murphey 36 (the periphrasis here is vague) = Déroche-Vatin 211–212 ("pénetrant dans la fortresse par les brèches étroites").
45. Doukas 39.4, 39.11.
46. Kritoboulos 1.59.2.
47. Philippides and Hanak, *Siege*, 619–623.
48. Posculo 4.951–962 = Ellisen 80 = Déroche-Vatin 391; Kritoboulos 1.51.2 (in a speech by the sultan) and 1.56.2 (in action); a general reference in Doukas 39.7. For the bridge before May 29, see p. 163 above.

49. Barbaro in Cornet 56–57 = Jones 66–67 = Déroche-Vatin 498–499 (truncated). The ladders are mentioned also by Doukas 39.6; Kritoboulos 1.51.1; Kastritsis, *An Early Ottoman History*, 179. The fleet activation in the final assault is mentioned more generally by Leonardo in Belgrano 252 = Melville-Jones 35 = Déroche-Vatin 721–722; Nestor-Iskander 52 (pp. 68–69).
50. For this Jewish quarter, see Majeska, *Russian Travelers*, 38, 268–269.
51. Ganchou, 'Sujets grecs crétois,' 372–373; Lane, *Venice*, 235.
52. R. C. Mueller, *The Venetian Money Market: Banks, Panics, and the Public Debt, 1200–1500* (Baltimore 1997) 212–213.
53. Ganchou, 'La *fraterna societas*,' 192–193.
54. See, indicatively, Philippides and Hanak, *Siege*, xvi–xvii, 486, 505, 567, and passim.
55. E.g., E. McGeer, 'The Defence of Constatinople,' in S. Bassett, ed., *The Cambridge Companion to Constantinople* (London and New York 2023) 117–131, here 123; Angold, *Fall*, 8.
56. Angold, *Fall*, 7.
57. Isidoros, *Letter to Bessarion* 12, in Philippides and Hanak, *Cardinal Isidore*, 201, 206.
58. Kritoboulos 1.31.3.
59. Metochites, *Byzantios* 60 (p. 482).
60. Tursun Bey in Inalcik-Murphey 35–36 = Déroche-Vatin 208.
61. Sphrantzes 36; for this factor generally, see E. Chrysos, 'Η Άλωση της Πόλης: Μια «έσωθεν» Άλωση;' in *Τιμητικός Τόμος Ελίζας Αλεξανδρίδου* (Athens 2016) 509–518, who, however, goes too far in saying that divisions among the defenders "paralyzed" the defense (510).

CHAPTER 9

1. Tursun Bey in Déroche-Vatin 212.
2. Tursun Bey in Déroche-Vatin 212.
3. Laonikos Chalkokondyles 8.21; resistance mentioned generally by Posculo 4.1064–1065 = Ellisen 82 = Déroche-Vatin 394; Tetaldi 18.2, in Philippides 194–195; and Nestor-Iskander 79 (pp. 88–89).
4. Isidoros, *Letter to Bessarion* 13, in Philippides and Hanak, *Cardinal Isidore*, 201, 206.
5. Doukas 39.14.
6. Laonikos Chalkokondyles 8.20 (the forum of Tauros should be that of Constantine; see below).
7. Doukas 39.24–25; Kritoboulos 1.63, 1.65–66.

8. Kritoboulos 1.61.2.
9. Paul, '*Urbs Capta*.'
10. Barbaro in Cornet 55 = Jones 66.
11. Barbaro in Cornet 57 = Jones 67 = Déroche-Vatin 499 (truncated).
12. Doukas 40.5; cf. Ioannes Anagnostes, *History of the Final Fall of Thessalonike* 14, for 1430.
13. Kritoboulos 1.61.5–6; also Leonardo in Belgrano 255 = Melville-Jones 39 = Déroche-Vatin 725; Barbaro in Cornet 56–57 = Jones 67; Isidoros, *Letter to Bessarion* 14, in Philippides and Hanak, *Cardinal Isidore*, 201, 206; Doukas 39.20.
14. Tursun Bey in Déroche-Vatin 214–216.
15. E.g., Leonardo in Belgrano 255 = Melville-Jones 39 = Déroche-Vatin 725.
16. Doukas 39.23. We do not know where this church was located: Philippides and Hanak, *Siege*, 266–286. By the Palaiologan era, Theodosia of Tyre (May 29: *Synaxarion of Constantinople*, col. 713–715) had apparently merged with the iconoclast-era martyr Theodosia of Constantinople, or the latter had taken over the former's feast day: E. Kountoura-Galake, '29 May 1453: The Fall of Constantinople and the Memory of the Enigmatic St. Theodosia. A Strange Coincidence,' in Motos Guirao and Morfakidis Filactós, eds., *Constantinopla*, v. 2, 75–82; A. Effenberger, 'Theodosia von Konstantinopel—Kult und Kultort,' *Jahrbuch der österreichischen Byzantinistik* 61 (2011) 121–134.
17. Master Henry of Soemmern, *The Fall and Sack of the City of Constantinople* 6, text and tr. in Philippides, *Mehmed II*, 124–125.
18. Isidoros in Pertusi, *Caduta*, v. 1, 60.
19. Laonikos Chalkokondyles 8.20.
20. Doukas 39.17.
21. B. Pentcheva, *Hagia Sophia: Sound, Space, and Spirit in Byzantium* (University Park, PA 2017) 3.
22. Doukas 39.18–19.
23. Barbaro in Cornet 55–56 = Jones 66 = Déroche-Vatin 498, with a note there on the location (I am not sure that the "tower" is the column).
24. Doukas 39.20.
25. Doukas 39.21.
26. Leonardo in Belgrano 254 = Melville-Jones 38 = Déroche-Vatin 725.
27. Isidoros, *Letter to Bessarion* 15, in Philippides and Hanak, *Cardinal Isidore*, 201, 206–207.
28. Niketas Choniates, *History* 573–576.
29. Isidoros, *Letter to Bessarion* 14, in Philippides and Hanak, *Cardinal Isidore*, 201, 206.

30. Tursun Bey in Inalcik-Murphey 37 = Déroche-Vatin 216. Bargain prices: Laonikos Chalkokondyles 8.23.
31. Barbaro in Cornet 57 = Jones 67.
32. Kritoboulos 1.67.4; cf. Leonardo in Belgrado 255 = Melville-Jones 38–39 = Déroche-Vatin 725, says that 60,000 were captured.
33. Text and tr. (modified) in Philippides, *Emperors*, 48–49.
34. Doukas 40.1.
35. V. Déroche, 'Le Bey sous le régard du Pantokratôr,' in E. Borromeo et al., eds., *Déchiffrer le passé d'un empire* (Paris 2022) 207–215.
36. Tursun Bey in Déroche-Vatin 217–218; Doukas 40.1; Kritoboulos 1.68.1–3.
37. Doukas 39.28.
38. Doukas 39.29–30 (quotation); and Barbaro in Cornet 57–58 = Jones 67–68 = Déroche-Vatin 499–500 (truncated).
39. Barbaro in Cornet 58 = Jones 68–69 = Déroche-Vatin 500–501 (truncated).
40. Barbaro in Cornet 58–59 = Jones 69 (quotation); Laonikos Chalkokondyles 8.25; Tetaldi 20.2–21.1, in Philippides 200–205; Tetaldi told the same story to the Venetian Senate later: see ibid. 23–24, with the information about his slave. For the Cretan ships and their captains, see Manoussakas, 'Les derniers défenseurs.'
41. Texts, translations, and discussions of this note also in R. Browning, 'A Note on the Capture of Constantinople in 1453,' *Byzantion* 22 (1952) 379–387; and Philippides, *Mehmed II*, 24–25.
42. Brown, *Venice and Antiquity*, 236–237; Philippides and Hanak, *Siege*, 472.
43. Barbaro in Cornet 59 = Jones 69–70; Doukas 39.31; Leonardo in Belgrano 256–257 = Melville-Jones 41 = Déroche-Vatin 727–728; Lomellino in Pertusi 46–47 = Melville-Jones 132–133 = Déroche-Vatin 528–529. Giustiniani's ships left at night: see Déroche-Vatin 649–650.
44. K. Mertzios, 'Περὶ τῶν ἐκ Κωνσταντινουπόλεως διαφυγόντων τὸ 1453 Παλαιολόγων καὶ ἀποβιβασθέντων εἰς Κρήτην,' in *Actes du XIIe Congrès International d'études byzantines*, v. 2 (Belgrade 1961) 171–176, here 172–173.
45. N. Necipoglu, 'Constantinopolitan Merchants and the Question of Their Attitudes toward Italians and Ottomans in the Late Palaiologan Period,' in C. Scholz and G. Makris, eds., *Πολύπλευρος Νούς: Miscellanea für Peter Schreiner* (Munich 2000) 251–263, here 261.
46. One of them is translated in Déroche-Vatin 509–511.
47. Tursun Bey in Inalcik-Murphey 37 = Déroche-Vatin 218–219.
48. Date: Ganchou, 'Le *prôtogéros* de Constantinople,' 240.

49. Laonikos Chalkokondyles 8.22; Doukas 40.4; Kritoboulos 1.64; Kastritsis, *An Early Ottoman History*, 179.
50. Doukas 39.25–26, 40.4.
51. Laonikos Chalkokondyles 8.24.
52. Master Henry of Soemmern, *The Fall and Sack of the City of Constantinople* 9, text and tr. (modified) in Philippides, *Mehmed II*, 128–129. For Isidoros' captivity and escape, see Philippides and Hanak, *Cardinal Isidore*, 212–221.
53. Laonikos Chalkokondyles 8.24.
54. Isidoros, *Letter to Bessarion* 16, in Philippides and Hanak, *Cardinal Isidore*, 202, 207; Leonardo in Belgrano 256 = Melville-Jones 40 = Déroche-Vatin 726–727; the anonymous Greek chronicle in Philippides, *Emperors*, 52–53. For Notaras in particular, see below. For the emendation of Goudeles' name, see Philippides and Hanak, *Siege*, 131–132.
55. Venetians: Philippides and Hanak, *Siege*, 12 n. 40, 39–40; Catalans: ibid. 157; and Déroche-Vatin 530, 727, 950.
56. Leonardo in Belgrano 256 = Melville-Jones 40 = Déroche-Vatin 726–727; Posculo 4.1075–1077 = Ellisen 82 = Déroche-Vatin 394; and the Venetian chronicle cited by Philippides and Hanak, *Siege*, 12 n. 40.
57. Lomellino in Pertusi 46–49 = Melville-Jones 132 = Déroche-Vatin 530. Concessions: Déroche-Vatin 530–531 n. 57; for the two men in general, see ibid. 704 n. 90 and 711 n. 114.
58. Déroche-Vatin 725 n. 168.
59. Leonardo in Belgrado 240, 255–256 = Melville-Jones 19, 39–40 = Déroche-Vatin 702, 726–727. For this accusation, see pp. 84–85 above.
60. Doukas 40.3–4; and Leonardo in Belgrado 255 = Melville-Jones 39 = Déroche-Vatin 726. For the empty City, see also Kritoboulos 1.67.
61. The relevant texts are collected and translated in Philippides and Hanak, *Siege*, 597–618. The first extant source giving the sexualized version of the execution is possibly the account of Nikolaos Sekoundinos, who visited Edirne in the summer of 1453 (probably also Constantinople, and he certainly spoke with many survivors of the siege); for his role in the process of creating the myth of Notaras, see Ganchou, 'Le rachat des Notaras,' 181. For the date ("on the third day" after the fall of the City), see Isidoros, *Letter to Bessarion* 16, in Philippides and Hanak, *Cardinal Isidore*, 202, 207. Isidore was there at the time, as he emphasizes in the letter, though in hiding. Iakobos: Philippides and Hanak, *Siege*, 41–44.
62. Ganchou, 'Le rachat des Notaras,' 155.
63. Kritoboulos 1.73.1.

64. Radu of Wallachia (a brother of Vlad III the Impaler): Laonikos Chalkokondyles 9.82; see, in general, Kaldellis, *New Herodotos*, 167–169.
65. Sphrantzes 35.11–12, 37.3; Ganchou, 'Le rachat des Notaras,' 154–155 n. 25. For Ilyas Bey, see A. Gallotta, 'Ilyas Beg, il mütevelli e le origini di Corizza (Korçë/Görice),' in E. Zachariadou, ed., *The Via Egnatia under Ottoman Rule (1380–1699)* (Rethymnon 1996) 113–122.
66. Kritoboulos 1.73.7–14 (also 1.76–77); see the analysis of the background in Inalcik, 'Policy of Mehmed II.'
67. Mehmed II, *Fetihname to the Sultan of Egypt*, in Déroche-Vatin 751–752.
68. Doukas 39.30; Laonikos Chalkokondyles 8.26.
69. "Terror": Leonardo in Belgrano 257 = Melville-Jones 41 = Déroche-Vatin 727–728; for Pagliuzzo, see p. 147 above.
70. Pallavicino's affidavit is introduced and translated in Déroche-Vatin 853–861.
71. For the Greek original and a nearly contemporary Italian translation of the *aman-name*, see Philippides, *Mehmed II*, 347–350; English translation in Melville-Jones 136–137; introduction and French translation in Déroche-Vatin 513–518; for the *protogeros*, see Ganchou, 'Le *prôtogéros* de Constantinople,' esp. 225.
72. Ganchou, 'Le *prôtogéros* de Constantinople,' 240.
73. Lomellino in Pertusi 46–47 = Melville-Jones 133 = Déroche-Vatin 529–530; Leonardo in Belgrano 257 = Melville-Jones 41 = Déroche-Vatin 727–728; Doukas 39.30, 42.2; Laonikos Chalkokondyles 8.26–27; Kritoboulos 1.67; for the evidence of Isidoros, see Philippides and Hanak, *Cardinal Isidore*, 240 n. 114. Notary (Lorenzo Calvi): Déroche-Vatin 657.
74. Balletto, 'Battista di Felizzano e Domenico di Novara,' 39–43.
75. Lomellino in Pertusi 50–51 = Melville-Jones 135 = Déroche-Vatin 533. Renegade: report by the Florentine ambassador to Genoa, Nicolò Soderini (August 20, 1453), in N. Iorga, *Notes et estraits pour servir à l'histoire des croisades au Xve siècle*, v. 2 (Paris 1899) 493; see Philippides and Hanak, *Siege*, 13–14, 466 n. 98, 518. A summer of unreliable news: Ganchou, 'Le rachat des Notaras,' 167–171.
76. Posculo 4.529–531 = Ellisen 71 = Déroche-Vatin 379 (where a note trying to explain this).
77. Captivity and book-buying: Philippides and Hanak, *Siege*, 16–17; Philippides, *Mehmed II*, 209 n. 26. Alleged harrassment: Déroche-Vatin 690; complaint to the pope against him: ibid. 741–744.
78. Doukas 42.1; Kritoboulos 1.62.3.
79. K. N. Konstantinides, 'Πρόσφυγες ἀπό τήν Κωνσταντινούπολη στὴν Κύπρο μετά τήν ἅλωση τοῦ 1453,' in E. Chrysos, ed., *Ἡ ἅλωση τῆς Πόλης*

(Athens 1994) 135–141, here 139. For the dispersal of the City's books, see Mondrain, 'Transfer.'

80. A. Turyn, *Dated Greek Manuscripts of the Thirteenth and Fourteenth Centuries in the Libraries of Italy*, 2 vols. (Urbana, IL 1972) v. 1, 122.
81. Madden, 'Fires.'
82. Lauro Quirini, *Letter to Pope Nicholas V*, in Pertusi, *Testi inediti*, 74 = Déroche-Vatin 631. For other sources that talk about the destruction of books, see Philippides and Hanak, *Siege*, 196 n. 9.
83. See the letter of Enea Silvio Piccolomini, who was later to become pope Pius II (1458–1464), in Pertusi, *Caduta*, v. 2, 45–49; for Enea (Aeneas) and others on this theme, see N. Bisaha, *Creating East and West: Renaissance Humanists and the Ottoman Turks* (Philadelphia 2004) 2, 60, 65–69, 75 (Ficino); Hankins, 'Renaissance Crusaders,' 122.
84. Konstantinos Laskaris, *De scriptoribus Graecis Patria Siculis* in *PG* 161: 917–918.
85. In general, see P. D. Mastrodimitris, *Νικόλαος Σεκουνδινὸς (1402–1464): Βίος καὶ ἔργον* (Athens 1970); C. Caselli, 'Interpreter, Diplomat, Humanist: Nicholas Sagundinus as a Cultural Broker in the 15th-Century Mediterranean,' in D. Slootjes and M. Verhoeven, eds., *Byzantium in Dialogue with the Mediterranean: History and Heritage* (Leiden, 2019) 226–244; and the *PLP* 25106.
86. For the embassy to Mehmed and importance of Sekoundinos' account, see Ganchou, 'Le rachat des Notaras,' 179–184; also Philippides and Hanak, *Siege*, 40. The speech to Alfonso is translated from the Latin, with annotation, in Déroche-Vatin 783–803; the Latin edition is by C. Caselli, *Ad serenissimum principem et invictissimum regem Alphonsum Nicolai Sagundini oratio* (Rome 2012).
87. For a translation and commentary on this work, see Philippides, *Mehmed II*, 6–16, 55–91; for a study, see M. Meserve, *Empires of Islam in Renaissance Historical Thought* (Cambridge, MA 2008) 106–116.
88. Barbaro in Cornet 61 = Jones 72. For the Senate's interest in the matter, see Halff, 'Nicolò Barbaro,' 15 n. 58, 25–26; Ganchou, 'Le rachat des Notaras,' 178, 213 (and passim); for ransom sizes, see ibid. 225–226; and idem, 'La *fraterna societas*,' 151–152.
89. Whitchurch, *The Constantinopolis*, 3–4, 7–8, 51.
90. Halff, 'Nicolò Barbaro, 25–26, 37 n. 6; Philippides and Hanak, *Siege*, 111, 454 n. 67; Manoussakas, 'Les derniers défenseurs,' 336, 339.
91. Kritoboulos 1.73.1–5; Doukas 23.9; crying out: Ioannes Anagnostes, *History of the Final Fall of Thessalonike* 14 (Thessalonike). Egypt:

Nikolaos Sekoundinos (Sagundini), *Oration for King Alfonso of Aragon*, in Déroche-Vatin 794. A fifth: Inalcik, 'Policy of Mehmed II,' 232, 235.

92. Agallianos: Blanchet, *Georges-Gennadios Scholarios*, 141–142; E. Zachariadou, 'Constantinople se repeuple,' in Kiousopoulou, ed., *1453*, 47–59, here 55–58.
93. Kritoboulos 1.73.1–5; for the exemptions, see also Inalcik, *The Survey of Istanbul*, 1455 617.
94. Ganchou, 'Le *prôtogéros* de Constantinople.'
95. For the letter, see Déroche-Vatin 811–815.
96. Leonardo in Belgrado 256 = Melville-Jones 40 = Déroche-Vatin 727; Doukas 42.1.
97. Barbaro in Cornet 55 = Jones 66; Perugia: Philippides and Hanak, *Siege*, 37, in a second-hand account by one Niccolò Tignosi da Foligno.
98. Lomellino in Pertusi 44–45 = Melville-Jones 132 = Déroche-Vatin 528; Laonikos Chalkokondyles 8.28.
99. Michael Apostoles, *Letters* 4 and 8, ed. R. Stefec, *Die Briefe des Michael Apostoles* (Hamburg 2013).
100. Georgakopoulos, *Μιχαήλ Ἀποστόλης*, 77, 201, 205, 219.
101. Philippides and Hanak, *Siege*, 75–77; J. Monfasani, 'Filelfo and the Byzantines,' in J. De Keyser, ed., *Francesco Filelfo, Man of Letters* (Leiden 2019) 13–21, here 13–14.
102. Ganchou, 'Le rachat des Notaras.'
103. Ganchou, 'La famille Koumousès,' 67, 70.
104. J. Harris, *Greek Emigres in the West, 1400–1520* (Camberley, UK 1995) 18–21.
105. For these documents, see Grant, *Greek Captives*, ch. 4.
106. Schreiner, *Die byzantinischen Kleinchroniken*, v. 1, 647–648. P. Rance usefully connects the dots on this Demetrios Leontares in 'Finding the Right Words: A Letter to the Emperor (Laur. Plut. 55.4, F. 197v). Books, Education and Rhetoric an a Late Byzantine Household,' *Parekbolai* 12 (2022) 27–56.
107. E.g., the cases in Ganchou, 'Le rachat des Notaras,' 212.
108. Philippides and Hanak, *Siege*, 73–74, 79–80, relying primarily on documents in J. Darrouzès, 'Lettres de 1453,' *Revue des études byzantines* 22 (1964) 72–127; see also Ganchou, 'Le *prôtogéros* de Constantinople,' 229; Grant, *Greek Captives*, 128–129.
109. The anonymous Greek chronicle in Philippides, *Emperors*, 76–78.
110. Doukas 40.9.
111. Inalcik, 'Policy of Mehmed II'; S. Gerasimou, 'Η επανοίκηση της Κωνσταντινούπολης μετά την άλωση,' in Kiousopoulou, ed., *1453*, 3–21; Kafescioğlu, *Constantinopolis/Istanbul*, ch. 4.

112. Gennadios Scholarios, *Funeral Oration for His Nephew Theodoros Sophianos*, in *Oeuvres*, v. 1, 279.
113. Gennadios Scholarios, *Pastoral Letter on the Fall of Constantinople*, in *Oeuvres*, v. 4, 224; French translation in Déroche-Vatin 913–914.
114. M. Angold, 'The Autobiographies of the Patriarch Gennadios II Scholarios,' in T. Shawcross and I. Toth, eds., *Reading in the Byzantine Empire and Beyond* (Cambridge 2018) 68–89, here 81–83.
115. Angold, *Fall*, 69–70.
116. For Gennadios, Basilikos, and other Romans (Greeks) at the Ottoman court, see Ganchou, 'Le rachat des Notaras,' 176–177, 208; 'La *fraterna societas*,' 132–134, 154, 180–181; 'Le *prôtogéros* de Constantinople,' 238 n. 82; and K.-P. Matschke, 'Leonhard von Chios, Gennadios Scholarios, and die "Collegae" Thomas Pyropulos and Johannes Basilikos vor, während and nach der Eroberung von Konstantinopel durch die Türken,' *Byzantina* 21 (2000) 227–236, esp. 230–232. For Basilikos and Pyropoulos before the siege, see p. 82 above. Venetian Crete: Angold, *Fall*, 97.

CHAPTER 10

1. For the dissemination of the news, see Philippides and Hanak, *Siege*, 110–111, 547–551.
2. Initial confusion in Italy: Ganchou, 'Le rachat des Notaras.'
3. The text is translated and insightfully studied by Kefala, *The Conquered*, ch. 4, quotation from 35; historical encounter: 41, and Philippides, *Mehmed II*, 205–207. For editions of many laments, see S. Lambros, 'Μονοδίαι καὶ θρήνοι ἐπὶ τῆς ἁλώσεως τῆς Κωνσταντινουπόλεως,' *Νέος Ἑλληνομνήμων* 5 (1908) 190–270; Pertusi, *Caduta*, v. 2, 293–341; for French translations, see Déroche-Vatin 865–980; for studies, see A. J. Goldwyn, '"I come from a cursed land and from the depths of darkness": Life after Death in Greek Laments about the Fall of Constantinople,' in I. Nilsson and P. Stephenson, eds., *Byzantium: The Desire for a Lost Empire* (Uppsala 2014) 93–108; A. Papayianni, '*He Polis healo*: The Fall of Constantinople in 1453 in Post-Byzantine Popular Literature,' *Al-Masaq* 22 (2010) 27–44; earlier studies are cited by Philippides, *Mehmed II*, 85 n. 33, 153 n. 7.
4. A. K. Sanjian, 'Two Contemporary Armenian Elegies on the Fall of Constantinople, 1453,' *Viator* 1 (1970) 223–262; Pertusi, *Caduta*, v. 2, 410–419; M. K. Krikorian und W. Seibt, *Die Eroberung Konstantinopels im Jahre 1453 aus armenischer Sicht: drei Elegien* (Graz 1981); A. Sharon, 'A Hebrew Lament from Venetian Crete on the Fall of Constantinople: Michael Ben Shabbetai Cohen Balbo,' *Dialogos* 7 (2000) 43–46.

5. J. Duindam, *Dynasties: A Global History of Power, 1300–1800* (Cambridge 2016) 278.
6. Legends about Konstantinos: Philippides and Hanak, *Siege*, 210–211, 235; D. M. Nicol, *The Immortal Emperor: The Life and Legend of Constantine Palaiologos, Last Emperor of the Romans* (Cambridge 1992) 95–108; martyr: Schreiner, *Die byzantinischen Kleinchroniken*, v. 1, 155 (no. 14.107).
7. P. Marciniak, 'Fantastic(al) Byzantium: The Image of Byzantium in Speculative Fiction,' in M. Kulhánková and P. Marciniak, eds., *Byzantium in the Popular Imagination: The Modern Reception of the Byzantine Empire* (London 2023) 249–260, here 252.
8. Mehmed II, *Fetihname to the Sultan of Egypt*, in Déroche-Vatin 750.
9. Early decision: Kafescioğlu, *Constantinopolis/Istanbul*, 16; first winter: ibid. 229 n. 5 and S. Gerasimou, 'Η επανοίκηση της Κωνσταντινούπολης μετά την άλωση,' in Kiousopoulou, ed., *1453*, 3–21, esp. 12–13. Delay: Angold, *Fall*, 149, 160–161.
10. Kafescioğlu, *Constantinopolis/Istanbul*, 84.
11. G. Necipoğlu, *Architecture, Ceremonial, and Power: The Topkapi Palace in the Fifteenth and Sixteenth Centuries* (Cambridge, MA 1991) 4–22.
12. Translation in G. Necipoğlu, 'The Life of an Imperial Monument: Hagia Sophia after Byzantium,' in R. Mark and A. Çakmak, eds., *Hagia Sophia from the Age of Justinian to the Present* (Cambridge 1992) 195–225, here 198.
13. Kafescioğlu, *Constantinopolis/Istanbul*, 86; and E. Piltz, 'Hagia Sophia and Ottoman Architecture,' *Byzantinoslavica* 72 (2014) 293–309 (to be used with caution).
14. I owe this formulation to Charis Messis, who suggested it as I was explaining this idea.
15. Kafescioğlu, *Constantinopolis/Istanbul*, 6, 174; for this tradition, see especially S. Yerasimos, *La fondation de Constantinople et de Sainte-Sophie dans les traditions turques* (Paris 1990) 1–23.
16. Isidoros, *Letter to Bessarion* 1, in Philippides and Hanak, *Cardinal Isidore*, 198, 203.
17. M. Stachowski and R. Woodhouse, 'The Etymology of *İstanbul*: Making Optimal Use of the Evidence,' *Studia Etymologica Cracoviensia* 20 (2015) 221–245.
18. S. Kennedy, *Two Works on Trebizond: Michael Panaretos, Bessarion* (Washington, DC 2019).
19. Kritoboulos 1.1.3.

20. C. J. Hilsdale, *Byzantine Art and Diplomacy in an Age of Decline* (Cambridge 2014); S. Çelik, *Manuel II Palaiologos (1350–1425): A Byzantine Emperor in a Time of Tumult* (Cambridge 2021).
21. S. Budak, 'Teaching Greek, Studying Philosophy, and Discovering Ancient Greek Knowledge at the Ottoman Court in the Fifteenth Century,' *Dumbarton Oaks Papers* 78 (2024) 355–396. The rather maximalist readings on p. 377 are tempered by important caveats on p. 390.
22. Wilson, *From Byzantium to Italy*, 29–33; Filelfo: Angold, *Fall*, 90. For the impact of 1453 on the movement of books (limited) vs. scholars (greater), see Mondrain, 'Transfer.'
23. Kaldellis, *Phantom Byzantium*, ch. 6.
24. For these attitudes among the German humanists of the sixteenth century, see A. Ben-Tov, *Lutheran Humanists and Greek Antiquity: Melanchthonian Scholarship between Universal History and Pedagogy* (Leiden 2009). The same attitudes were endorsed by Gibbon in the late eighteenth century: see *History of the Decline and Fall of the Roman Empire*, ch. 62, ed. D. Womersley, 3 vols. (London 1994), here v. 3, 765.
25. Bodnar, *Cyriac of Ancona*, 298–301, 329–331.
26. See the Florentine Donato Acciaiuolo in N. Bisaha, *Creating East and West: Renaissance Humanists and the Ottoman Turks* (Philadelphia 2004) 124; for many more cases, see Lamers, *Greece Reinvented*.
27. For one case study, see A. Kaldellis, 'The Byzantine Role in the Making of the Corpus of Classical Greek Historiography: A Preliminary Investigation,' *Journal of Hellenic Studies* 132 (2012) 71–85.
28. Georgakopoulos, *Μιχαήλ Ἀποστόλης*, 207–209.
29. L. Miletti, 'La Riscoperta dei classici greci nel Rinascimento in Italia meridionale: La Napoli di Alfonso il Magnanimo,' *I Quaderni di Atene e Roma* 8 (2023) 429–445.
30. B. Figliuolo, 'Notizie su traduzioni e traduttori greci alla corte di Alfonso il Magnanimo,' *Italia medioevale e umanistica* 53 (2012) 359–374, here 370–371.
31. B. Laourdas, 'Μιχαὴλ Ἀποστόλη λόγος περὶ Ἑλλάδος καὶ Εὐρώπης,' *Ἐπετηρὶς Ἑταιρείας Βυζαντινῶν Σπουδῶν* 19 (1949) 235–244, here 243.
32. Kafescioğlu, *Constantinopolis/Istanbul*, 199, 204–206, 225.
33. E. N. Boeck, *The Bronze Horseman of Justinian in Constantinople: The Cross-Cultural Biography of a Mediterranean Monument* (Cambridge 2021) 330–334.
34. F. Clark, 'From the Rise of Constantine to the Fall of Constantinople: Defining Byzantium and the "Middle Age" in Early Modern Scholarship,'

in N. Aschenbrenner and J. Ransohoff, eds., *The Invention of Byzantium in Early Modern Europe* (Washington, DC 2021) 323–348, here 341–344.

35. W. H. McNeill, 'The Age of Gunpowder Empires, 1450–1800,' in M. Adas, ed., *Islamic and European Expansion: The Forging of a Global Order* (Philadelphia 1993) 103–139.
36. B. Simms, *Europe: The Struggle for Supremacy from 1453 to the Present* (New York 2013) 7–8.
37. Angold, *Fall*, 96.
38. Hankins, 'Renaissance Crusaders.'
39. W. Brandes, 'Der Fall Konstantinopels als apokalyptisches Ereignis,' in S. Kolditz and R. C. Müller, eds., *Geschehenes und Geschriebenes: Studien zu Ehren von Günther* S. Henrich *und Klaus-Peter Matschke* (Leipzig 2005) 453–469. For a survey of western attitudes toward the Ottomans, see N. Malcolm, *Useful Enemies: Islam and the Ottoman Empire in Western Political Thought, 1450–1750* (Oxford 2019).
40. I. Hasiotes, 'Marchar contra Constantinopla: Η Κωνσταντινούπολη στη σταυροφορική φιλολογία του 15ου, 16ου και 17ου αιώνα,' in *Constantinopla*, v. 3, 15–34.
41. P. E. Chevedden, '"A Crusade from the First": The Norman Conquest of Islamic Sicily, 1060–1091,' *Al-Masaq* 22 (2010) 191–225.
42. C. Kafadar, *Between Two Worlds: The Construction of the Ottoman State* (Berkeley 1995) 19–20.
43. Kefala, *The Conquered*.
44. The link between 1453 and Atlantic exploration is asserted by scholars in widely different fields, e.g., F. Cervantes, *Conquistadores: A New History* (New York 2021) 5; M. Balard, 'Le grande commerce,' in A. Laiou and C. Morrisson, eds., *Le monde byzantin*, v. 3: *L'Empire grec et ses voisins (XIIIème–XVème siècle)* (Paris 2011) 117–127, here 127; M. Nystazopoulou-Pelekidou, "Η ἅλωση τῆς Κωνσταντινούπολης: Διεθνὴς συγκυρία καὶ διεθνεῖς ἐπιπτώσεις,' in *Constantinopla*, v 2., 127–135, here 131–132 n. 14 (citing more studies). A full recent study can be found in Rohan, *Transforming Empire*, esp. ch. 5–6 (see 258–259 for Salvago). Continued Genoese presence in Pera after 1453 was advocated by K. Fleet, *European and Islamic Trade in the Early Ottoman State: The Merchants of Genoa and Turkey* (Cambridge 1999) 122–133. Decline of the Genoese east: S. A. Epstein, *Genoa and the Genoese, 958–1528* (Chapel Hill, NC 1996) 273–274, 285.
45. Matthew 24:36; Mark 13:32; Acts of the Apostles 1:7; 1 Thessalonians 5:1–2.
46. Psalm 90:4; 2 Peter 3:8.

47. Ioseph Bryennios, *First Oration on the Coming Judgment*, p. 371, ed. E. Voulgaris, *Ἰωσὴφ μοναχοῦ τοῦ Βρυεννίου τὰ εὑρεθέντα*, v. 2 (Leipzig 1768).
48. Important studies of this tradition include A. Rigo, 'L'anno 7000, la fine del mondo e l'impero Cristiano: Nota su alcuni passi di Giuseppe Briennio, Simeone di Tessalonica e Gennadio Scholario,' in G. Ruggieri and A. Gallas, eds., *La cattura della fine: Variazioni dell'escatologia in regime di cristianità* (Genoa 1992) 153–185; and M.-H. Congourdeau, 'Byzance et la fin du monde: Courants de pensée apocalyptiques sous les Paléologues,' in B. Lellouch and S. Yerasimos, eds., *Les traditions apocalyptiques au tournant de la chute de Constantinople* (Paris 1999) 55–97.
49. Angold, *Fall*, ch. 5, does as much as one can.
50. For a survey of the alleged links between Russia and Byzantium and the modern schools of thought about them (minimalists vs. maximalists), see J. Kusber, 'Autocracy as a Form of Political Theology? Ruler and Church in Early Modern Muscovy (1450s–1725),' in M.-D. Grigore and V. N. Makrides, eds., *Orthodoxy in the Agora: Orthodox Christian Political Theologis across History* (Göttingen 2024) 83–101, here 87–96. I am persuaded by the minimalists, including S. Ivanov, 'The Second Rome as Seen by the Third: Russian Debates on "the Byzantine Legacy",' in P. Marciniak and D. C. Smythe, eds., *The Reception of Byzantium in European Culture since 1500* (London 2016) 55–79.
51. A. Kaldellis, 'From "Empire of the Greeks" to "Byzantium": The Politics of a Modern Paradigm Shift,' in N. Aschenbrenner and J. Ransohoff, eds., *The Invention of Byzantium in Early Modern Europe* (Washington, DC 2021) 349–367, here 363.

Bibliography

Abbreviations

Constantinopla	E. Motos Guirao and M. Morfakidis Filactós, eds., *Constantinopla: 550 años de su caida*, 3 vols. (Granada 2006).
Déroche-Vatin	V. Déroche and N. Vatin, eds., *Constantinople 1453: Des Byzantins aux Ottomans. Textes et documents* (Toulouse, 2016).
Melville-Jones	J. R. Melville Jones, *The Siege of Constantinople: Seven Contemporary Accounts* (Amsterdam 1972).
PG	J.-P. Migne, ed. *Patrologia Graeca*, 161 vols. (Paris 1857–1866).
ΠΠ	*Παλαιολόγεια καὶ Πελοποννησιακά*, ed. S. Lambros, 4 vols. (Athens, 1912–1930).

PRIMARY SOURCES

(In most cases, I use my own translations when quoting Greek texts, but, where they are available, I reference published translations here too. When I quote non-Greek texts, I use published translations, also referenced here, but often condense them.)

Anagnostes, Ioannes, *History of the Final Fall of Thessalonike*, ed. I. Tsaras, *Ἰωάννου Ἀναγνώστου Διήγησις περὶ τῆς τελευταίας ἁλώσεως τῆς Θεσσαλονίκης* (Thessalonike 1958); English tr. J. R. Melville-Jones, *Venice and Thessalonica 1423–1430: The Greek Accounts* (Padua 2006) 149–179.

Antonio Ivani da Sarzana, *The Fall of Constantinople*, ed. P. Pontari and S. Marcucci, *Antonio Ivani da Sarzana: Opere storiche* (Florence 2006) 253–267; older ed. and Italian tr. Pertusi, *Testi inediti*, 143–165.

Barbaro, Nicolò, *Diary of the Siege of Constantinople*, ed. E. Cornet, *Giornale dell'assedio di Costantinopoli 1453* (Vienna 1856); ed. A. Codato, *Il Diario dell'assedio di Costantinopoli di Nicolò Barbaro* (Canterano 2017) (this inaccessible edition is not cited in my notes); partial ed. Pertusi, *Caduta*, v. 1, 5–38; English tr. J. R. Jones, *Nicòlo Barbaro: Diary of the Siege of Constantinople 1453* (New York 1969); partial French tr. D-V 455–501.

Benvenuto of Ancona, *Report on the Siege of Constantinople*, ed. Pertusi, *Testi inediti*, 4–5; English tr. M. Philippides, *Byzantium, Europe, and the Early Ottoman Sultans, 1373–1513: An Anonymous Greek Chronicle of the Seventeenth Century (Codex Barberinus 111)* (New Rochelle 1990) 197–199; French tr. Déroche-Vatin 563–568.

Bertrandon de la Broquière, *The Voyage d'Outremer*, English tr. G. R. Kline (New York 1988).

Buondelmonti, Cristoforo, ed. G. R. L. von Sinner, *Cristoforo Buondelmonte: Liber Insularum Archipelagi* (Leipzig 1824); ed. K. Bayer, *Cristoforo Buondelmonti: Liber insularum archipelagi* (Wiesbaden 2007); *Description of the Aegean & Other Islands*, ed. and English tr. E. Edson (New York 2018).

Choniates, Niketas, *History*, ed. J.-L. van Dieten, *Nicetae Choniatae Historia* (Berlin and New York 1975); English tr. H. J. Magoulias, *O City of Byzantium, Annals of Niketas Choniates* (Detroit 1984).

Chortasmenos, Ioannes, ed. H. Hunger, *Johannes Chortasmenos (ca. 1370–ca. 1436/37)* (Vienna 1969).

Chrysoloras, Manuel, *Comparison of Old Rome and New Rome*, ed. C. Billò, 'Manuele Crisolora, Confronto tra l'Antica e la Nuova Roma,' *Medioevo greco* 0 (2000) 6–26; English tr. in C. Smith, *Architecture in the Culture of Early Humanism: Ethics, Aesthetics, and Eloquence 1400–1470* (New York 1992) 199–215.

de Clavijo, Ruy González, *Embajada a Tamorlán*, ed. F. López Estrada (Madrid 1943); *Embassy to Tamerlane*, tr. G. Le Strange (London 1928).

Doukas, *History*, ed. S. Kotzabassi, *Ducae Historia* (Berlin and New York 2024); English tr. H. Magoulias, *Decline and Fall of Byzantium to the Ottoman Turks, by Doukas* (Detroit 1975).

Gennadios (Georgios Scholarios), *Oeuvres complètes de Georges (Gennadios) Scholarios*, ed. M. Jugie, L. Petit, and X.A. Siderides, 8 vols. (Paris 1928–1936).

Geoffroi de Villehardouin, *Conquest of Constantinople*, ed. and modern French tr. E. Faral, *Villehardouin: La conquête de Constantinople*, 2 vols., 2nd ed. (Paris 1961); English tr. M. R. B. Shaw, *Joinville and Villehardouin: Chronicles of the Crusades* (London 1963).

Gregoras, Nikephoros, *Roman History*, ed. I. Bekker and L. Schopen, *Nicephori Gregorae historiae Byzantinae*, 3 vols. (Bonn 1829–1855).

Kananos, Ioannes, *The Siege of Constantinople*, ed. and English tr. A. M. Cuomo, *Ioannis Canani de Constantinopolitana obsidione relatio* (Boston and Berlin 2016).

Kantakouzenos, Ioannes, *History*, ed. L. Schopen, *Ioannis Cantacuzeni eximperatoris historiarum libri IV*, 3 vols. (Bonn 1831–1832).

Kastritsis, D. J., *An Early Ottoman History: The Oxford Anonymous Chronicle (Bodleian Library, Ms Marsh 313)* (Liverpool 2017).

Kinnamos, Ioannes, *History*, ed. A. Meineke, *Ioannis Cinnami epitome rerum ab Ioanne et Alexio Comnenis gestarum* (Bonn 1836); English tr. C. Brand, *John Kinnamos: Deeds of John and Manuel Comnenus* (New York 1976).

Konstantin Mihailović, *Memoirs of a Janissary*, ed. S. Soucek and English tr. B. Stolz (Ann Arbor, MI 1975); partial French tr. Déroche-Vatin 441–447.

Kritoboulos of Imbros, *History*, ed. D. R. Reinsch, *Critobuli Imbriotae historiae* (Berlin and New York 1983); English tr. C. T. Riggs, *Kritovoulos: History of Mehmed the Conqueror* (Princeton 1954).

Kyriacus of Ancona, *Letters*, ed. and English tr. E. D. Bodnar, *Cyriac of Ancona: Later Travels* (Cambridge, MA 2003).

Laonikos Chalkokondyles, *The Histories*, ed. and English tr. A. Kaldellis (Cambridge, MA, and London 2014).

Leonardo of Chios, *Letter to Pope Nicholas V*, ed. J.-P. Migne, ed. *Patrologia Graeca*, 161 vols. (Paris 1857–1866) v. 159: 925–941; ed. L. T. Belgrano, 'Prima serie di documenti riguardanti la colonia di Pera,' *Atti della società ligure di storia patria* 13 (1877) 233–257; partial ed. Pertusi, *Caduta*, v. 1, 124–170; English tr. Melville-Jones 11–41; French tr. Déroche-Vatin 681–728.

Lomellino, Angelo Giovanni, *Letter to Antonio Lomellino*, ed. Pertusi, *Caduta*, v. 1, 42–51; English tr. Melville-Jones 131–135; French tr. Déroche-Vatin 519–534.

Majeska, G. P., *Russian Travelers to Constantinople in the Fourteenth and Fifteenth Centuries* (Washington, DC 1984).

Manuel II Palaiologos, *Funeral Oration on his Brother Theodoros*, ed. and English tr. J. Chrysostomides, *Manuel II Palaeologus: Funeral Oration on his Brother Theodore* (Thessalonike 1985).

Metochites, Theodoros, *Byzantios*, ed. I. Polemis and E. Kaltsogianni, *Theodorus Metochites: Orationes* (Berlin 2019) 430–552.

Nestor-Iskander, *The Tale of Constantinople (Of Its Origin and Capture by the Turks in the Year 1453)*, ed. and English tr. W. K. Hanak and M. Philippides (New Rochelle, NY 1998); French tr. Déroche-Vatin 397–439. My citations refer to the Hanak and Philippides edition.

Pertusi, A., *La caduta di Costantinopoli*, 2 vols. (Milan 1976).

Pertusi, A., *Testi inediti e poco noti sulla caduta di Costantinopoli*, ed. A. Carile (Bologna 1983).

Posculo, Ubertino, *Constantinople*, ed. A. Ellissen, *Analekten der mittel- und neugriechischen Literatur*, v. 3 (Leipzig 1857) 12–83; partial ed. and Italian tr. Pertusi, *Caduta*, v. 1, 198–225; partial French tr. Déroche-Vatin 359–395; partial English tr. B. A. Whitchurch, *The Constantinopolis of Ubertino Posculo: Translation and Commentary, Book 4* (PhD dissertation: Fordham University 2019).

Scalamonti, Francesco, *Life of Cyriac of Ancona*, ed. and tr. C. Mitchell et al., *Cyriac of Ancona: Life and Early Travels* (Cambridge, MA 2015) 2–171.

Schiltberger, Johann, *The Bondage and Travels of Johann Schiltberger: A Native of Bavaria, in Europe, Asia, and Africa, 1396–1427*, tr. J. B. Telfer (London 1879).

Schreiner, P., *Die byzantinischen Kleinchroniken*, 3 vols. (Vienna 1975–1979).

Sphrantzes, Georgios, *Brief Chronicle*, ed. R. Maisano, *Giorgio Sfranze: Cronaca* (Rome 1990); English tr. M. Philippides, *The Fall of the Byzantine Empire: A Chronicle by George Sphrantzes, 1401–1477* (Amherst 1980).

Synaxarion of Constantinople, ed. H. Delehaye, *Synaxarium Ecclesiae Constantinopolitanae* (Brussels 1902).

Tafur, Pero, *Andanças e viajes*, ed. M. A. Pérez Priego (Seville 2009); English tr. M. Letts, *Pero Tafur: Travels and Adventures, 1435–1439* (New York and London 1926).

Tetaldi, Giacomo, *Treatise on the Fall of Constantinople*, ed. and English tr. M. Philippides, *Mehmed II the Conqueror and the Fall of the Franco-Byzantine Levant to the Ottoman Turks: Some Western Views and Testimonies* (Tempe, AZ 2007) 133–217.

Tursun Beg, *The History of Mehmed the Conqueror*, fascimile ed. and English paraphrase H. Inalcik and R. Murphey (Minneapolis and Chicago 1978); French tr. Déroche-Vatin 187–231; Italian tr. L. Berardi, *Tursun Bey: La conquista di Costantinopoli* (Milan 2007).

MODERN SCHOLARSHIP

(Items that are cited only once in the notes are referenced fully there and not here. The following bibliography is for items that are cited more than once in the notes.)

Agoritsas, D., *Κωνσταντινούπολη: Η πόλη και η κοινωνία της στα χρόνια των πρώτων Παλαιολόγων (1261–1328)* (Thessalonike 2016).

Angold, M., *The Fall of Constantinople to the Ottomans: Context and Consequences* (London and New York 2012).

Asutay-Effenberger, N., *Die Landmauer von Konstantinopel-Istanbul* (Berlin and New York 2007).

Babinger, F., *Mehmed the Conqueror and His Time*, tr. R. Manheim (Princeton 1978).

Balard, M., *La Romanie génoise: XIIe–début du XVe siécle*, 2 vols. (Rome 1978).

Balivet, M., *Byzantins et Ottomans: relations, interaction, succession* (Istanbul 1999).

Balletto, L., 'Battista di Felizzano e Domenico di Novara fra Genova ed il Vicino Oriente a metà dil Quattrocento,' in A. Guiance and P. Ubierna, eds., *Sociedad y memoria en la Edad Media* (Buenos Aires 2005) 35–54.

Bisaha, N., *From Christians to Europeans: Pope Pius II and the Concept of the Modern Western Identity* (New York and London 2023).

Blanchet, M.-H., *Georges-Gennadios Scholarios (vers 1400–vers 1472): un intellectuel orthodoxe face à la disparition de l'empire Byzantin* (Paris 2008).

Bodnar, E. D., *Cyriac of Ancona: Later Travels* (Cambridge, MA 2003).

Brown, P. F., *Venice and Antiquity: The Venetian Sense of the Past* (New Haven 1996).

Emecen, F. M., *Fetih ve Kyamet 1453: lstanbul'un Fethi ve Kıyamet Senaryoları* (Istanbul 2016).

Estangüi Gómez, R., *Byzance face aux Ottomans: Exercise du pouvoir et contrôle du territoire sous les derniers Paléologues* (Paris 2014).

Fleet, K., *European and Islamic Trade in the Early Ottoman State: The Merchants of Genoa and Turkey* (Cambridge 1999).

Fodor, P., 'Ottoman Warfare, 1300–1453,' in K. Fleet, ed., *The Cambridge History of Turkey*, v. 1: *Byzantium to Turkey, 1071–1453* (Cambridge 2009) 192–225.

Ganchou, T., 'Le rachat des Notaras après la chute de Constantinople ou les relations «étrangères» de l'élite byzantine au XVe siècle,' in M. Balard and A. Ducellier, eds., *Migrations et diasporas méditerranéennes (Xe–XVIe siècles)* (Paris 2002) 149–229.

Ganchou, T., 'La famille Koumousès (Κουμούσης) à Constantinople et Négrepont, avant et après 1453,' in C. A. Maltezou, C. E. Papakosta, eds., *Venezia-Eubea, da Egripos a Negroponte* (Venice 2006) 45–107.

Ganchou, T., 'La *fraterna societas* des crétois Nikolaos et Geôrgios Pôlos (Polo), entre Constantinople et Moncastro: affairs, dévotion et humanisme,' in *Thesaurismata* 39–40 (2011) 111–227.

Ganchou, T., 'Le *prôtogéros* de Constantinople Laskaris Kanabès (1454): À propos d'une institution ottomane méconnu,' *Revue des études byzantines* 71 (2013) 209–258.

Ganchou, T., 'Sujets grecs crétois de la sérénissime à Constantinople à la veille de 1453 (Iôannès Tortzélos et Nikolaos Pôlos): une ascension sociale brutalement interrompue,' in G. Ortalli et al., eds., *Il Commonwealth veneziano tra 1204 e la fine della Repubblica: Identità e peculiarità* (Venice 2015) 339–389.

Ganchou, T., '"La tour d'Irène" (Eirene Kulesi) à Istanbul: Le palais de Loukas Notaras?' *Travaux et mémoires* 21 (2017) 169–256.

Georgakopoulos, D. S., *Μιχαὴλ Ἀποστόλης: Ὁ βυζαντινὸς λόγιος καὶ τὸ ἔργο του στὴ βενετοκρατούμενη Κρήτη (1453–1478)* (Athens 2022).

Grant, A. C., *Greek Captives and Mediterranean Slavery, 1260–1460* (Edinburgh 2024).

Halff, M., 'Nicolò Barbaro and the Lists of Venetian Noblemen in his Account of the Siege of Constantinople (1453),' *Archivio Veneto*, ser. 6, 22 (2021) 5–49.

Hankins, J., 'Renaissance Crusaders: Humanist Crusade Literature in the Age of Mehmed II,' *Dumbarton Oaks Papers* 49 (1995) 111–207.

Imber, C., *The Ottoman Empire, 1300–1650: The Structure of Power* (New York 2002).

İnalcık, H., 'The Policy of Mehmed II toward the Greek Population of Istanbul and the Byzantine Buildings of the City,' *Dumbarton Oaks Papers* 23/24 (1969/1970) 229–249.

İnalcık, H., *The Survey of Istanbul 1455: The Text, English Translation, Analysis of the Text, Documents* (Istanbul 2012).

Jacoby, D., 'Constantinople as Commercial Transit Center, Tenth to Mid-Fifteenth Century,' in P. Magdalino and N. Necipoğlu, eds., *Trade in Byzantium* (Istanbul 2016) 193–210.

Janin, R., *Les églises et les monastères = La géographie ecclésiastique de l'empire byzantin*, pt. 1: *Le siège de Constantinople et le patriarcat oecuménique*, v. 3: *Les églises et les monastères* (Paris 1969).

Kafescioğlu, C., *Constantinopolis / Istanbul: Cultural Encounter, Imperial Vision, and the Construction of the Ottoman Capital* (University Park, PA 2009).

Kaldellis, A., *A New Herodotos: Laonikos Chalkokondyles on the Ottoman Empire, the Fall of Byzantium, and the Emergence of the West* (Cambridge, MA 2014).

Kaldellis, A., *Phantom Byzantium: Europe, Empire and Identity from Late Antiquity to World War I* (Chicago 2026).

Kefala, E., *The Conquered: Byzantium and America on the Cusp of Modernity* (Washington, DC 2020).

Kiousopoulou, T., *Βασιλεύς ή οικονόμος: Πολιτική εξουσία και ιδεολογία πριν την άλωση* (Athens 2007).

Kiousopoulou, T., ed., *1453: Η άλωση της Κωνσταντινούπολης και η μετάβαση απί τους μεσαιωνικούς στους νεώτερους χρόνους* (Herakleio 2013).

Kolovos, I., *Στους καιρούς των σουλτάνων: Οι κοινωνίες της ελληνικής χερσονήσου υπό οθωμανική κυριαρχία (14ος–19ος αιώνας)* (Athens 2023).

Külzer, A., ed., *Ostthrakien (Eurōpē)* (Vienna 2008 = *Tabula Imperii Byzantini* v. 12).

Lamers, H., *Greece Reinvented: Transformations of Byzantine Hellenism in Renaissance Italy* (Leiden 2015).

Lane, F. C., *Venice: A Maritime Republic* (Baltimore 1973).

Lowry, H. W., *The Nature of the Early Ottoman State* (New York 2003).

Madden, T., 'The Fires of the Fourth Crusade in Constantinople, 1203–1204,' *Byzantinische Zeitschrift* 84–85 (1991–1992) 72–93.

Majeska, G. P., *Russian Travellers to Constantinople in the Fourteenth and Fifteenth Centuries* (Washington, DC 1984).

Manoussakas, M., 'Les derniers défenseurs crétois de Constantinople d'après les documents véntitiens,' *Akten des XI. Internationalen Byzantinisten-Kongress* (Munich 1960) 331–340.

Mergiali-Sahas, S., 'Οι Βυζαντινοί ως εμπορεύσιμο αγαθό στο δουλεμπόριο της Μεσογείου,' in V. Leontaritou et al., eds., *Αντικήνσωρ: Τιμητικός τόμος Σπύρου Ν. Τρωιάνου* (Athens 2013) v. 2, 971–996.

Mondrain, B., 'Der Transfer griechischer Handschriften nach der Eroberung Konstantinopels,' in F. Fuchs, ed., *Osmanische Expansion und europaïscher Humanismus* (Wiesbaden 2005) 109–122.

Motos Guirao, E., and M. Morfakidis Filactós, eds., *Constantinopla: 550 años de su caida*, 3 vols. (Granada 2006).

Moustakas, K., 'Μεθοδολογικά ζητήματα στην προσέγγιση των πληθυσμιακών μεγεθών της υστεροβυζαντινής πόλης,' in T. Kiousopoulou, ed., *Οι βυζαντινές πόλεις (8ος–15ος αιώνας)* (Rethymno 2012) 225–251.

Necipoğlu, N., 'Ottoman Merchants in Constantinople during the First Half of the Fifteenth Century,' *Byzantine and Modern Greek Studies* 16 (1992) 158–169.

Necipoğlu, N., *Byzantium between the Ottomans and the Latins: Politics and Society in the Late Empire* (Cambridge 2009).

Nicol, D. M., The *Byzantine Family of Kantakouzenos (Cantacuzenus) ca. 1100–1460* (Washington, DC 1968).

Nicol, D. M., *Byzantium and Venice: A Study in Diplomatic and Cultural Relations* (Cambridge 1994).

Paul, G. M., '*Urbs Capta*: Sketch of an Ancient Literary Motif,' *Phoenix* 36 (1982) 143–155

Pertusi, A., *La caduta di Costantinopoli*, 2 vols. (Milan 1976).

Pertusi, A., *Testi inediti e poco noti sulla caduta di Costantinopoli*, ed. A. Carile (Bologna 1983).

Philippides, M., *Emperors, Patriarchs, and Sultans of Constantinople: An Anonymous Greek Chronicle of the Sixteenth Century* (Brookline, MA 1990).

Philippides, M., *Mehmed II the Conqueror and the Fall of the Franco-Byzantine Levant to the Ottoman Turks: Some Western Views and Testimonies* (Tempe, AZ 2007).

Philippides, M., *Constantine XI Dragaš Palaeologus (1404–1453): The Last Emperor of Byzantium* (London and New York 2019).

Philippides, M., and W. K. Hanak, *The Siege and the Fall of Constantinople in 1453: Historiography, Topography, and Military Studies* (Farnham, UK 2011).

Philippides, M., and W. K. Hanak, *Cardinal Isidore, c. 1390–1462: A Late Byzantine Scholar, Warlord, and Prelate* (London 2018).

Polemis, I., *Theodore Metochites: Patterns of Self-Representation in Fourteenth-Century Byzantium* (London 2024).

Oikonomidès, N., *Hommes d'affaires grecs et latins à Constantinople (XIIIe–XIVe siècle)* (Montreal 1979).

Rohan, P., *Transforming Empire: The Genoese from the Mediterranean to the Atlantic, 1282–1492* (PhD dissertation: Stanford University, 2021).

Setton, K. M., *The Papacy and the Levant (1204–1571)*, v. 2: *The Fifteenth Century* (Philadelphia 1971).

Shukurov, R., *The Byzantine Turks, 1204–1461* (Leiden 2016).

Van Millingen, A., *Byzantine Constantinople: The Walls of the City and Adjoining Historical Sites* (Cambridge 1899).

Whitchurch, B. A., *The Constantinopolis of Ubertino Posculo: Translation and Commentary, Book 4* (PhD dissertation: Fordham University 2019).

Wilson, N. G., *From Byzantium to Italy: Greek Studies in the Italian Renaissance*, 2nd ed. (London 2017) 29–33.

Wright, C., *The Gattilusio Lordships and the Aegean World, 1355–1462* (Leiden 2014).

Index

For the benefit of digital users, indexed terms that span two pages (e.g., 52–53) may, on occasion, appear on only one of those pages.

The present index excludes the terms and names basileus, Byzantium, Constantinople (and the City), Genoa and the Genoese, Greeks, Italy and Italians, Konstantinos XI Palaiologos, Mehmed II, Ottomans and Ottoman empire, Romans, sultan, Theodosian Walls, Turks, Venice and Venetians, which occur throughout the book.